I0722084

Dinosaurs and other Felonious Mischief:

The Art of Jason C. Poole

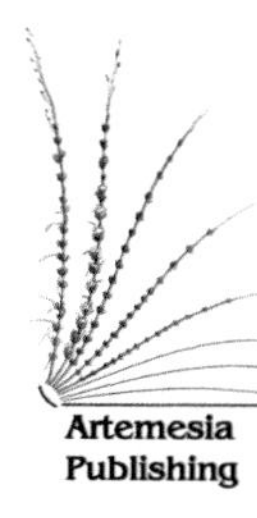

Artemesia
Publishing

ISBN: 978-1-963832-08-2 (paperback)
LCCN: 2025933517
Text and Artwork Copyright © 2025 by Jason C. Poole
Foreword Copyright © 2025 by Jason P. Schein

Please Note: There are some images in this collection that show violence and traumatic events There are images of bones and skeletons as well. Please use care when viewing the images.

Artemesia Publishing
9 Mockingbird Hill Rd
Tijeras, New Mexico 87059
www.apbooks.net
info@artemesiapublishing.com

Introduction

This book has been an incredible experience for me. The excitement of a new project, the worry of relatability, the introspection of getting the words to best explain things that are largely stored in my mind emotionally. The terror of deadlines that are closer on the calendar than they appear.

I started with an idea to share sketches from the last few years. The first years of my life living full time in Montana. My friend and publisher had grander ideas which led us to where we are now.

The book remains an art book at its core but it also explores the headspace of the artist as "life changes" affect the art, from style to amounts.

The message is simple. Find people, places and things that inspire and lift you up and your art will grow and change and have more meaning to you.

Jason C. Poole

Foreword

I am a classic "left-brain thinker," which is to say—if you subscribe to the now scientifically outdated concept—logic, reason, and details come naturally to me. Black and white data is my jam. Art, creativity, and music are the domain of "right-brain thinkers," and therefore, completely outside my wheelhouse, or even my realm of possibility. Only on a good day can I draw a reasonably realistic stick figure.

That is not to say I don't appreciate the arts. Untrained as they may be, my eyes and ears are filled with warmth and inspiration in the presence of masterpieces, whether they be hanging on a museum wall or emanating from a concert hall stage.

But these are the final products. It's easy to recognize and appreciate greatness when only the final, polished product is presented. What I find more compelling is the story of the master behind the masterpiece—the struggles in life that were essential to developing and nurturing that talent and the art itself. As right-brained polymath, Thomas Merton, once said, "art enables us to find ourselves and lose ourselves at the same time." I am most intrigued by the losing and the finding of oneself, and how those create the artist and the art. I want their origin story.

In the ensuing pages, you'll follow along with Jason as he very honestly shares his wanderings, both emotional and geographic, amid great triumphs and profound losses, among struggles and successes. Throughout it all, art has helped him find himself again and again. Some might say that was by random, lucky chance. Perhaps that is true, but knowing him as I do, and being in constant awe of his talents, I think it was inevitable. Jason and art, art and Jason—the two are inseparable, no matter what life throws at him. Either way, all of us—left and right brainers alike—we are the beneficiaries.

Jason P. Schein, Executive Director, Elevation Science Institute

"Art is a jealous lover."

I hypothesize that there is a great percentage of our population that do art as young people, but only a few stick with it for life. We get a good bit of positive feedback from folks that art is a gift which makes us special. Art is not a gift, art is a struggle. Early recognition given to a young artist is often what gives the push to continue on this path, so eat it up. That early recognition of your ability will hopefully give you the desire to push and do more art. It is the desire to be an artist that makes an artist grow. This is what eventually weeds out those who find more drive to do other things. So remember that those incredible artists that other artists hold in the highest esteem have earned that recognition through incredible amounts of drive to do the work.

My art journey of almost 50 years has taught me a lot about the state of being an artist. Being an artist, let alone a "successful" artist, relies heavily on two things: you get out of it what you put into it and you must manage your expectations and temper them with real observations of how the world really works. So it is really important to find your happy balance.

A quote that I love and will cling to and pass on for the rest of my life was said by fellow paleontologist, Ken Lacovara. We were talking about accomplishing some huge tasks. I voiced a bit of doubt to which he replied, "A PERSON did that. We are persons. We can do it." Which is a great way of saying that we are limited only by the limits we place on ourselves. So look around and see what has been done by others before limiting yourself.

Finally, you must know what you want from your art. Glory, money, fame. "Yes please." Or will it be a fun way to spend time doing something creative?

For me, I think I want it to matter. This is why teaching art has become so much a part of my life. How else do I make it matter? I tie it to things that I care about. For me nature and paleontology are at the top of my list, and that brings me to the big story I want to pen here.

This is my story of a life lived with art.

I grew up in East Oak Lane in Philadelphia. There were big houses on tree lined streets with old sneakers hanging from the telephone lines. We played stickball and kick-the-can. We built forts in the backyard and knocked on friends' doors to see if they could come out and play. When I was young, we (my brother and I) had to be home before the streetlights came on. We drank from garden hoses and ran through neighborhood yards rather than use the sidewalks. We were mostly well behaved, we knew that the neighbors were watching and mom and dad would hear it if we weren't.

I had a hard time in school early on, in fact I was a lousy student. I was also not very motivated to play sports. So, I really didn't stand out, except when I was drawing. When I was sketching or doodling my peers could see that there was something I could be noticed for. That was how I was hooked. I don't know that I really thought it through on any real level, but I liked when people looked at my drawings.

I drew from comics, and took inspiration from movies like Star Wars, Indiana Jones, and Alien. I also enjoyed making up places. It's called world building now, but the idea of creating my own worlds was wicked cool! Creatures, dinosaurs, bizarre machines, strange places and heroes, these things filled my sketchbooks.

In 1984 I was accepted to the High School of Creative and Performing Arts in Philadelphia where my formal training in visual arts started. The school was at 13th and Catherine Streets in the old "Plumbo" building in South Philly.

I like South Philadelphia. The rows of homes on one lane streets, some with cobblestones and old poplar trees. Family-owned restaurants and the bustle of people with the true Philadelphia accent.

CAPA, as the school was known, drew its students from all over Philadelphia. Two great friends and I took the subway each day and walked to get to and from school. These two friends were my anchors and inspirations. Luis had a great mind for fantasy and a great evolving style that inspired me to try new things and to push myself to keep up. Russell got images in his mind and seemed to know what each line was to look like before putting pencil to paper. His clean and precise style was something to see and something I still admire today.

I think that the three of us learned a great deal from each other. Both Luis and Russell got into doing pen and ink work before me. But I quickly fell in love with that medium. It is still my favorite medium today. I love the way line and the human mind work together to create and see a series of lines that represent a three-dimensional reality in a two-dimensional format. Picture a comic book illustration. Lines of varied thickness create the illusion of tone, representing light and shadows cast on an object. There is a visual language in that which is instinctively understood by the viewer. There is a certain magic in that.

In high school, we had classes like graphic design, illustration, drawing and sketching, painting and sculpture. I look back and realize how invested the teachers were and how amazingly lucky I was to have access to them. I do regret not being in more studious in my quest to be an artist at that point, but what I learned there has been the core of skills that moves me forward.

In 1988 I graduated high school, and at my father's behest, I attended Antonelli Institute of Commercial Art and Photography. My father had it in his head that commercial art was the only real way an artist could make money. Which was probably picked up by him from our neighbors who did just that and were making a good living.

There were some good classes, but also some good new friends. My style of art was becoming more refined and detail oriented. The pull to illustration was more definitely being felt by me and the idea of spending my life making dynamic illustrations seemed much more attractive than spending my life basically trying to trick people into buying stuff. But at least I knew that now.

The curve ball...

Being fresh out of school and working towards being a notable illustrator is a challenge for anyone. There is a good bit to figure out. You must have studio time, and it must be productive, you have to figure out the best way to get your art seen, but you must also have a job that pays the bills until your art can do that, if ever. I took another direction. I had a kid.

1990

I was 19 years old when my first child was born. All of what I thought I would be doing shifted, hard. My wife, who I met during the summer before high school, was a good mother to my child and I loved them both fiercely. But our little family needed money. So, I took all sorts of jobs and art took a backseat to everything. My wife took a couple of jobs, but I think she was hard wired to being a stay-at-home mom.

The early 1990s were hard for commercial artists as about half of the commercial art houses in Philadelphia closed up shop. The glut of now out of work commercial artists hitting the pavement looking for jobs were massively more experienced than the students like me just entering the job market.

My marriage fell apart. My relationship with my art was also not good as I spent less, and less time focused on it. I sketched when I could and would do little projects here and there for extra cash. It is the strangest thing to experience letting go of something so much a core of your being. The loss of myself was beginning to be a habit. This was an incredibly dark place in my life. I lost way too much of me.

But don't stop here, it gets better.

Academy of Natural Sciences of Philadelphia

My mother always said that it was important to do something with your life that you believed in, that you could be proud of.

I fell into a great job at the Academy of Natural Science of Philadelphia after spending a brief time as a volunteer fossil preparator. The Education Department needed someone to run the Safari Overnight program and to teach lessons in the museum. This place changed my life and taught me another life lesson. When an interesting door opens, walk through that door.

What changed about my life? Stability. I had a full-time job with a salary (although crappy) and benefits. I had a place where I could grow, and I found that I enjoyed teaching. I also found that I managed people well. Lastly, it gave me a little more time for art.

The Academy of Natural Sciences shared a circle on the Benjamin Franklin Parkway with the Franklin Institute and the Philadelphia Free Library. The circle was crowned by a beautifully sculpted fountain surrounded by a wide walkway and well-kept garden. Cars raced around the circle headed towards City Hall, while kids splashed in the fountain enjoying the spray of the water jets. I walked by this fountain each day and often ate lunch there.

The museum was like a family. There was plenty of dysfunction, but the people I worked closest with were the best!

This was a huge time of growth for me. I still battled what I realize now was depression, and several bridges with my past were burnt or burning, but I got up each morning and got to work.

There were also dinosaurs and other extinct creatures.

The museum opened opportunities for me to do dinosaur art for education materials, exhibits, and scientific publications. More and more illustrations were being commissioned for decent money. Other institutions and individuals were requesting art as well.

This sounds like a cascade to overnight success, but in reality it took years and still the art was earning a small percentage of my yearly income. I was dissatisfied, but going in the right direction.

This time rekindled a love of paleontology and science and most of all exploration. As the art opportunities continued to grow, so did my involvement in field excavation of dinosaurs and fossil preparation in a publicly viewable lab in Dinosaur Hall, which I was asked to manage.

Dinosaur Hall went through several refits while I worked at the museum, but it remained the flagship exhibit of the Academy. The hall itself was large and had a slight cathedral like feel with its mezzanines and wide main floor. The hall displayed massive skeletons of mostly Cretaceous dinosaurs, pterosaurs, and some aquatic reptiles. The bones of *Tyrannosaurus rex* proudly ruled the space. At the far end of the hall was my fossil lab.

There was a second marriage during that time. It was an extremely, personally harmful relationship that I will not focus on here but to say that it happened and that I vowed to never remarry.

As my second marriage came to an end. I was working on a massive dinosaur in Argentinian Patagonia with a great bunch of folks who shared my need to explore and interest in paleontology. It also gave me distance and head space to start thinking about who I was and wanted to be. Another life-changing relationship formed in the friendship with a then graduate student named Jason. Jason has become like a brother, so many hours of field work and great conversation have bound me to our common goals and moments of profound discoveries, both our own and of the students and dig participants we work with.

Jason and I work primarily in Montana. In some of the most beautiful natural spaces I have ever encountered. I am never happier than when I am there. Digging with our team or sketching the world around me at those times.

I have been working in Montana almost every summer since 1999.

Right around the time I was working in Patagonia on the then unnamed *Dreadnoughtus*, the 200-year-old Academy of Natural Sciences was merging with Drexel University.

Another key friendship rekindled with one of the coolest people I have ever met. She would eventually cause me to break my vow to never marry again. Happily. Stacy would also gift me a second child, Izzy. Surrounding myself with great people who get who I am and are positive influences is the best thing I have done for myself. For an artist in general, it is key.

So at this point in my life I was employed at the museum running Dinosaur Hall and the fossil preparation lab. I also worked as an adjunct professor teaching "Dinosaurs and their World" and "Intro to Geology" for Drexel University, as well as teaching sketching and drawing at Fliesher's Art Memorial in South Philadelphia. I had also done a bit of time illustrating for National Geographic.

We had a big house in East Oak Lane where I grew up, with plenty of rooms for a big studio and lots of family. Things were tight, but good. Stacy, Izzy, and my father lived in the house, as well as my great friend David and a revolving stream of young paleo interns.

Dad was having issues with what a life of heavy smoking will do to you, but he was still getting around. My daughter Izzy had started school and Stacy's career was doing great!

Then the first stories of Covid quietly crept into the media. People were just starting to say the word pandemic. The Academy "restructured" and I was offered a job, but it had nothing to do with the one I had built over 27 years. It was time to go. It was massively strange that as I walked through my dinosaur hall for the last time, I realized that I didn't really know who I was without the museum.

I finished up the last few weeks of the semester as the university planned to move all of its classes online. Students were fleeing the city in droves. I was told that adjuncts would be contacted when the university needed them.

My city was deserted. No kids at the fountain, very few cars on the road, and shops with closed signs as far as you could see.

Dad's health was declining, so I took care of him and tried to help my daughter do 5th grade online. I don't even remember sketching much at that time, although I know I must have as a large body of art was created.

We skipped our field season that year. It was the first time since 1999 that I did not spend at least a few weeks digging in the Bighorn Basin, which had become a great recentering time each year. The act of discovery is incredible. There are times when things are extremely hard or uncomfortable and then BAM! there is a fossil or wildlife sighting, or even just the moment that you stop and look around at the "big sky", rocky outcrops of various colors, or the face of a friend or colleague who just had an incredible "ah ha" moment. These things refill my mental batteries.

Time passed slowly and strangely. Dad would say "well boy we are strangers in a strange land." He ate the same thing every morning and afternoon. Two over easy eggs with grits, toast and coffee for breakfast and a PB&J for lunch with a glass of milk. Dinner was whatever I cooked, but his favorites were chili and hotdogs and beans so we did those often.

Covid got crazy then it died down. We had to be extra careful due to dad being in a high-risk state of health so we were slower to socialize. What a strange time it was. When dad's health really got bad, we decided that I could not keep taking care of him. At that point he really could not do anything for himself. I became worried about bed sores and just getting him to try to move and do little things. So it was decided he needed to go into assisted living. My brother took over Dad's care. Jonathan spent time with him almost daily and I packed for the field season.

My home and my city no longer felt like where I wanted/needed to be. The house was well over a hundred and fifty years old and was constantly needing repair. Prospects for employment were few and far between.

So we put the house up for sale. It sold super fast, and we moved to Montana.

Montana

We looked at opportunities in Red Lodge, Montana. There were no jobs and property was far too expensive as was the cost of living. My son Logan suggested checking out Missoula, which is a town/city with a thriving arts culture, a great nonprofit focus with good schools and incredible access to beautiful natural spaces. We found a small place to rent in the Moose Can Gully area of the South Hills.

The move to Montana was epic. Two dogs, a cat, a teenager, my wife, and mother-in-law in a rental box truck and a Honda Insight driving across the country. This drive took place after a masterful purging of stuff and packing of the old house, all of which I had practically no part in, as I was teaching in the field. I came to unload the truck and get Stacy settled as best I could before returning to the field. I was amazed at all my wife had accomplished and felt horrible for not being there.

The summer ended and I returned to my family. We spent the next few months exploring the incredible places to be in nature that are fifteen minutes or less from our house. Our first trip out of our fifteen minute bubble took us to the National Bison Range. We took the top off the Jeep and went African Safari style into the range. I sketched and took loads of photos of bison, elk, Whitetail and

Mule deer, coyotes and birds. It was an experience that has caused a deep fascination with bison which have appeared in several of my paintings and drawings.

The impact of Montana and its newness to me, awakened my mind and with it the need to do more with my art. My "studio urges" grew more often as did my desire to sketch outside.

Missoula can be a hard place to find your place, but sit down at Ruby's Cafe at the counter and people will start up a conversation. It's a great way to meet folks and figure out what Missoula has to offer. Not to mention Ruby's has the best breakfasts around.

There is a great arts focus in Missoula. I have found a great place for nature and inspiration in the Montana Natural History Center. I have had art exhibits on display and taught classes on dinosaurs, drawing, and nature journaling. I have found a home.

Doing art outside has a long history and takes many forms. (Plein-air, outdoor sketching, nature journalling) I have enjoyed nature journaling and sketching the most. Spending time two or three times per week in nature with a sketch book making observations both written and sketched in pen and watercolor has been massively inspiring. I find that the time I spend out of the studio in nature has reawakened a childlike curiosity and fascination that informs and fuels my time in the studio painting and drawing.

I like the format of the nature journal, especially when I keep a calendar as part of the book. I record phases of the moon, temperature, place, time, and observations all on a calendar. But the biggest benefit of keeping track of the calendar is the gentle push that it gives to continue. Seeing blank spaces on my calendar drives me to get back to being outside.

There are a good number of folks doing "Urban Sketching," which is great fun and provides different opportunities in subject matter. Often artists do their art alone. And I do enjoy a full day in the studio, but I find other artists to be great for inspiration and just trading techniques and ideas, and cool comradery.

Two of my friends and I started a Missoula based sketch group called "Missoula Sketchy Folks" for people who enjoy structured event sketching. We send an invite to meet two or three times a month to sketch in parks, coffee shops, or just cool spots in town. The events are all free and often we share our work with each other afterwards. It is the sharing that inspires people most. In fact, many "Sketchy Folks" will post work to our social media page for comments and constructive criticism. This sort of thing has been a great way to keep myself from isolation and stagnation.

Final thoughts. Art can be an all-encompassing life choice or a fun way to spend some time with a beloved hobby. Be honest with your needs and expectations and you will enjoy it all the more especially when you find yourself where you need to be.

For me sketching, drawing, and painting has provided a record of a life lived with art as my voice of choice.

~Jason C. Poole
Admitted Sketchy Folk

Prehistoric World

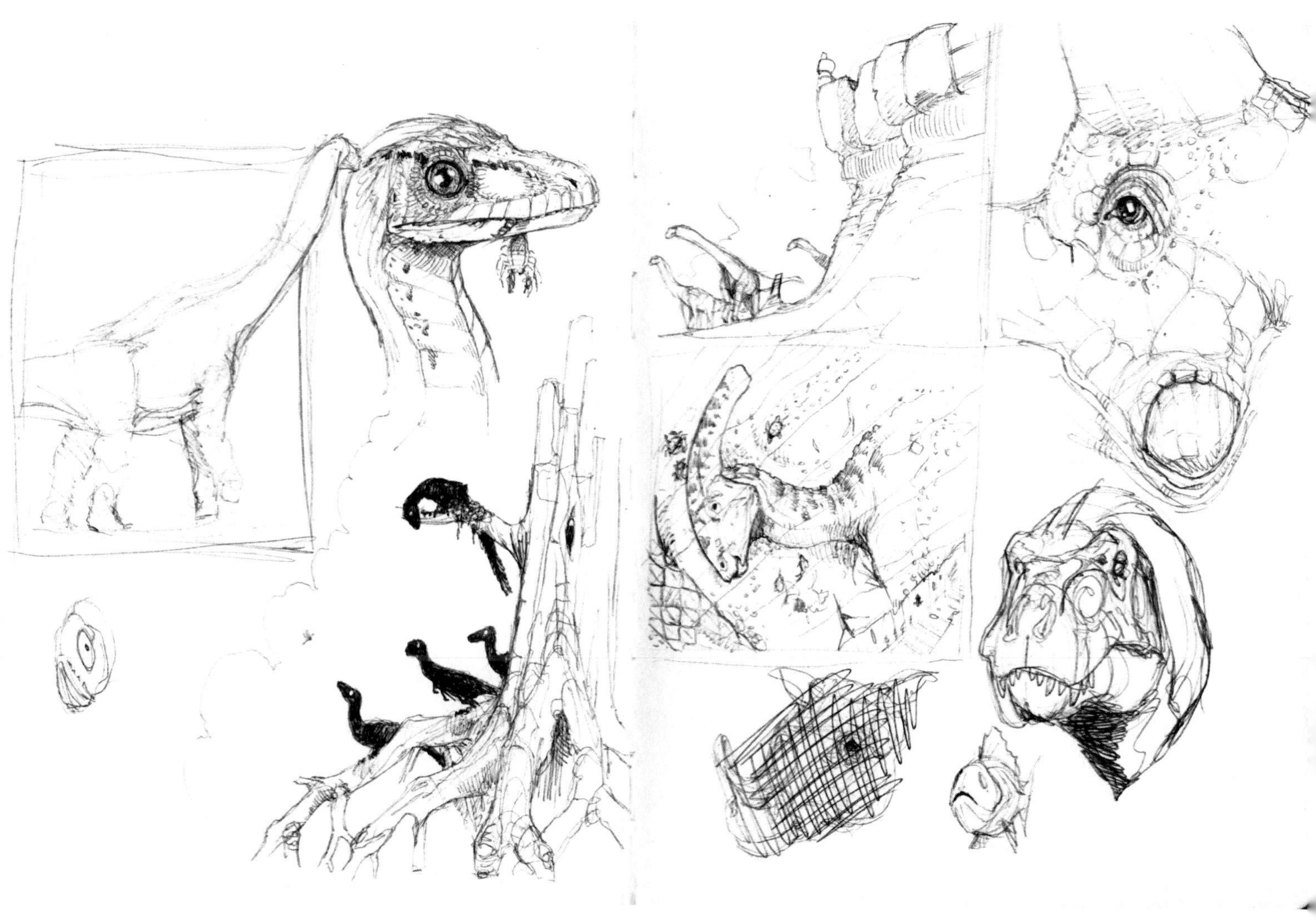

Non-Dinosaurs

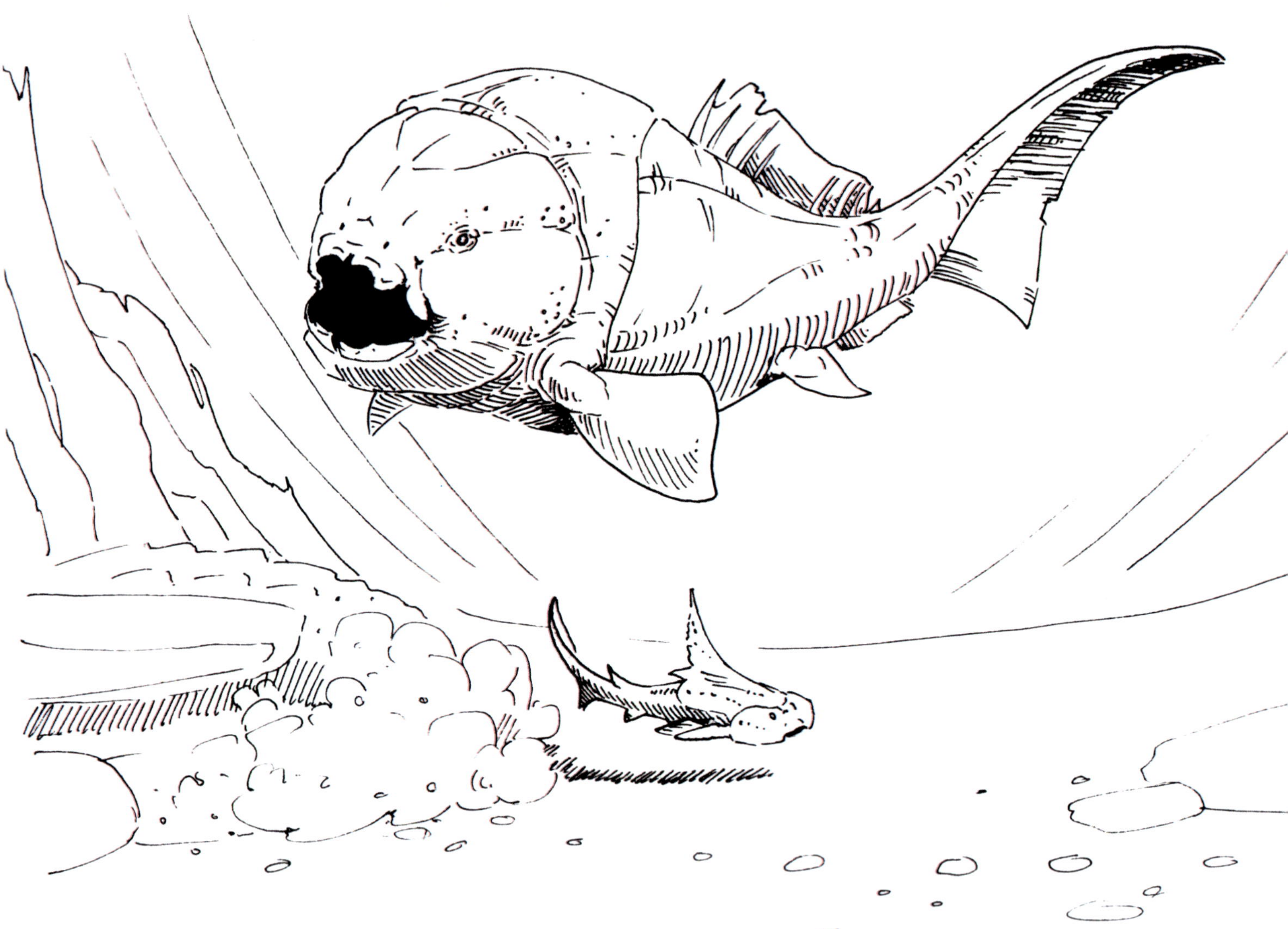

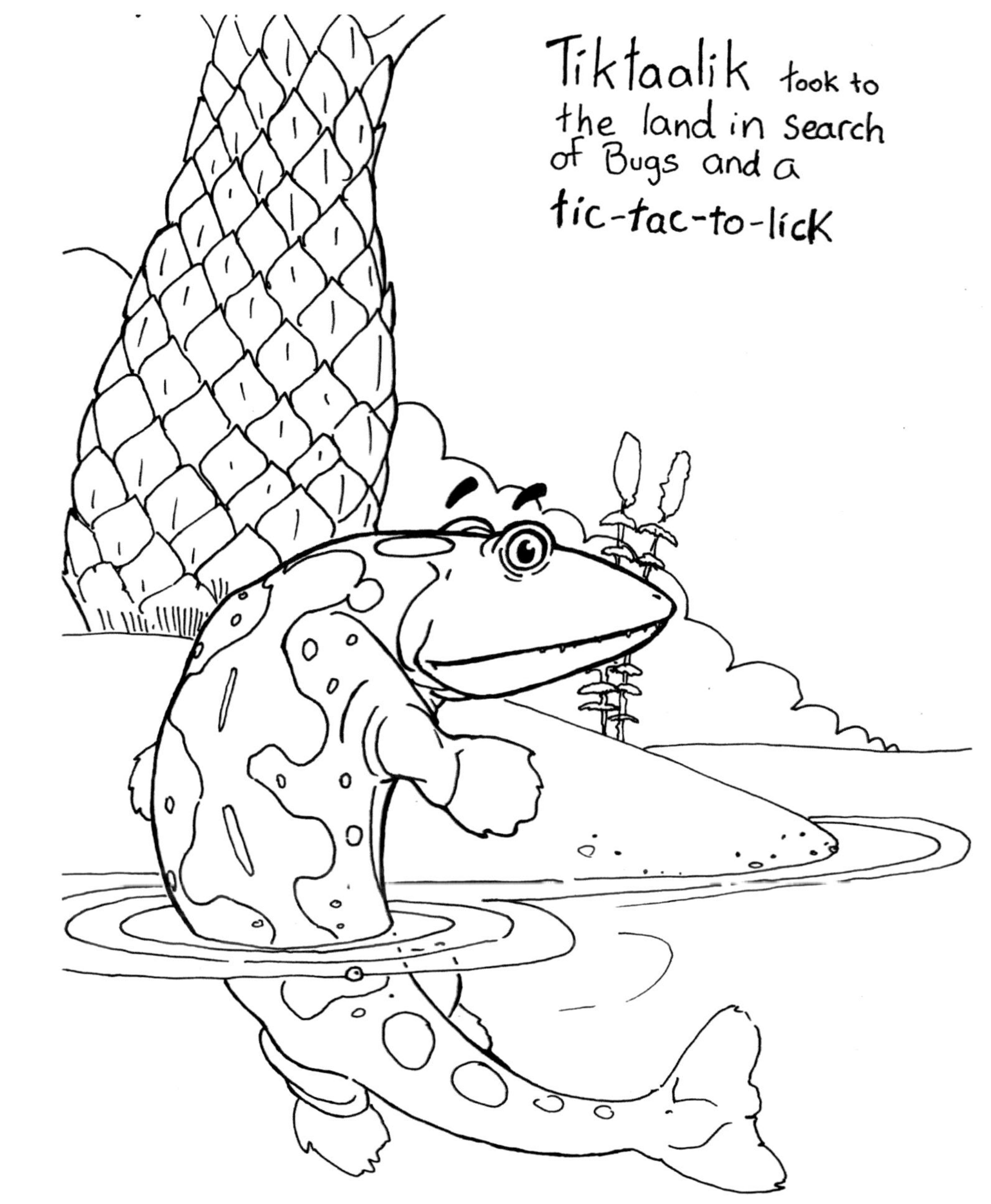

Tiktaalik took to the land in search of Bugs and a
tic-tac-to-lick

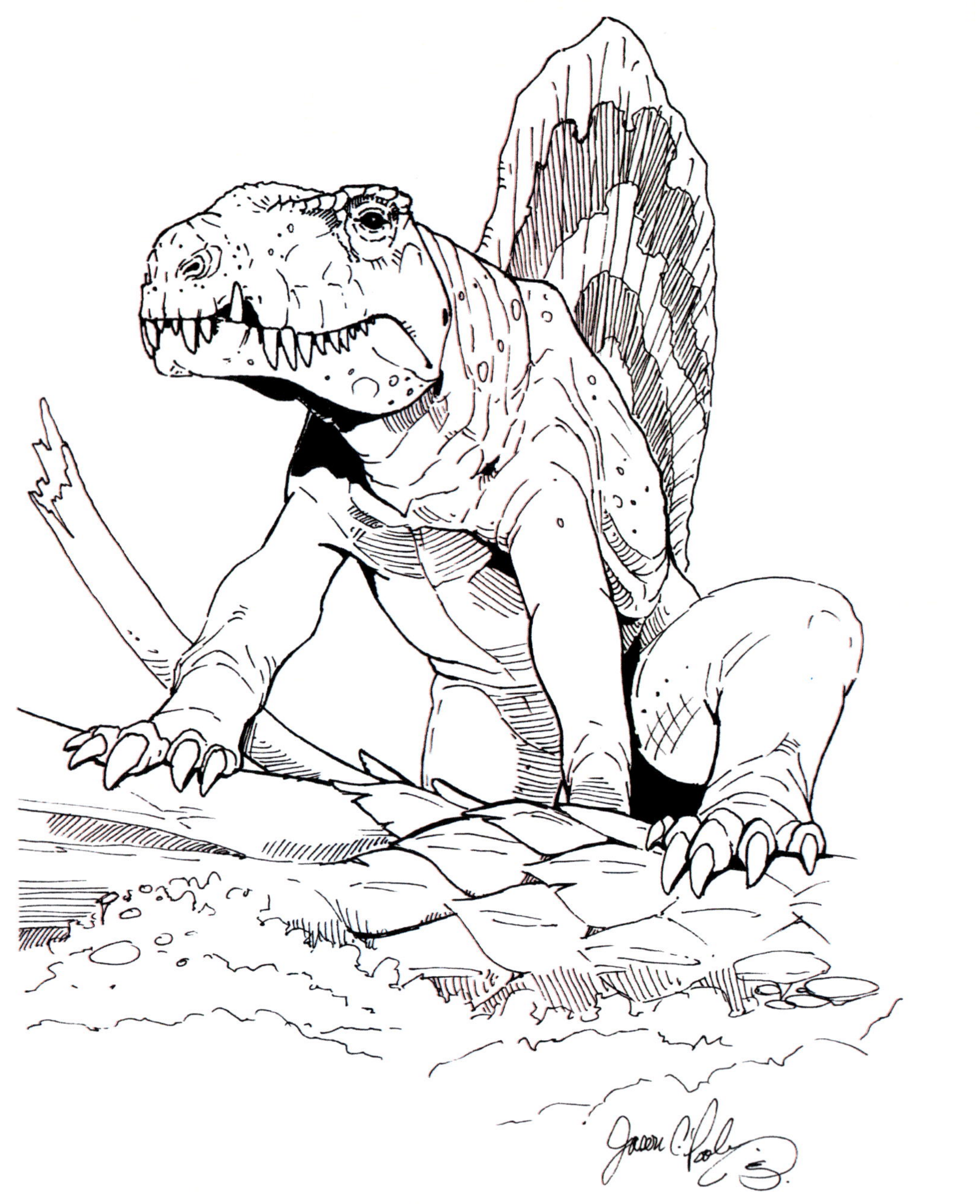

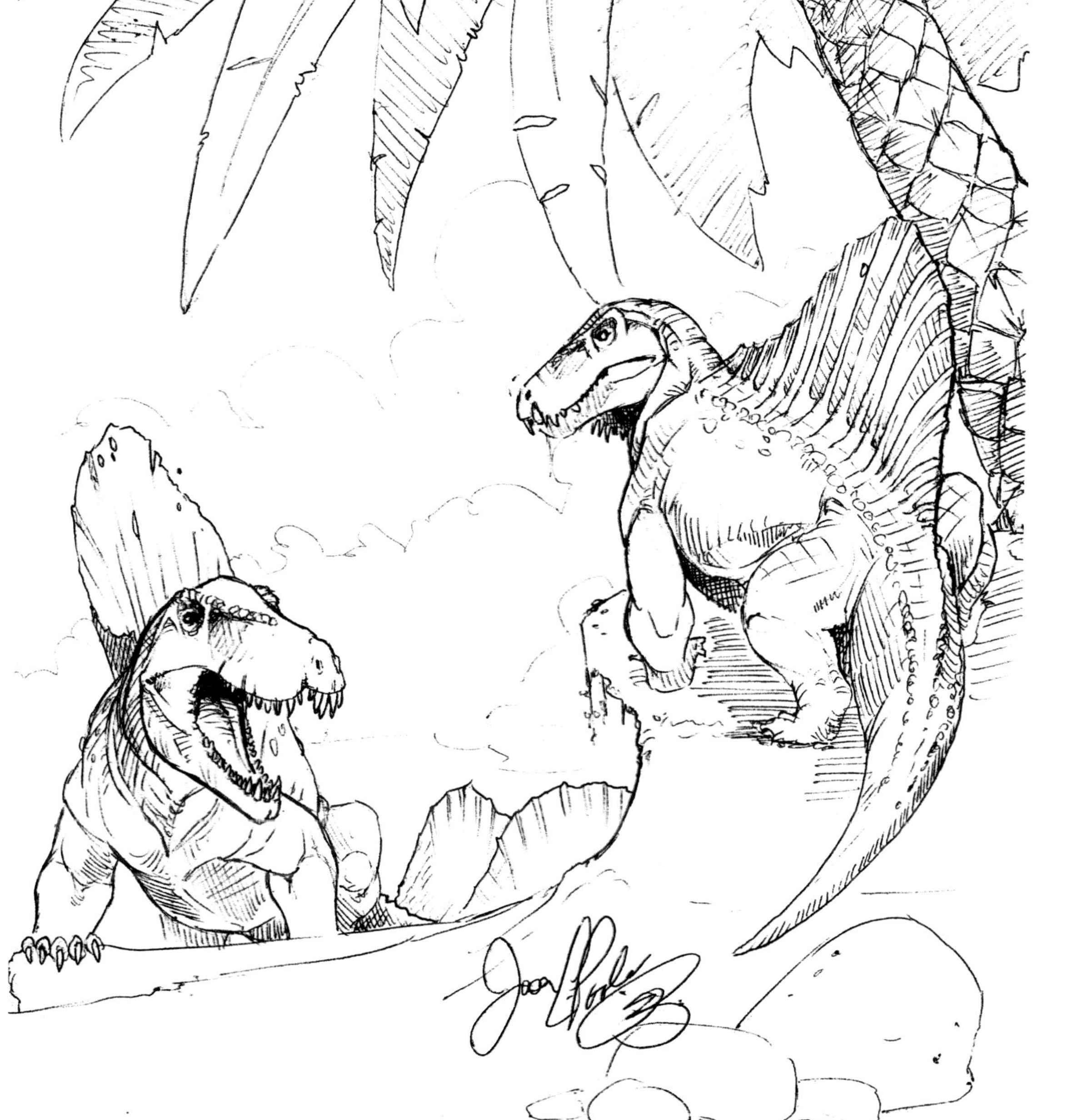

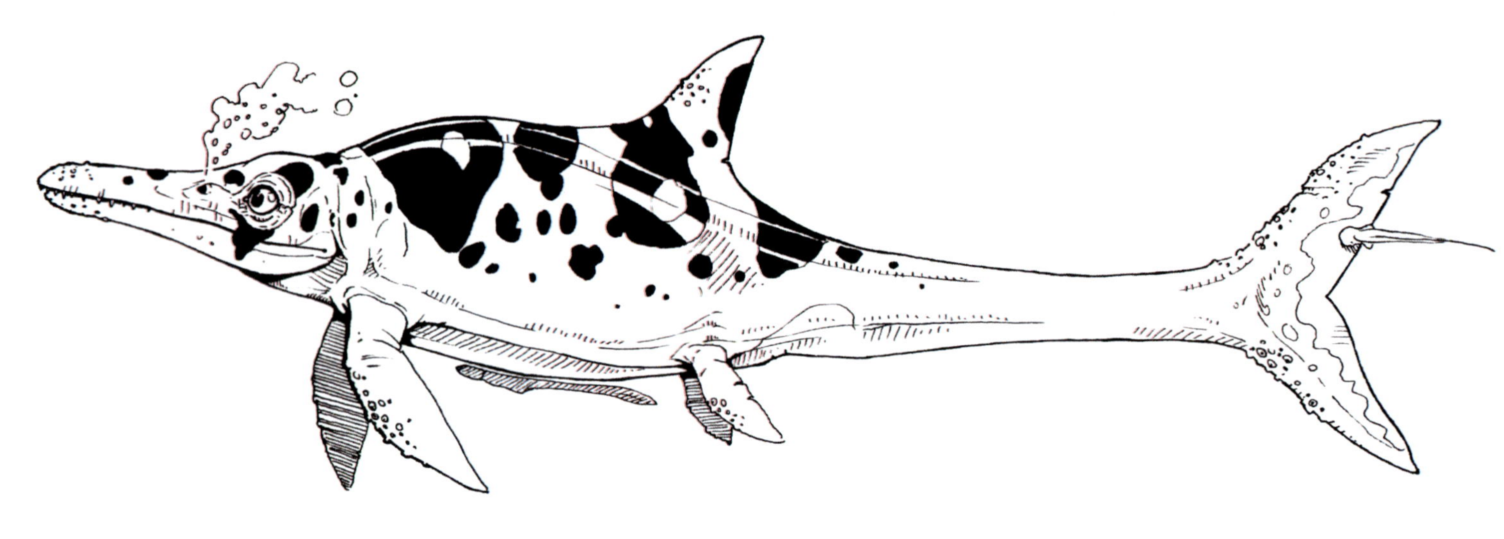

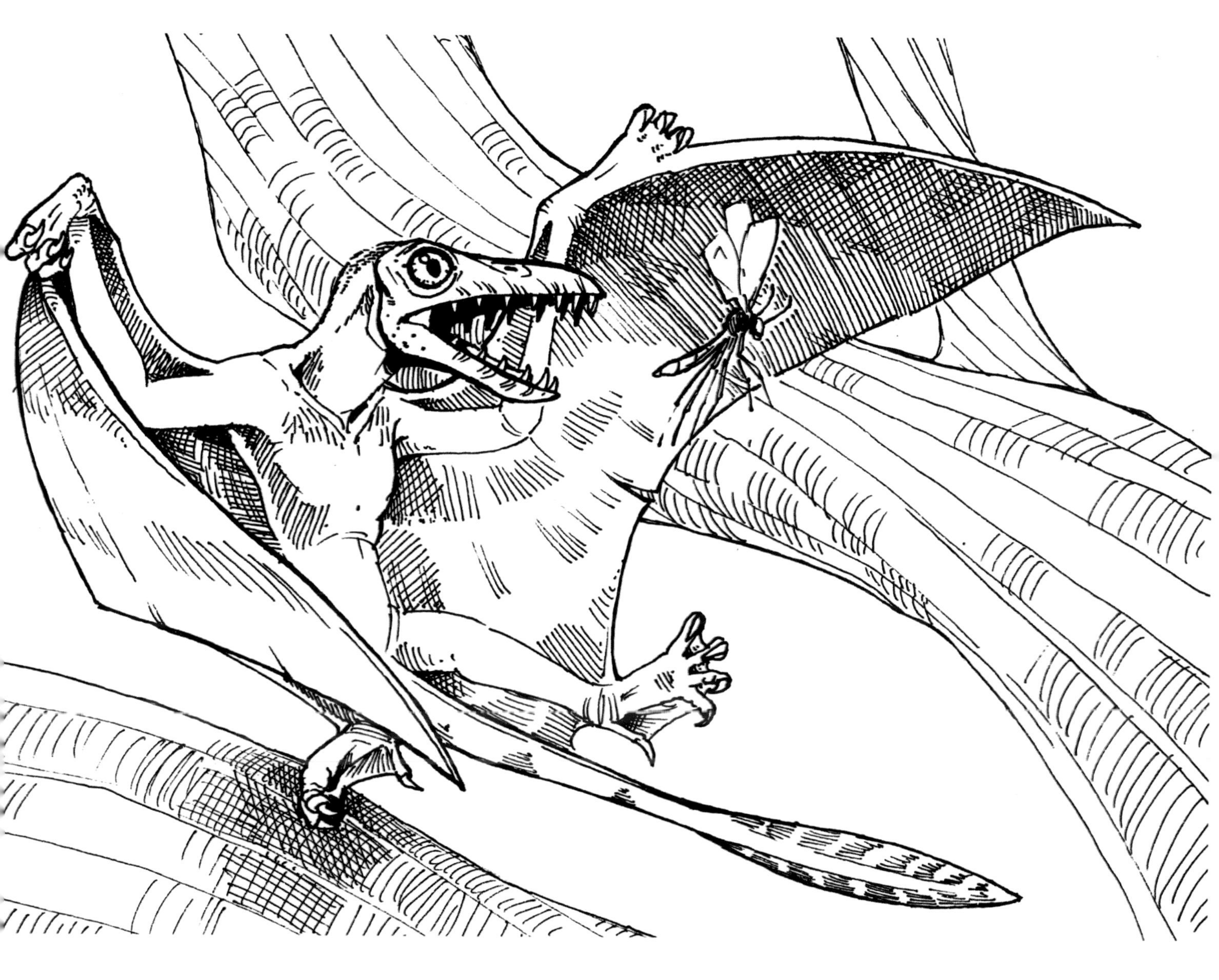

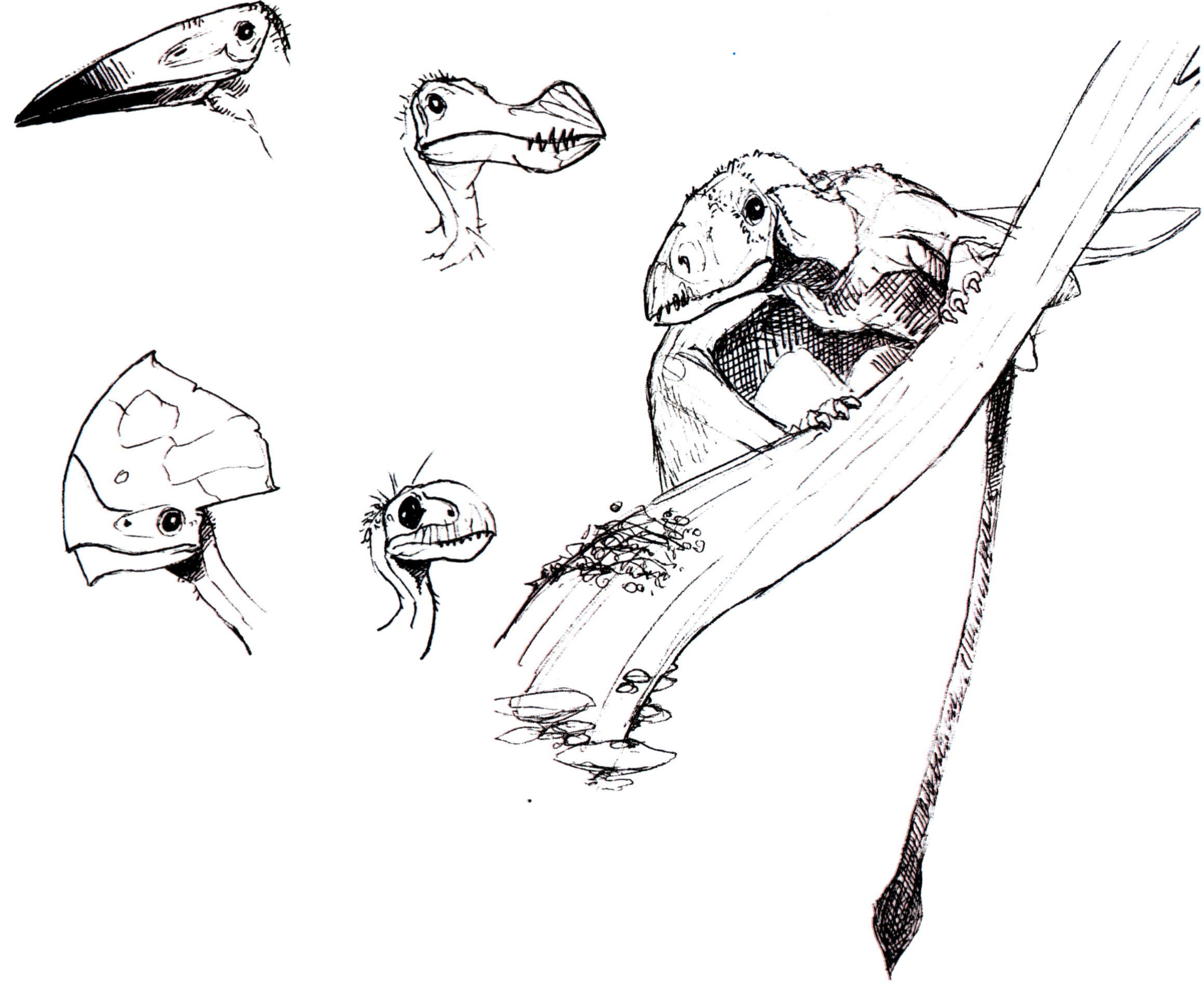

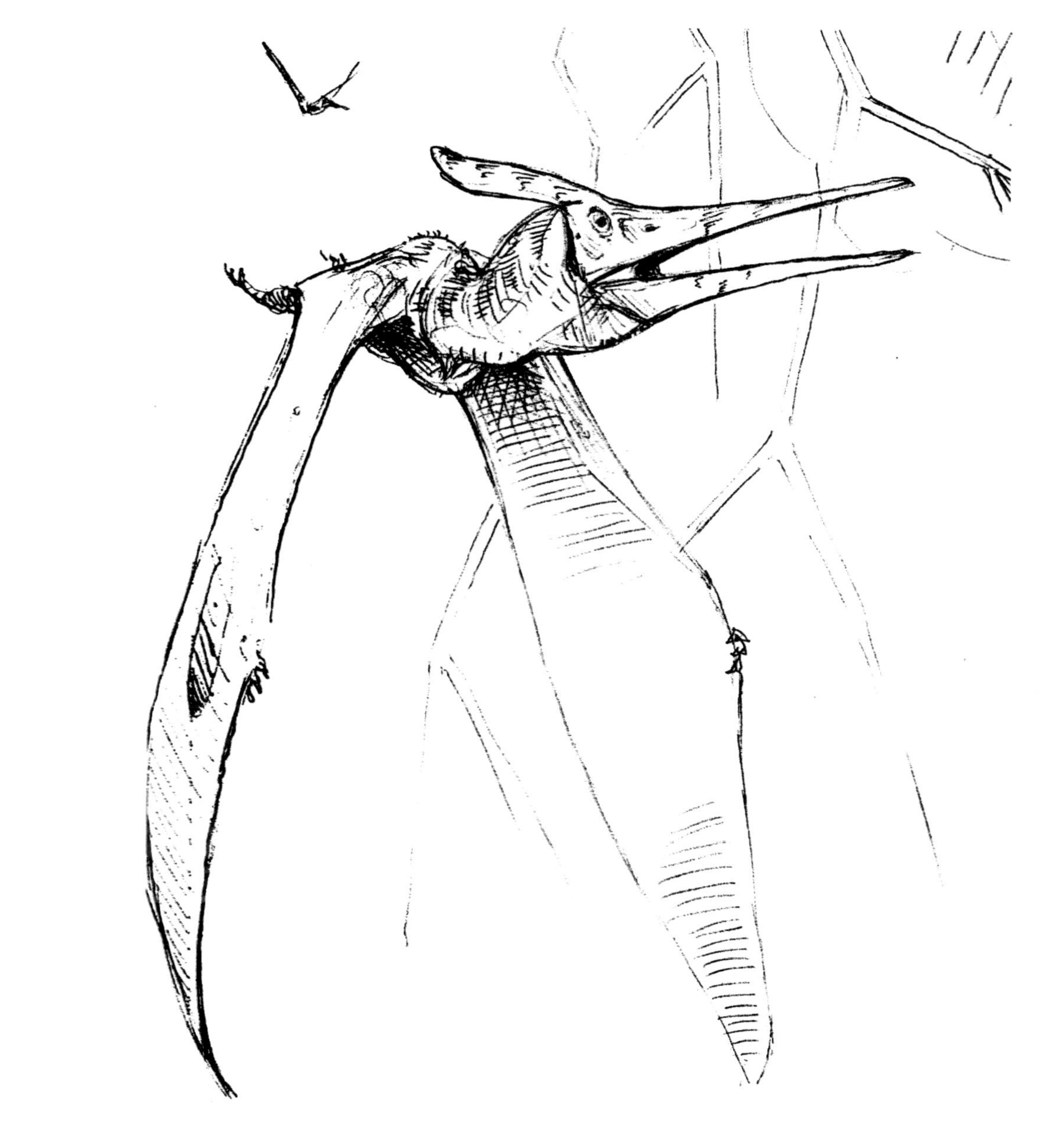

Prehistoric Scenes

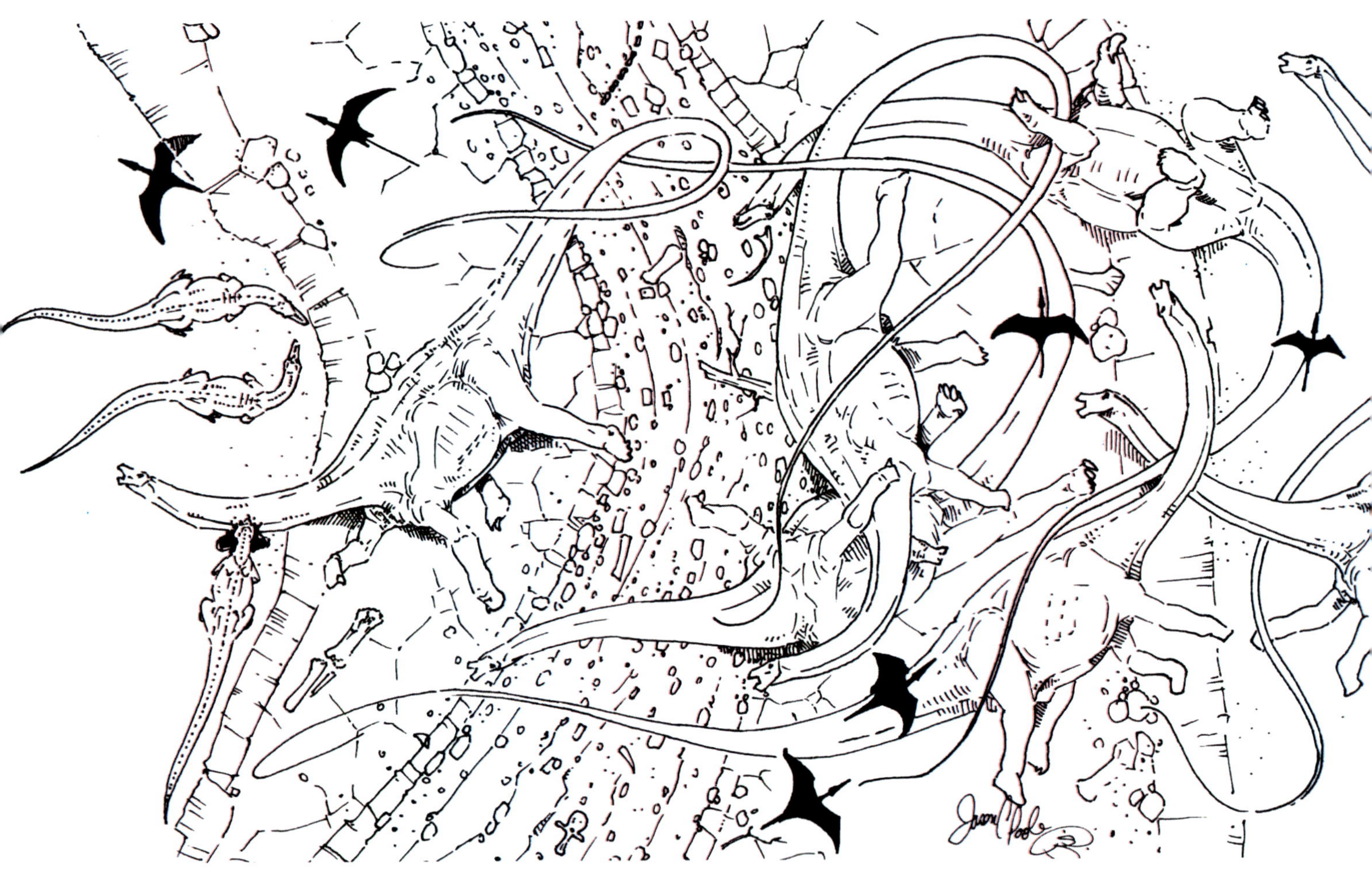

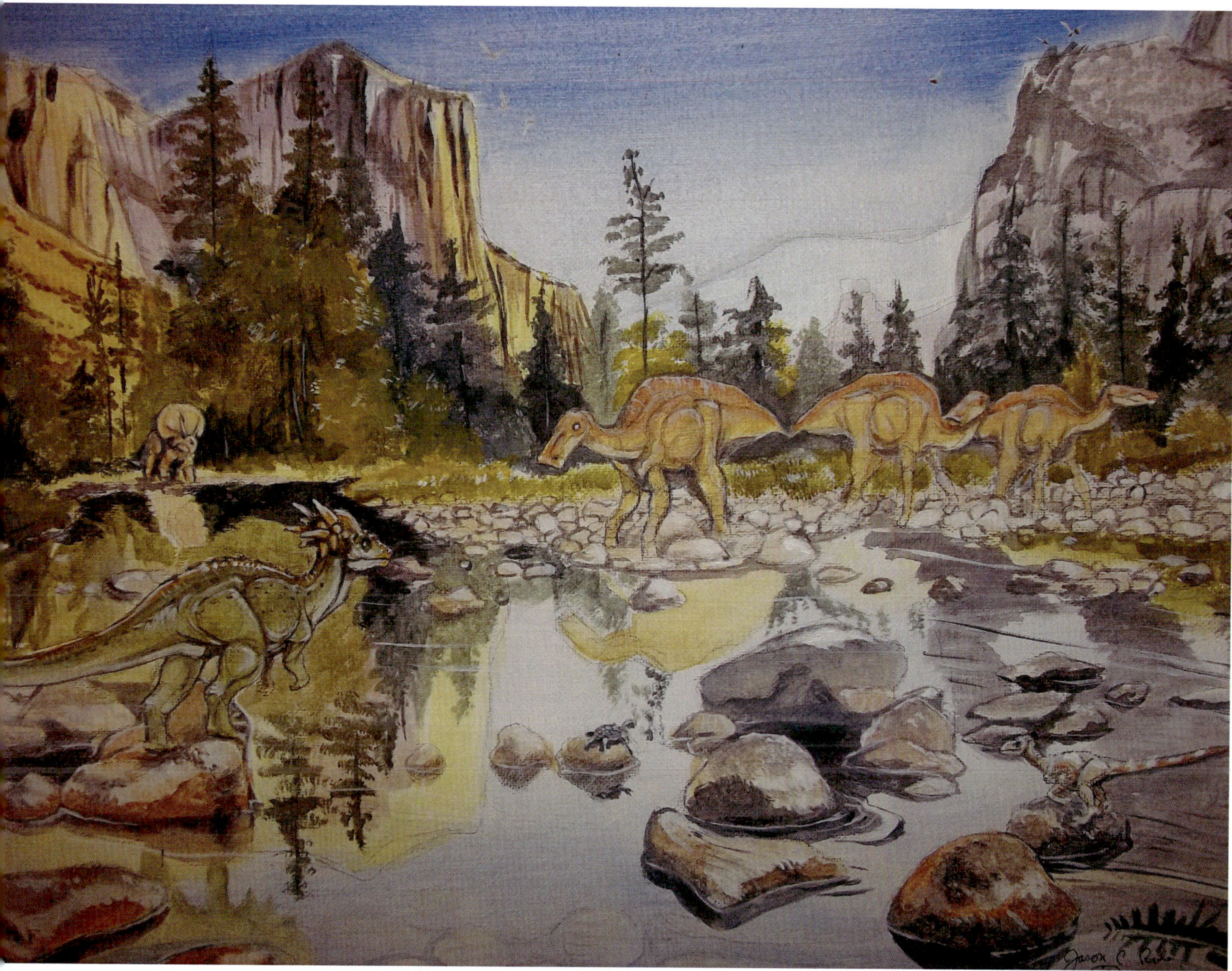

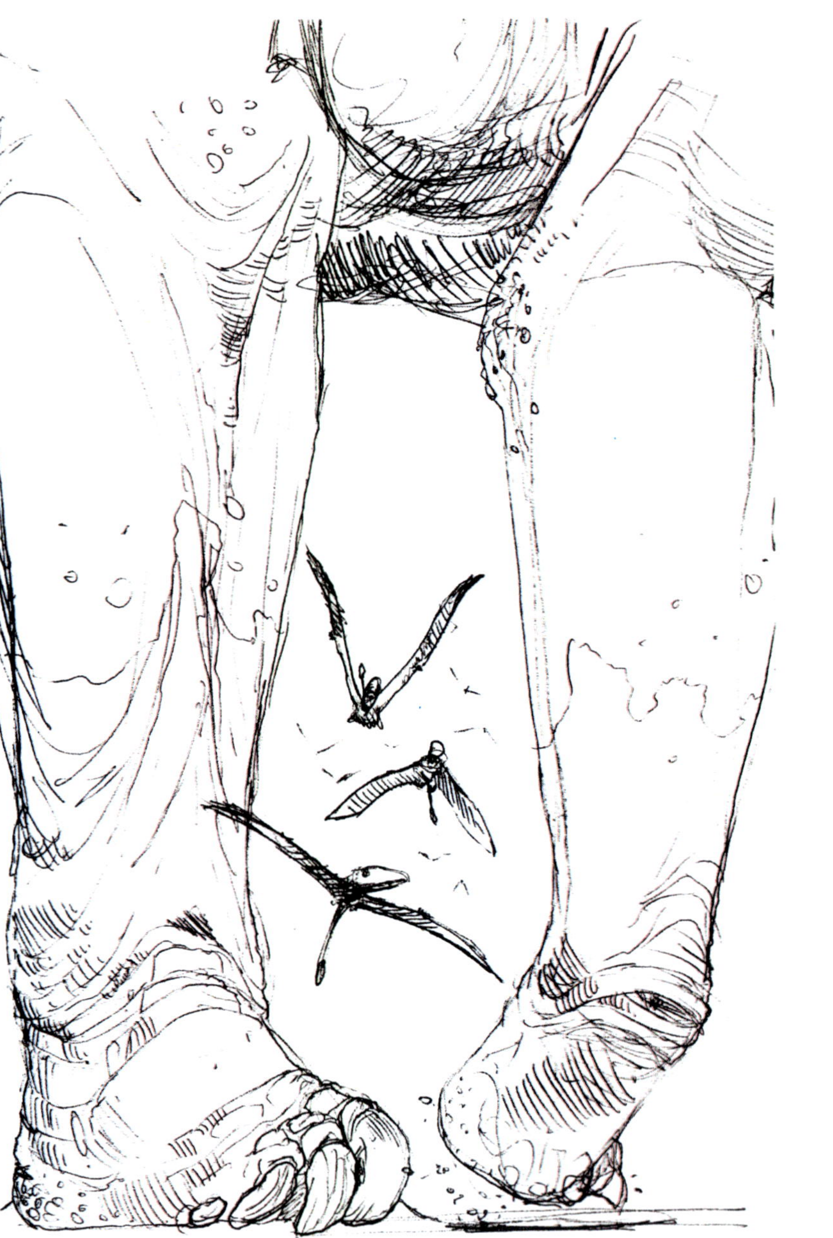

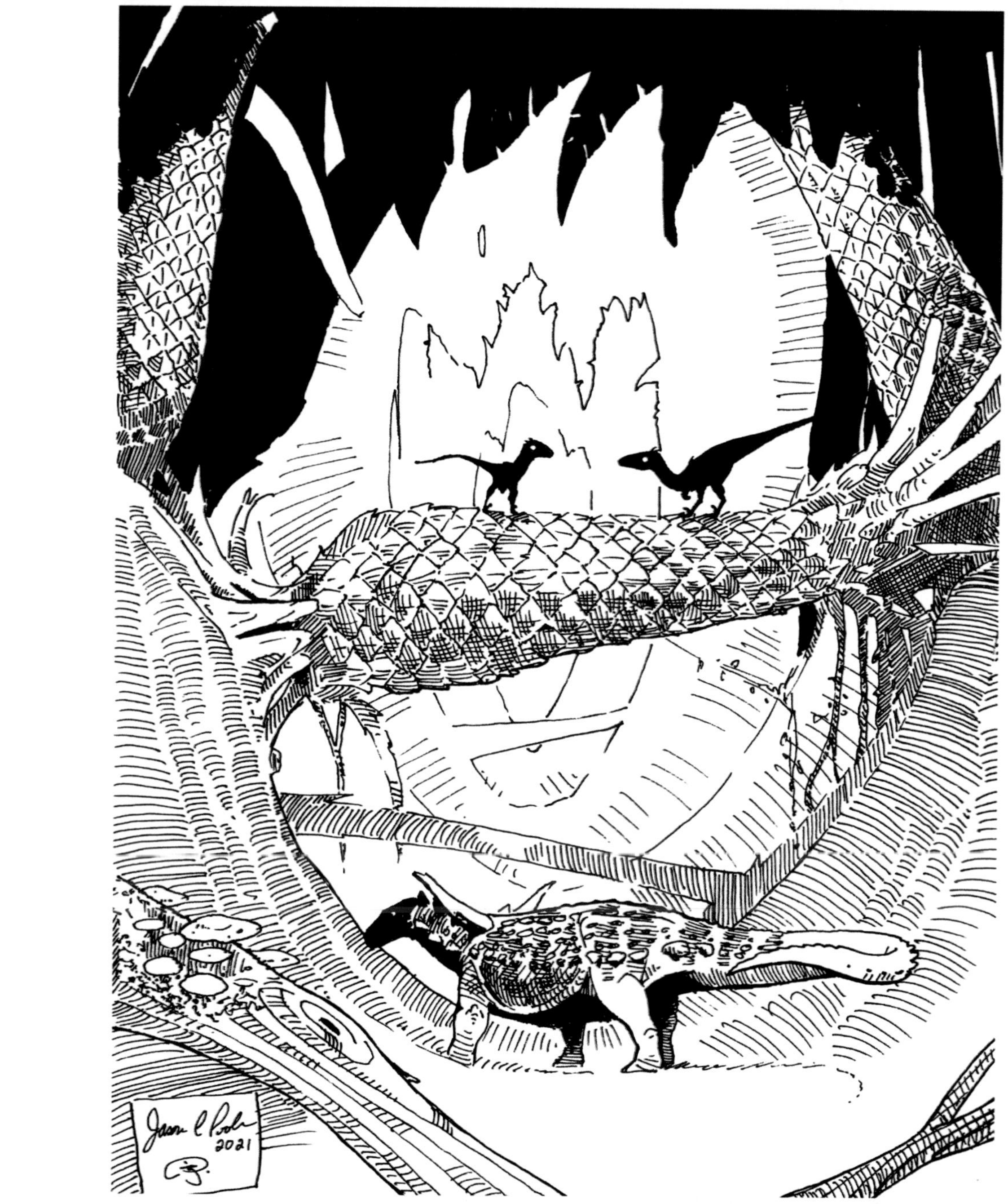

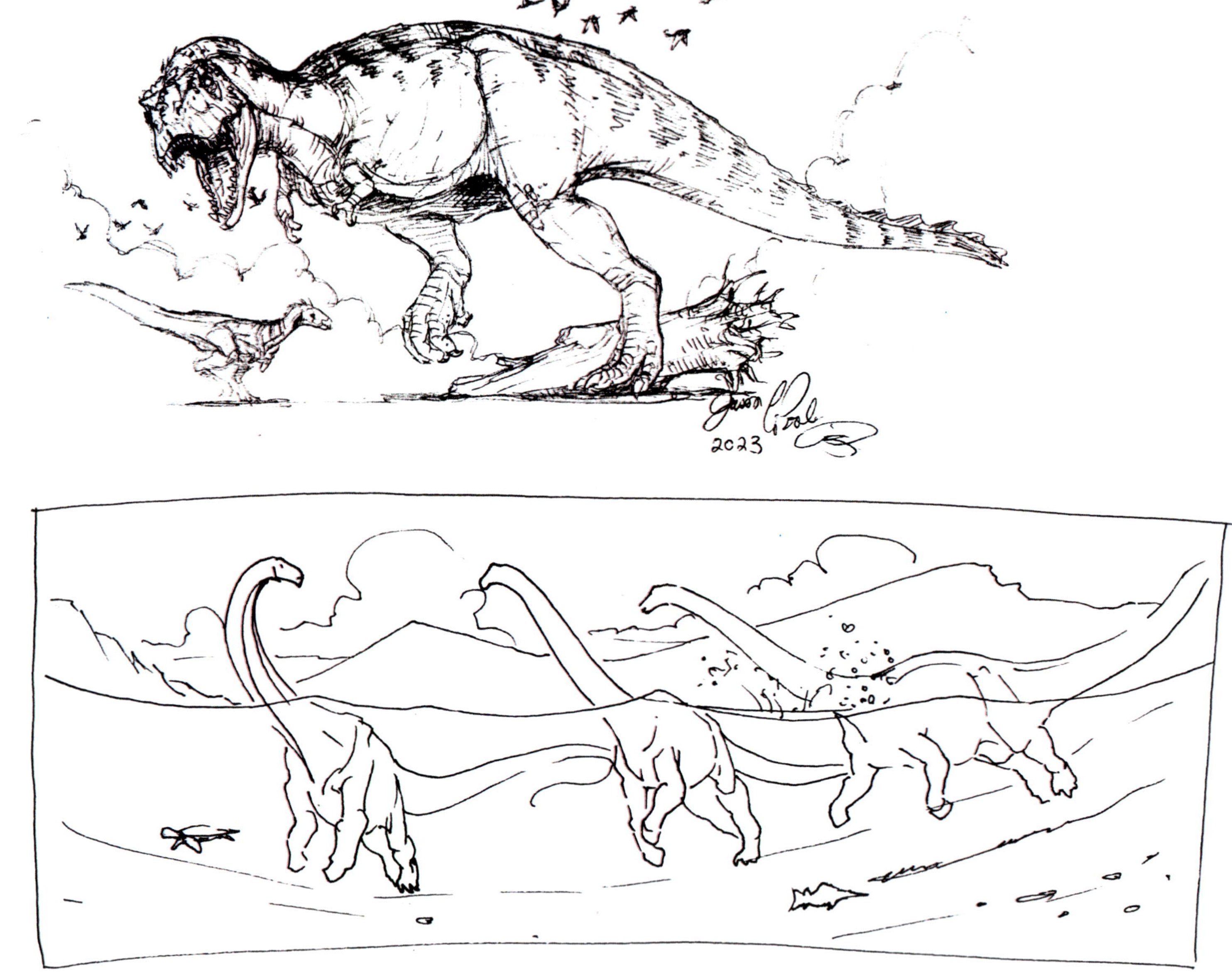

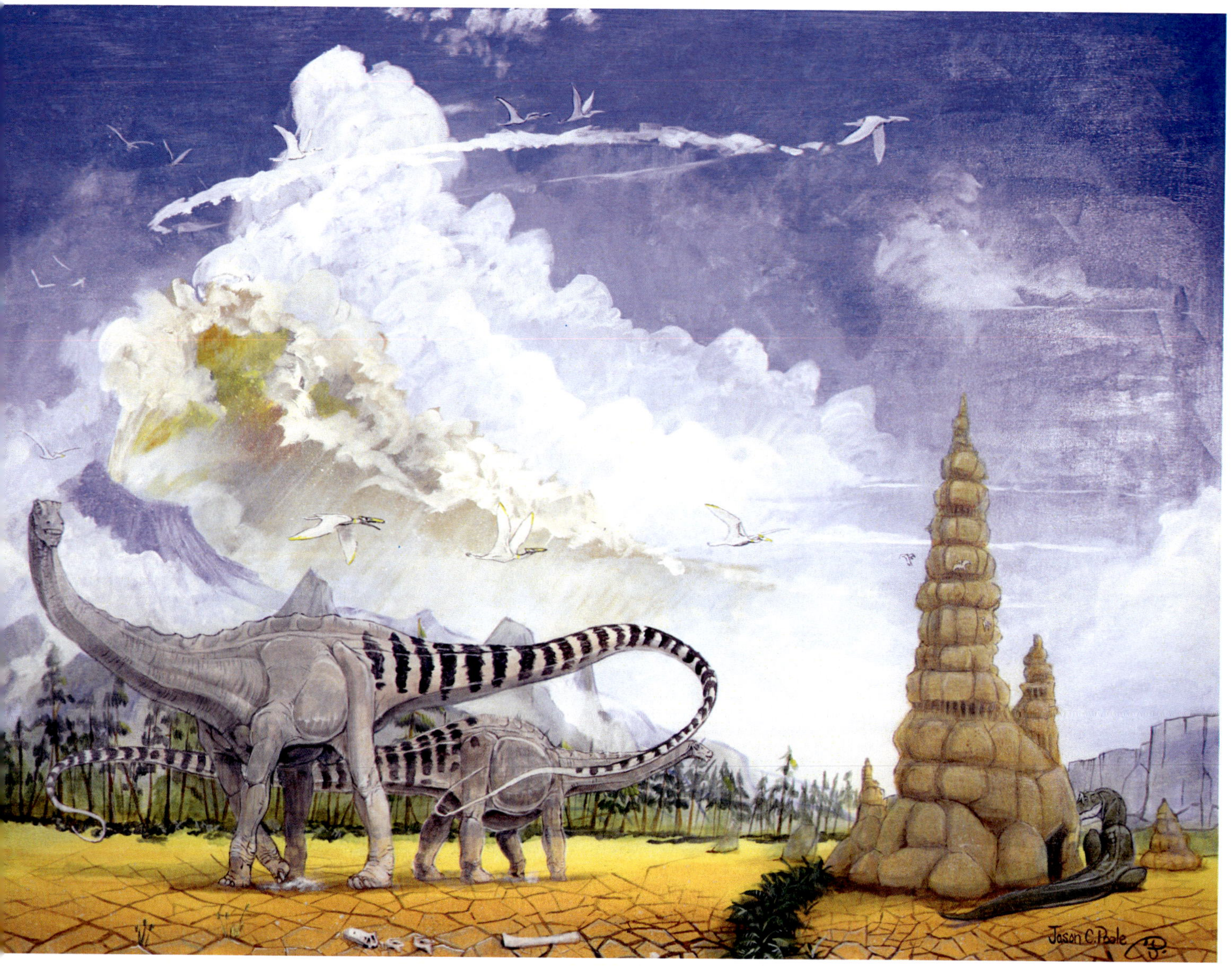

Jason C. Poole

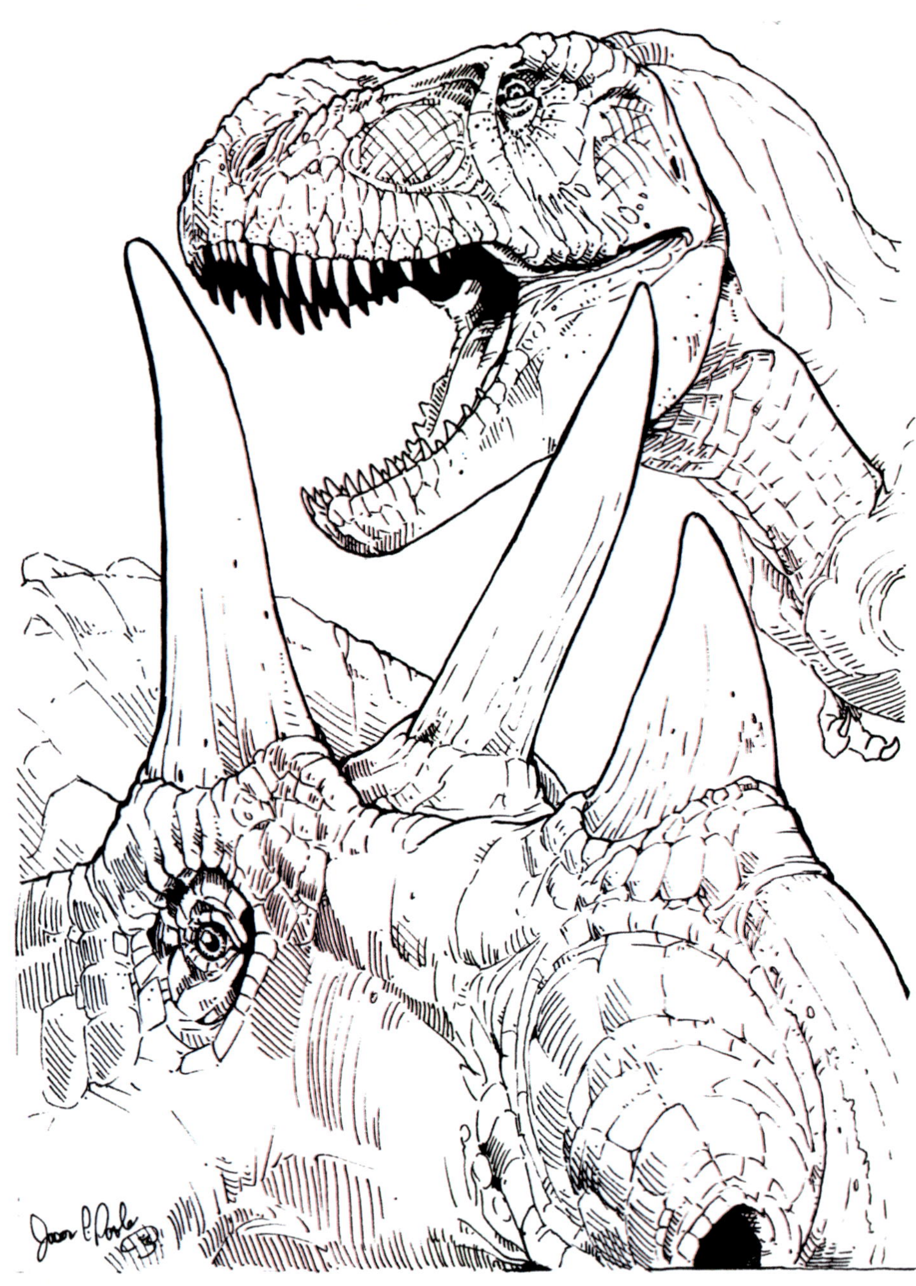

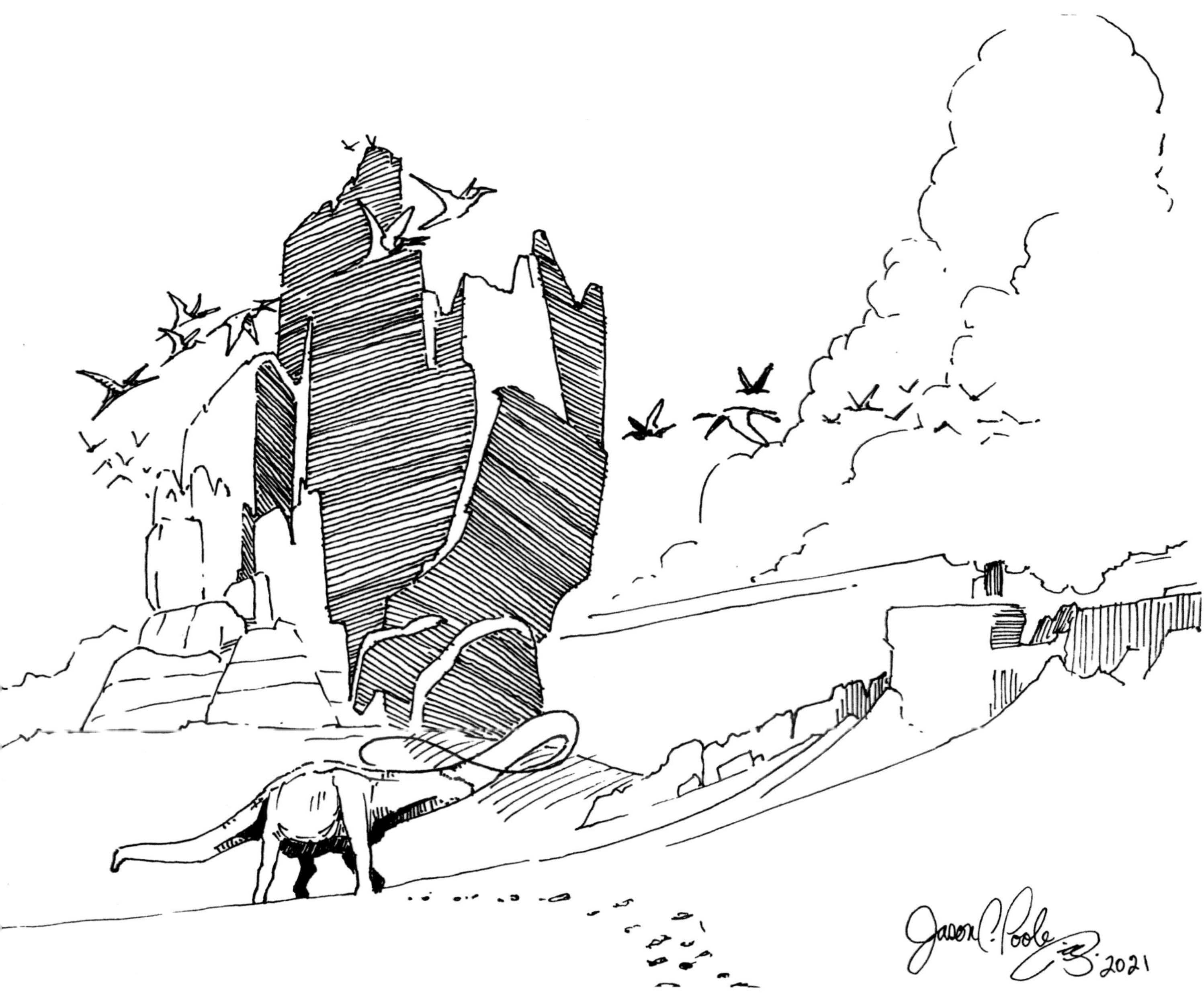

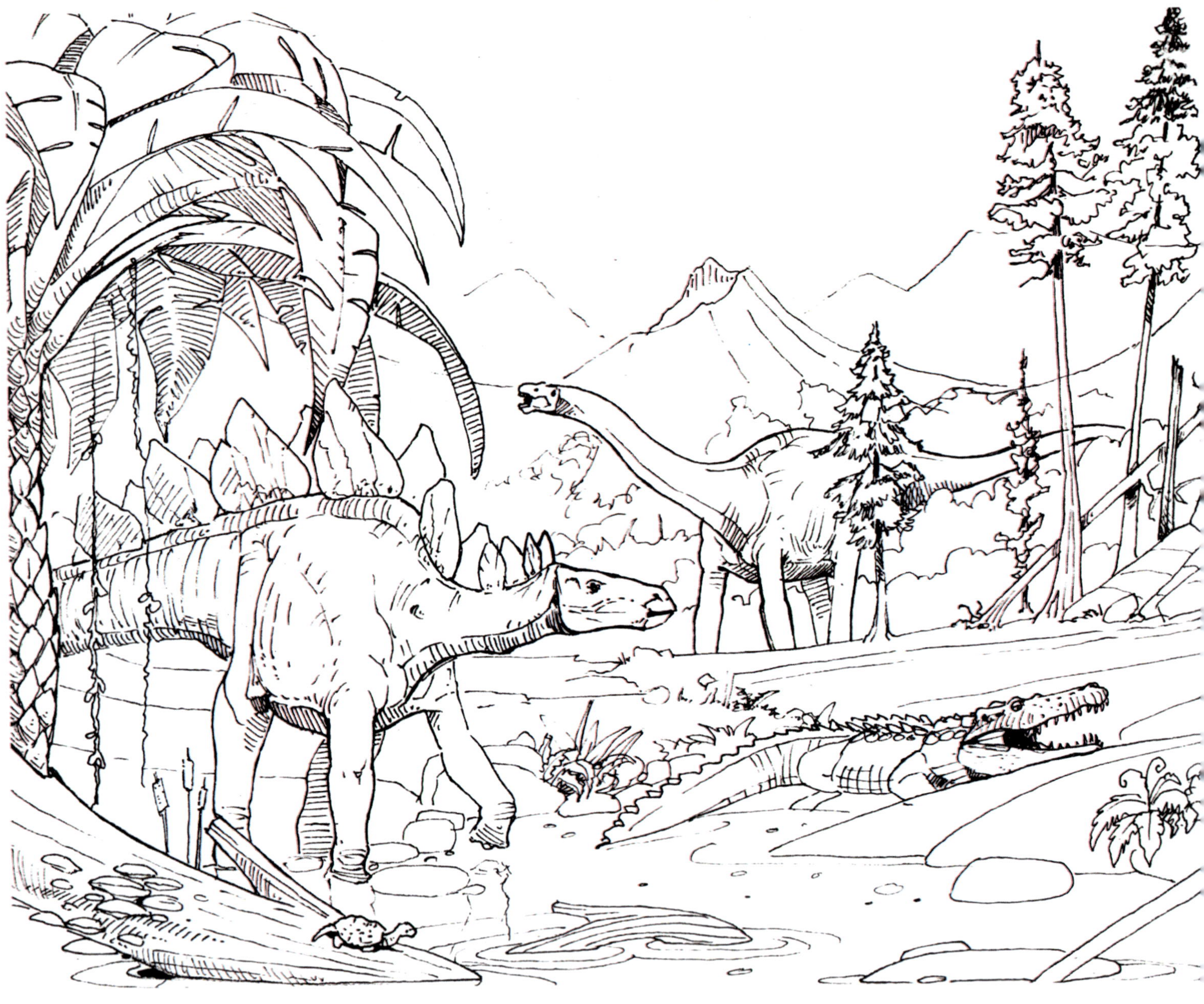

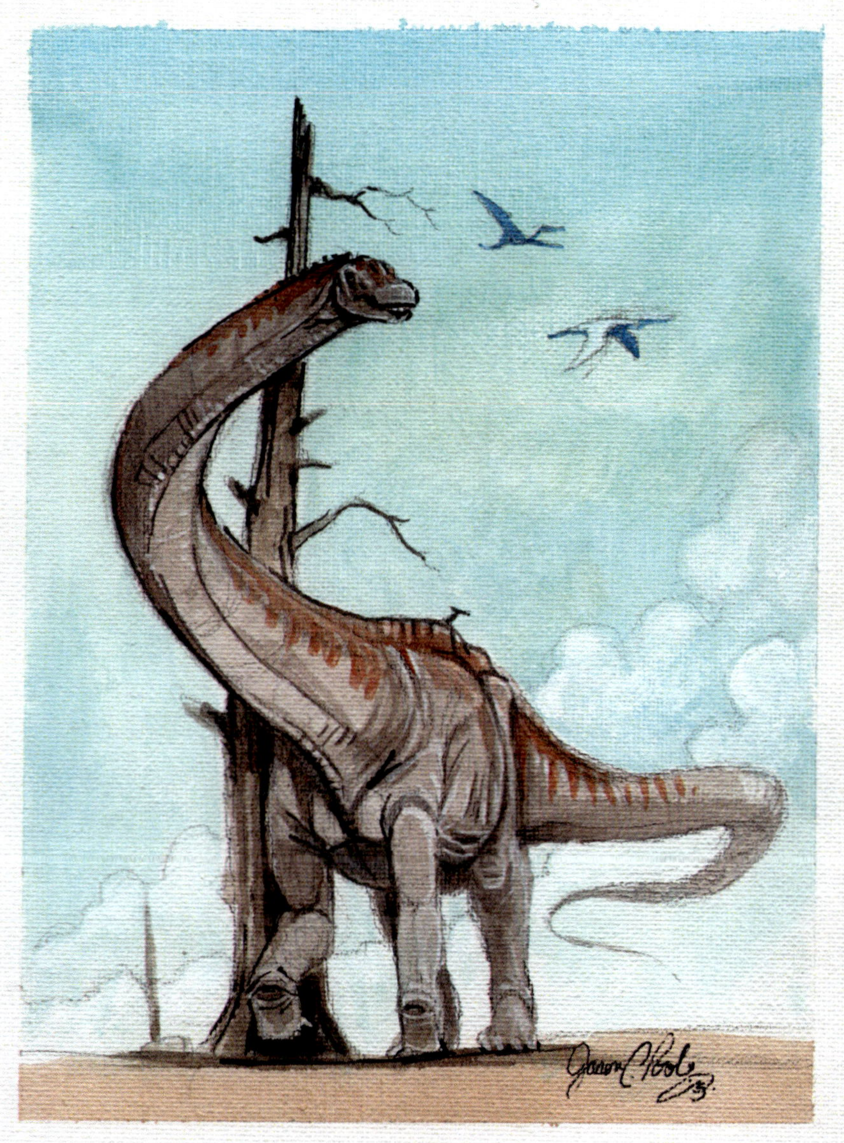

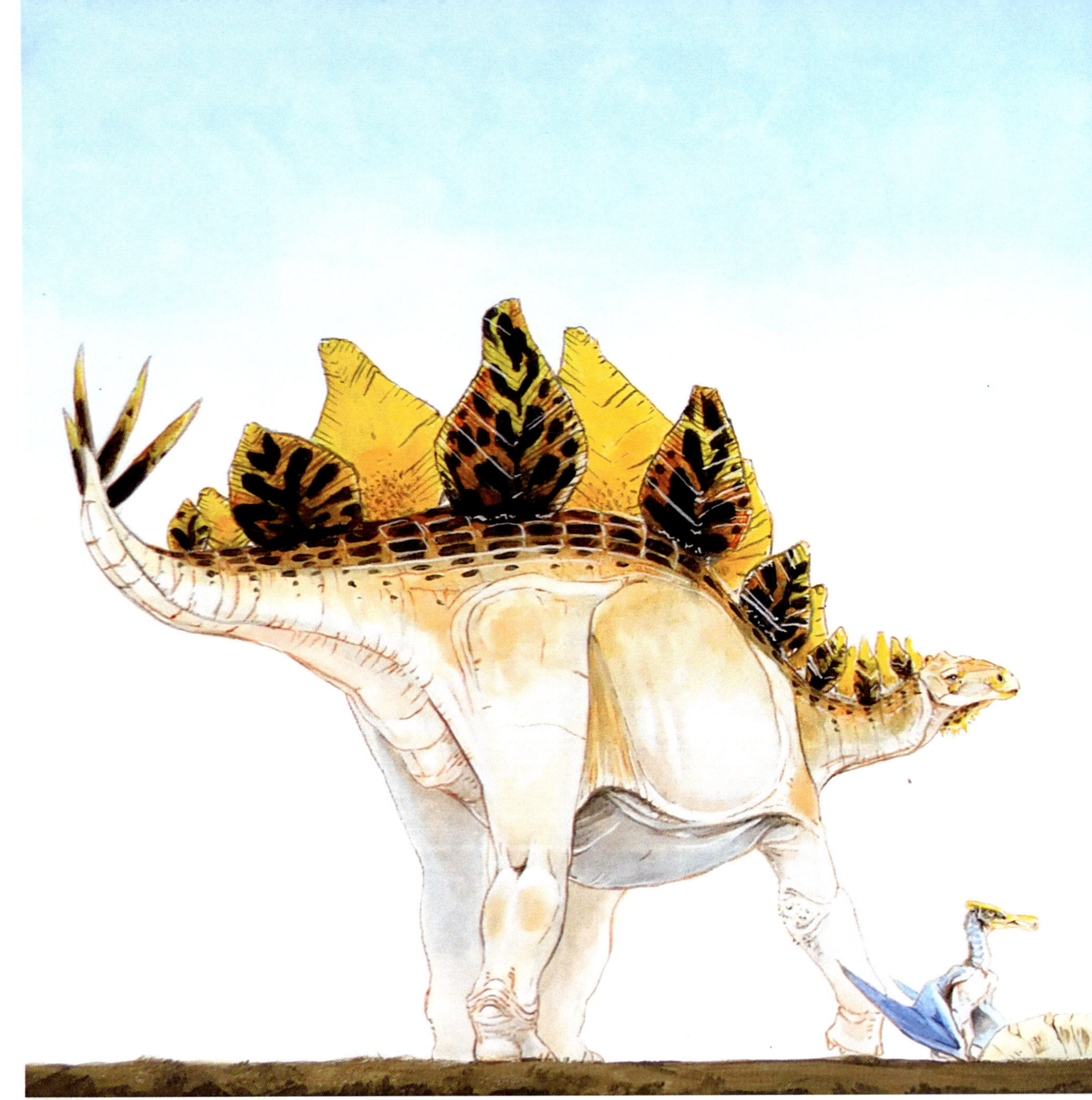

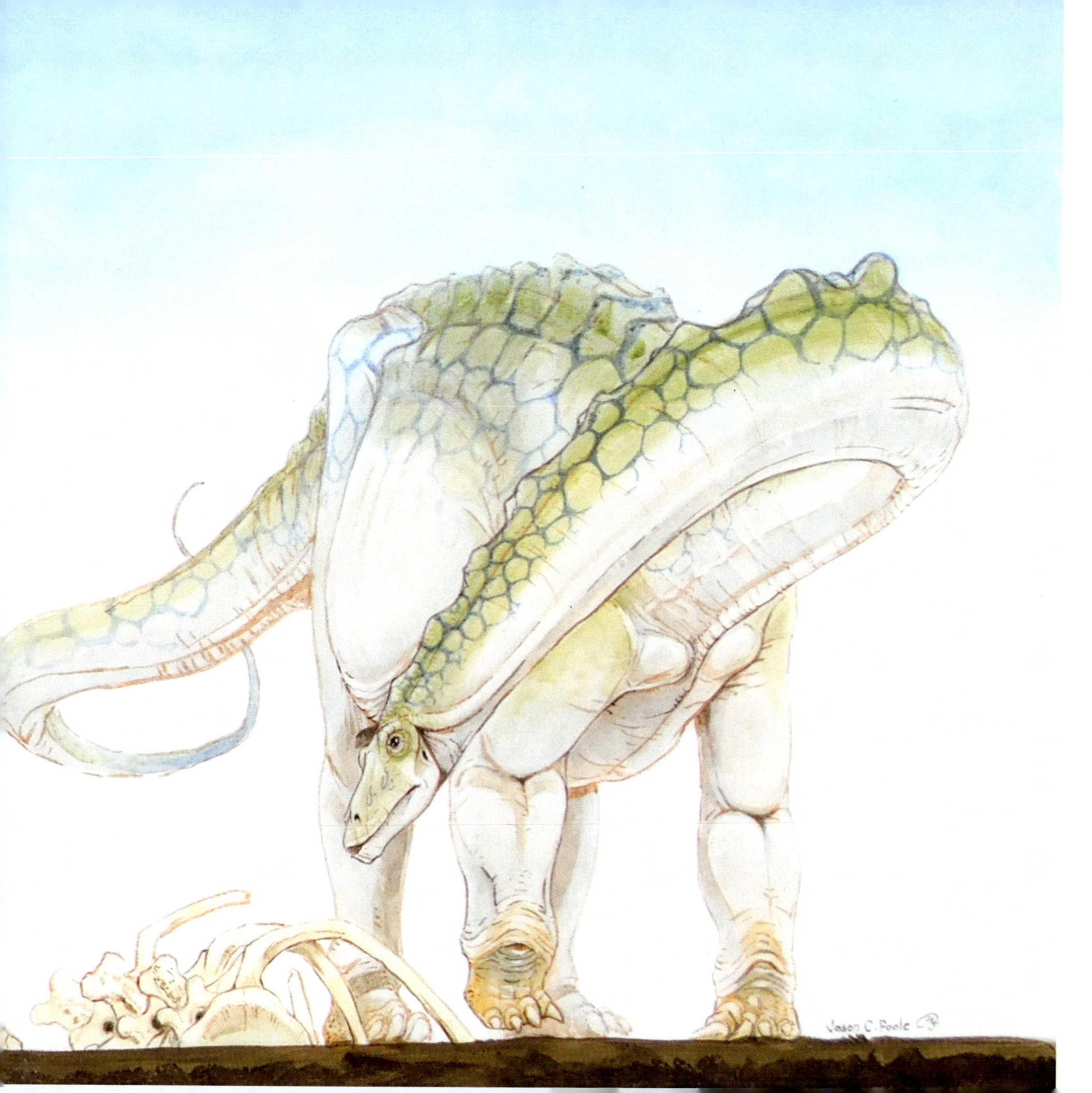
Jason C. Poole

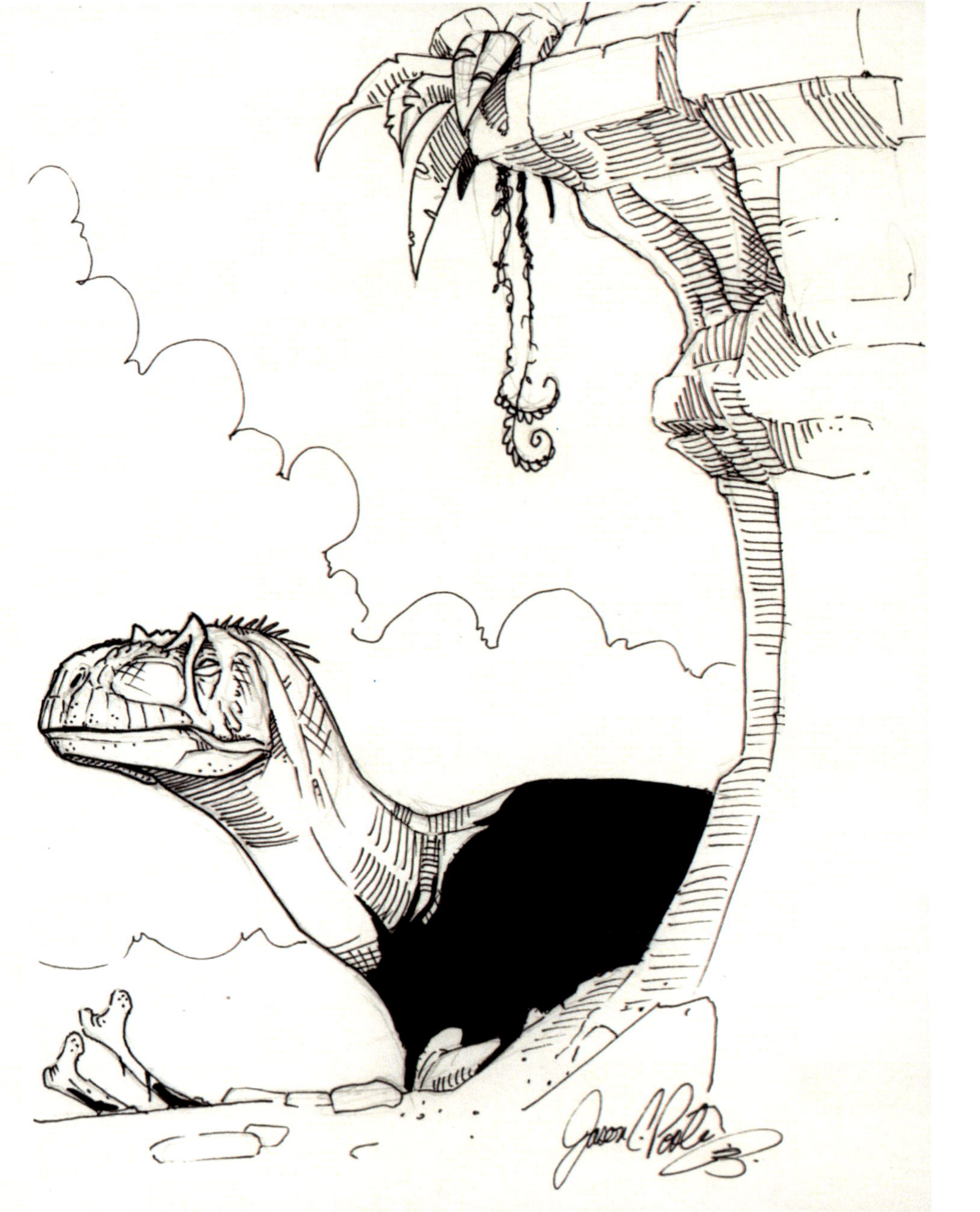

Ceratopsians

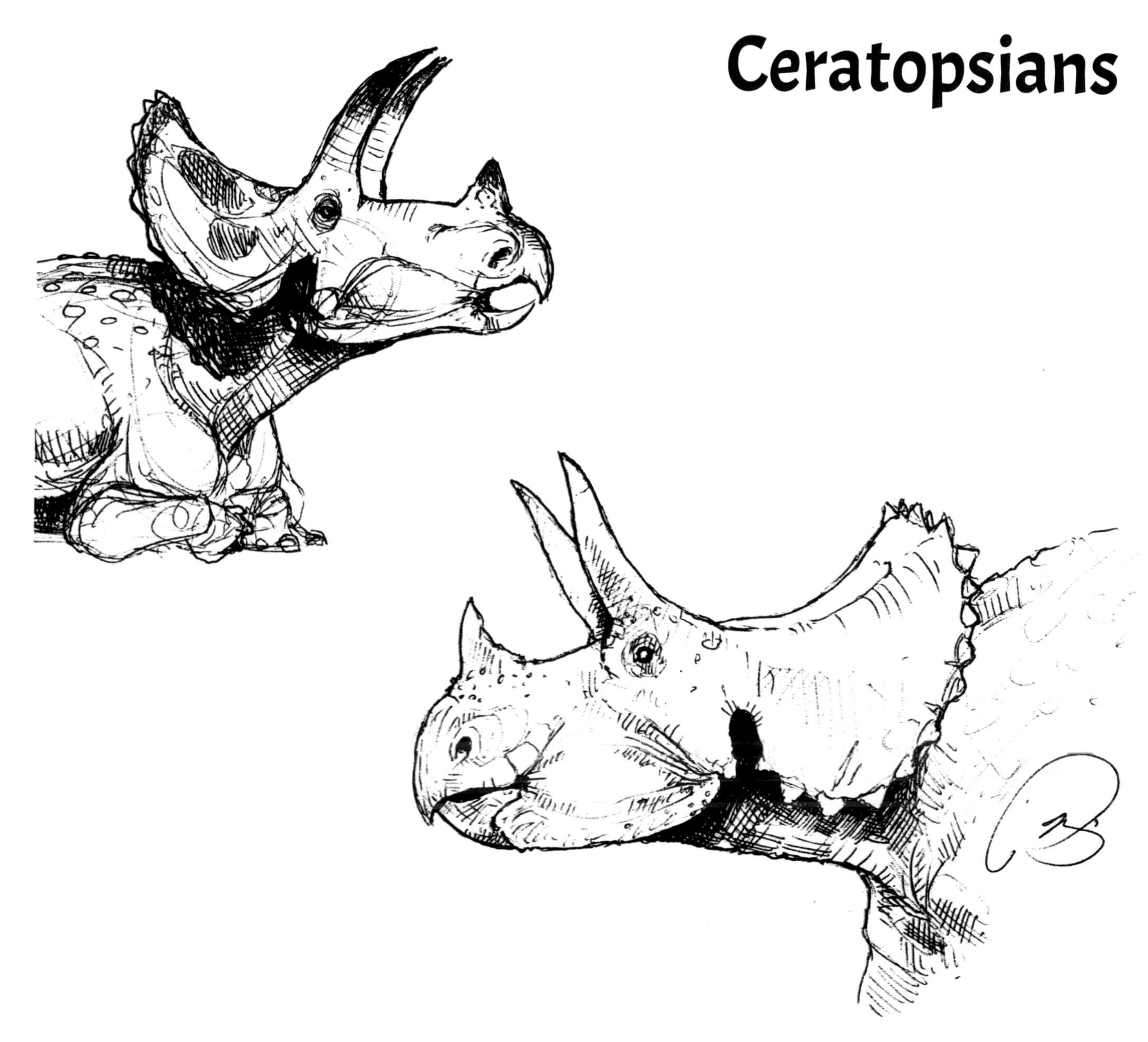

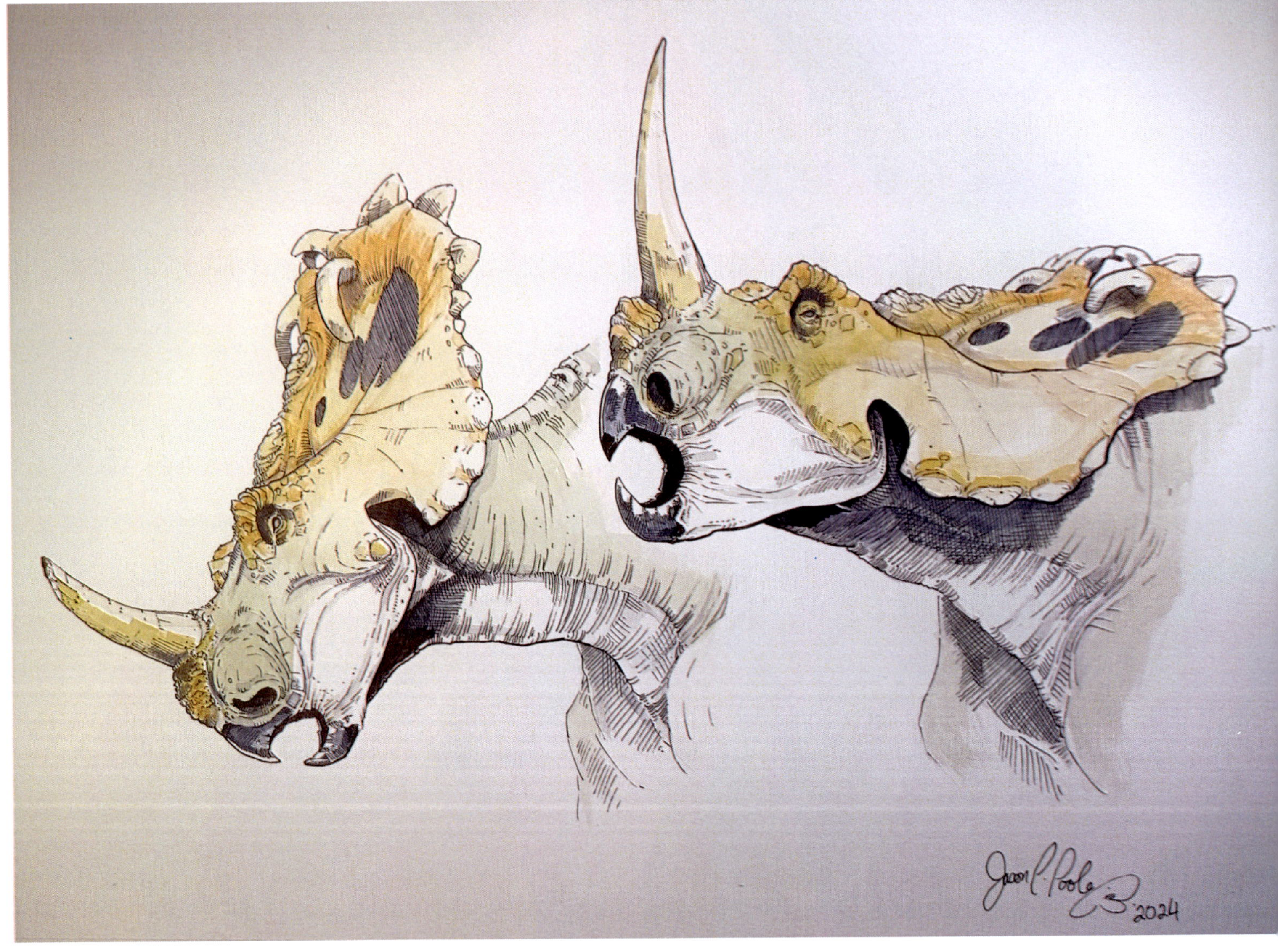

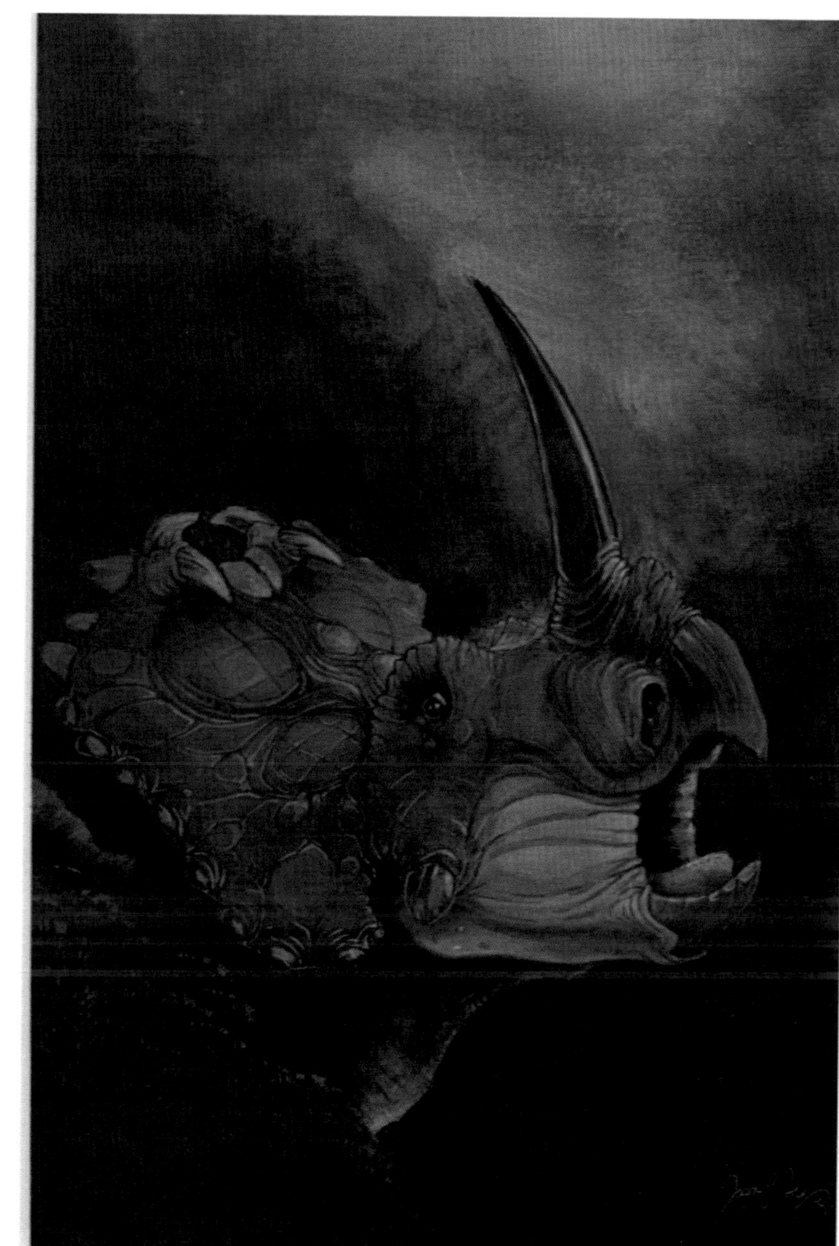

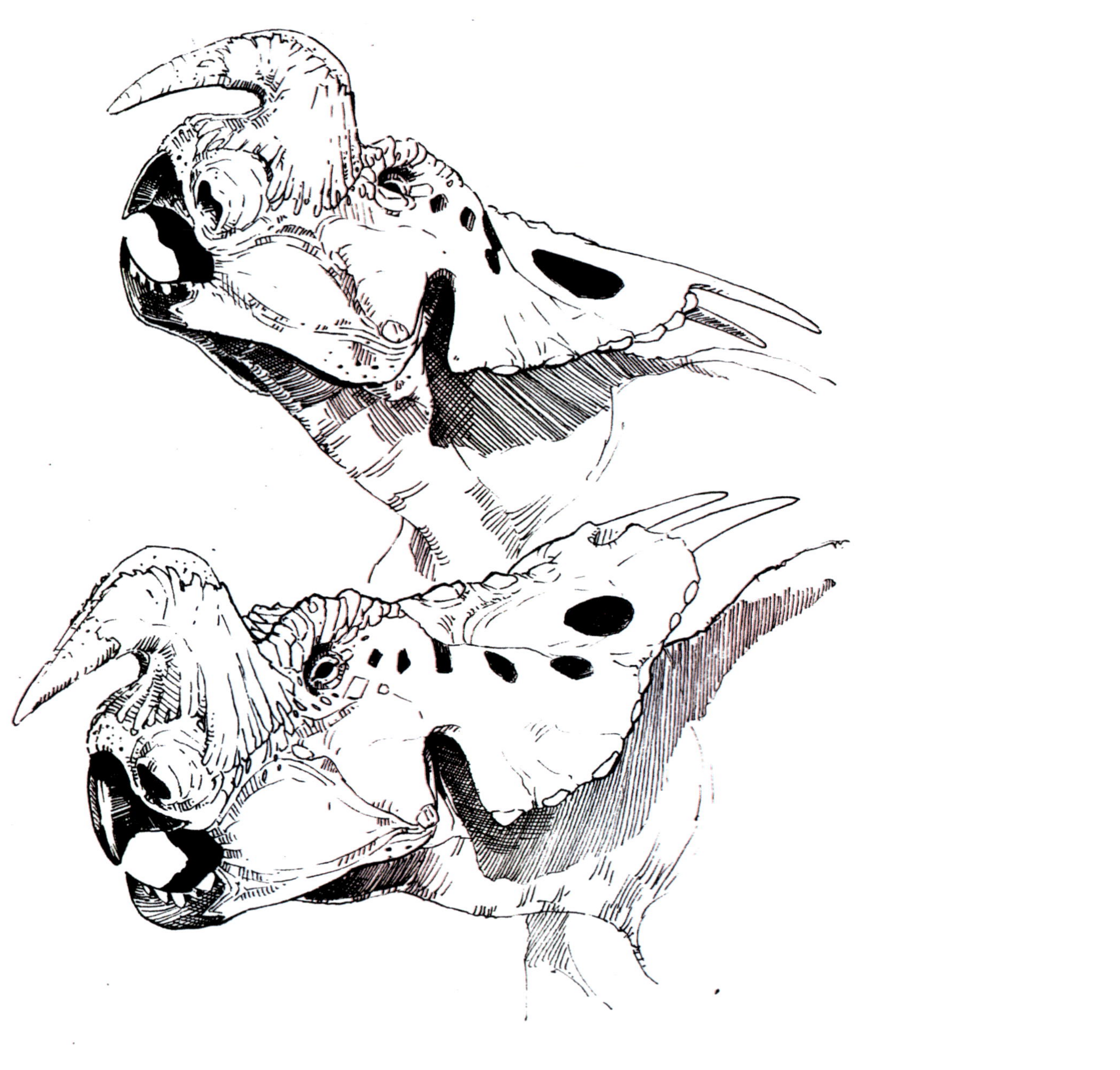

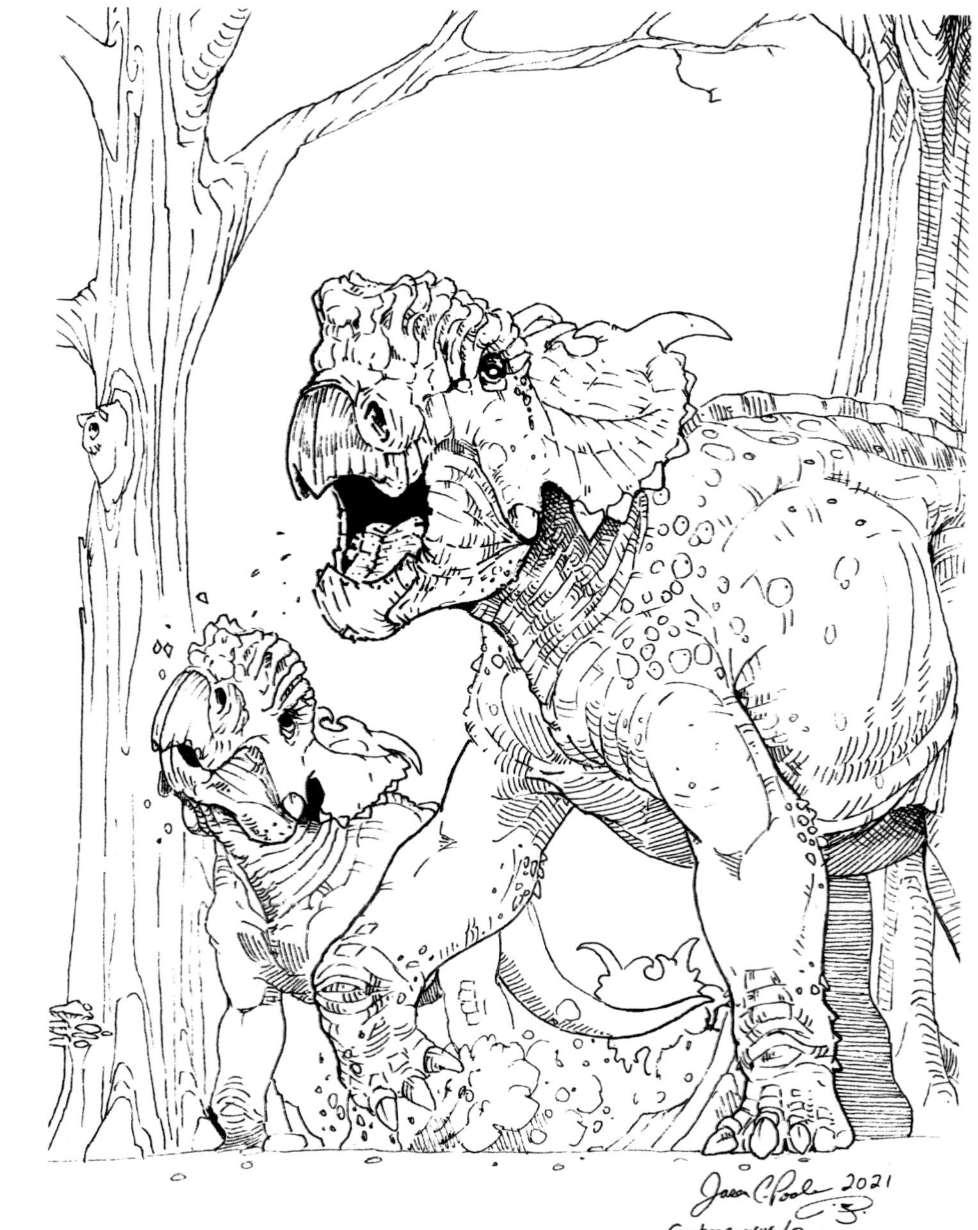

Jason C. Poole 2021
Centrosaurus/Pachyrhinosaurus

Psittacosaurus

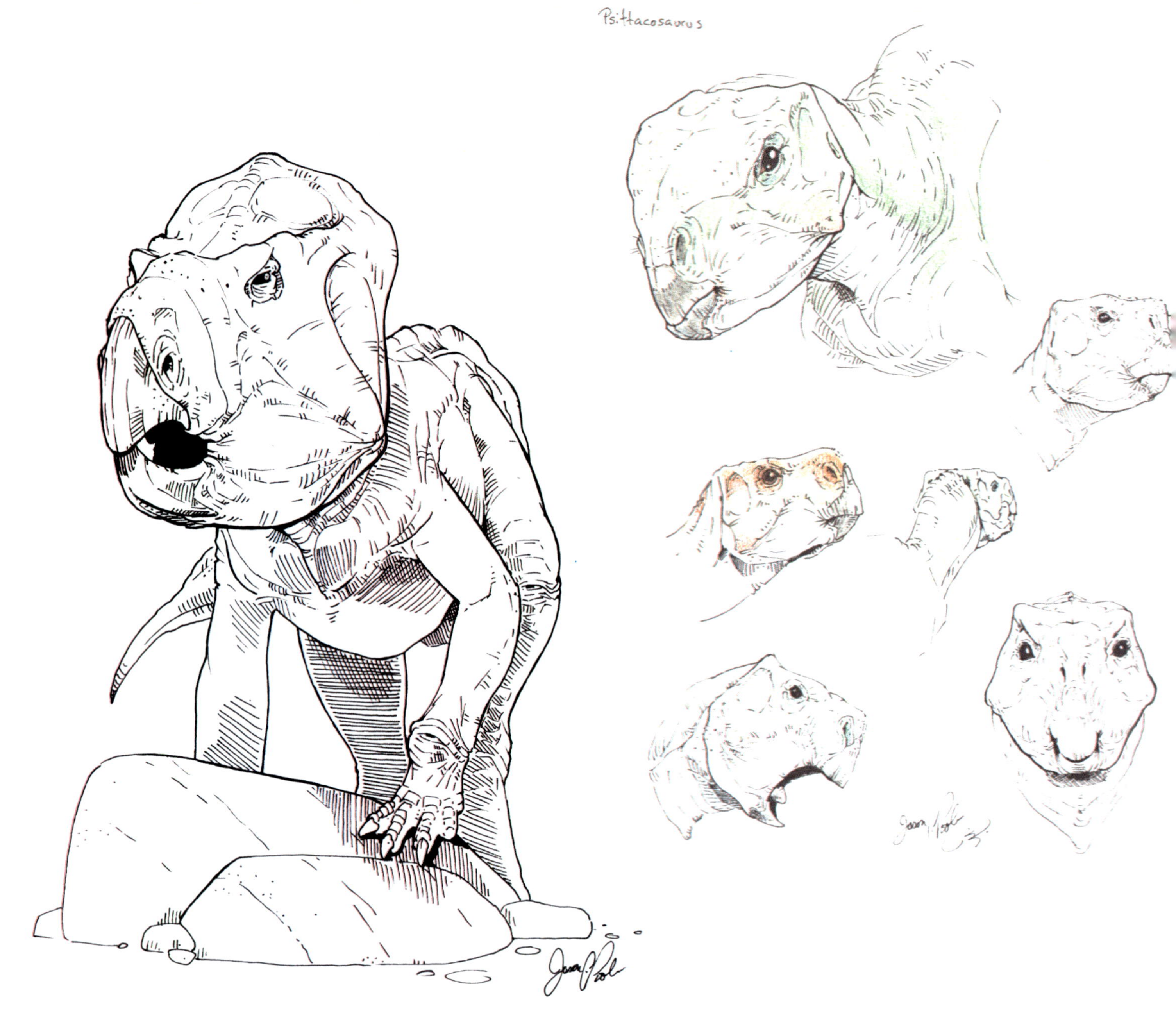

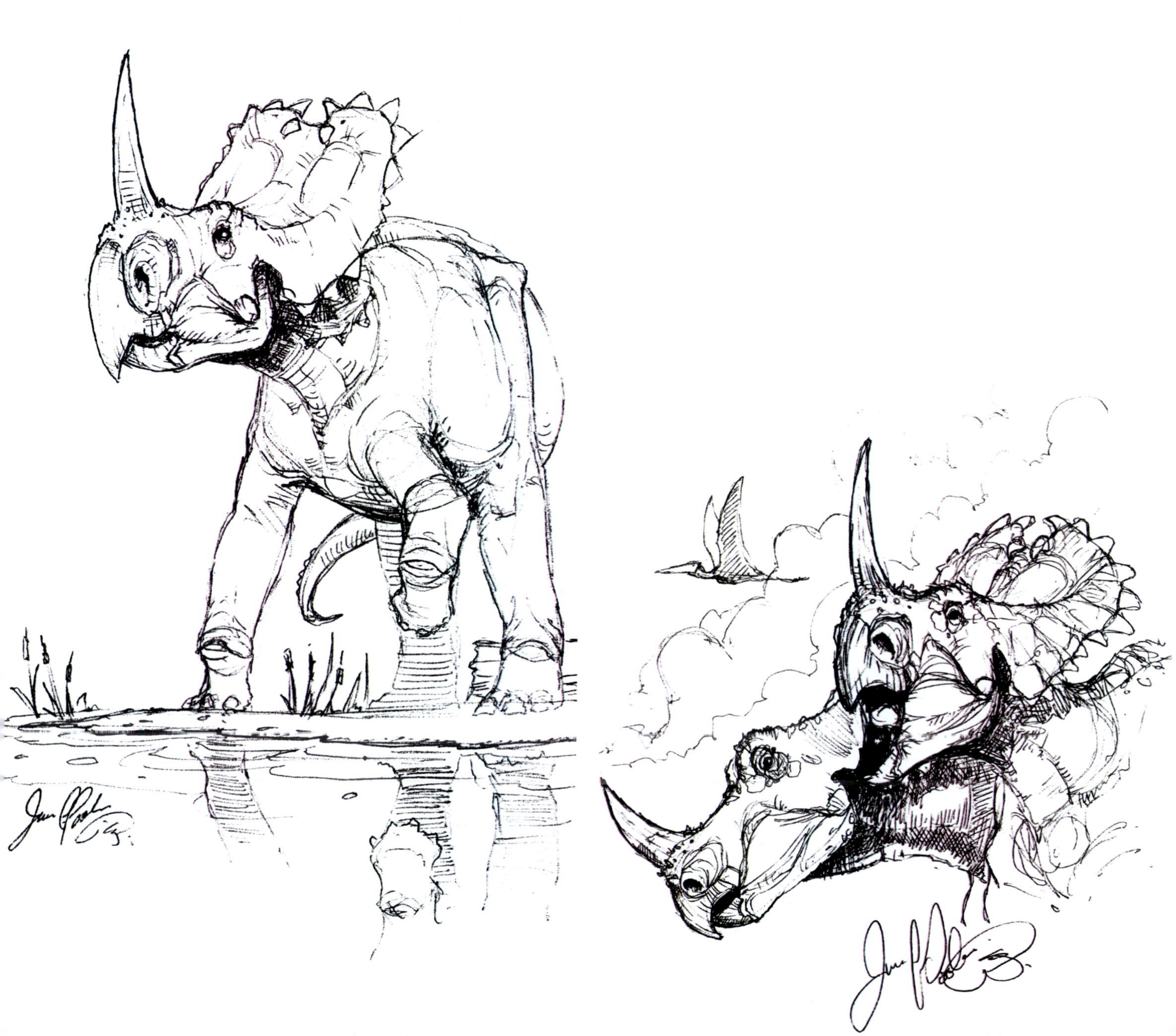

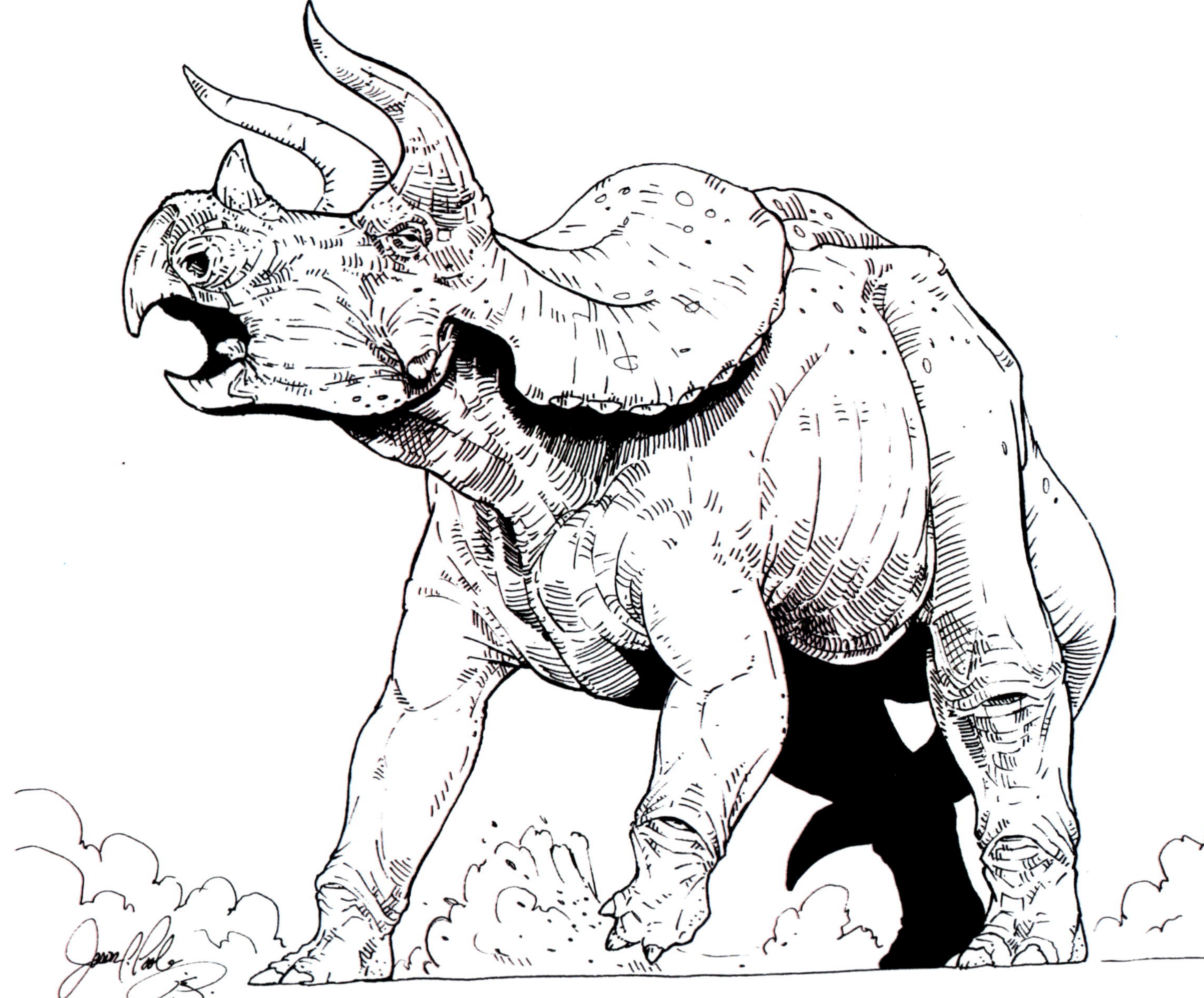

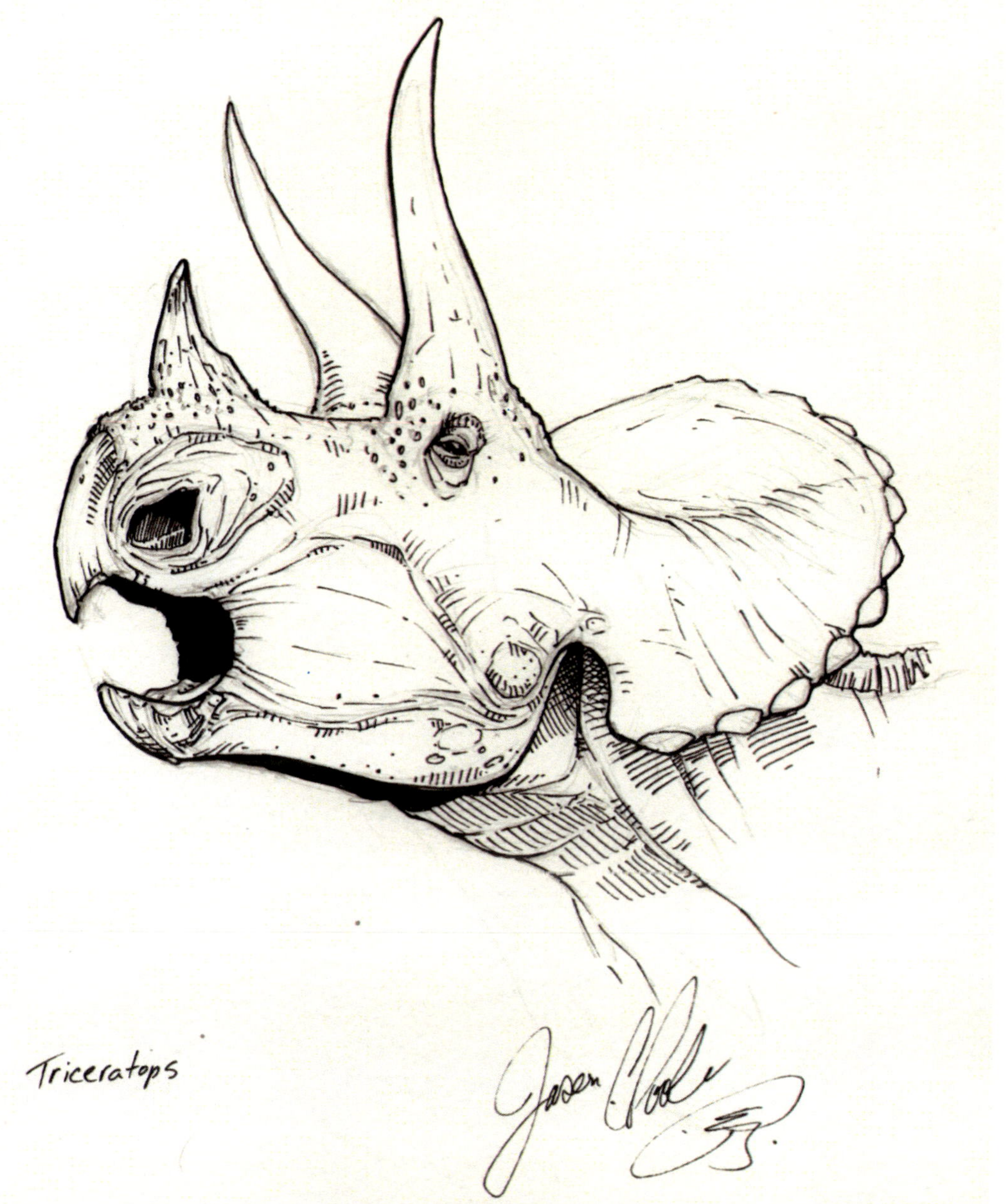

Triceratops

Hadrosaurs

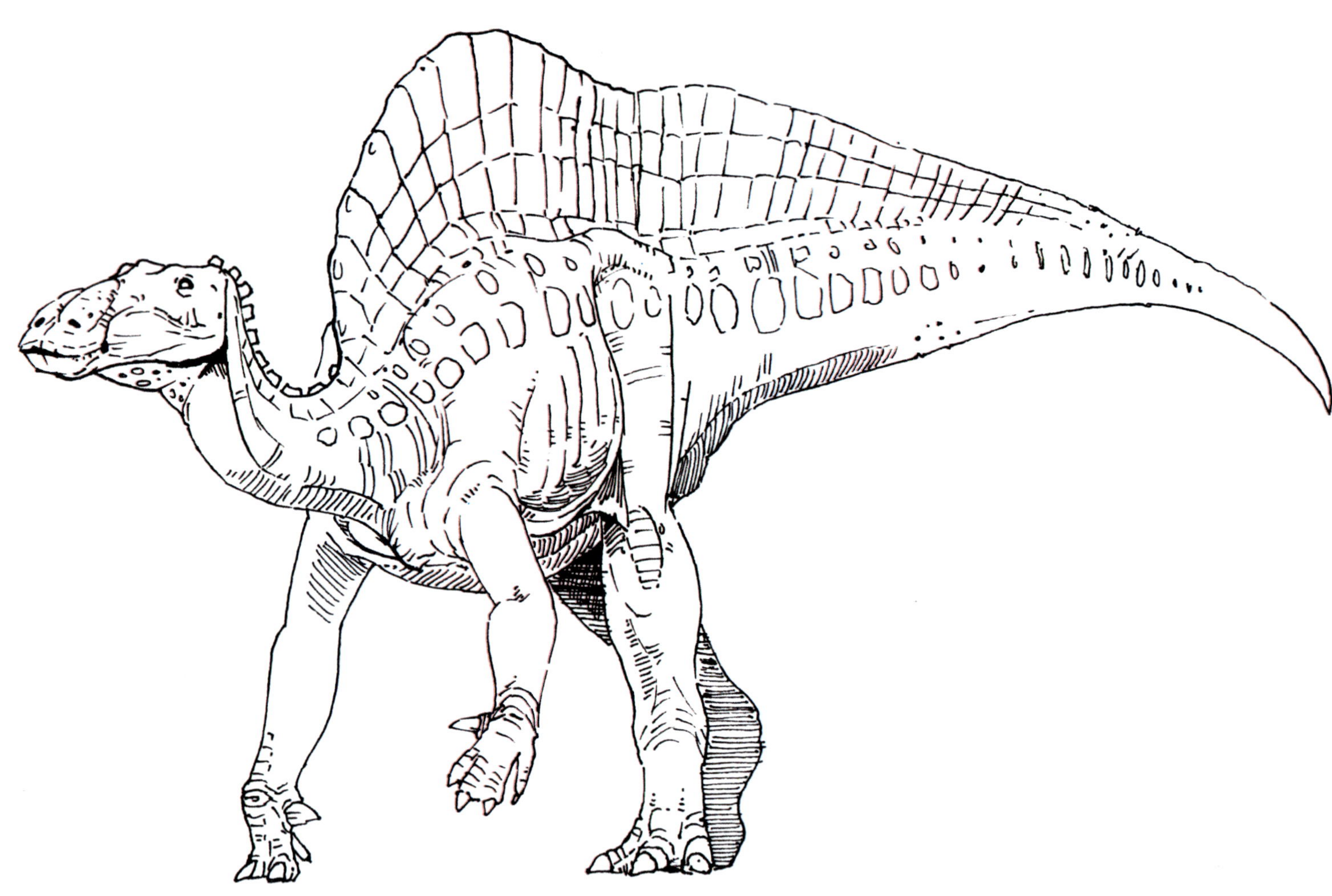

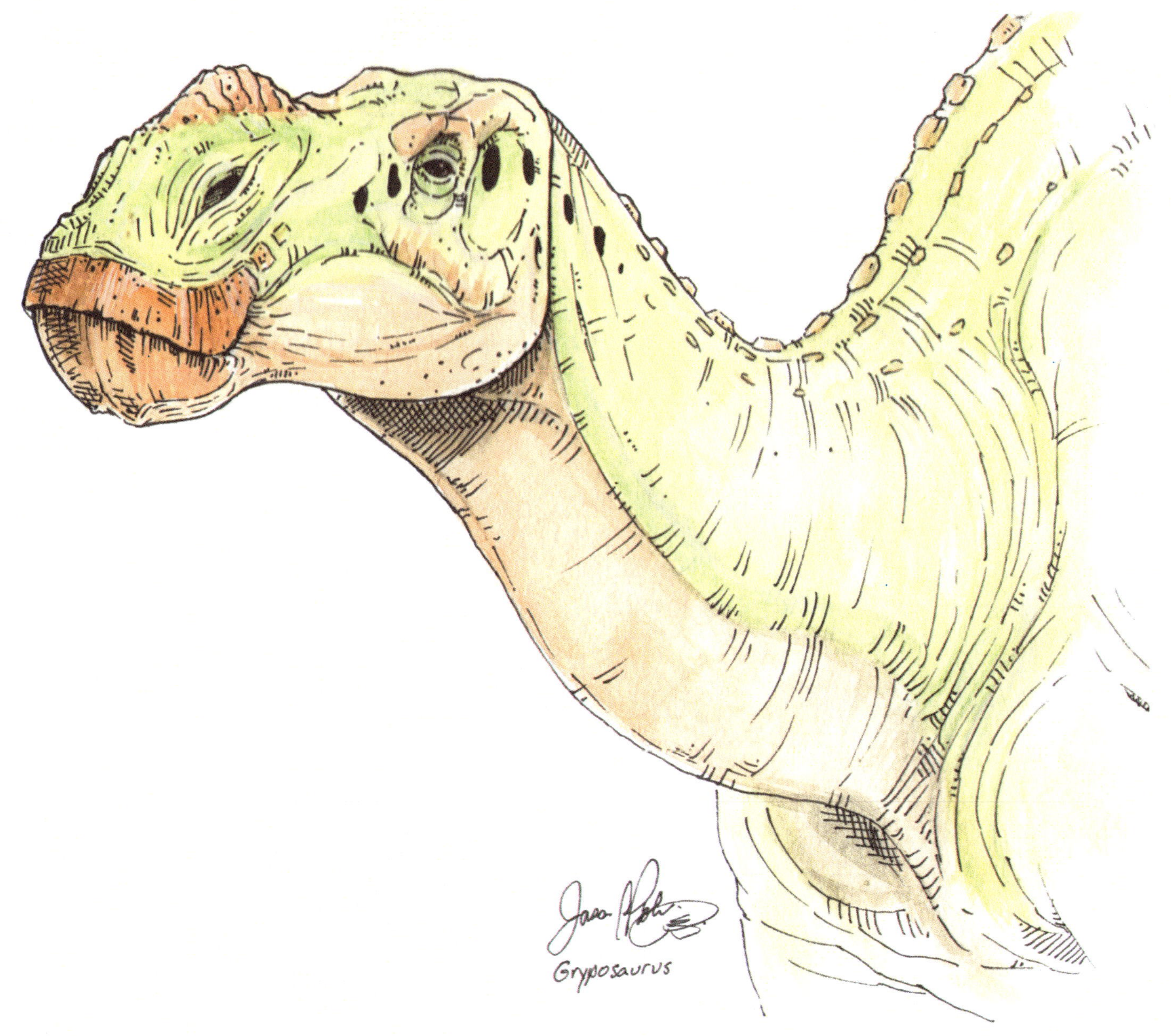

Gryposaurus

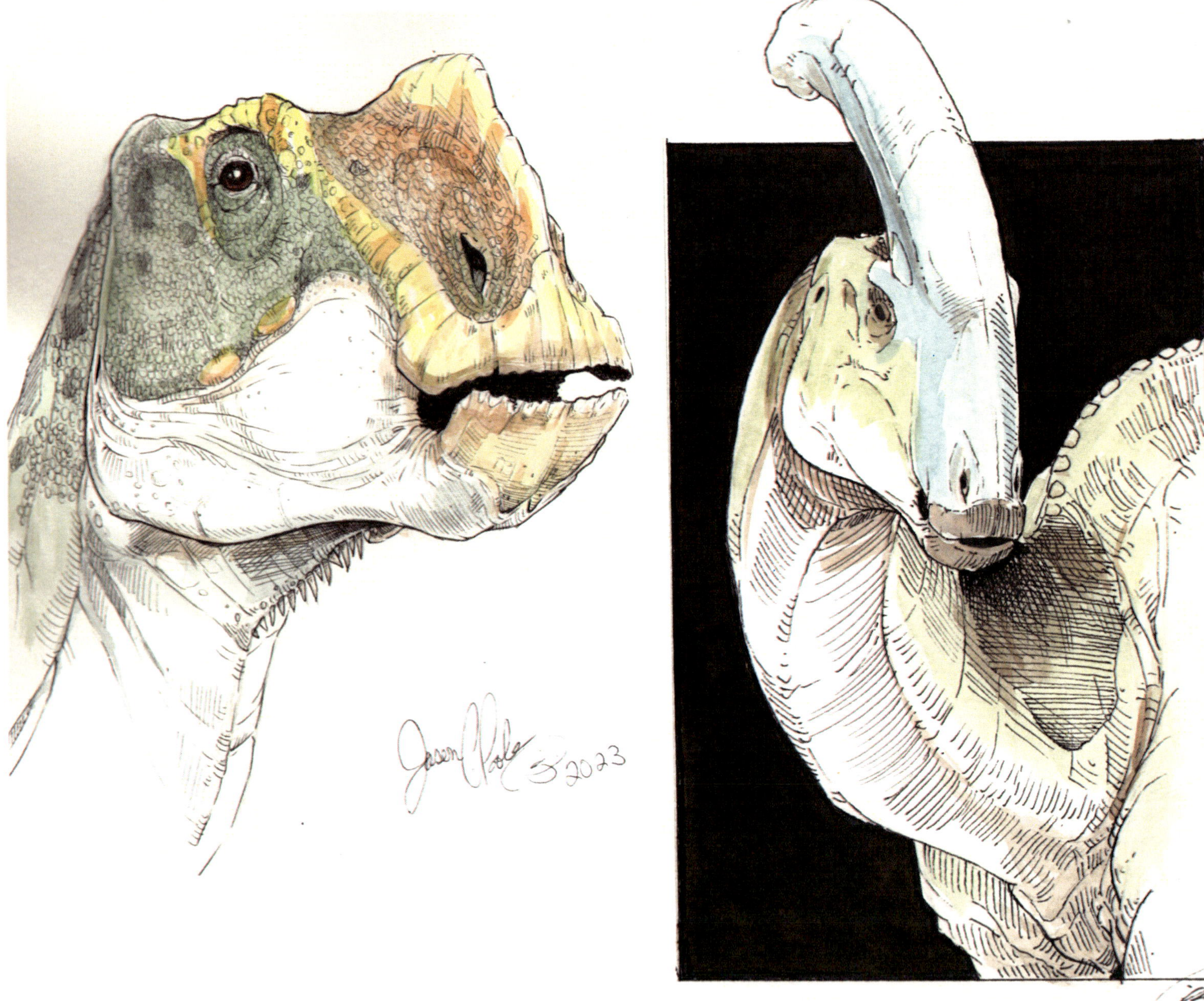

Jason Poole
3/2023

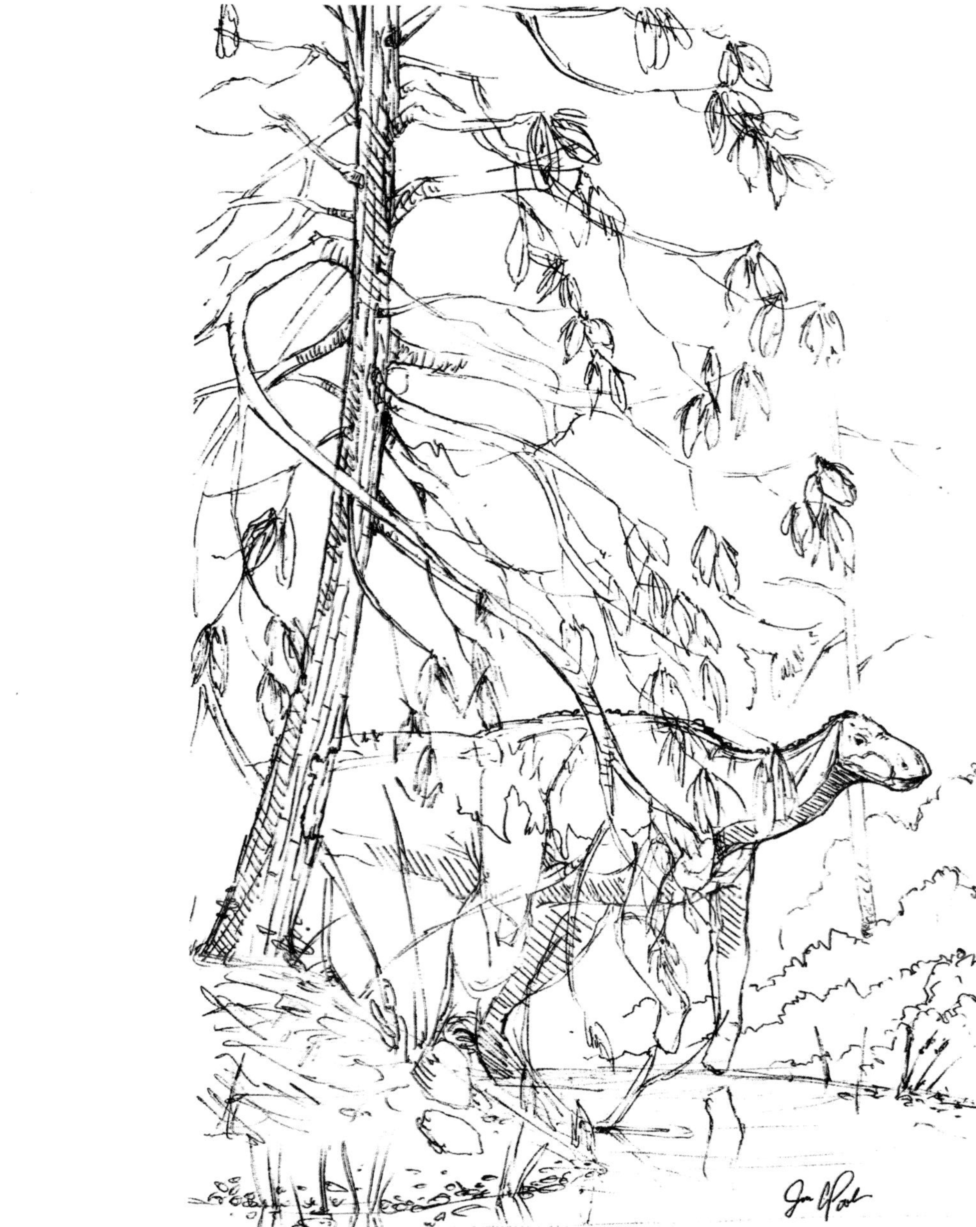

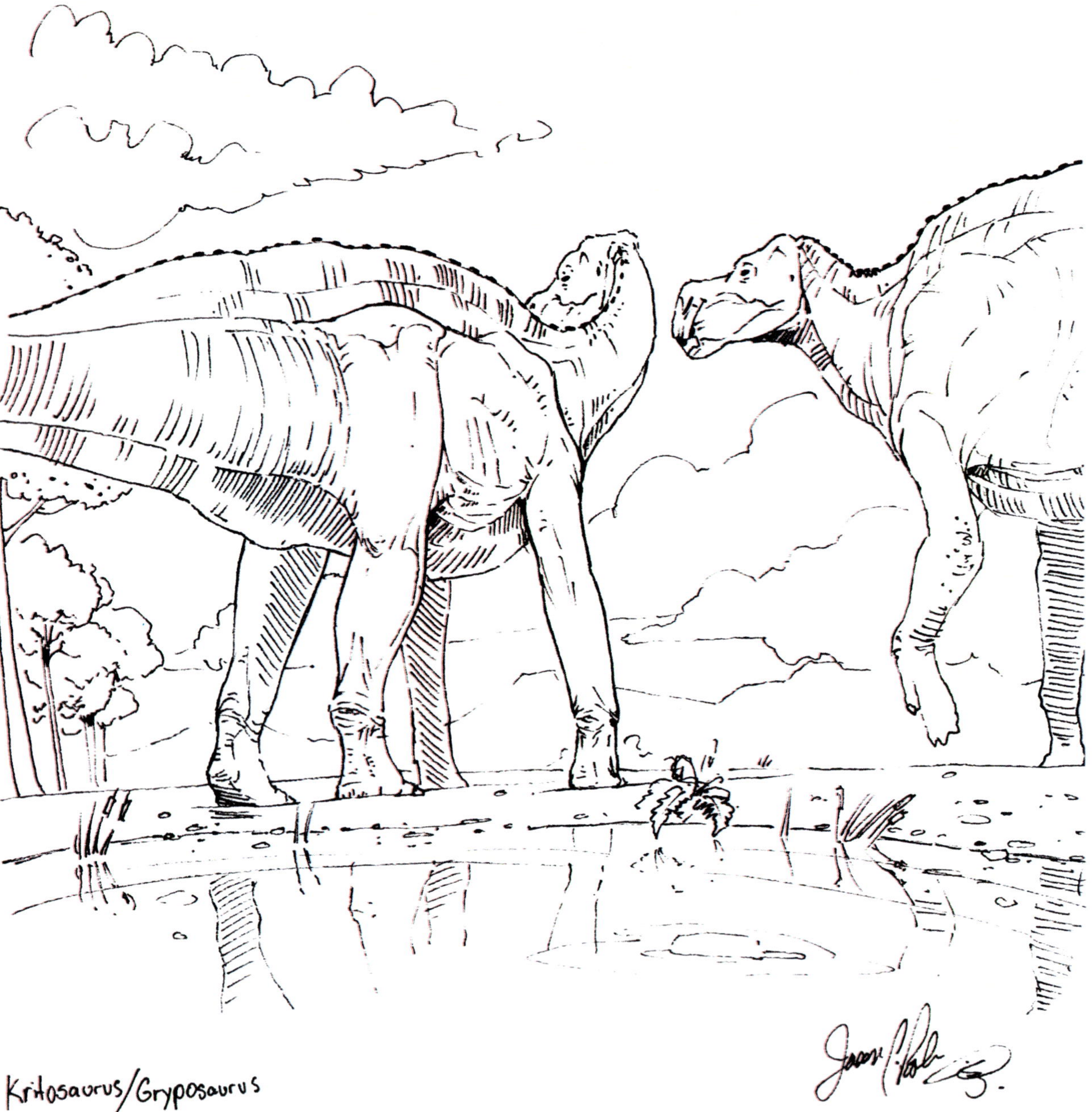

Kritosaurus/Gryposaurus

Kritosaurus

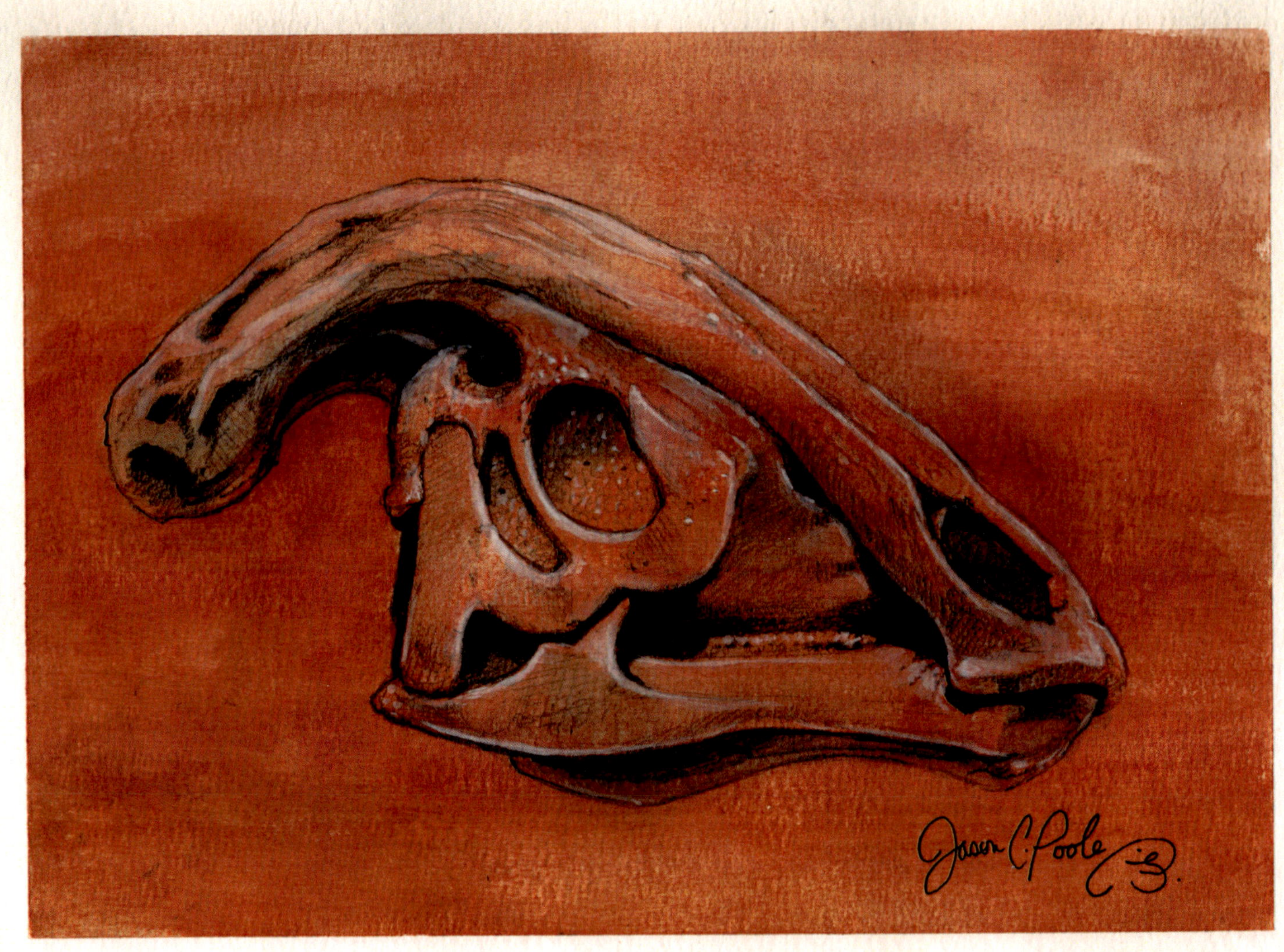

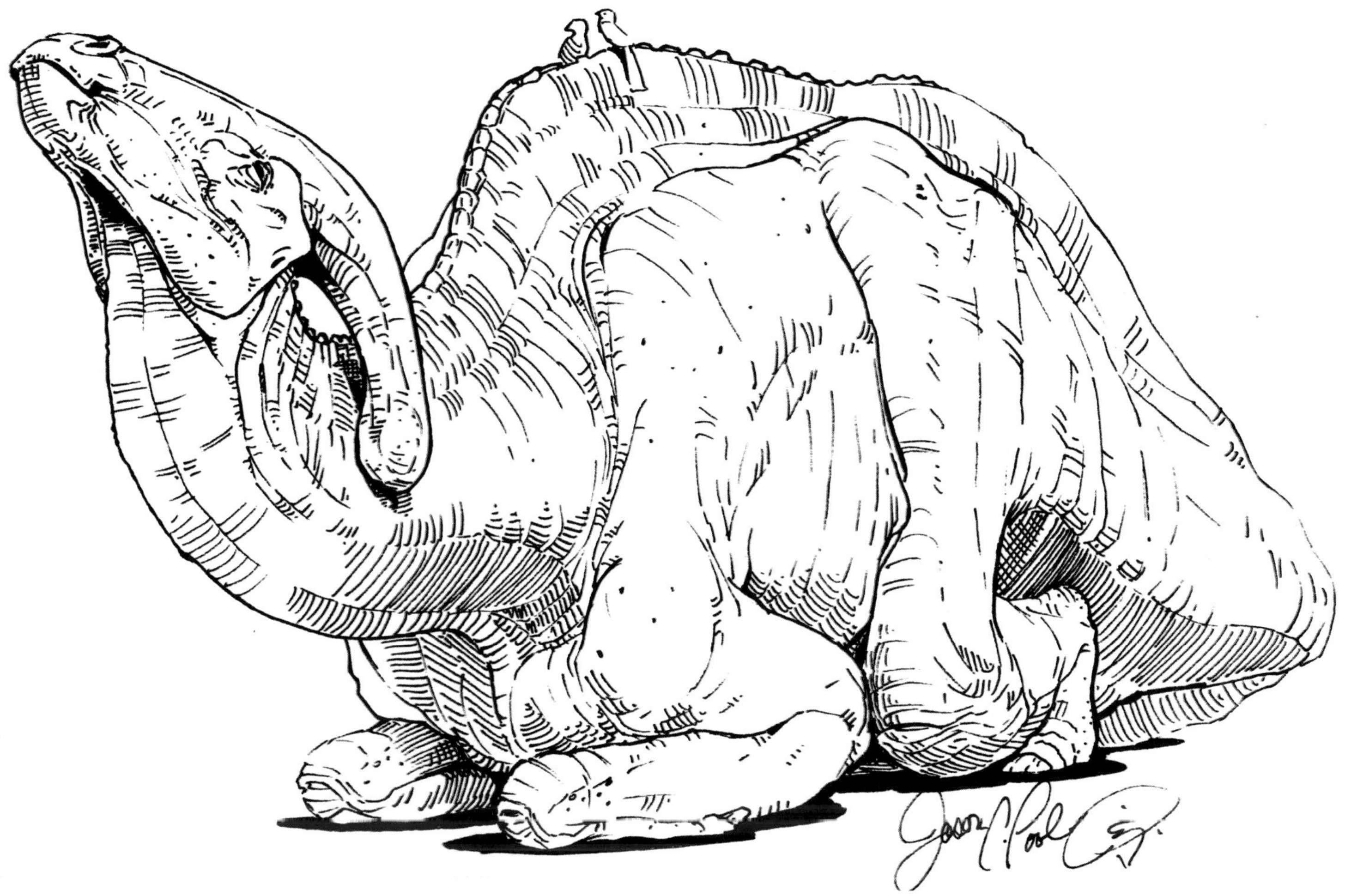

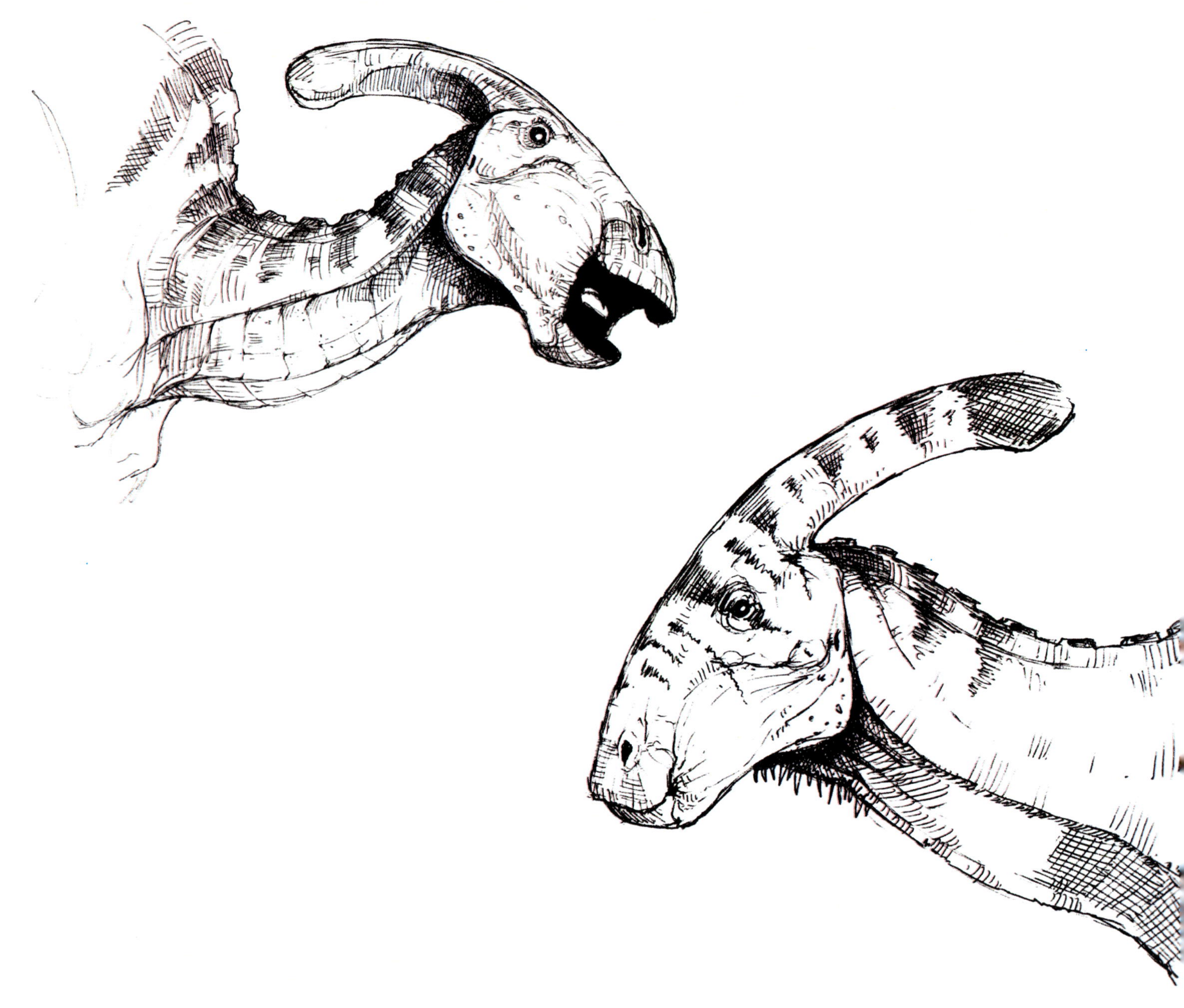

Miscellaneous Dinosaurs

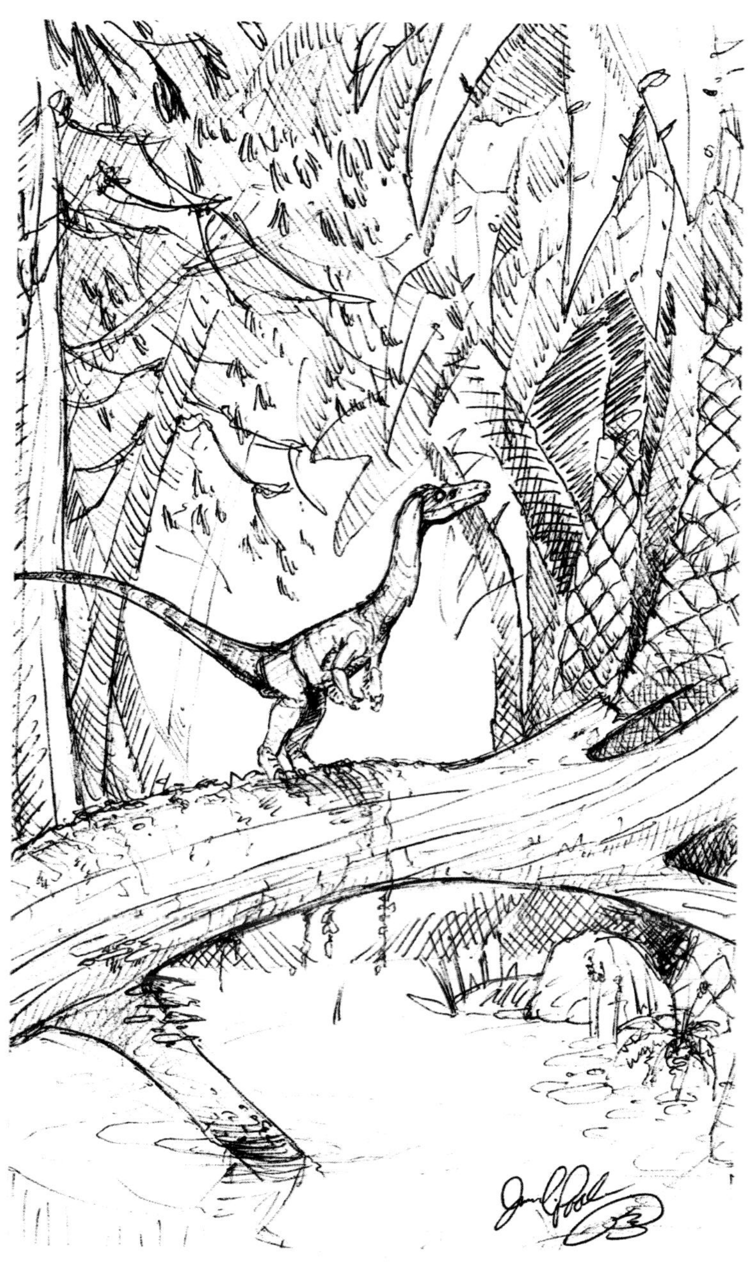

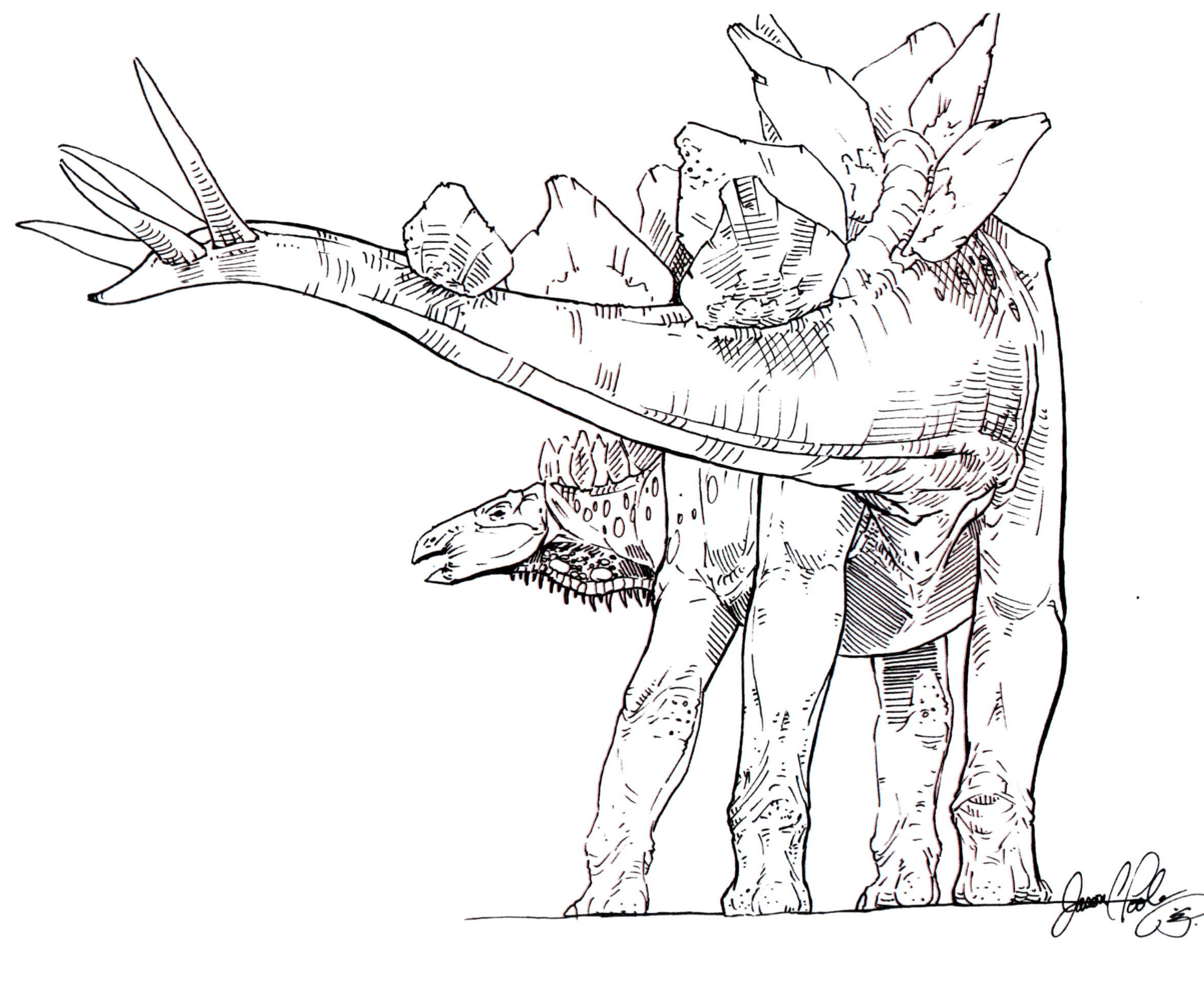

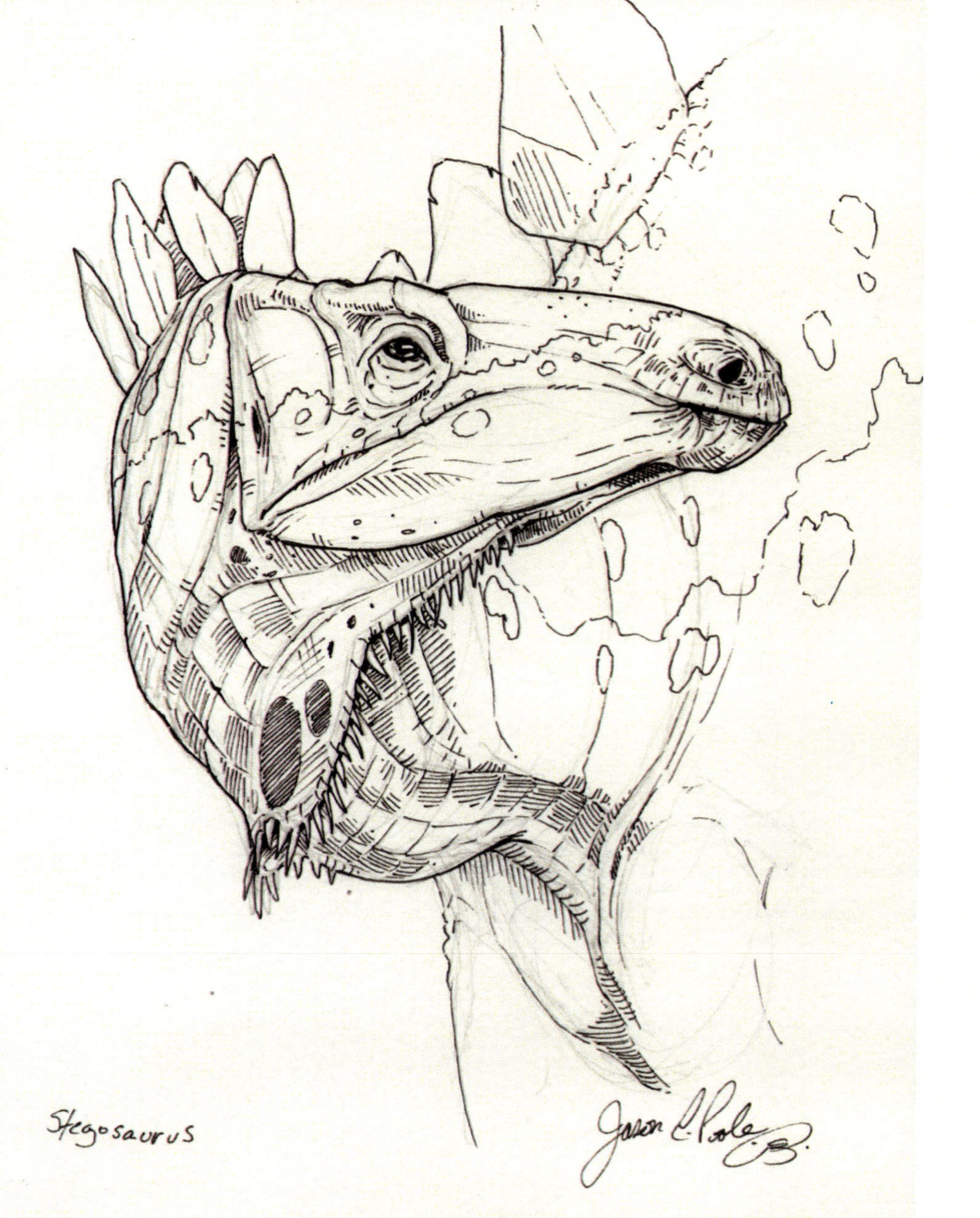

Stegosaurus

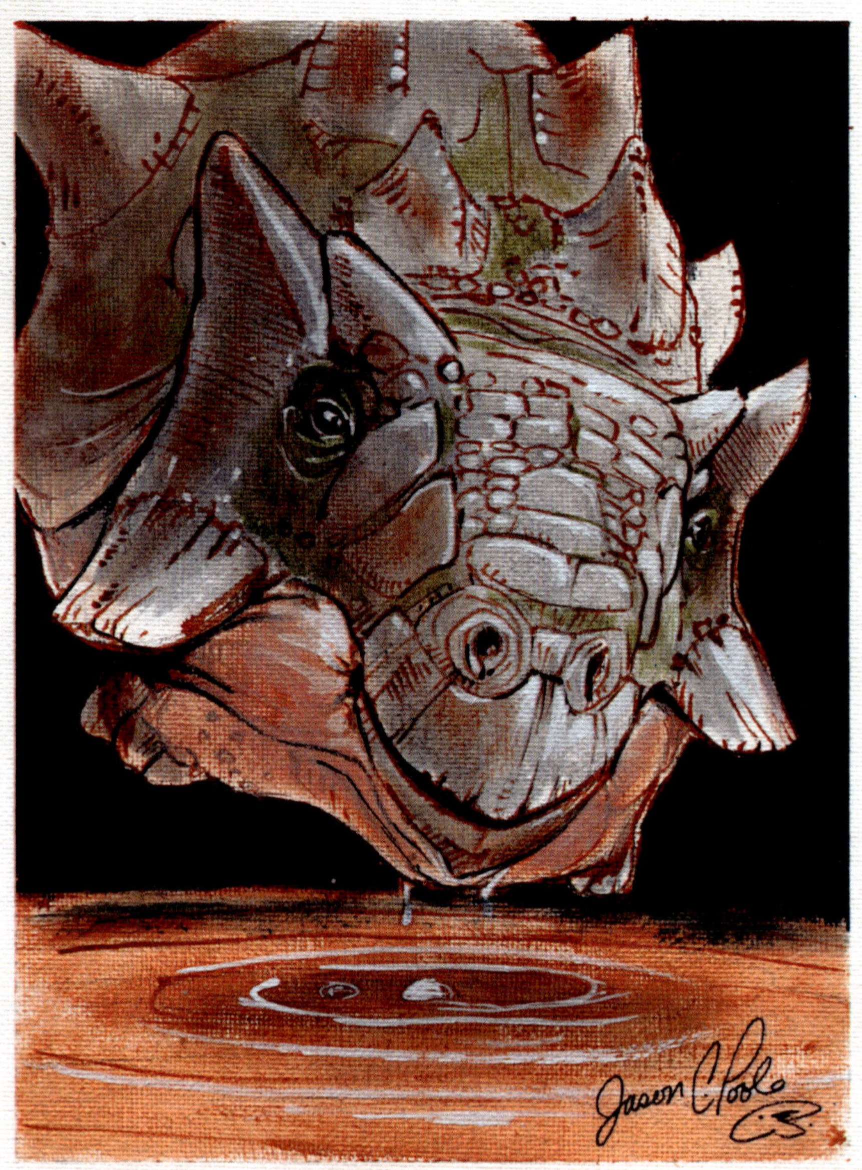

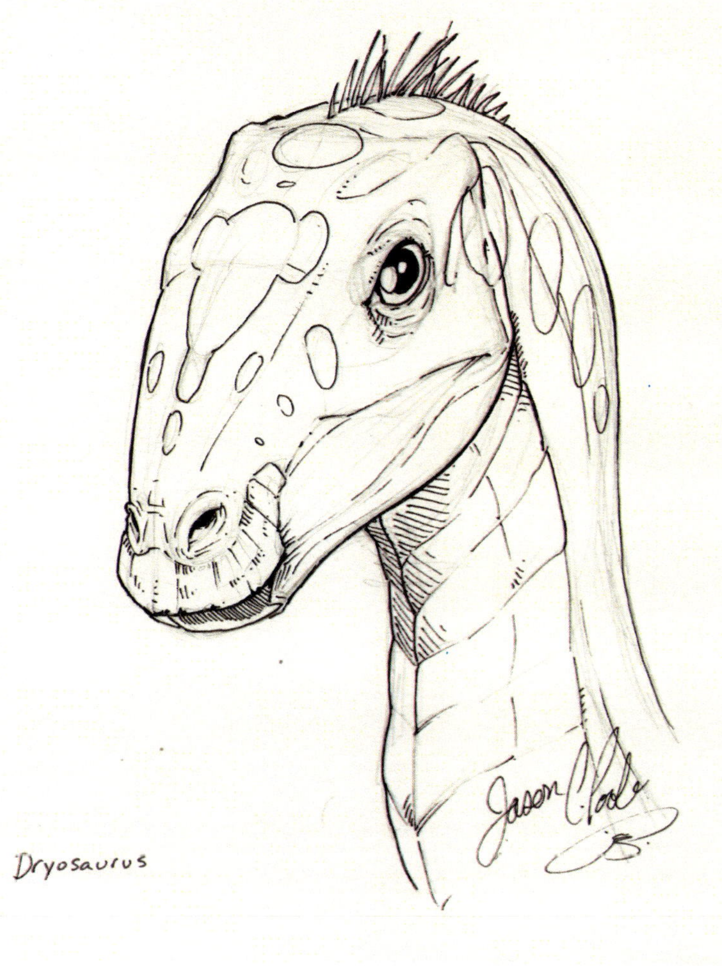

Dryosaurus

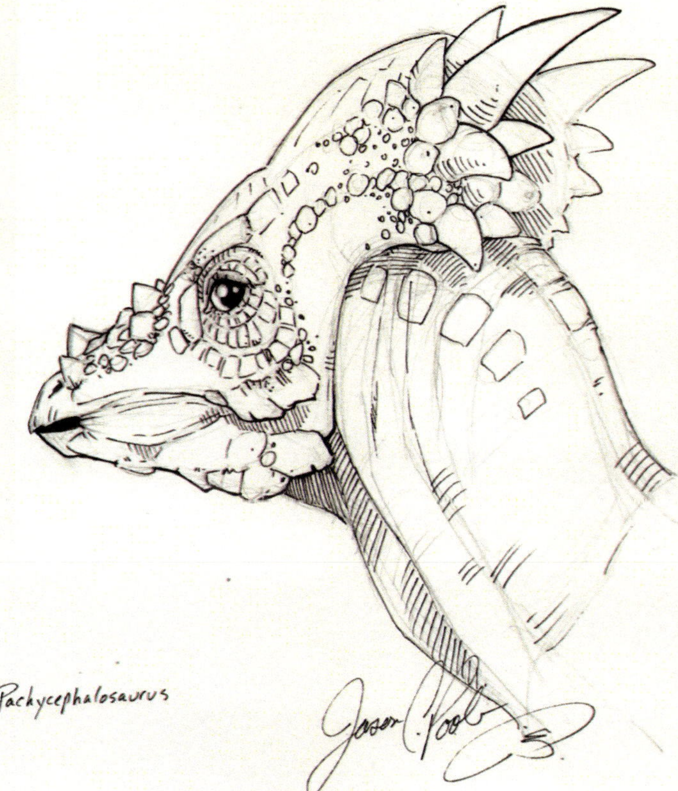

Pachycephalosaurus

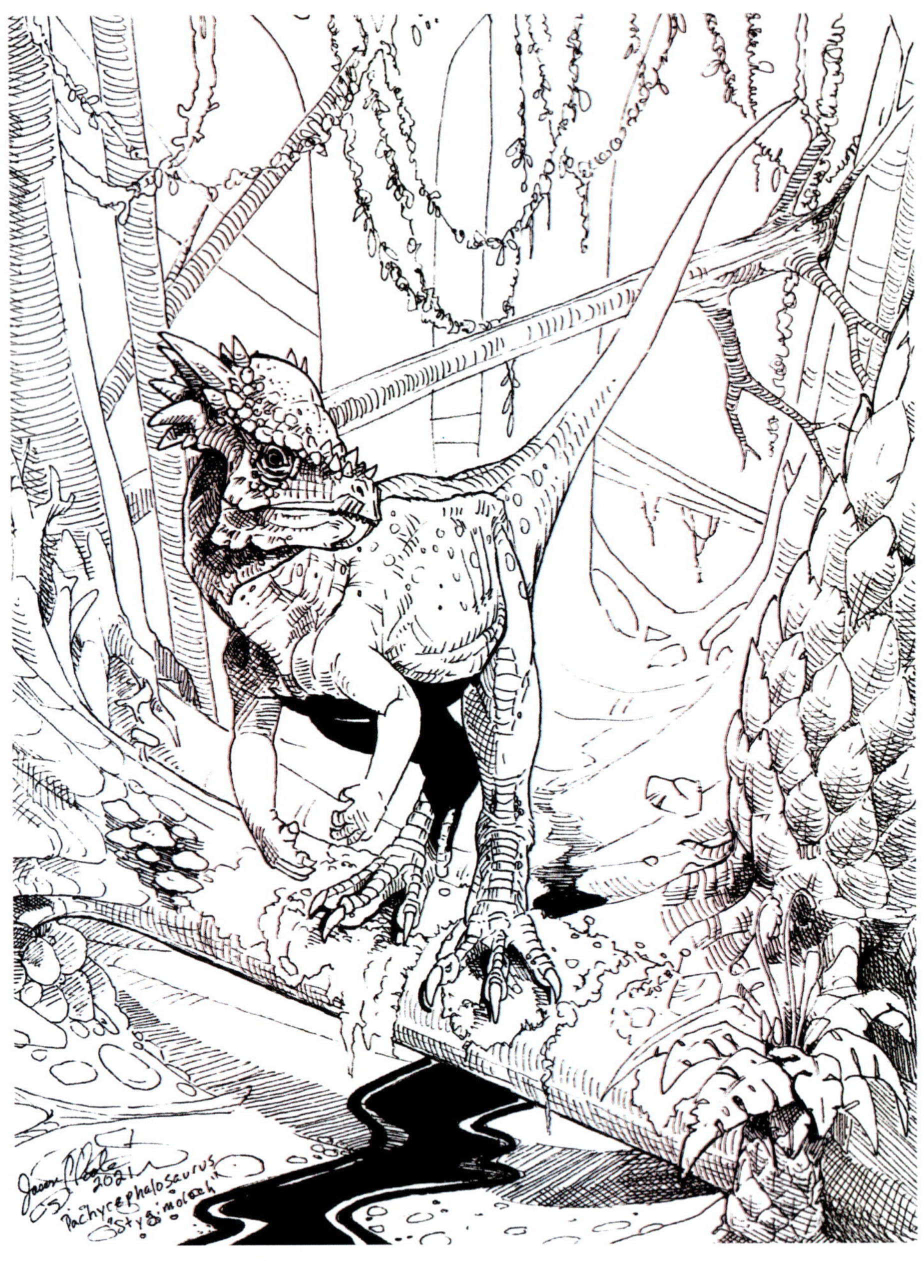

Jason Poole 2021
Pachycephalosaurus
"Stygimoloch"

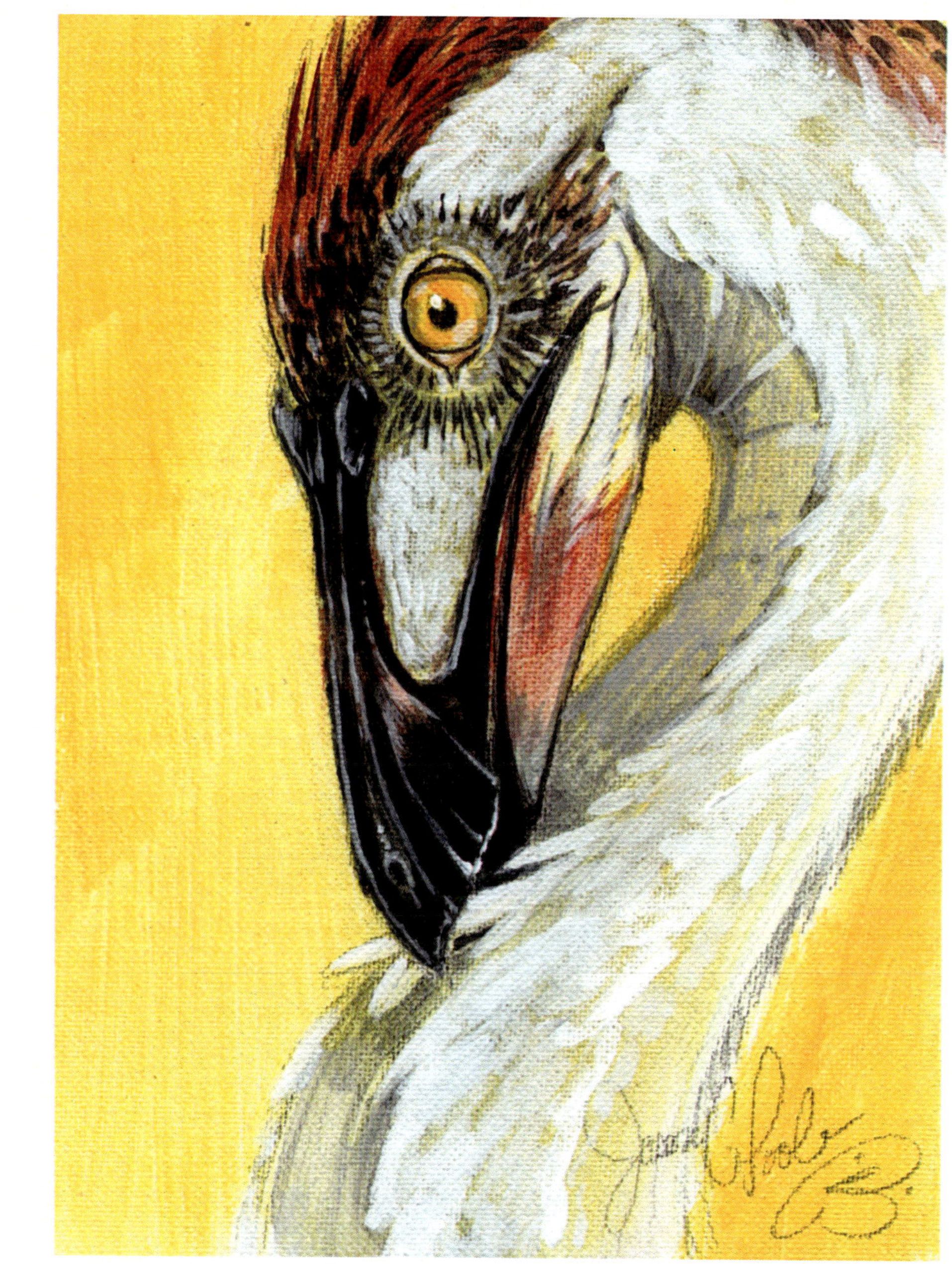

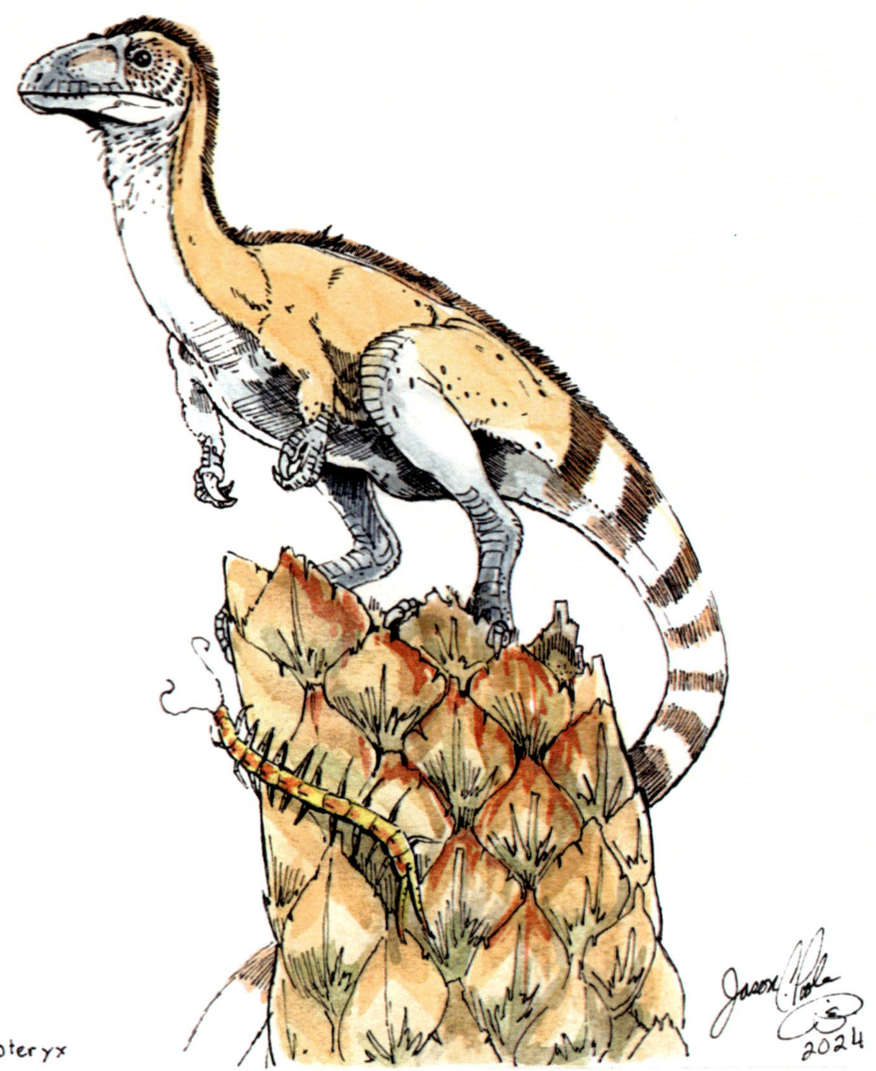

Sinosauropteryx

Sauropods

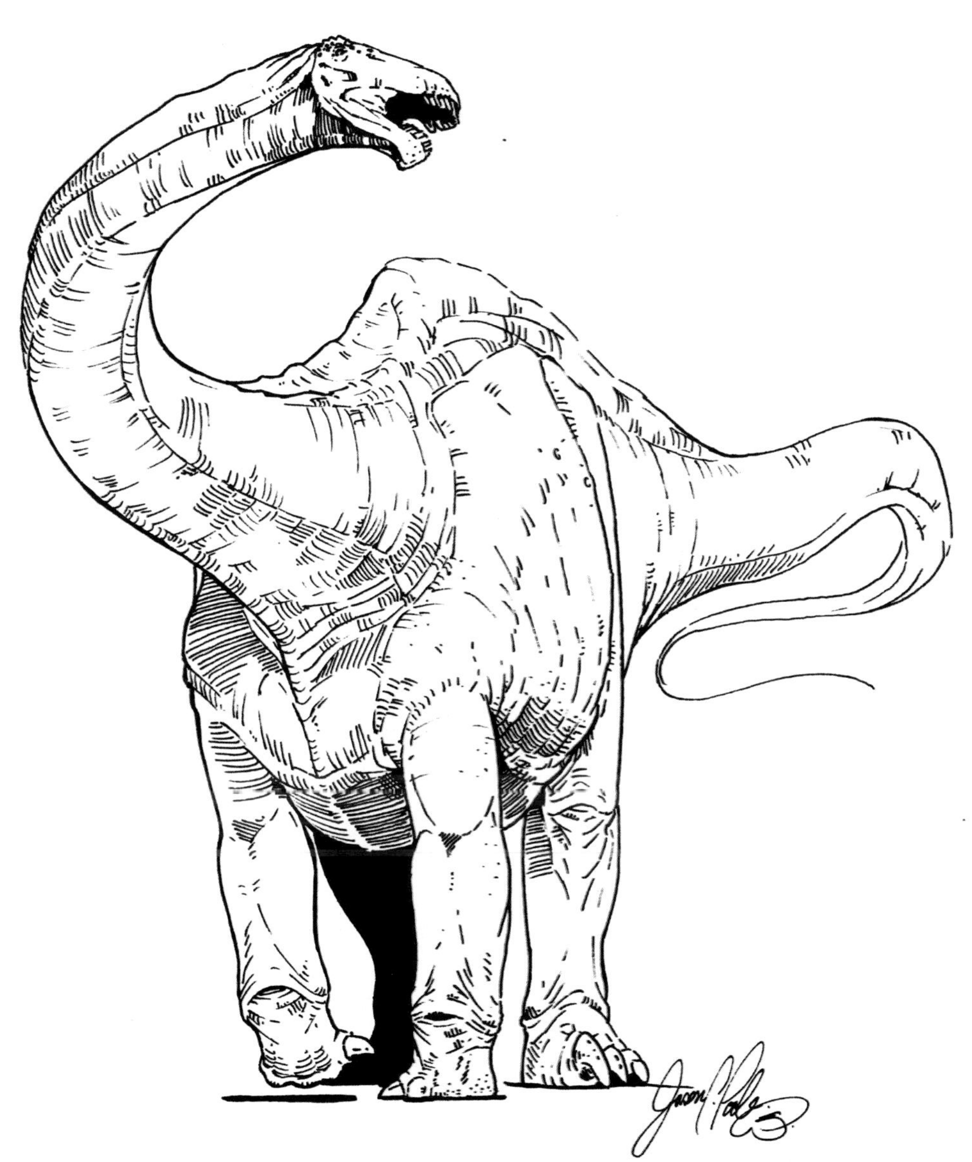

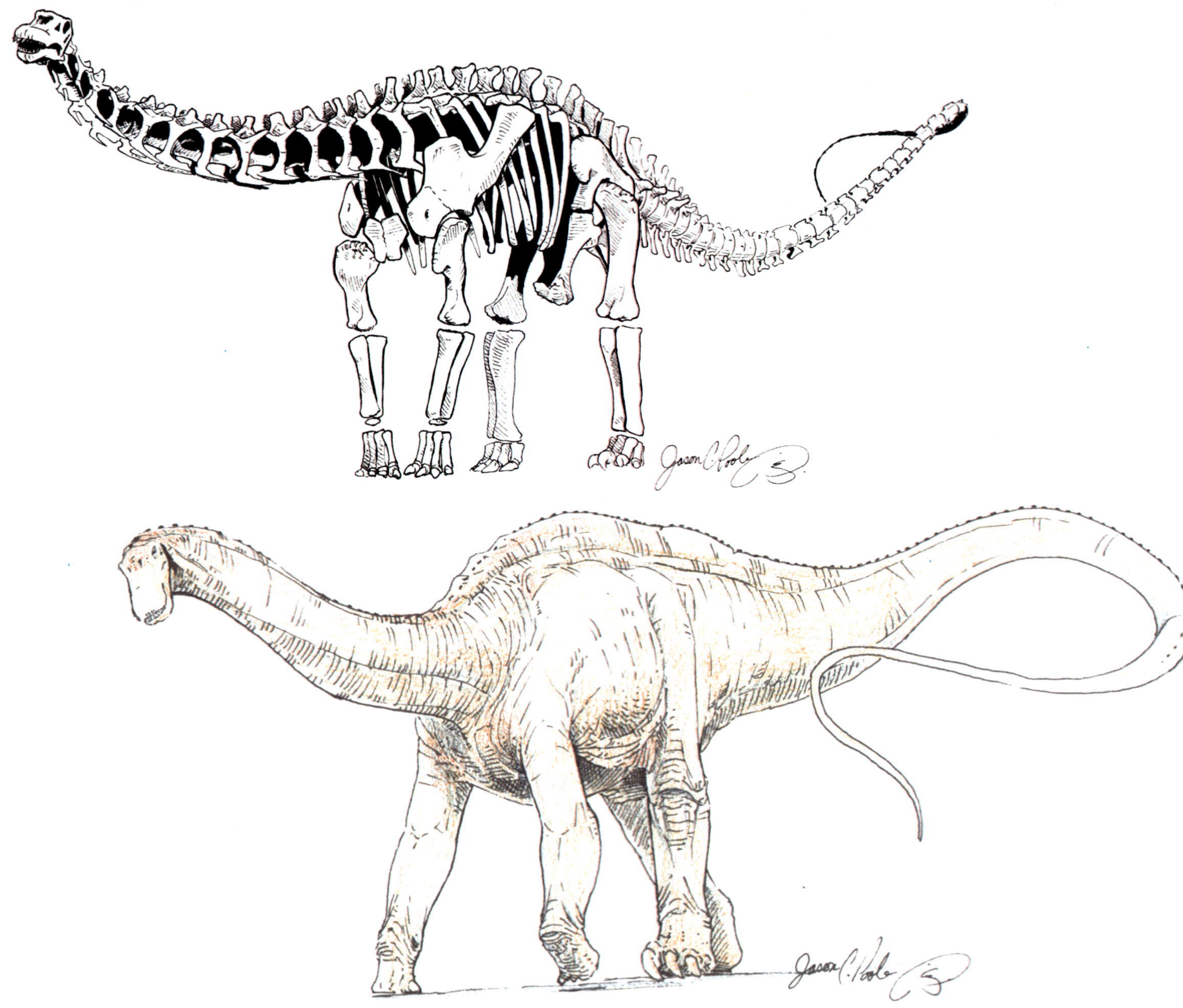

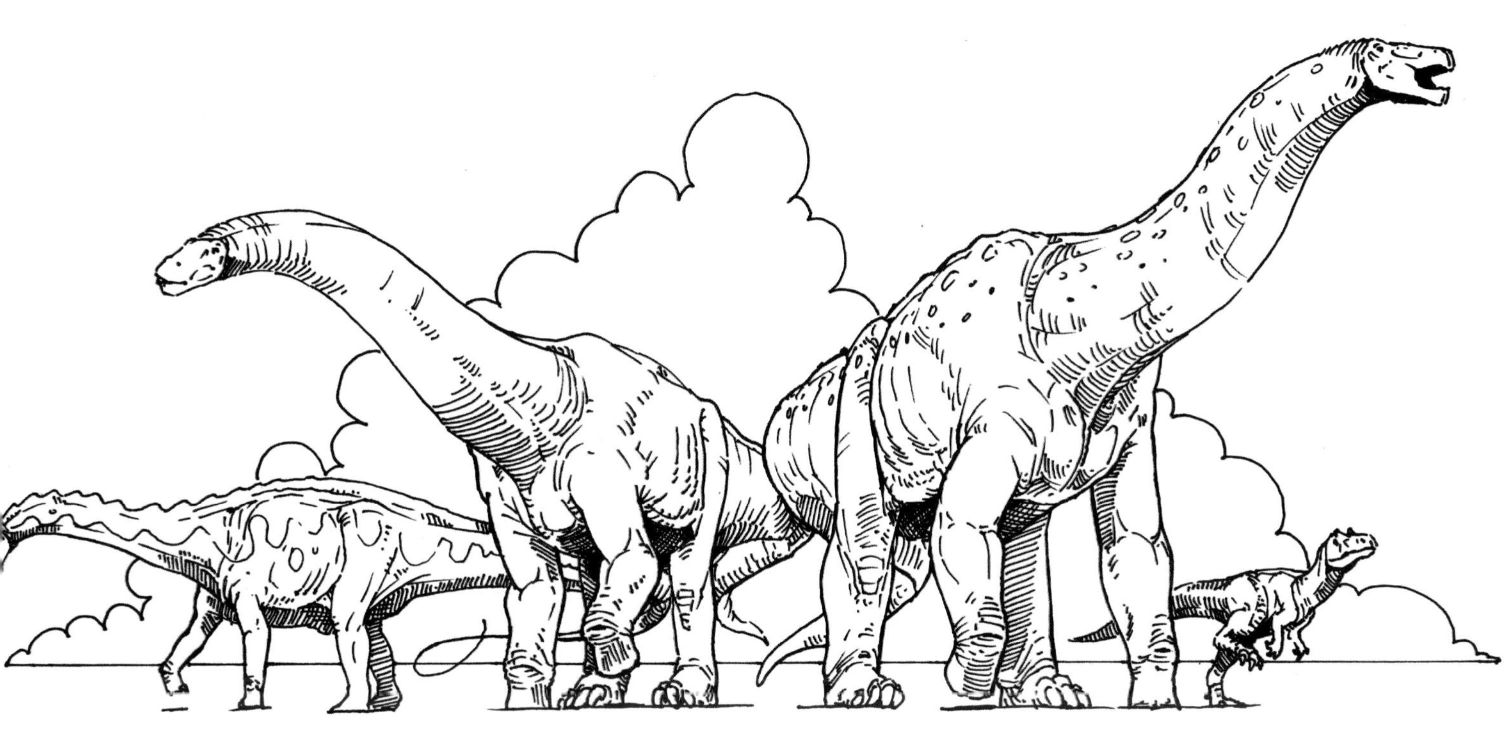

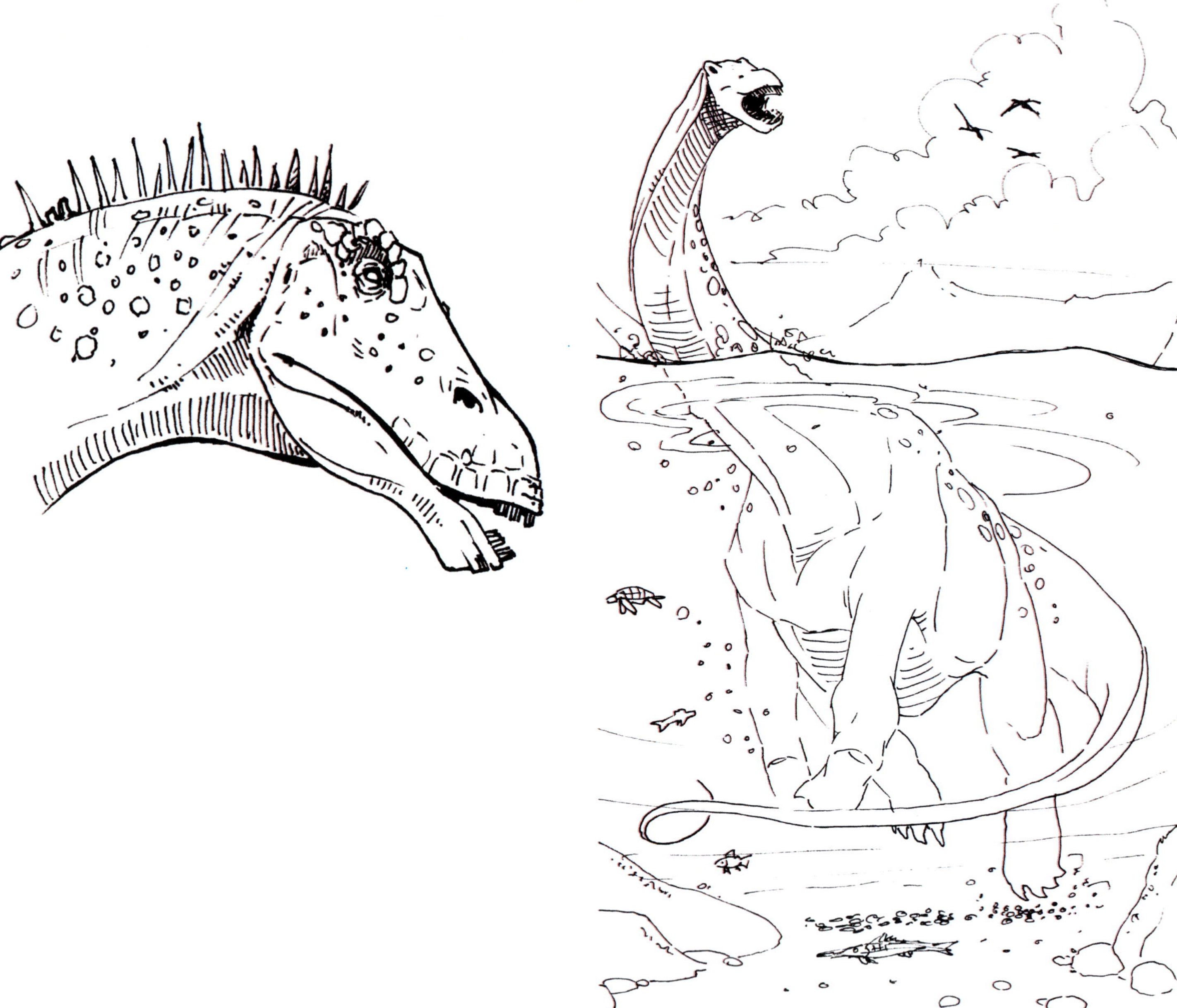

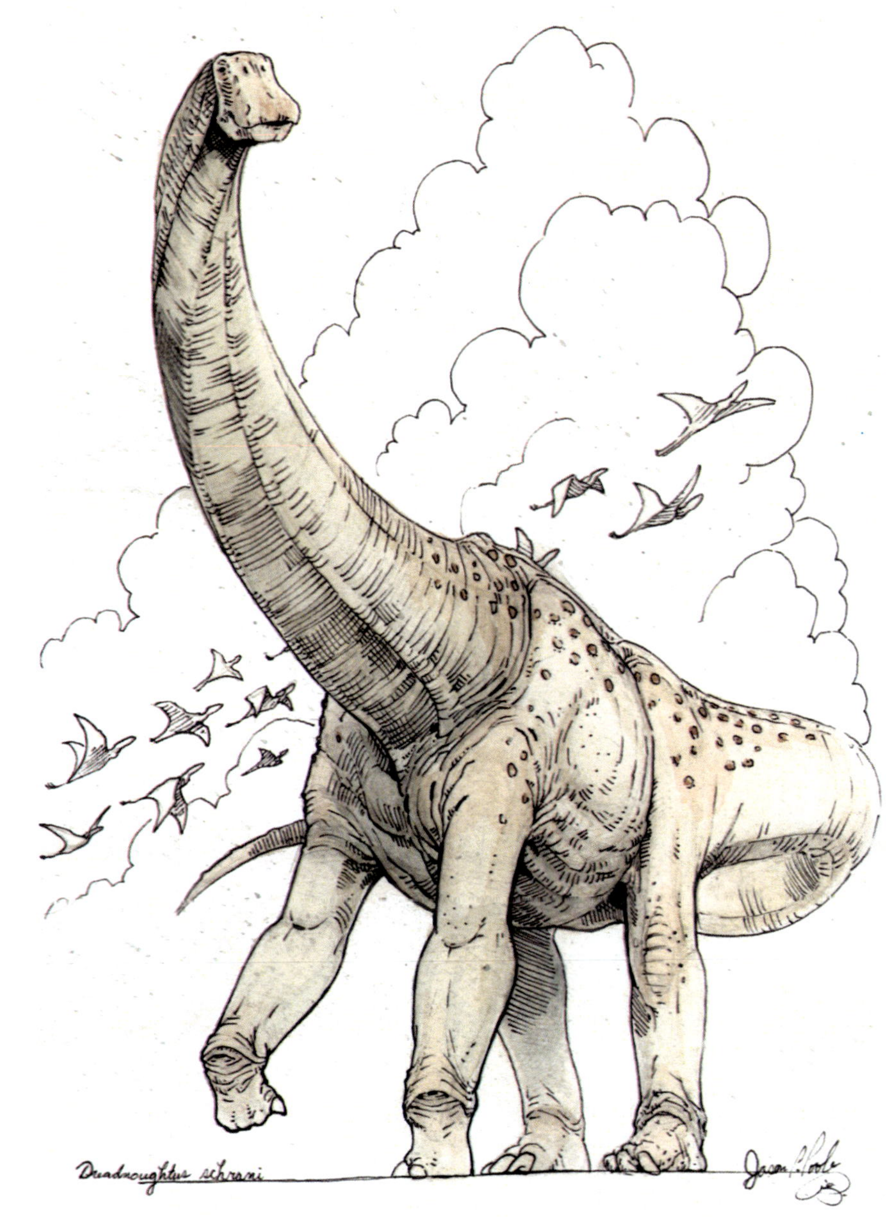

Dreadnoughtus schrani
Jason Poole

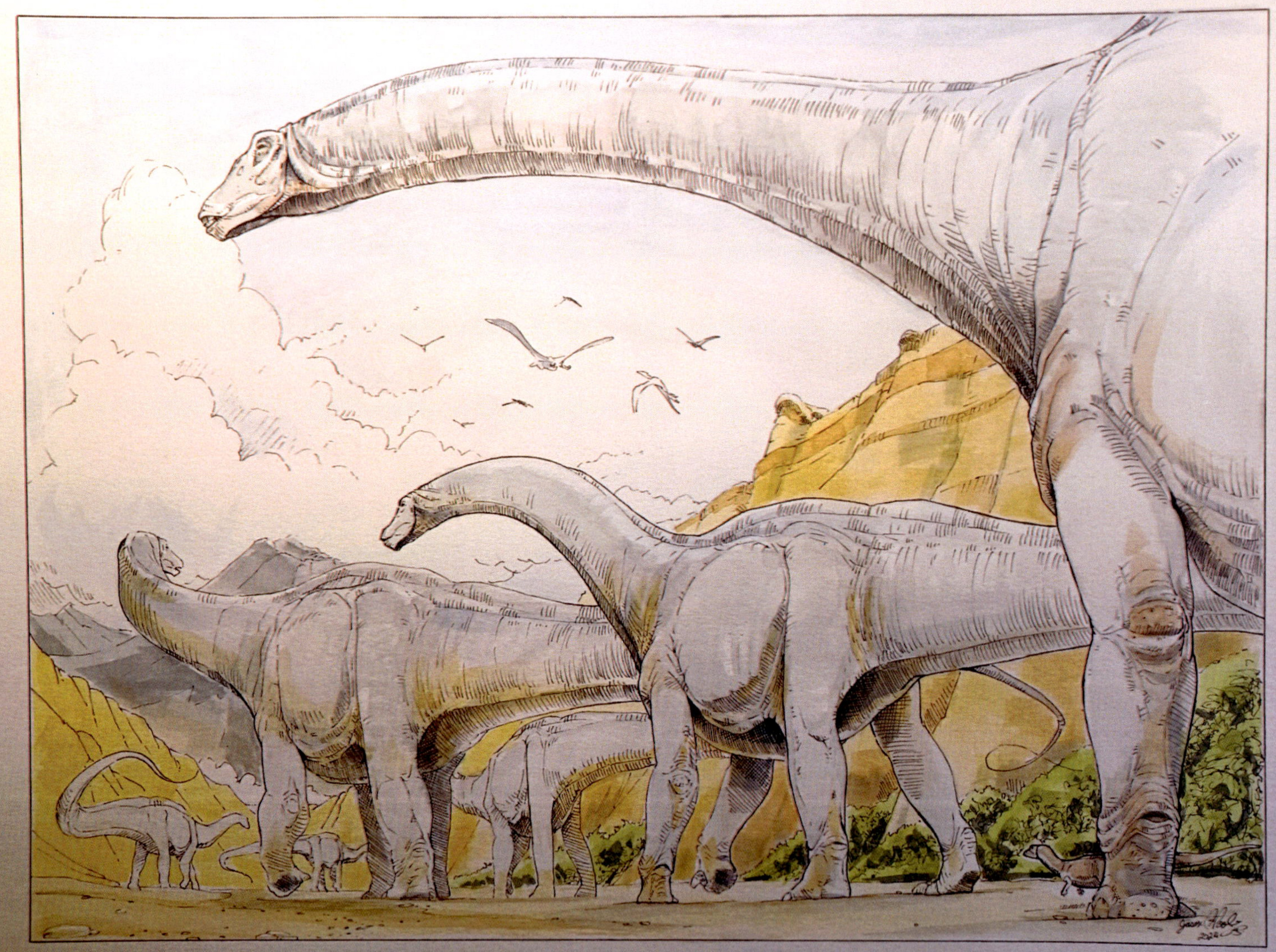

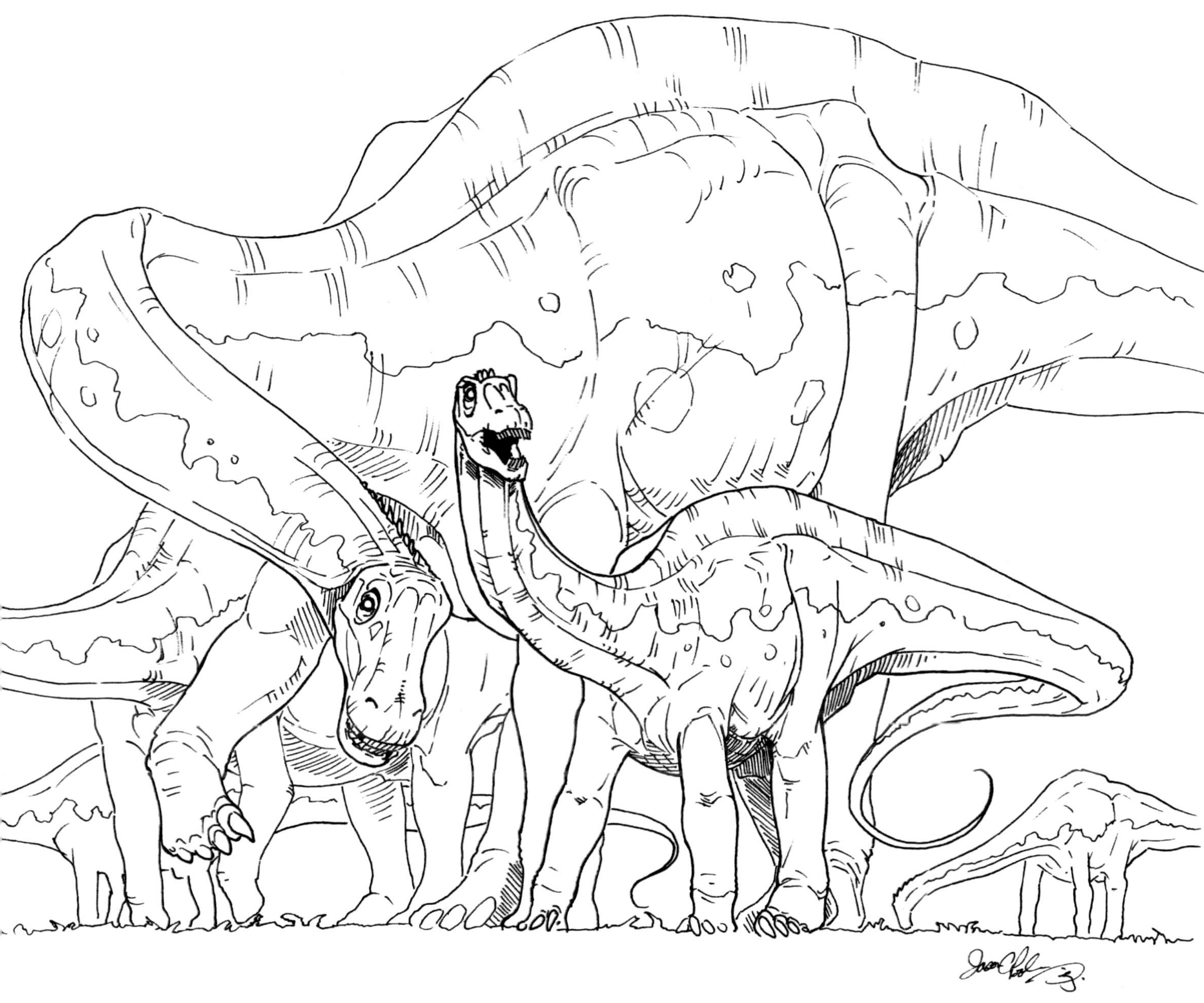

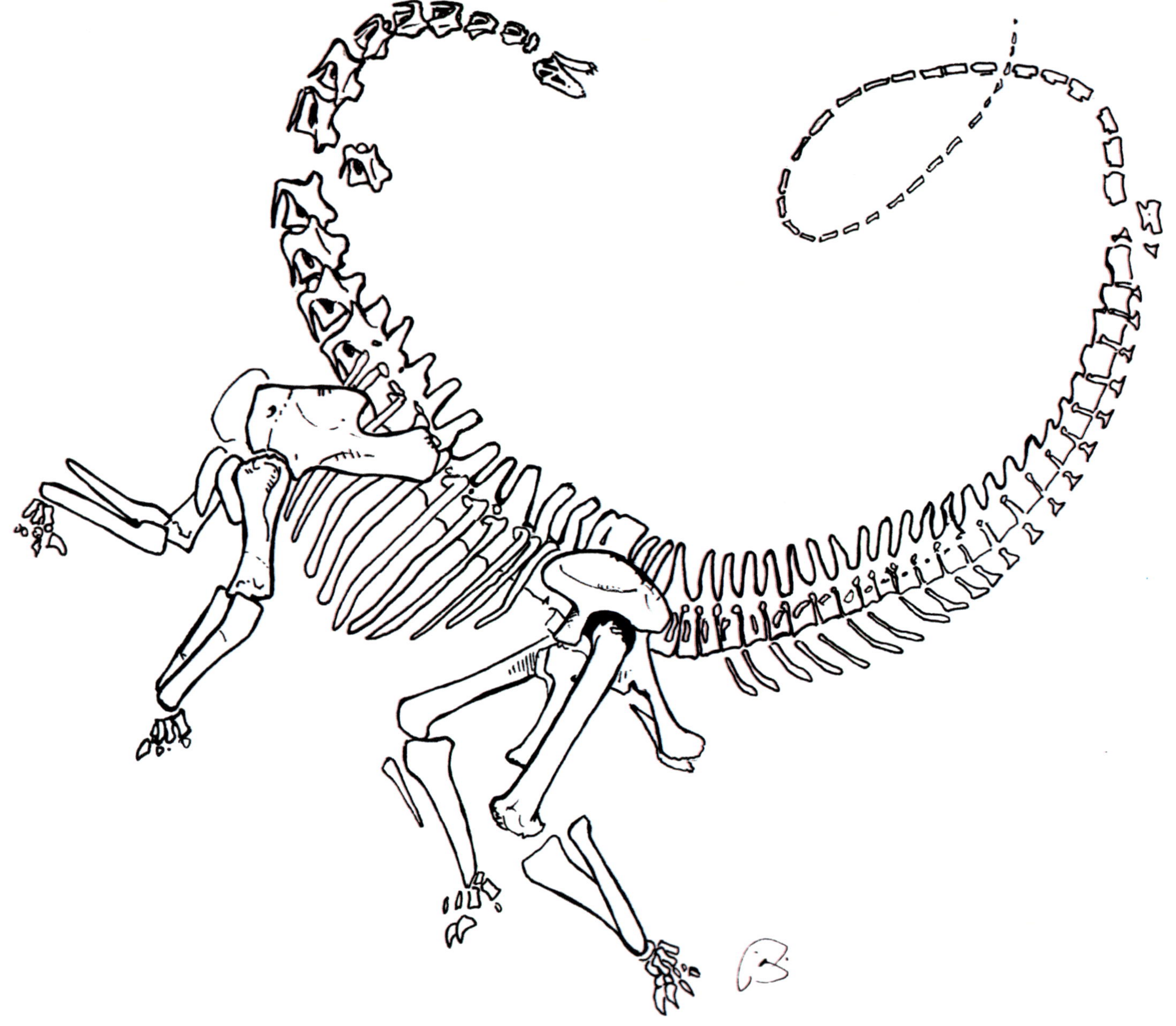

Apatosaurus

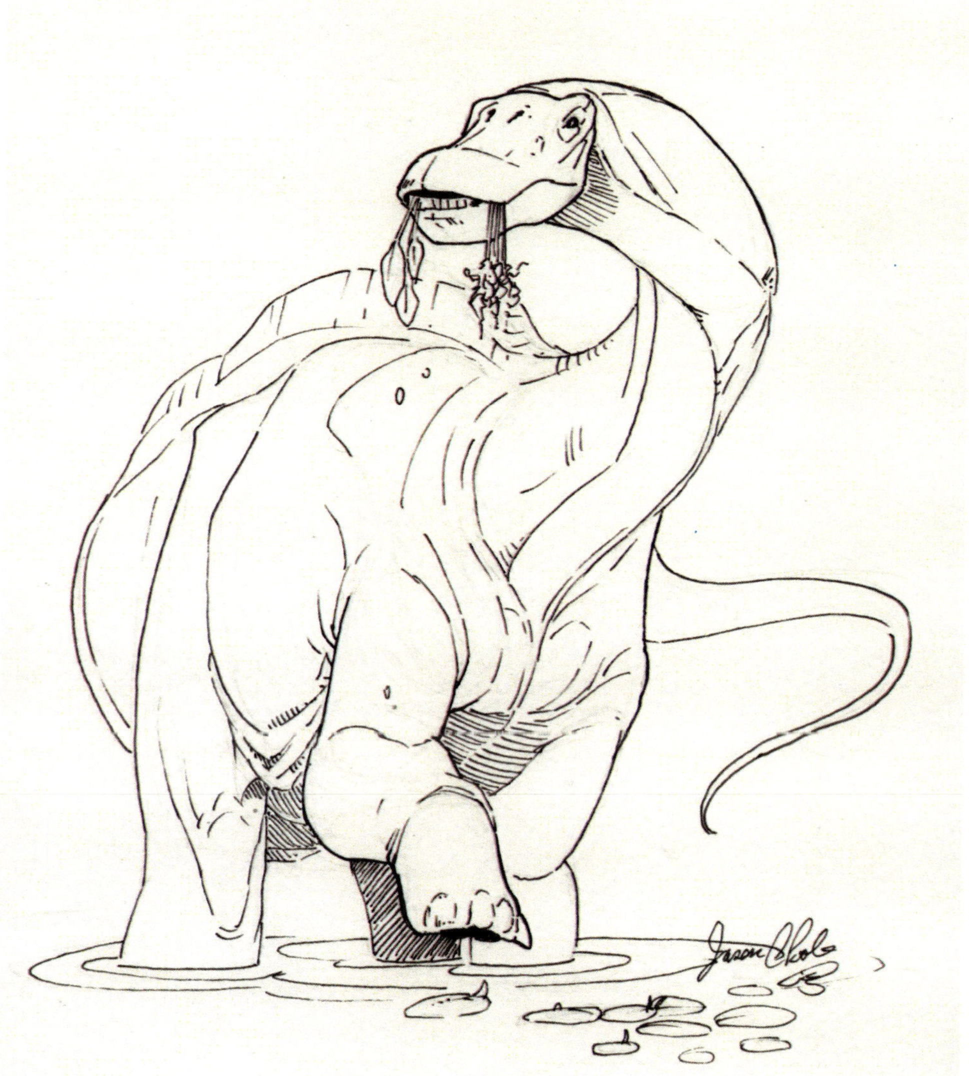

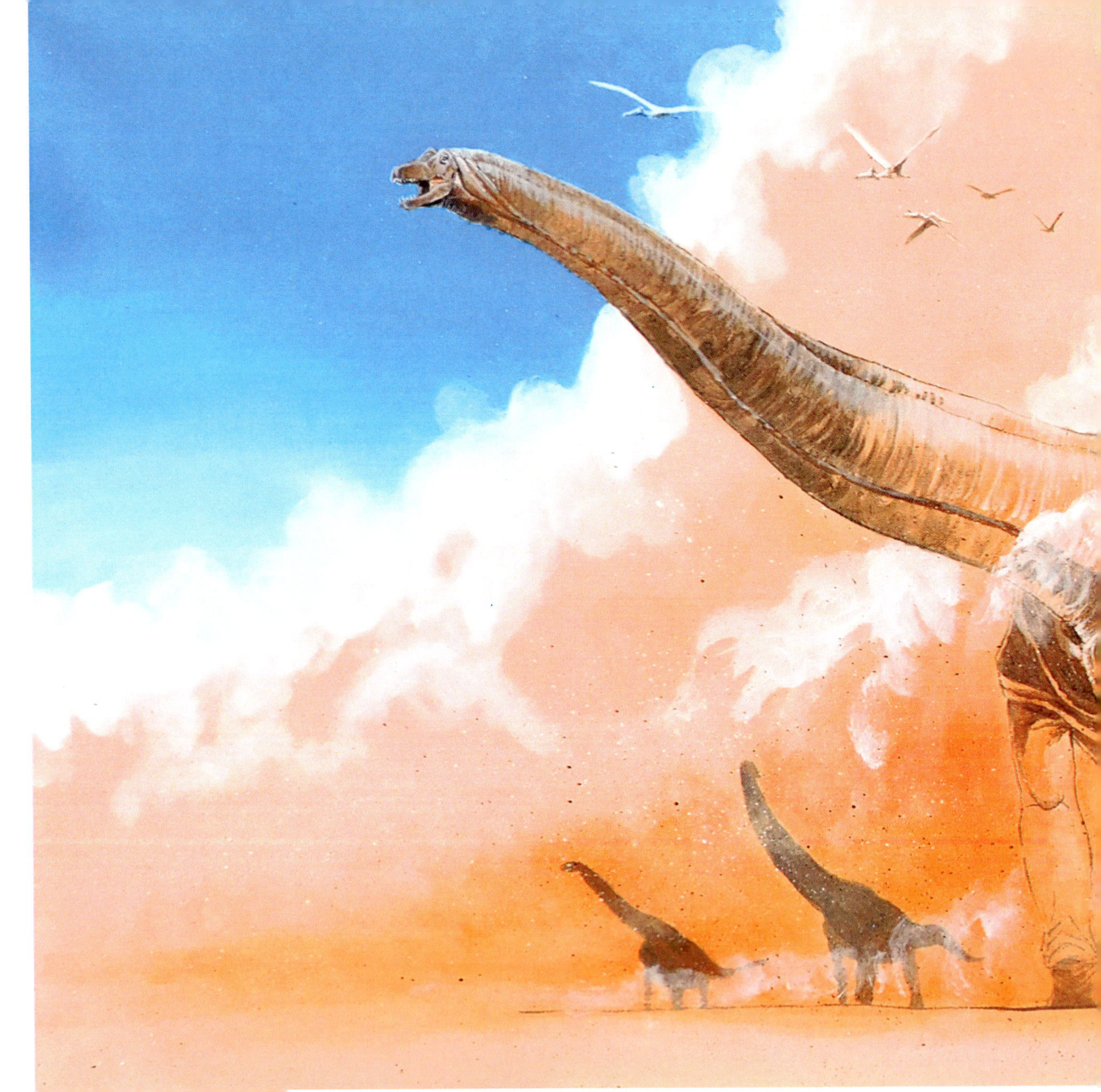

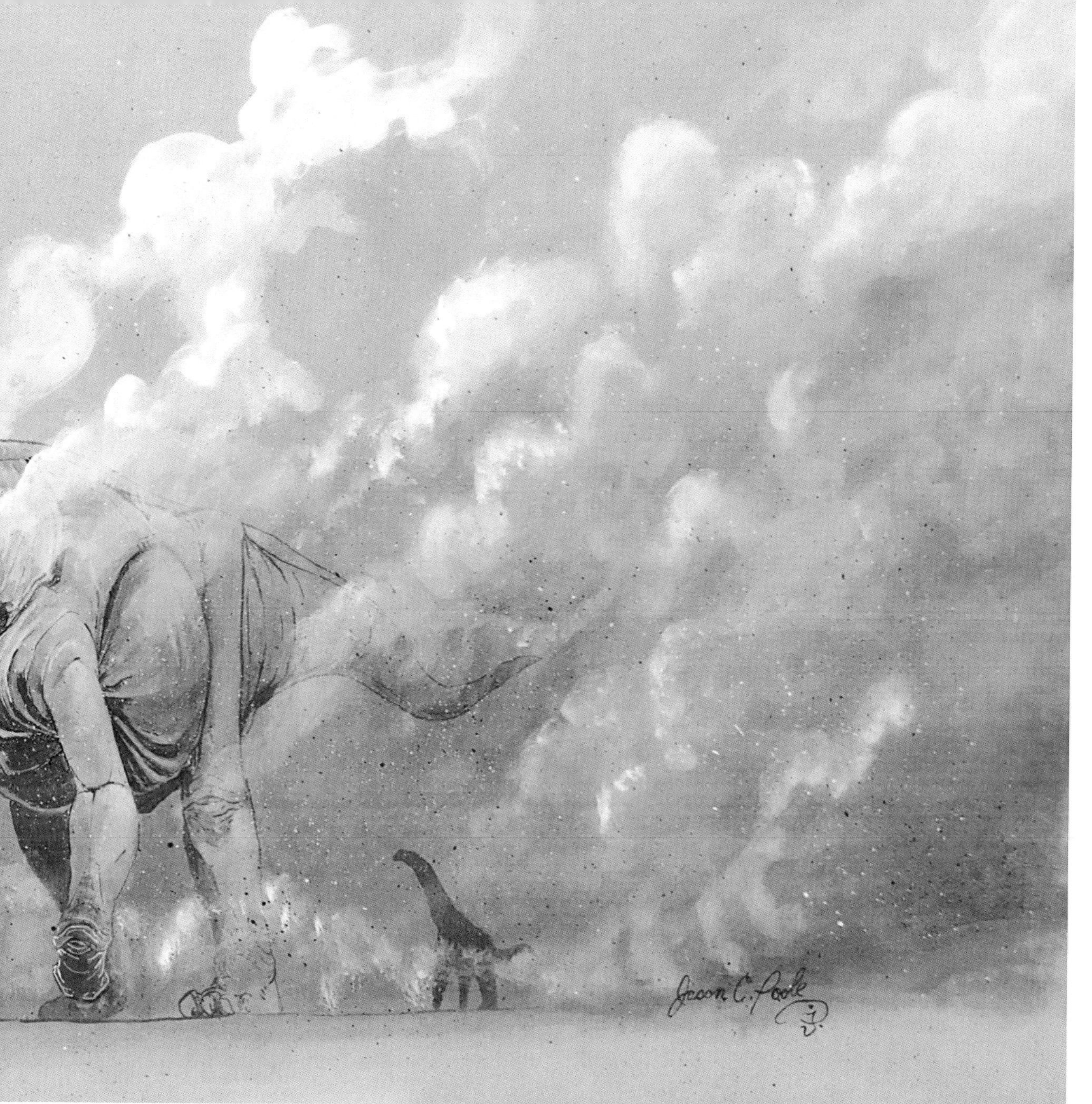

Jason C. Poole

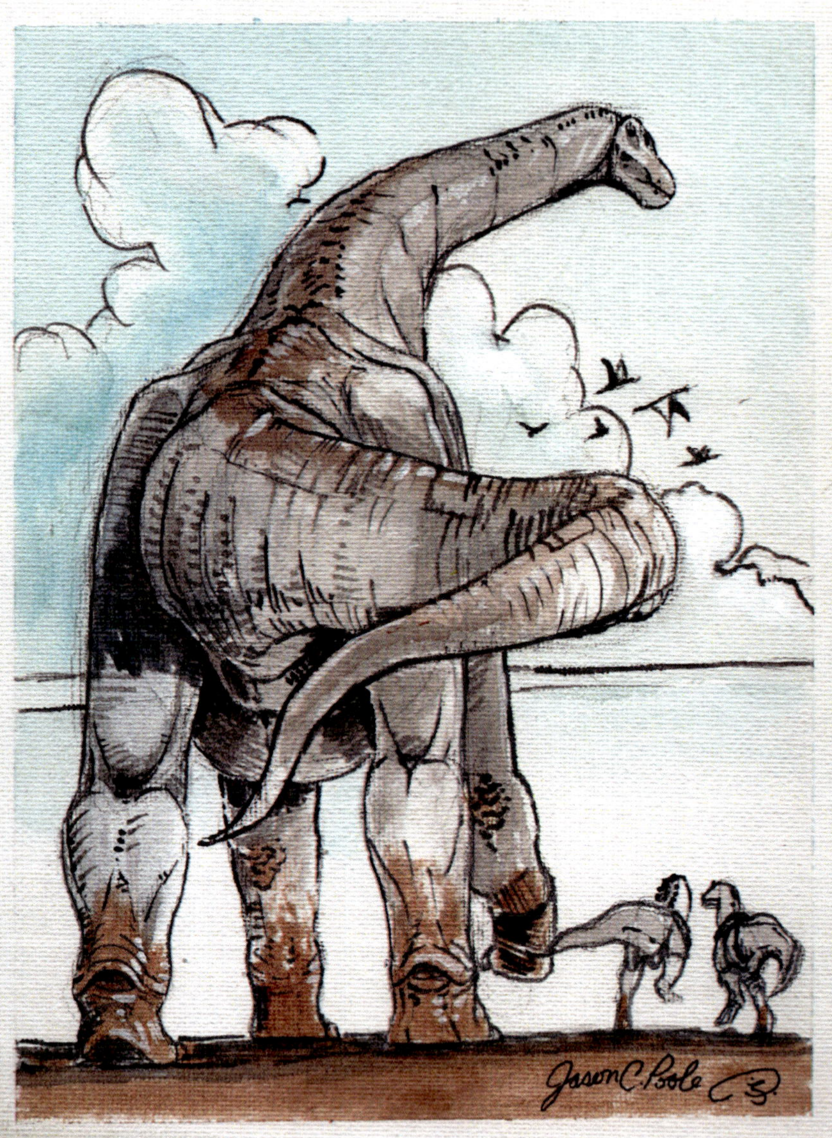

Jason C. Poole

Theropods

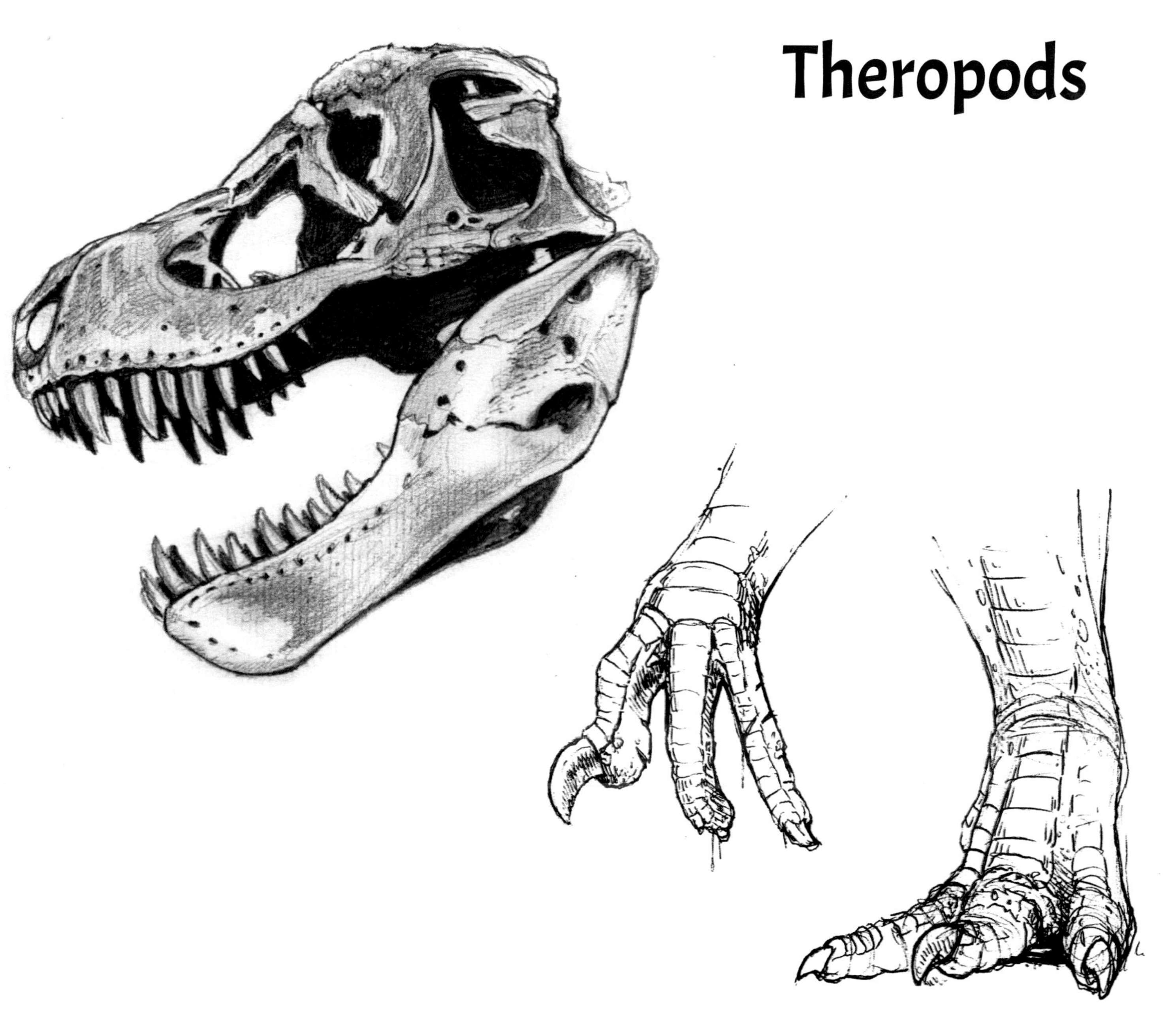

Allosaurus
M+M site

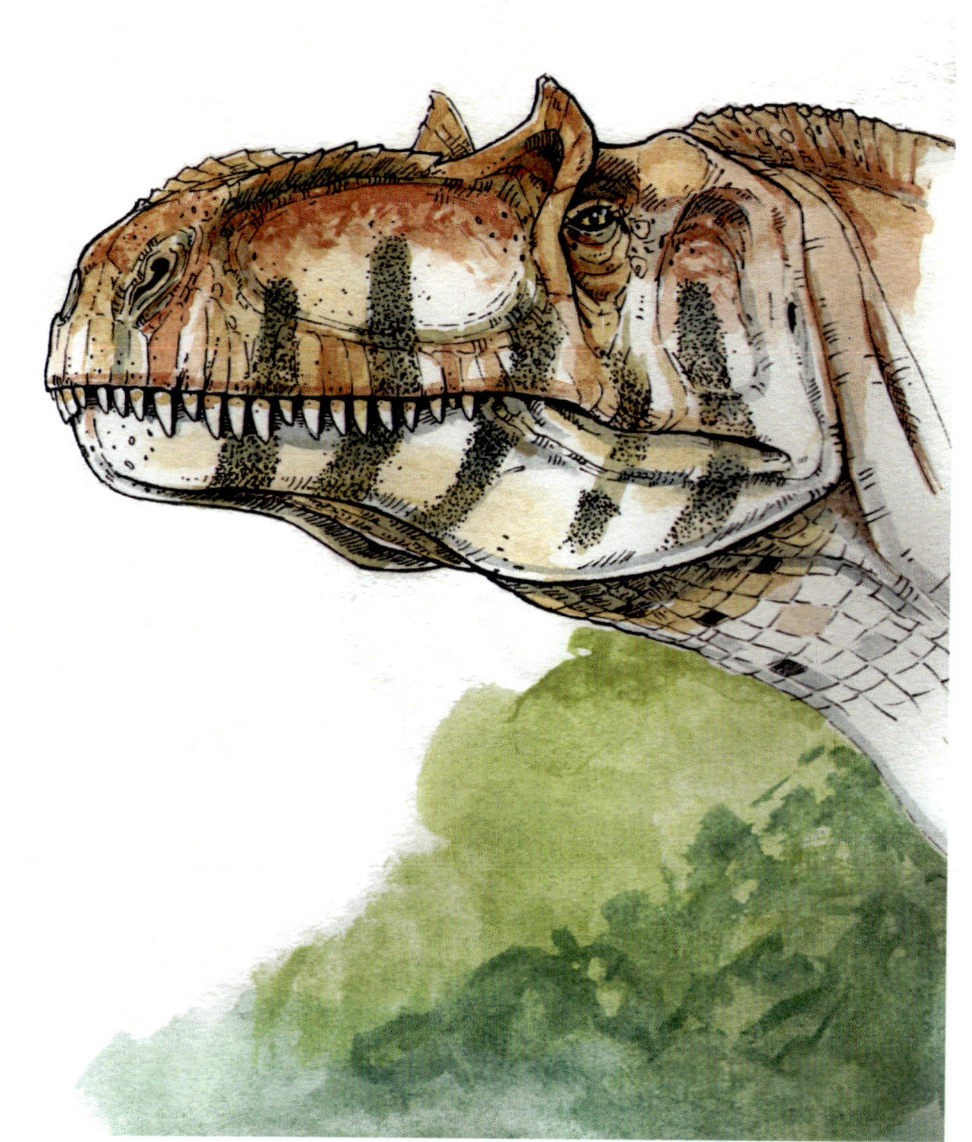

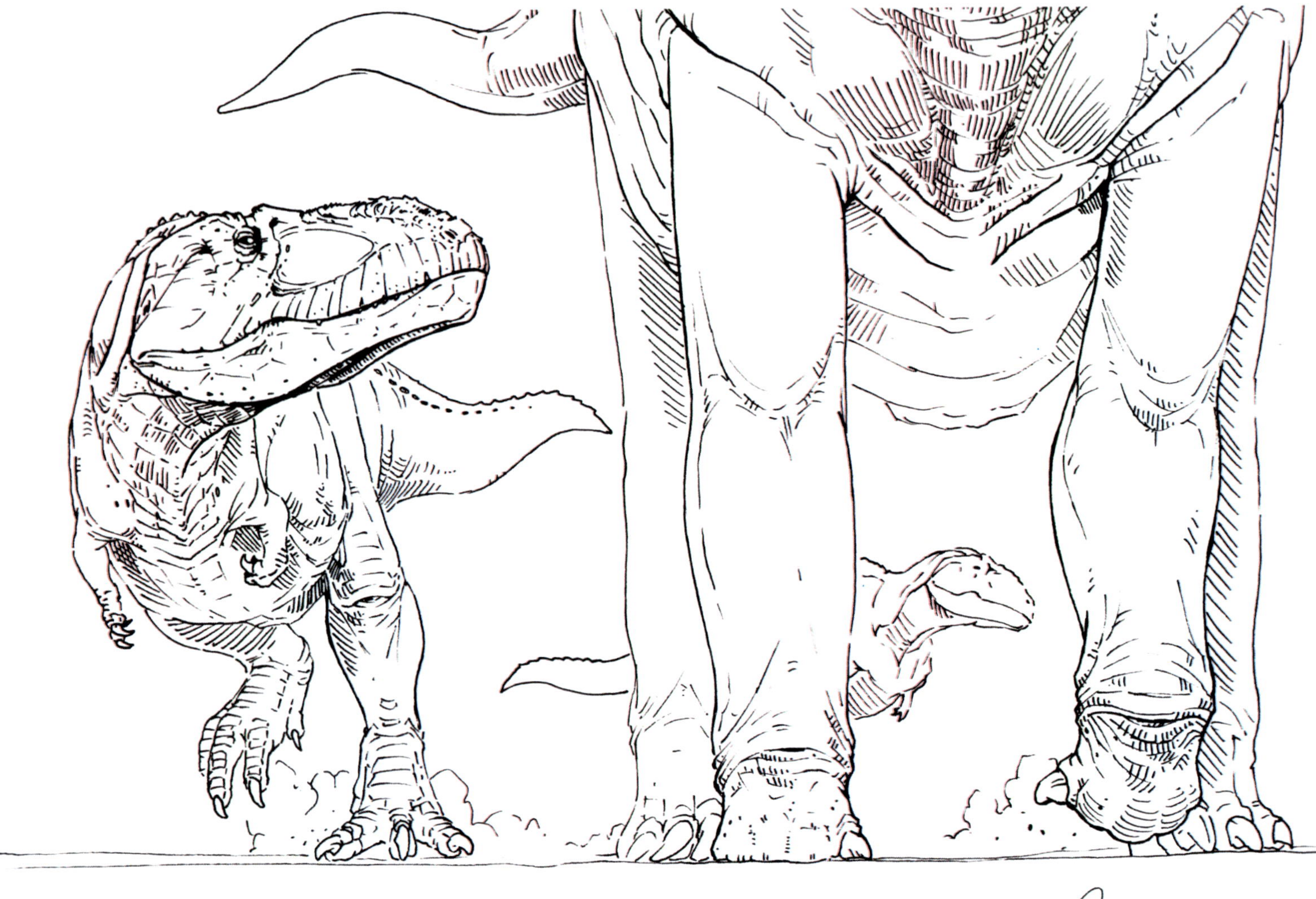

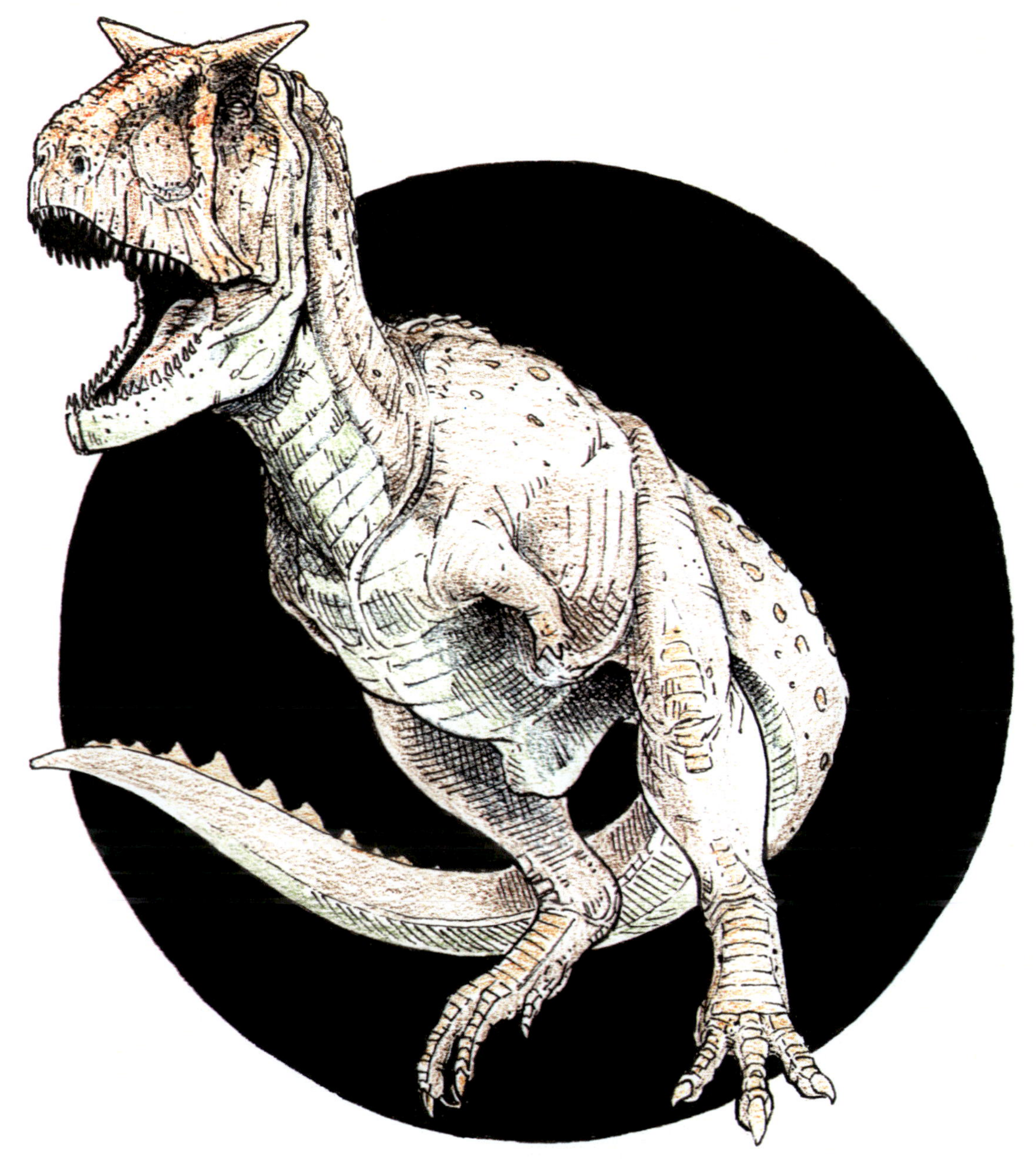

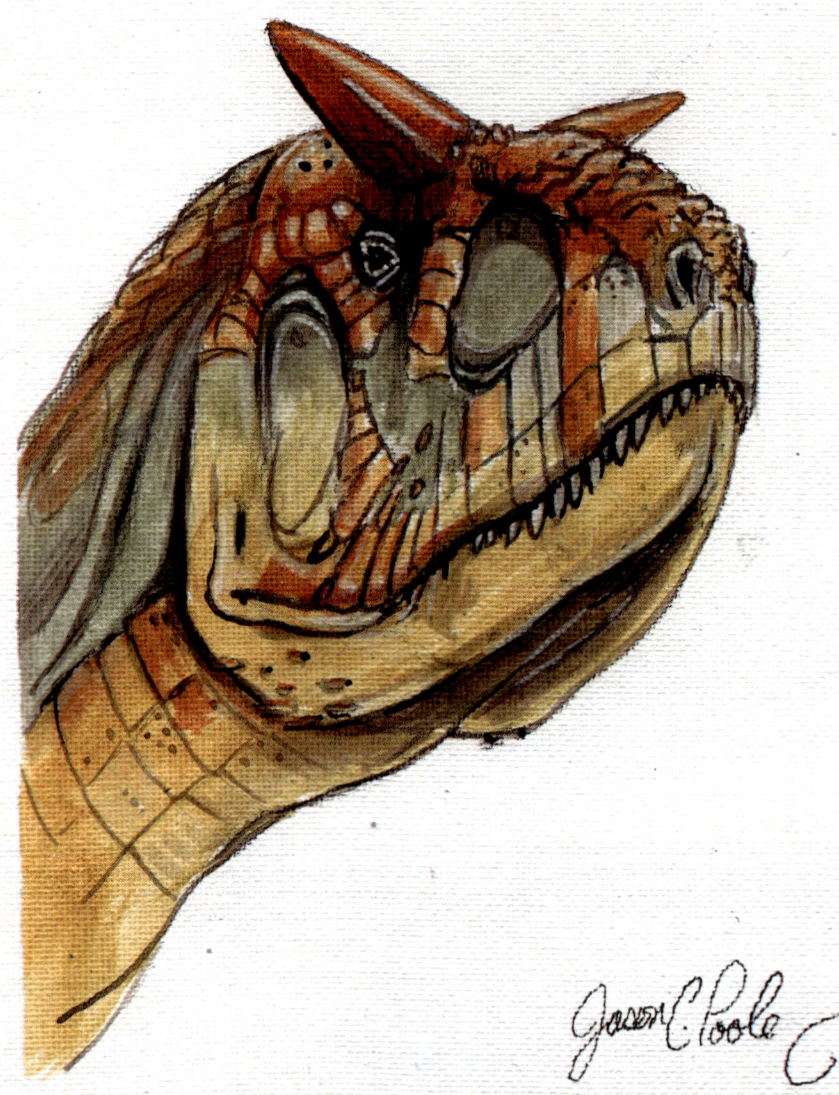
Jason C Poole

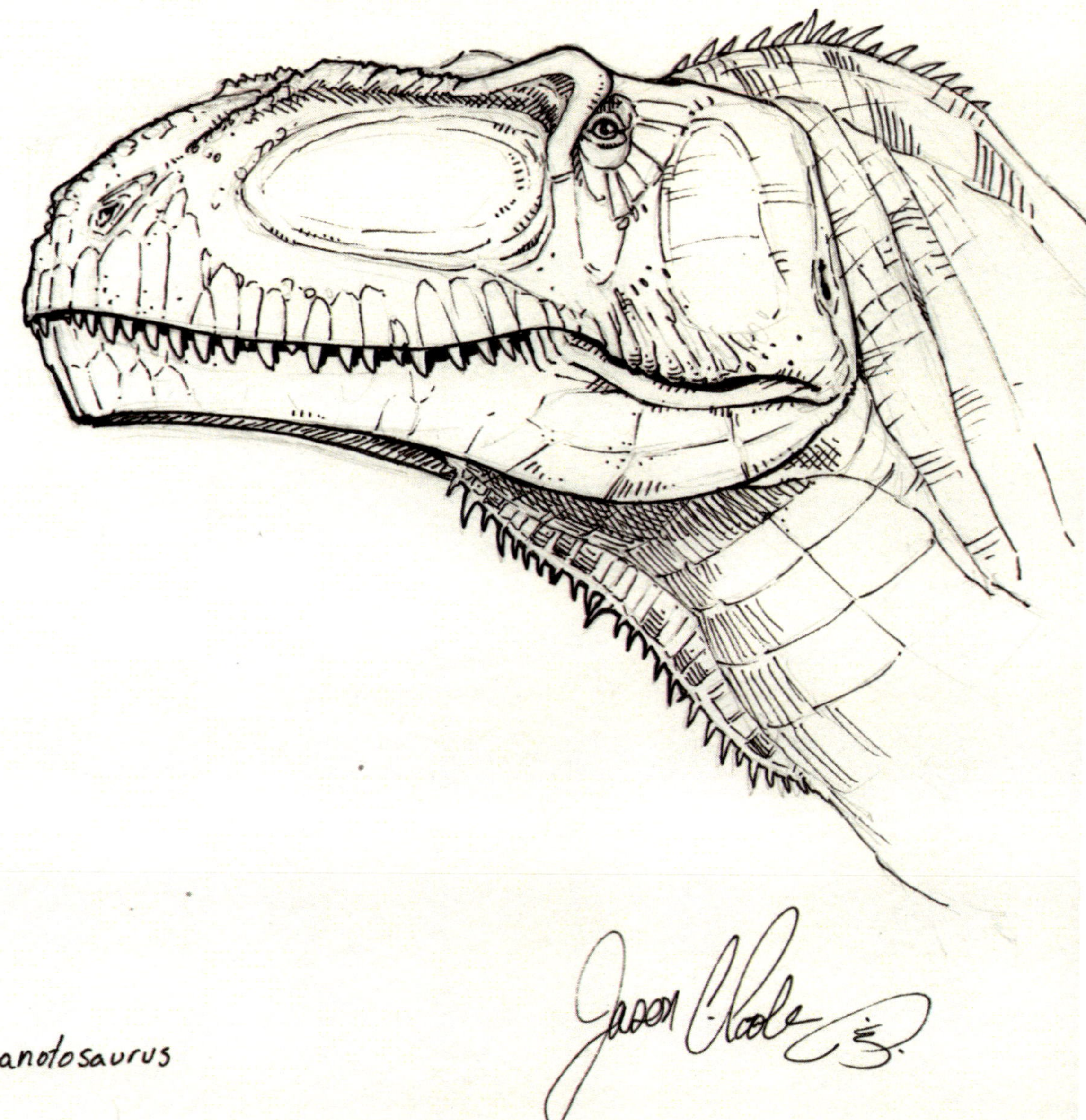

Giganotosaurus

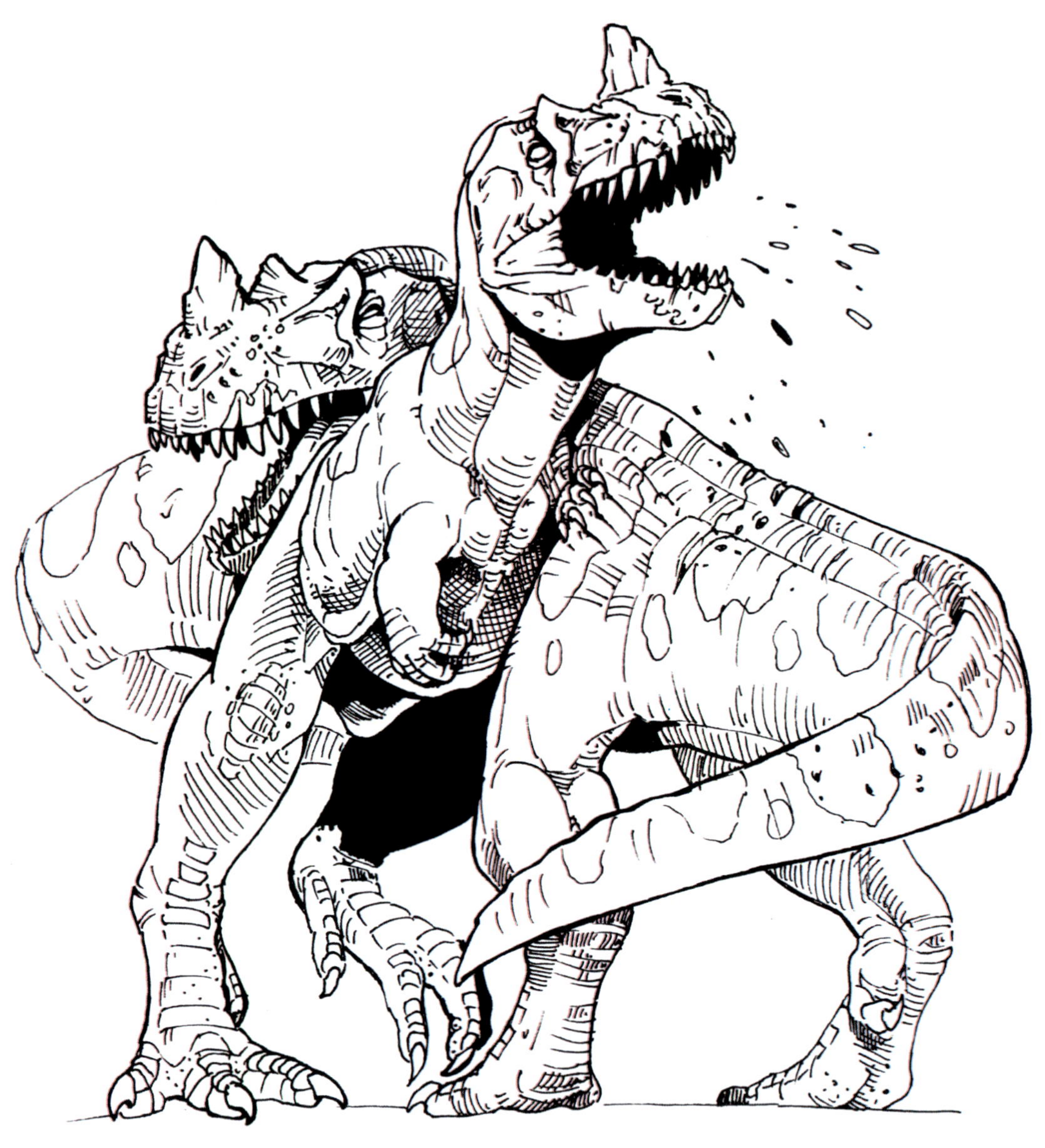

Jason C. Poole

Ceratosaurus

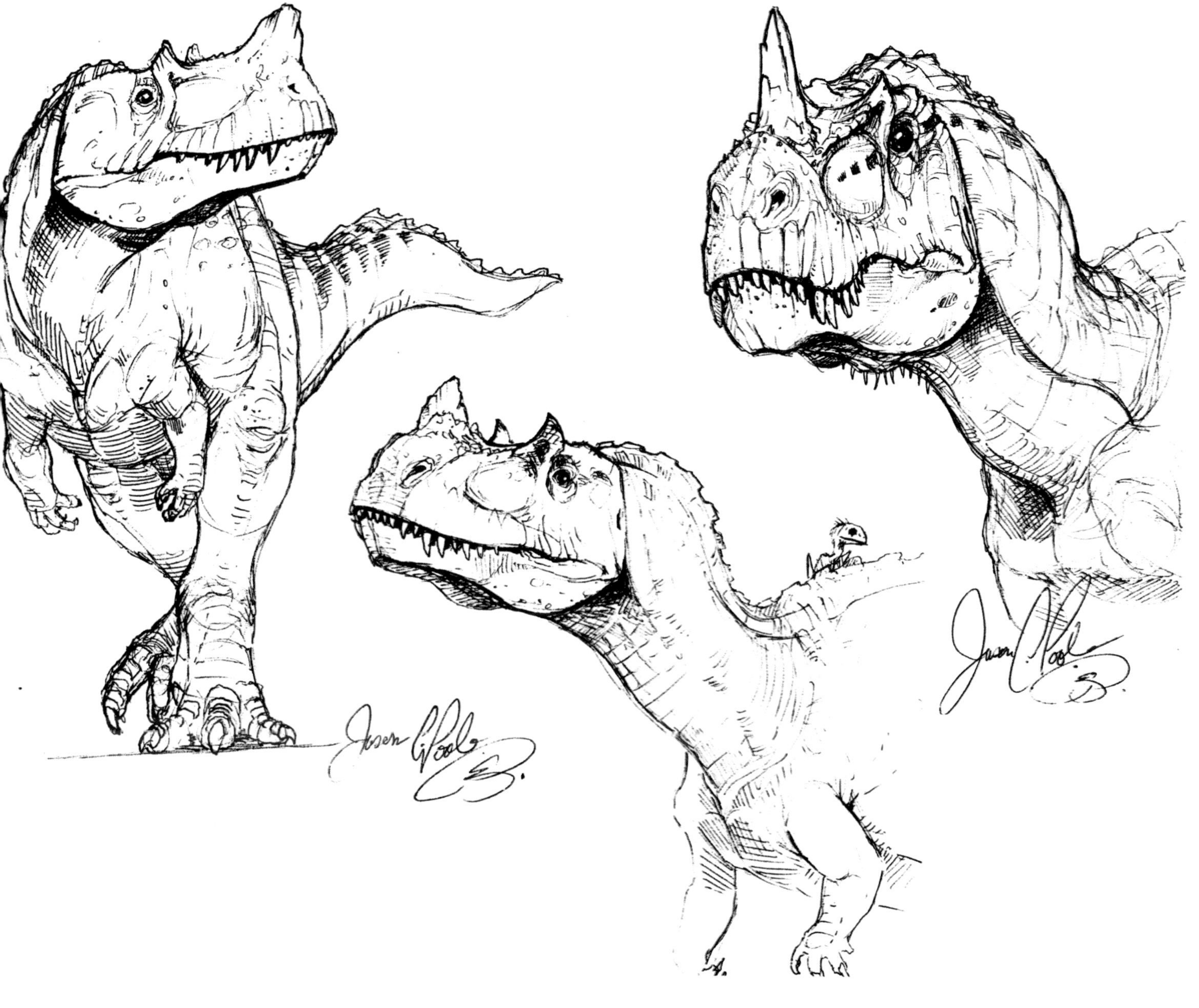

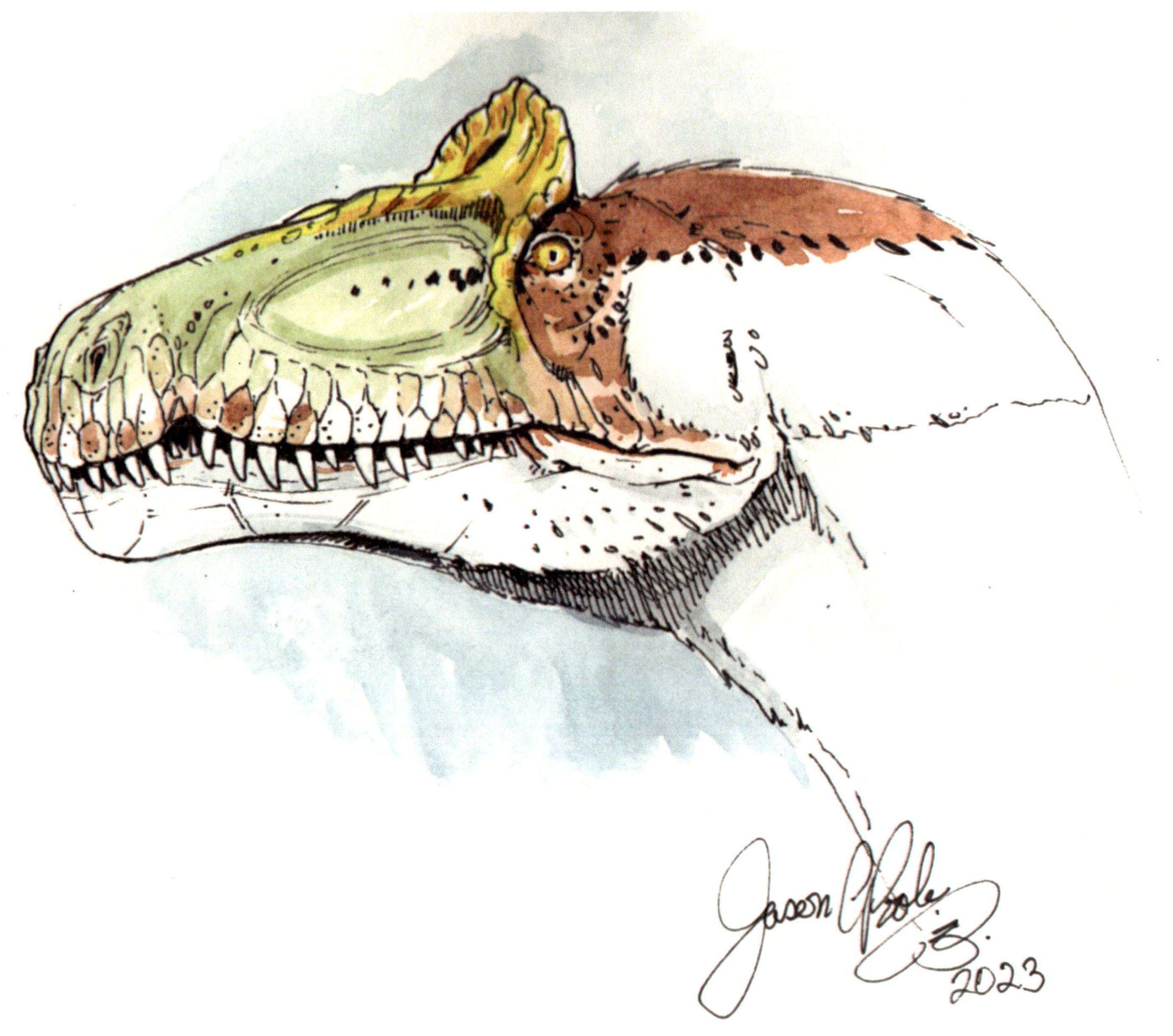

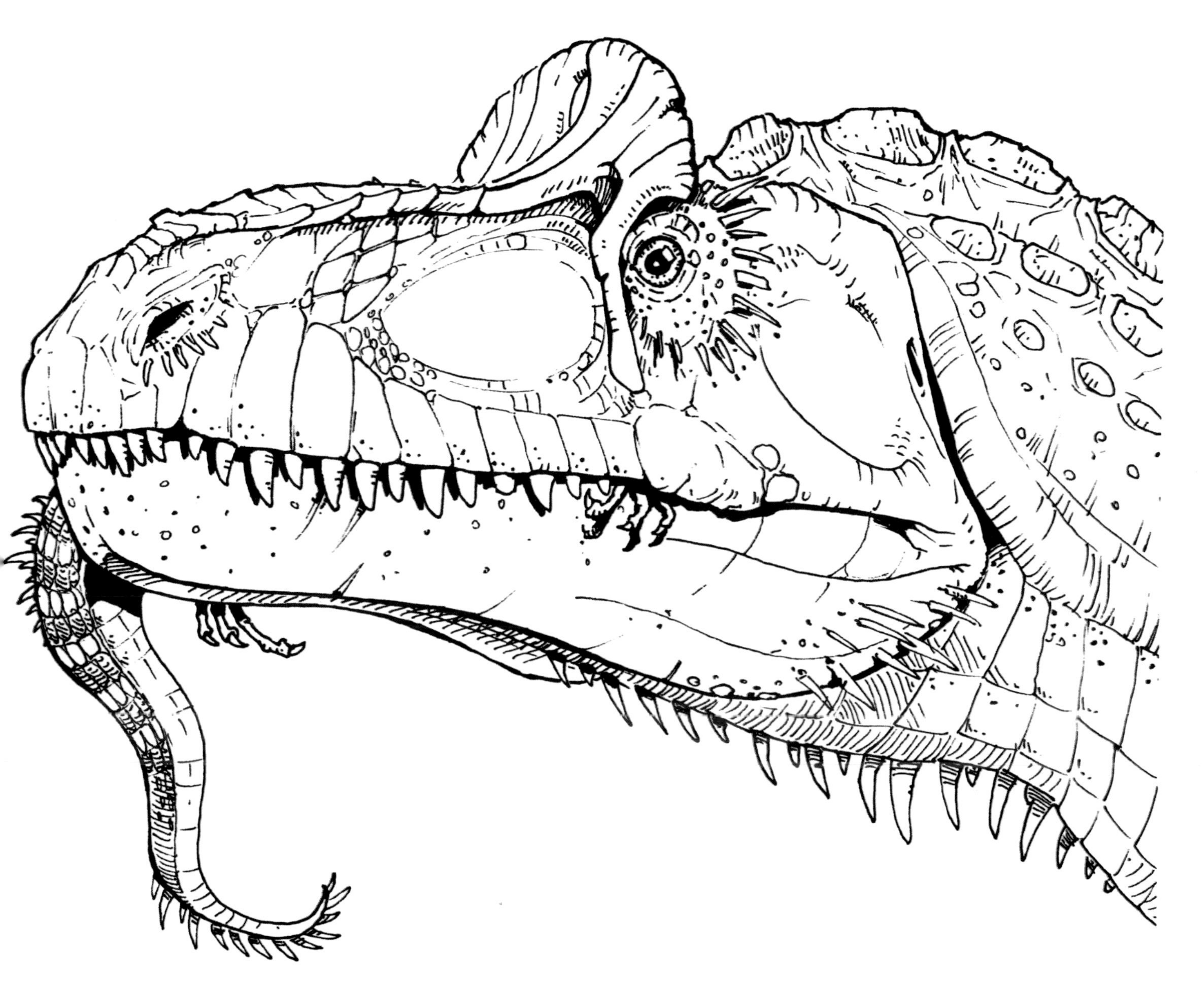

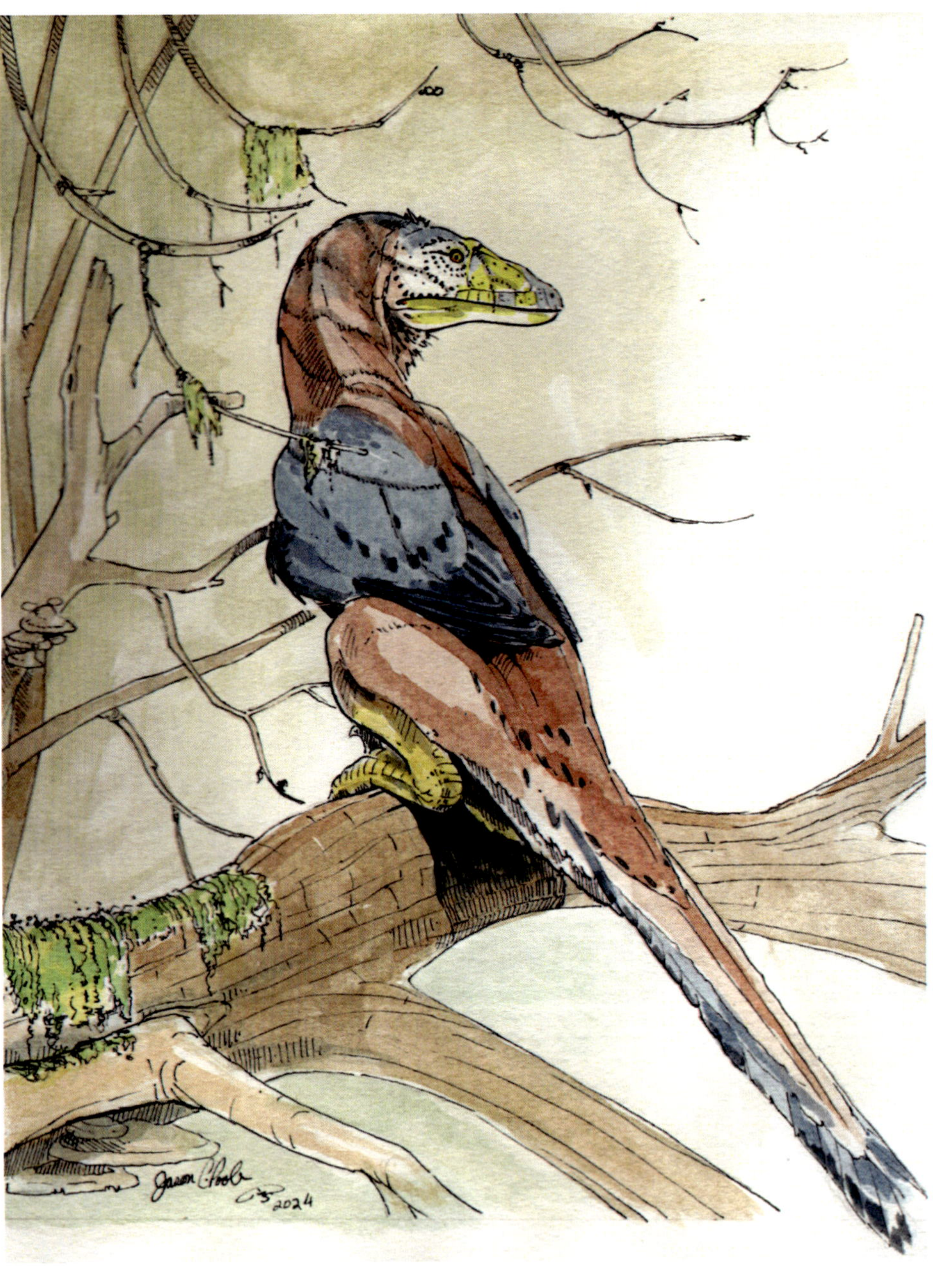

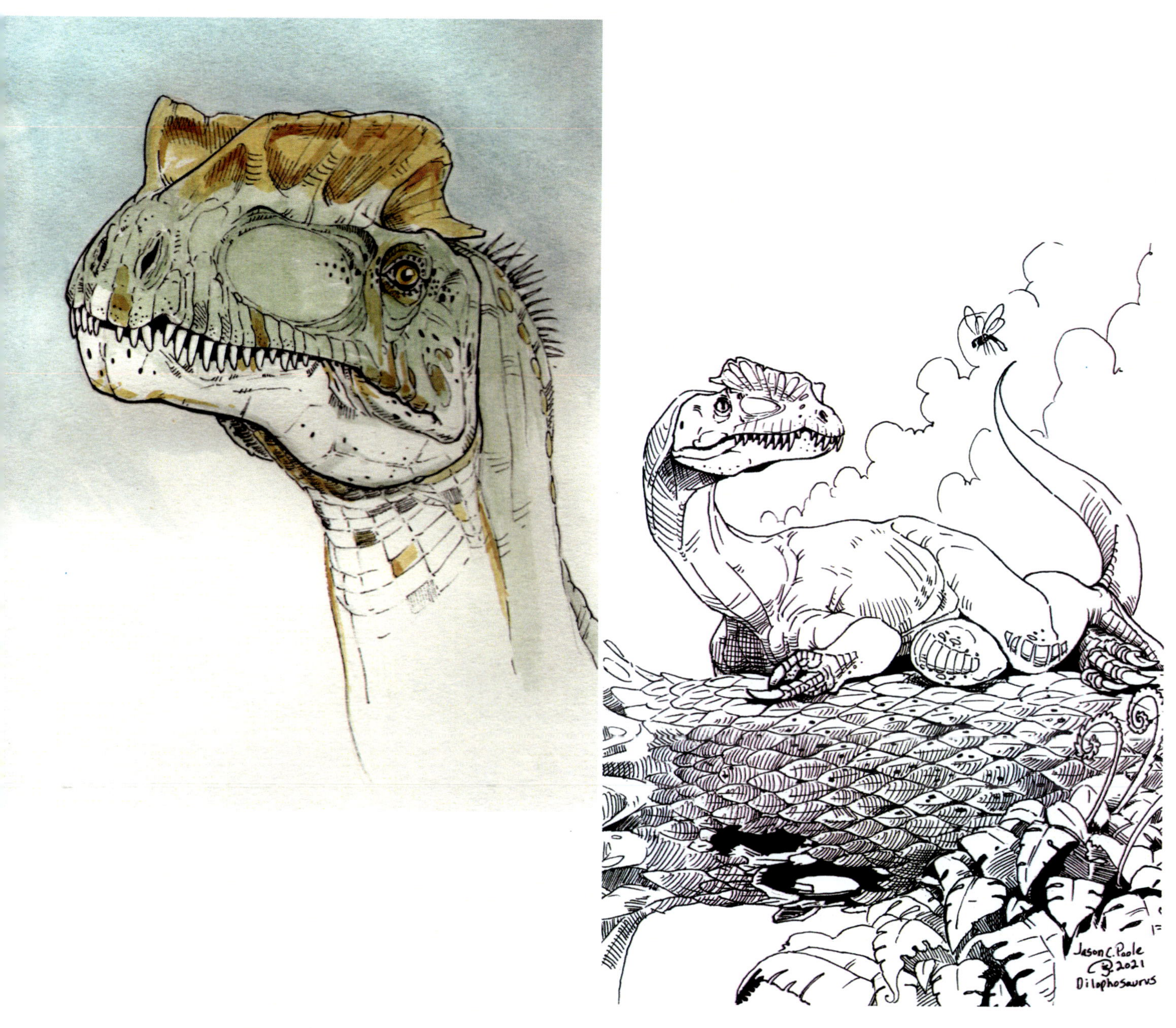

Jason C. Poole
© 2021
Dilophosaurus

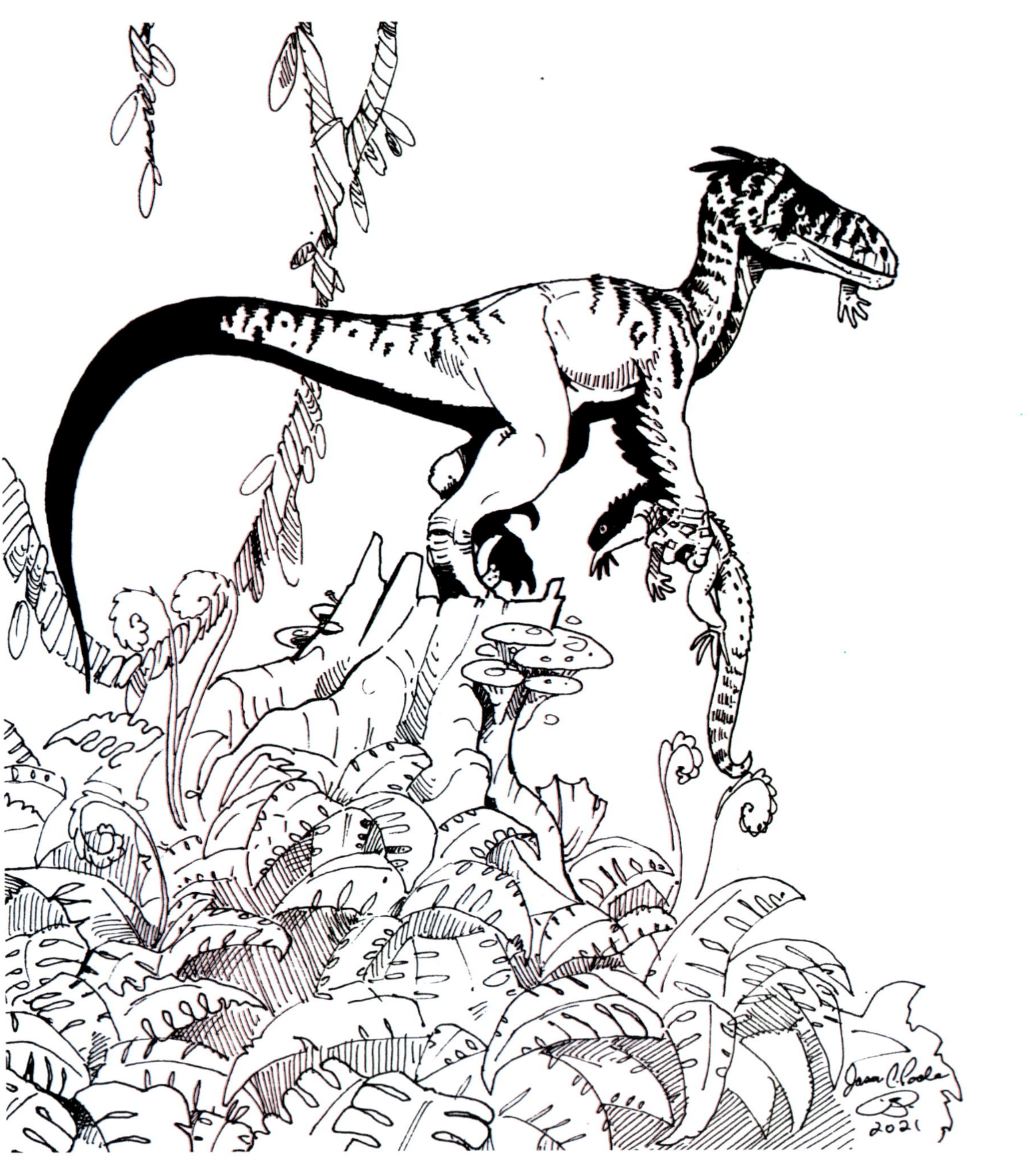

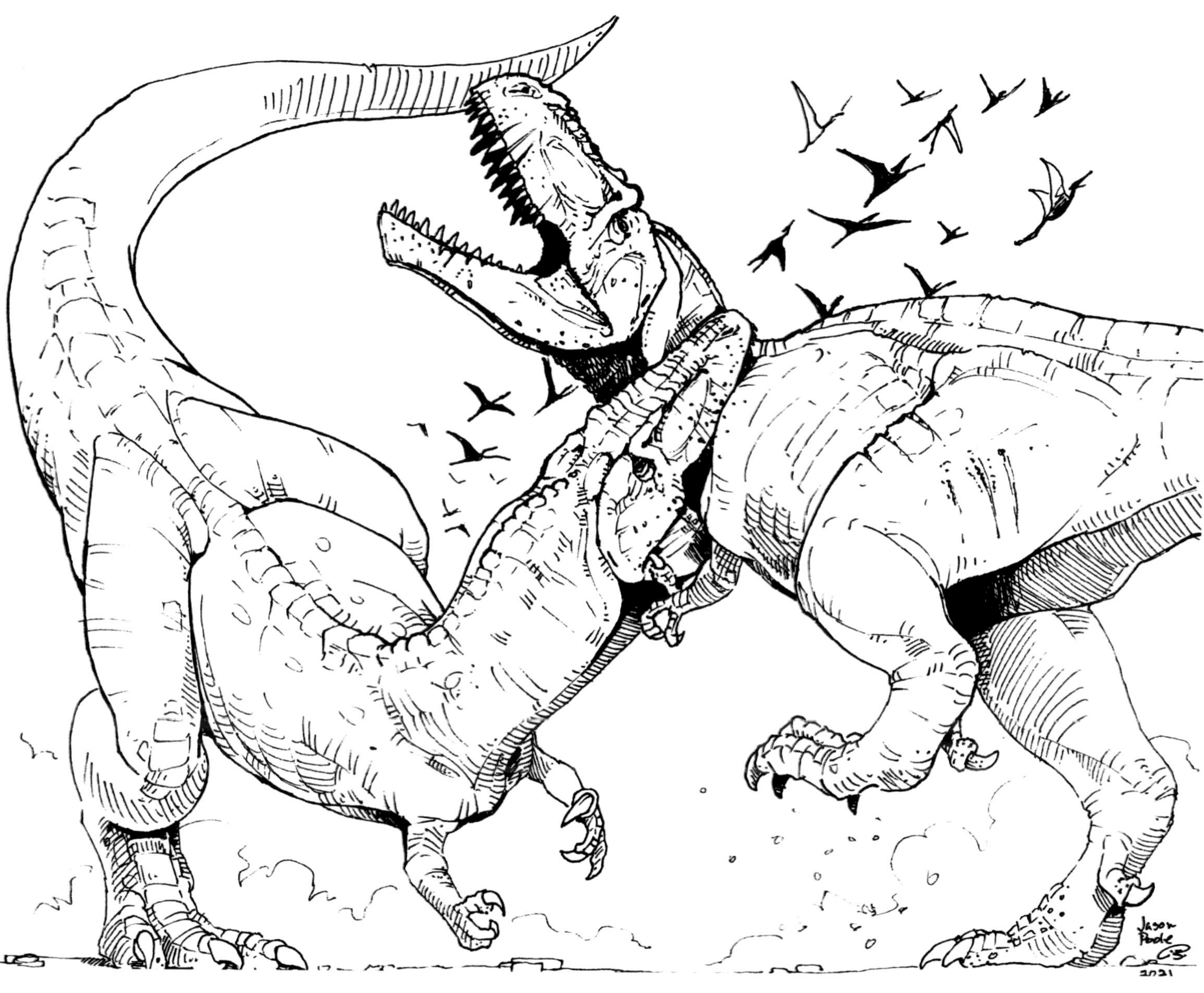
Jason Poole
2021

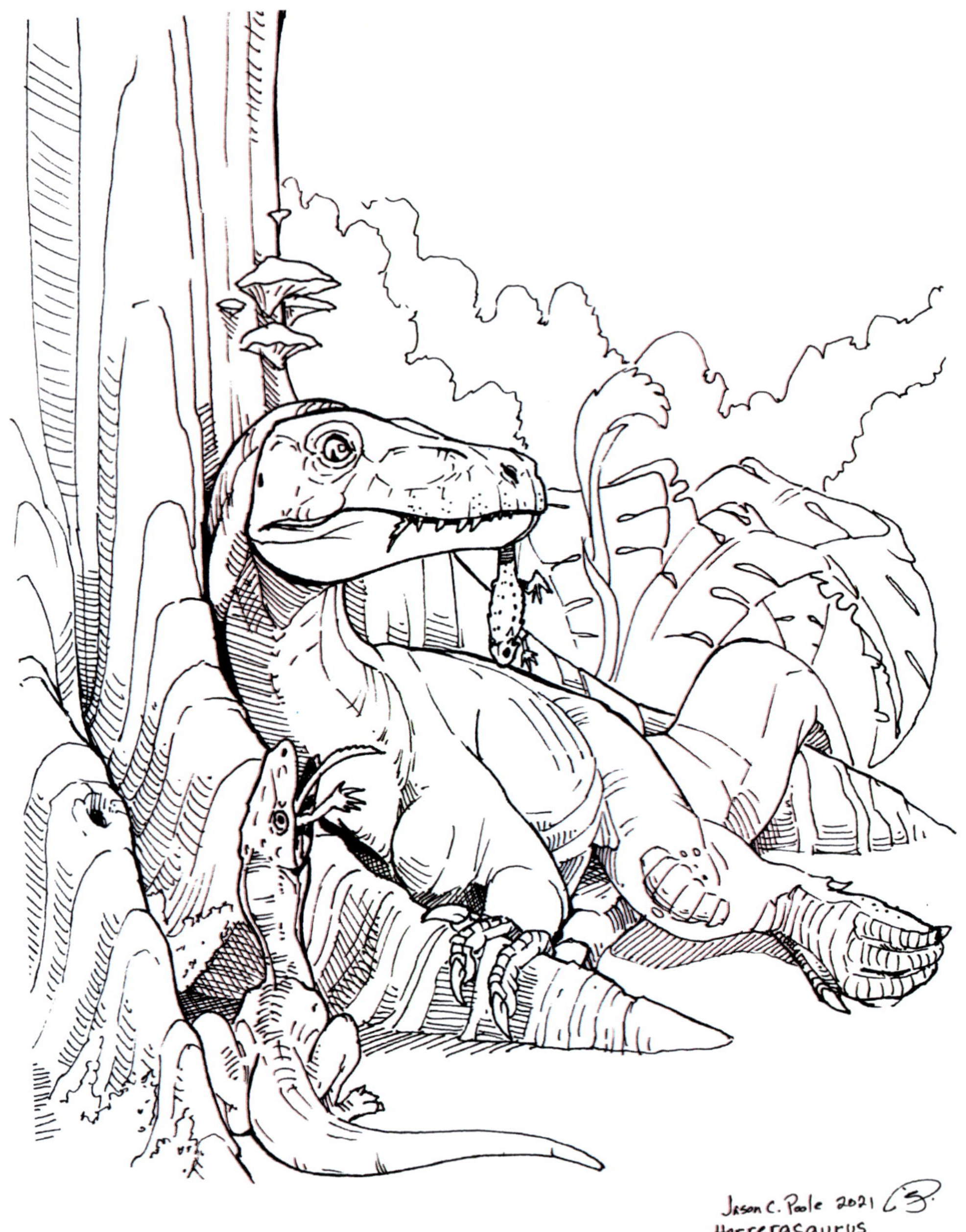

Jason C. Poole 2021
Herrerasaurus

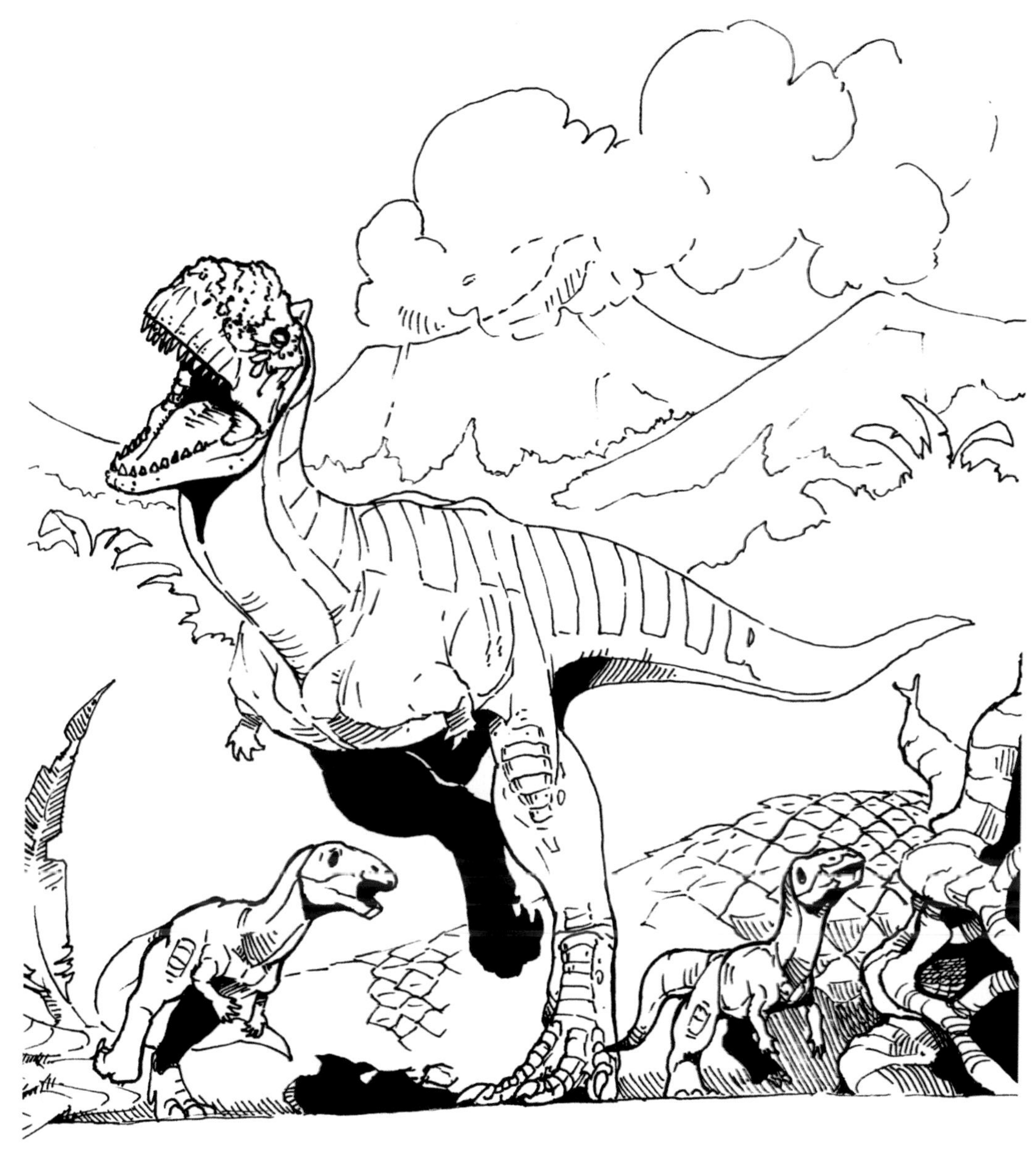

Jason C. Poole
majungasaurus

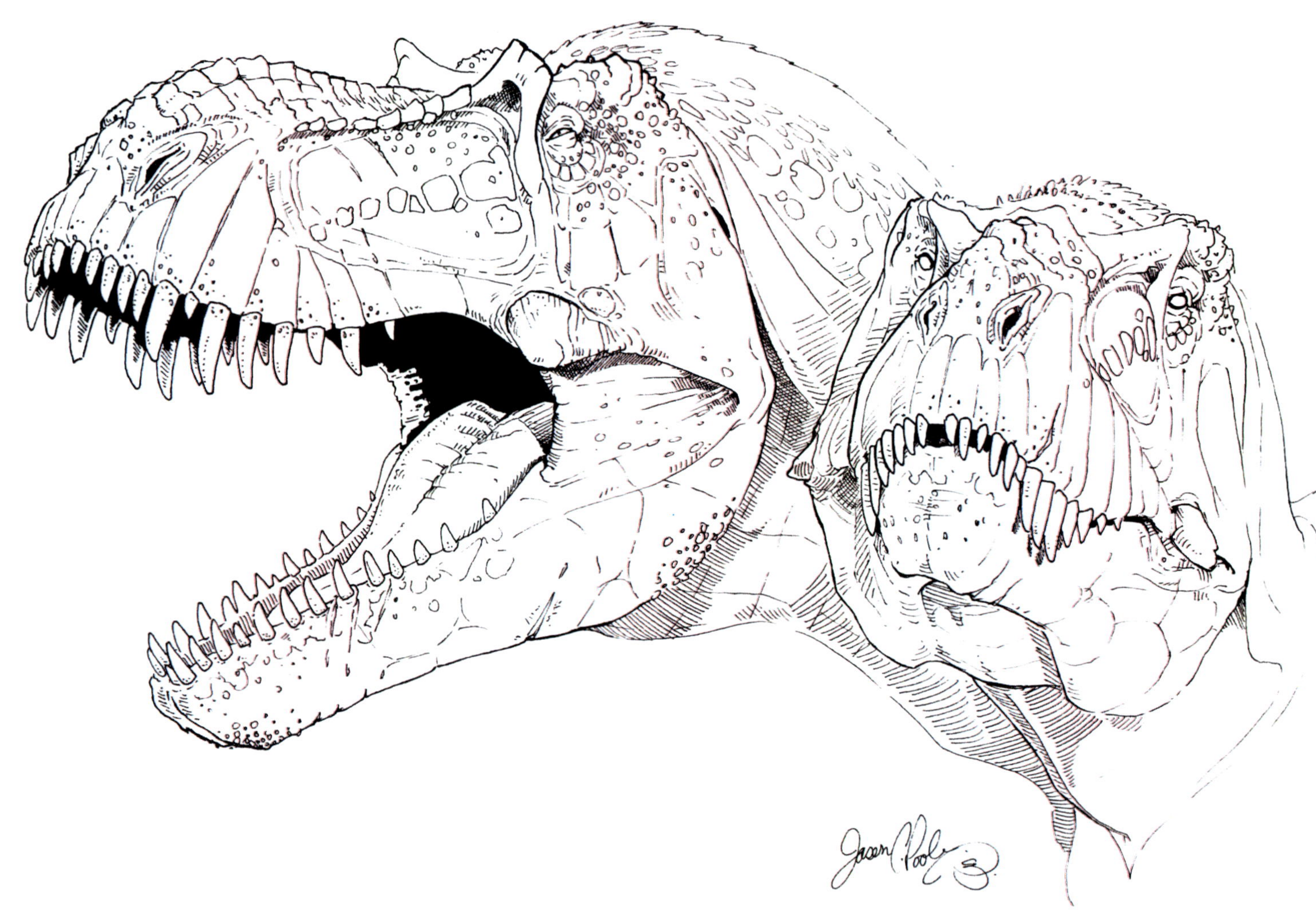

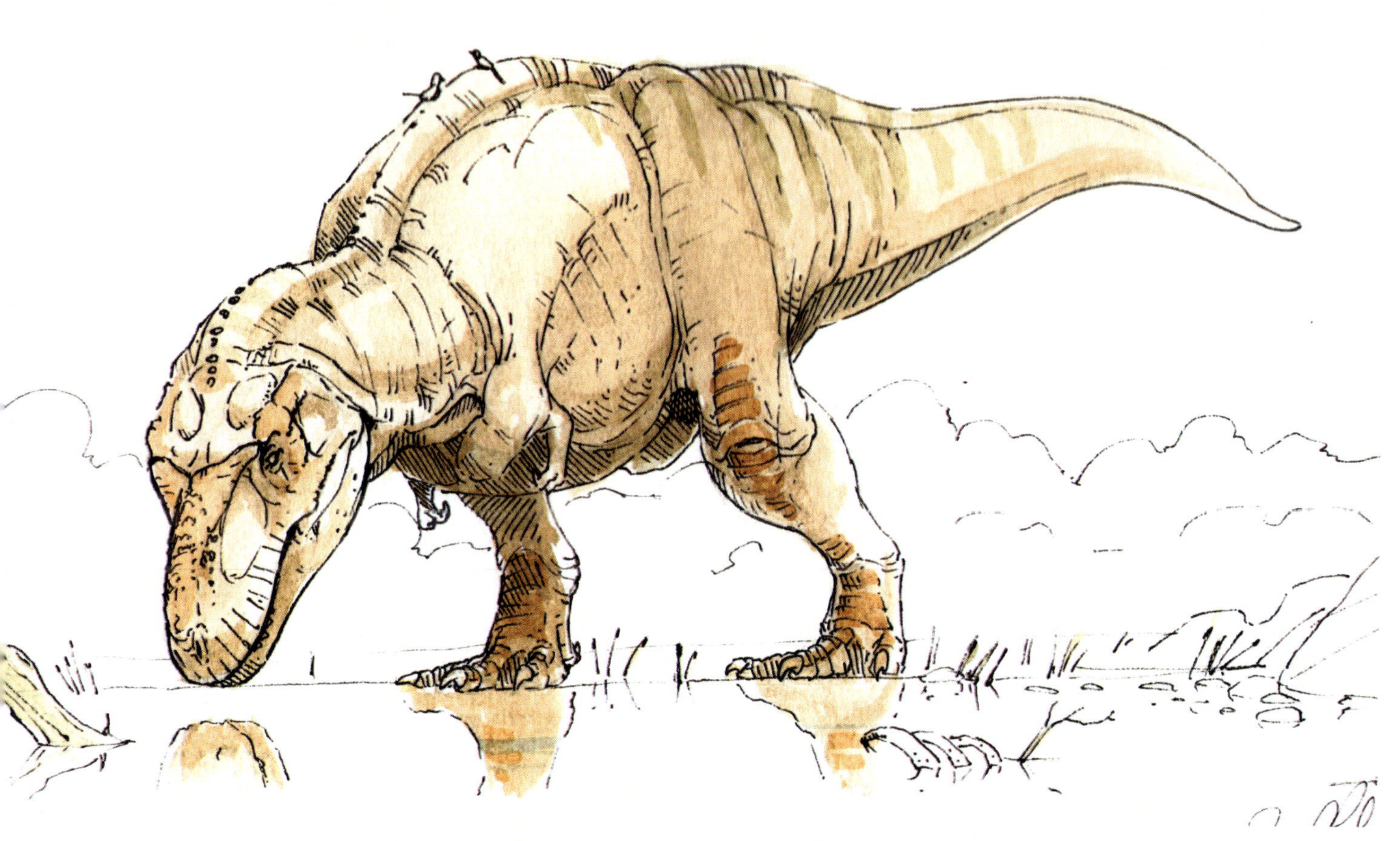

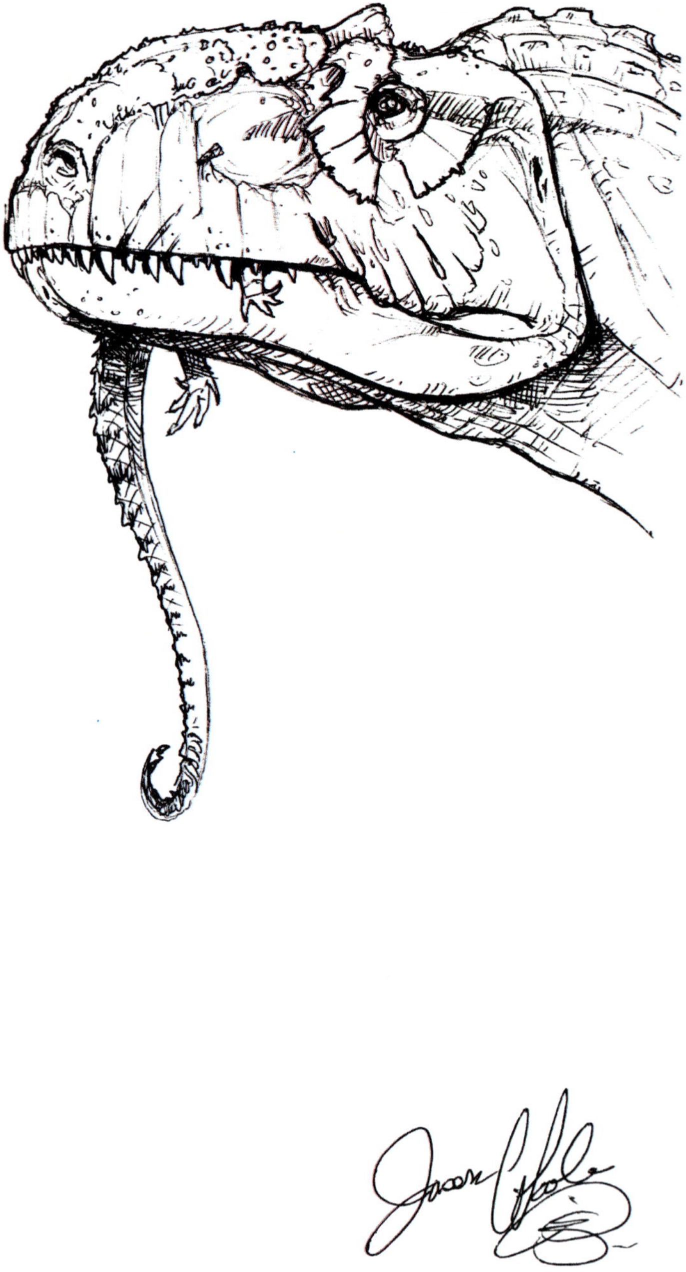

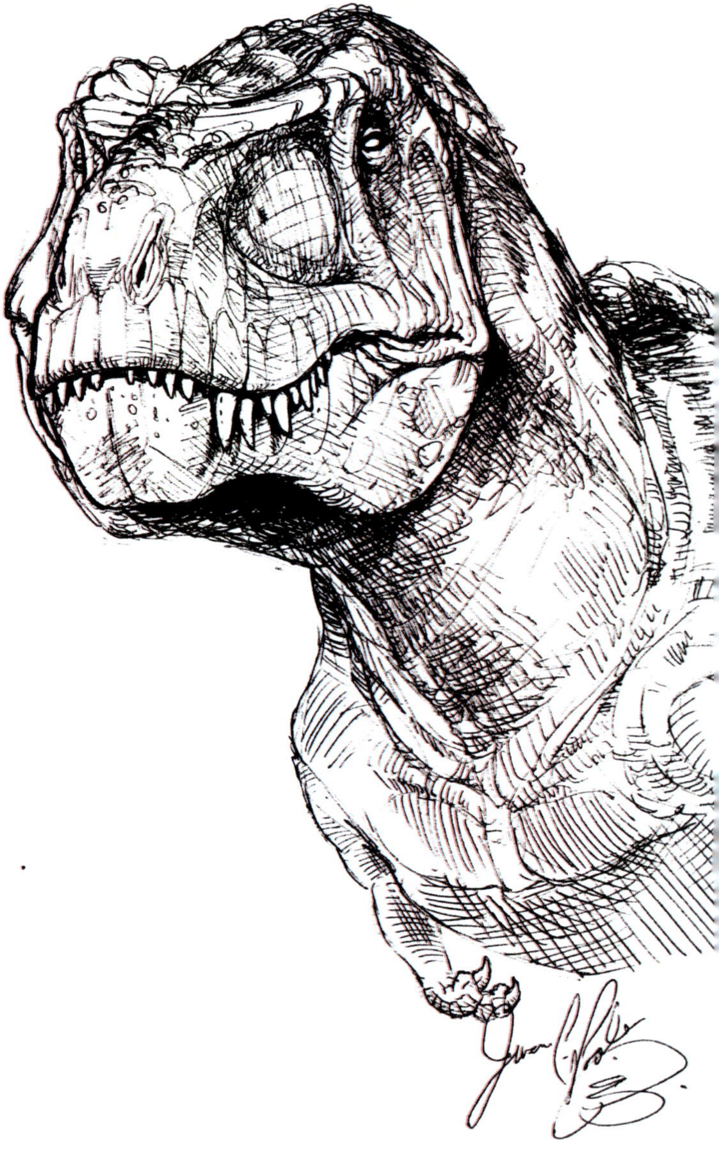

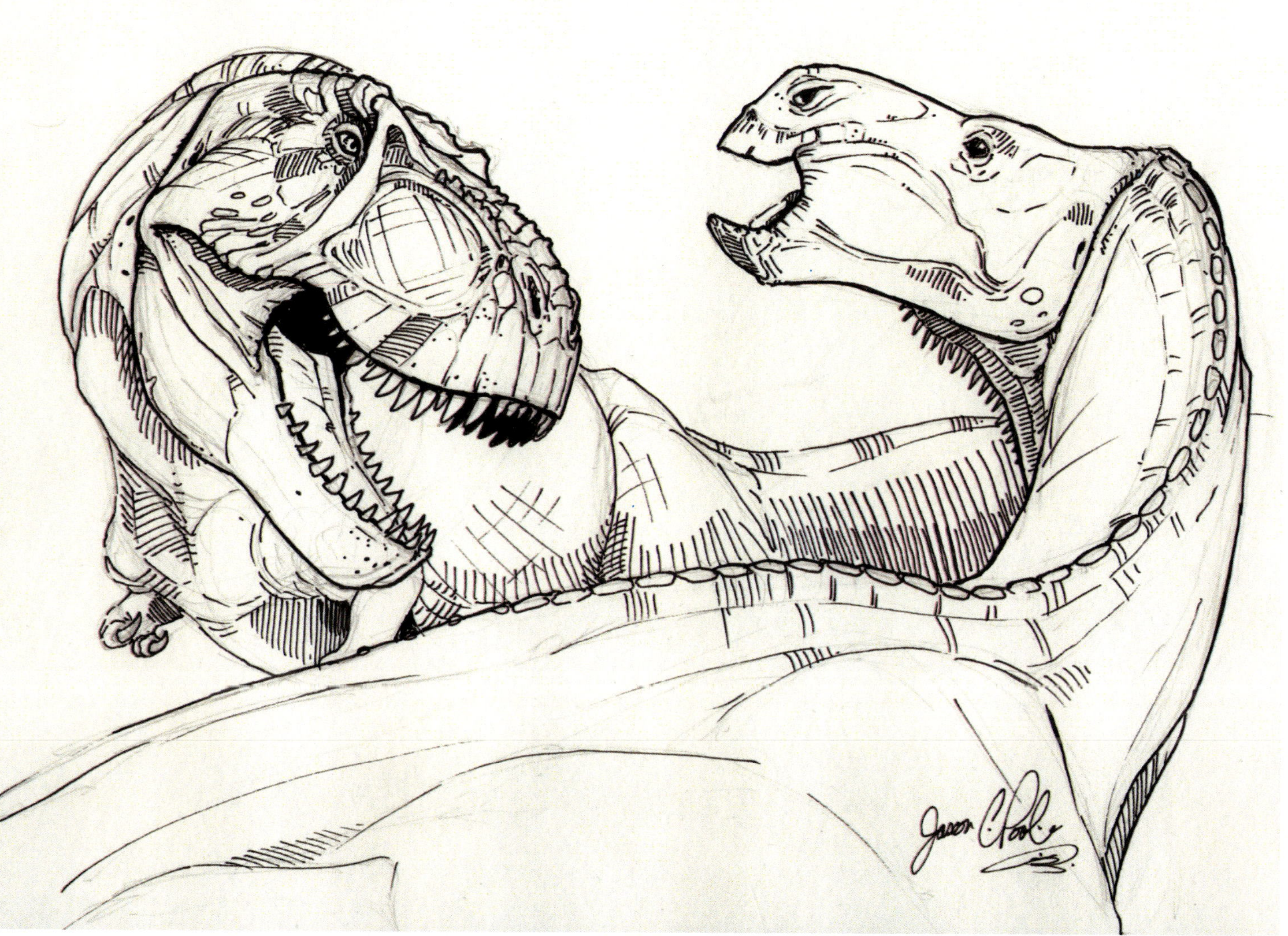

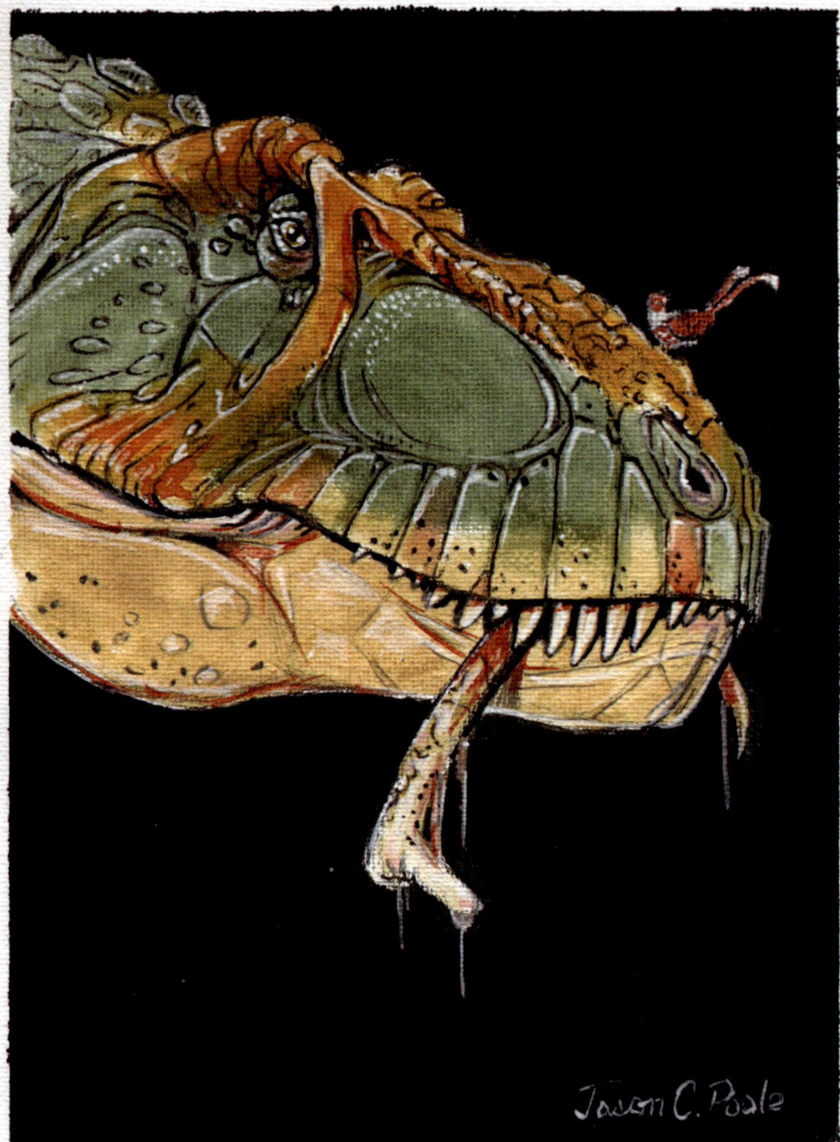
Jason C. Poole

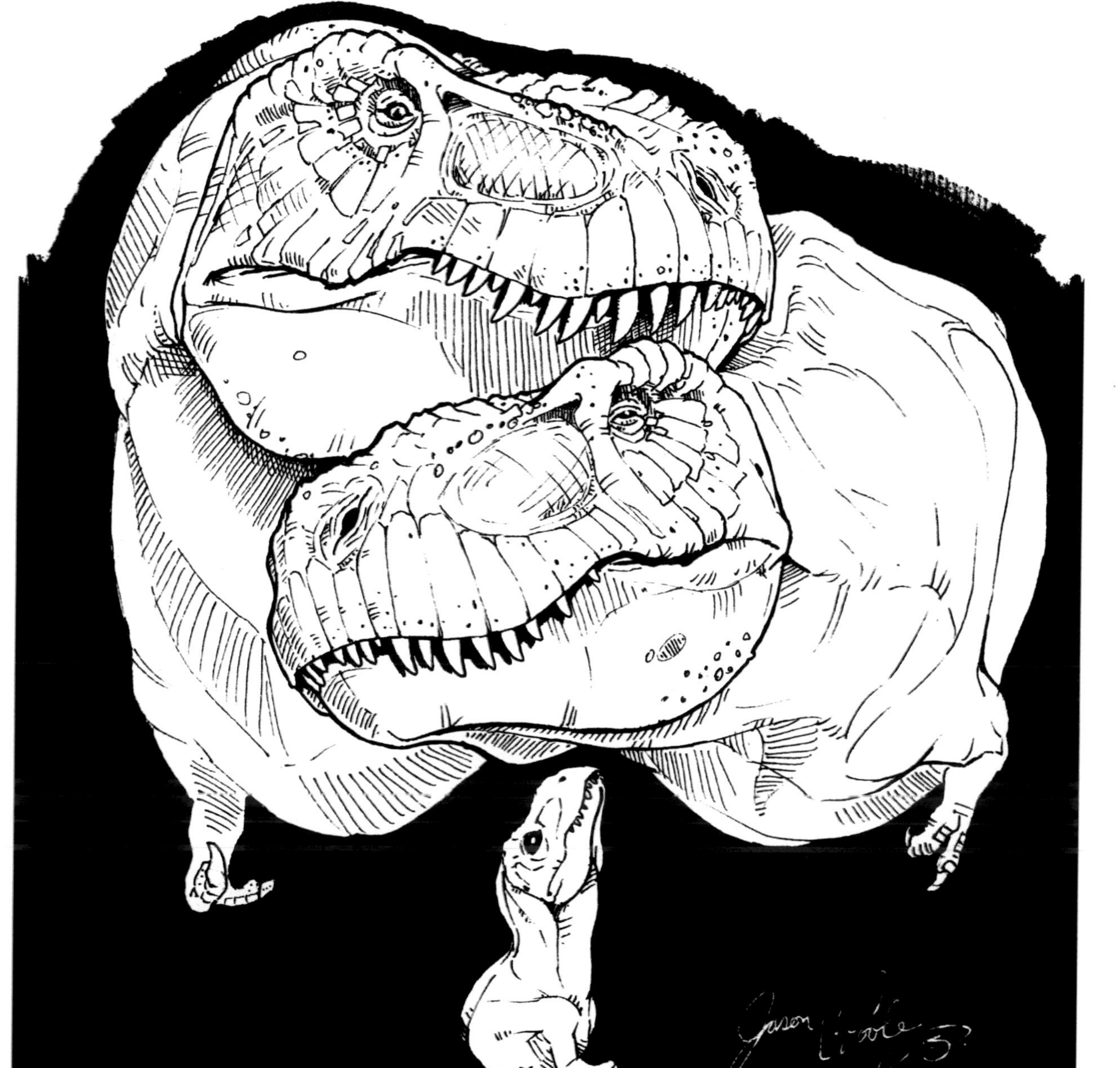

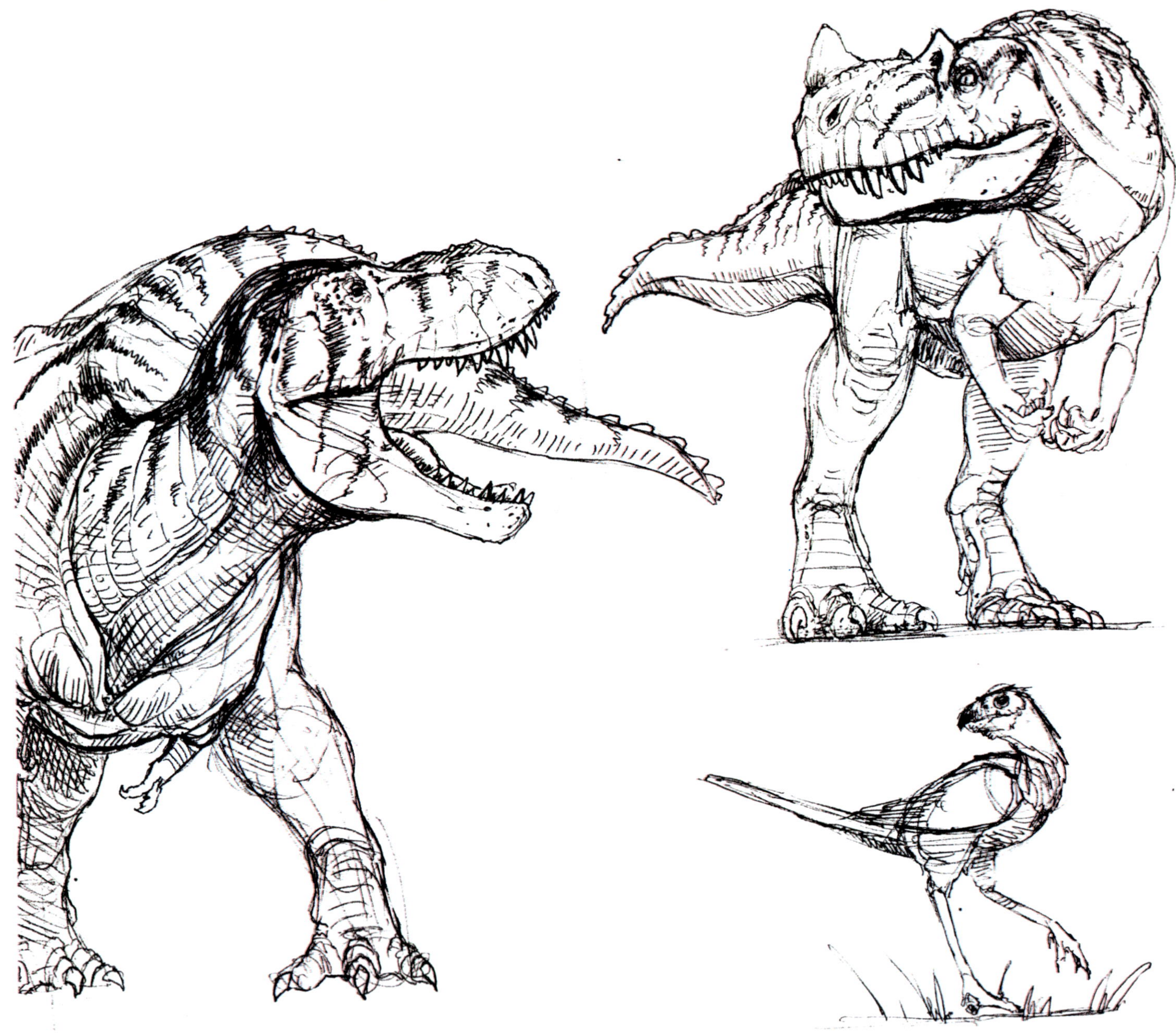

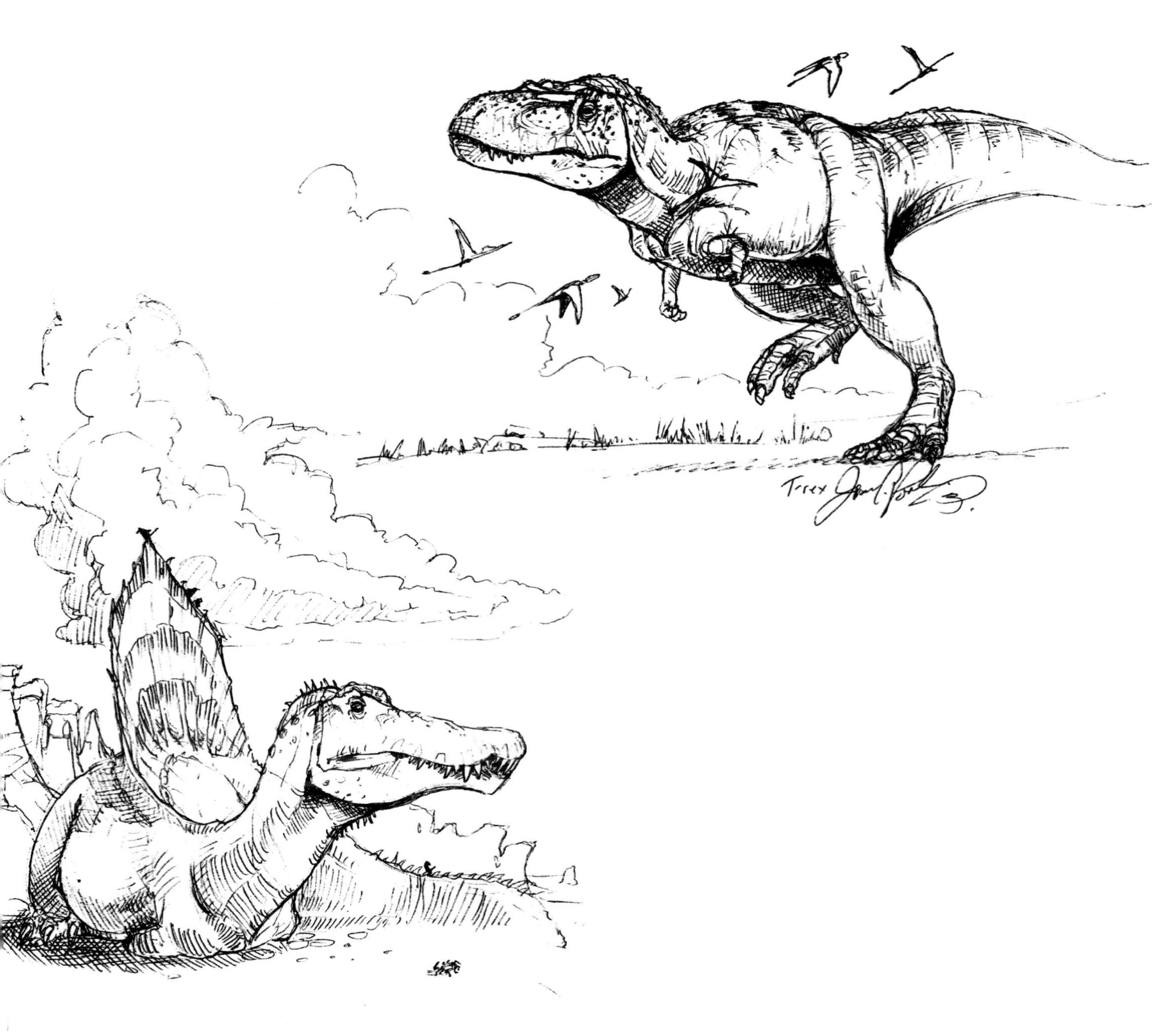

T-rex

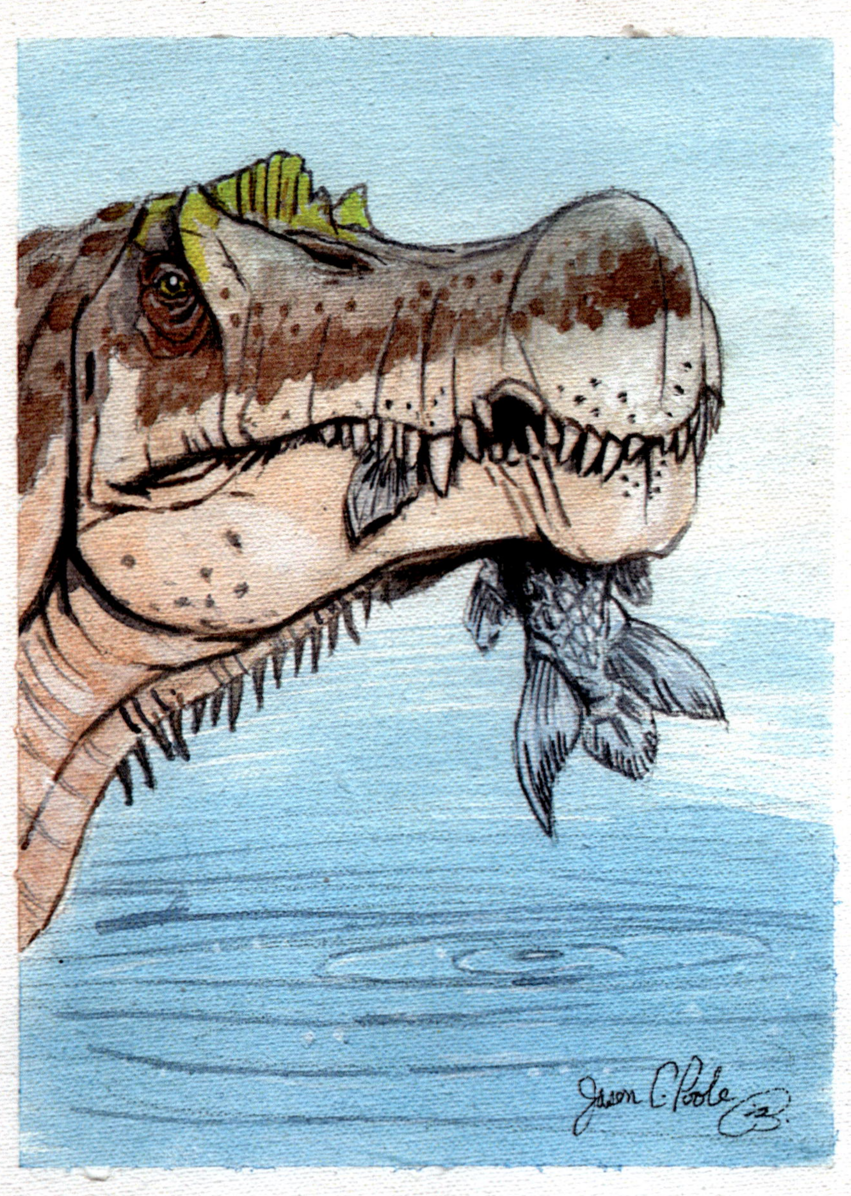
Jason C Poole

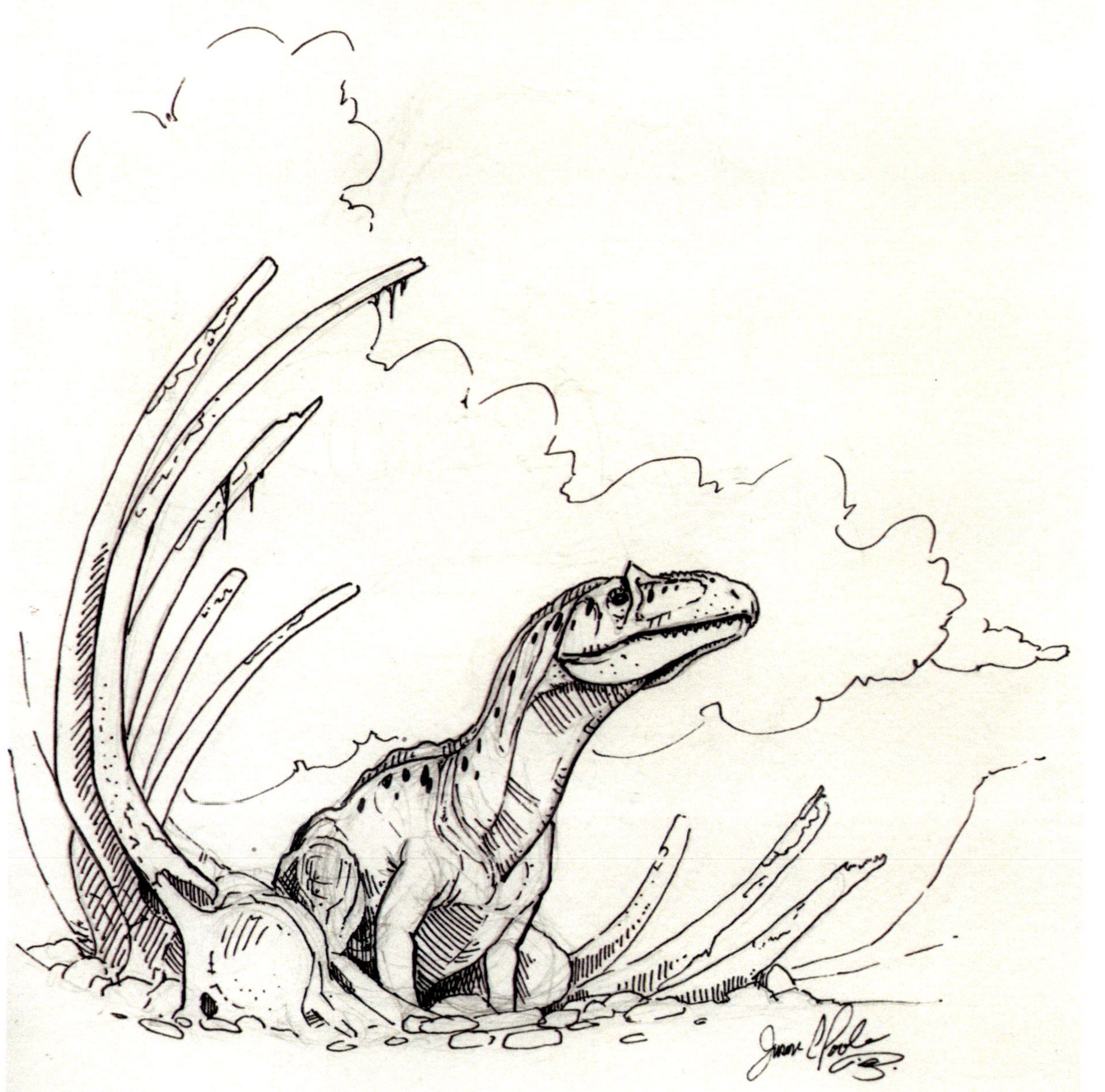

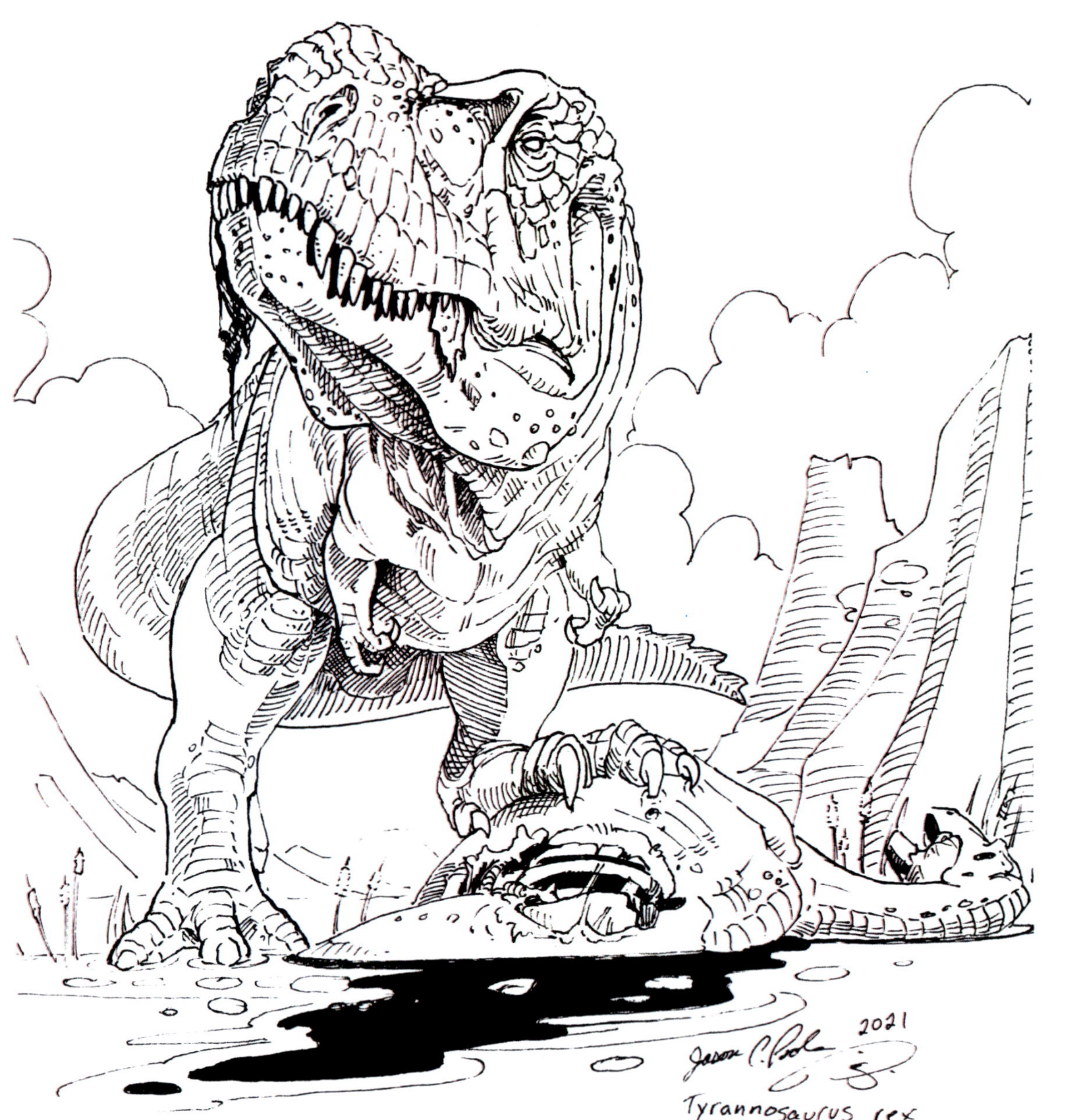

Jason C. Poole
2021
Tyrannosaurus rex

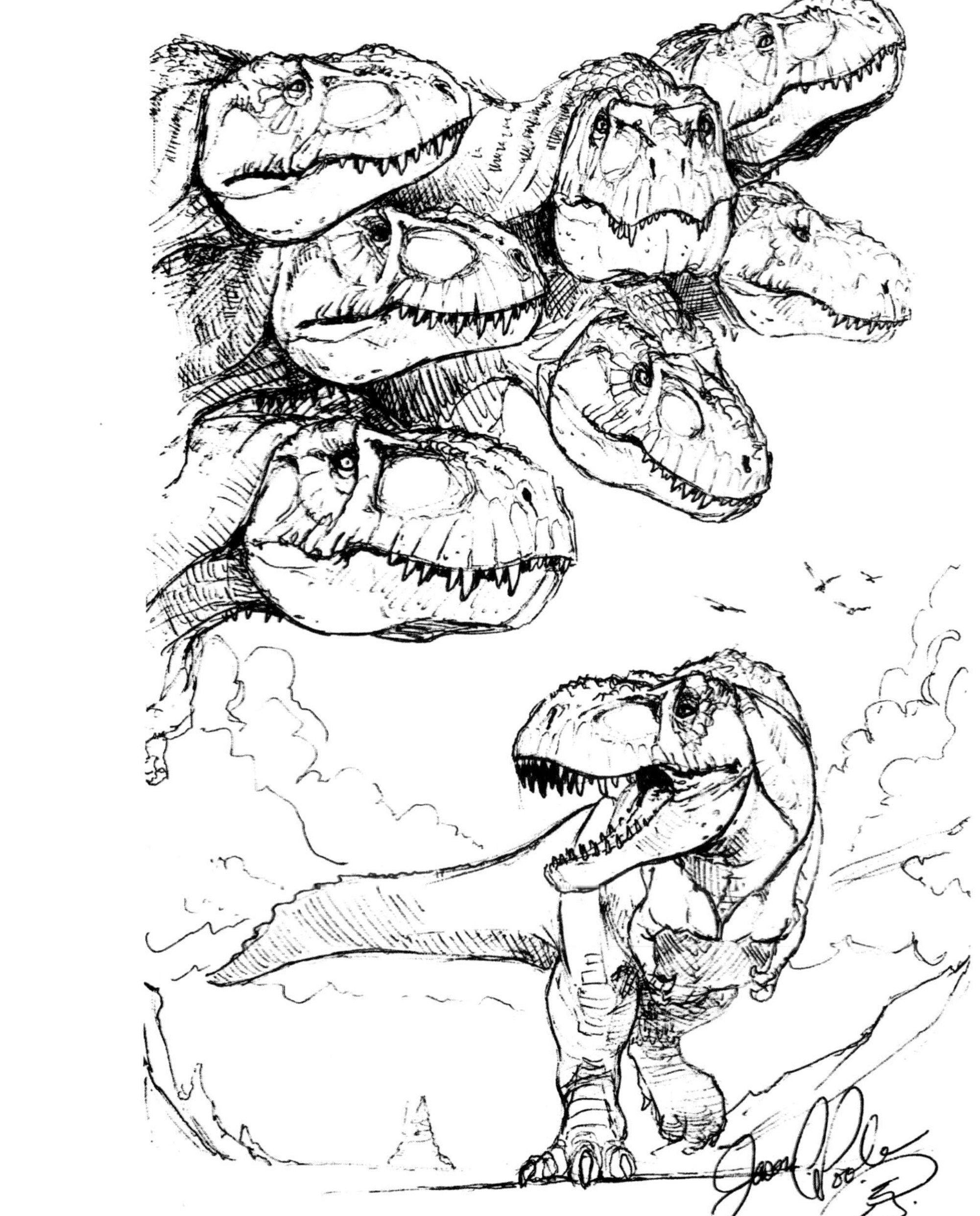

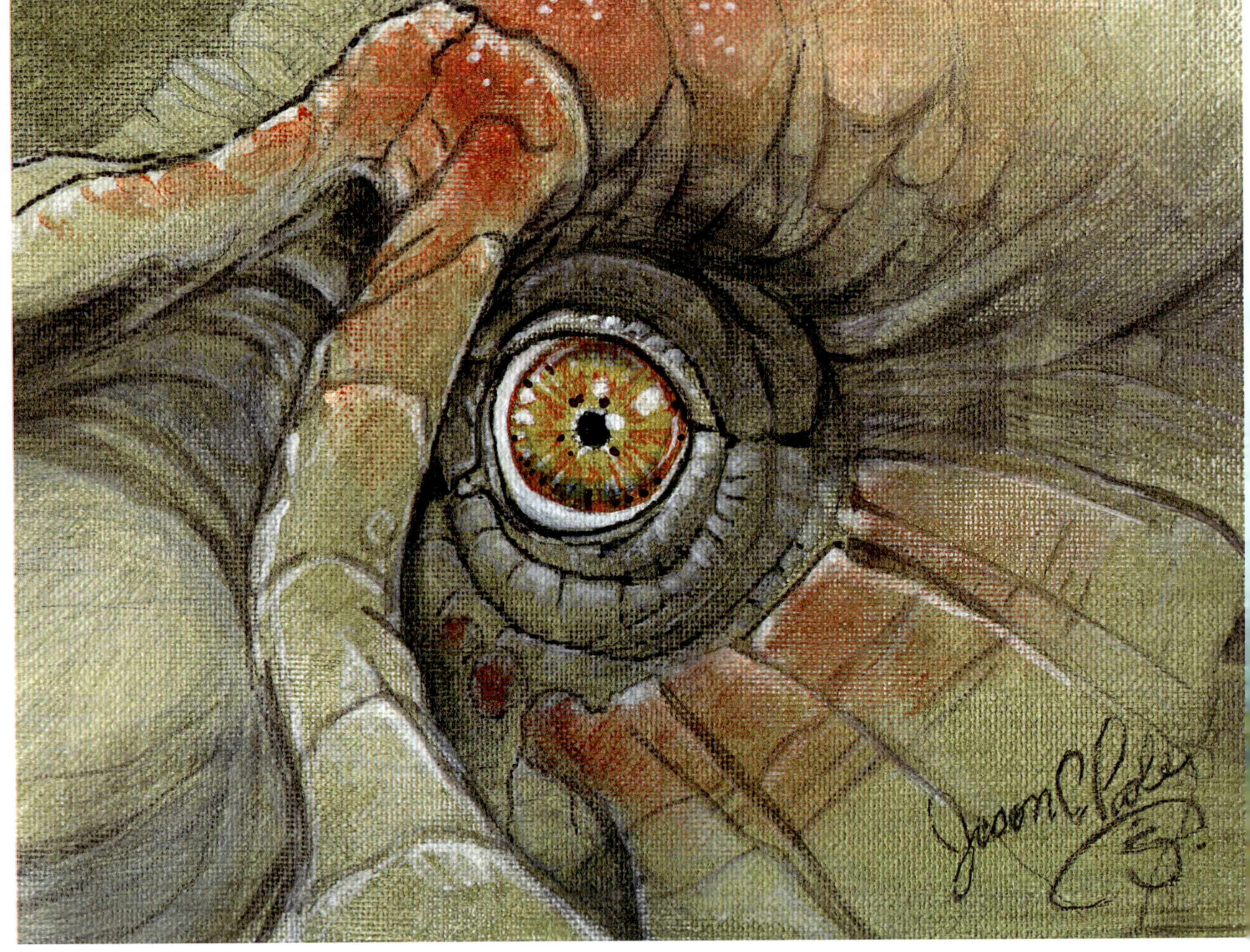

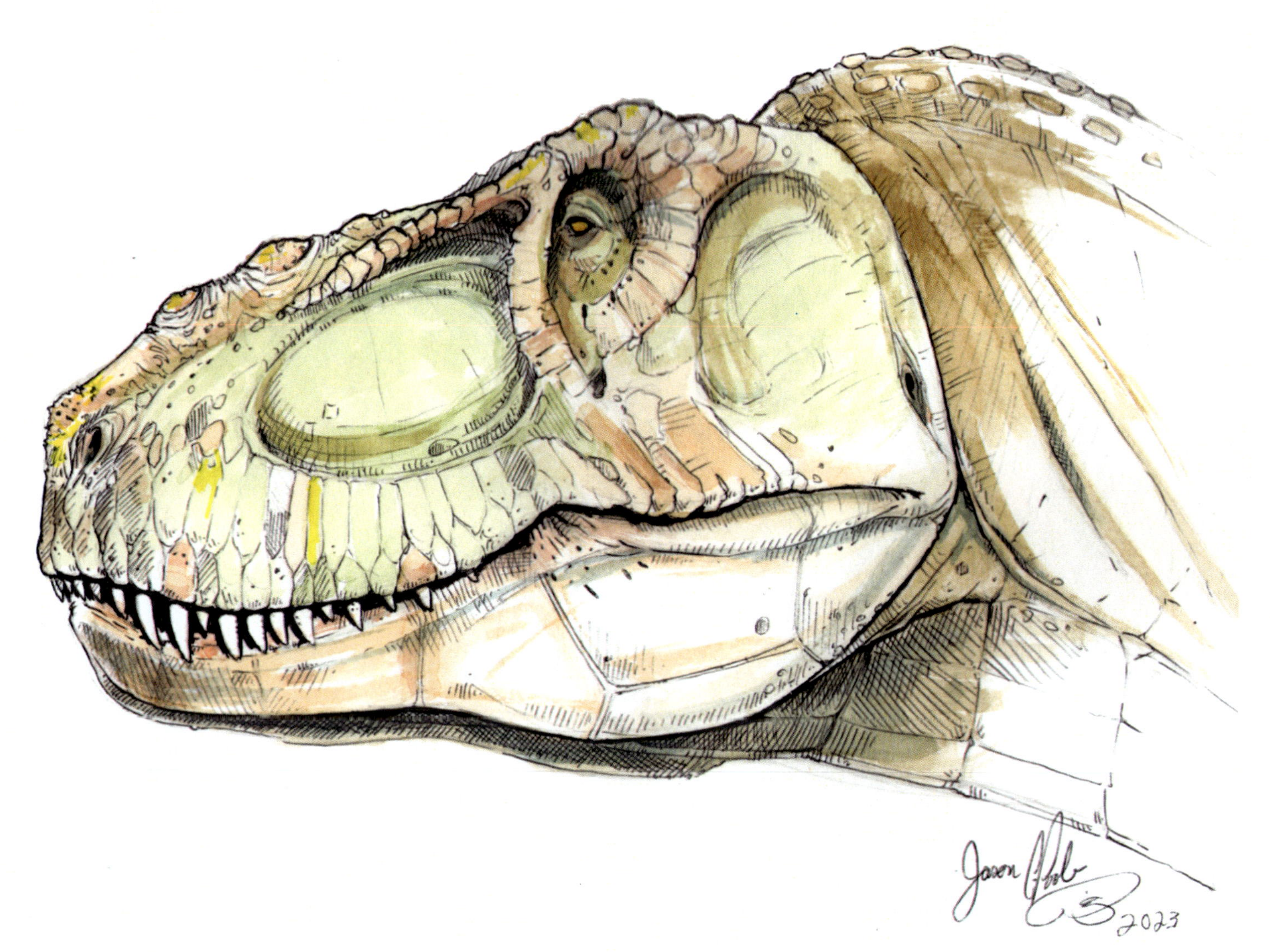

Jason Poole
2023

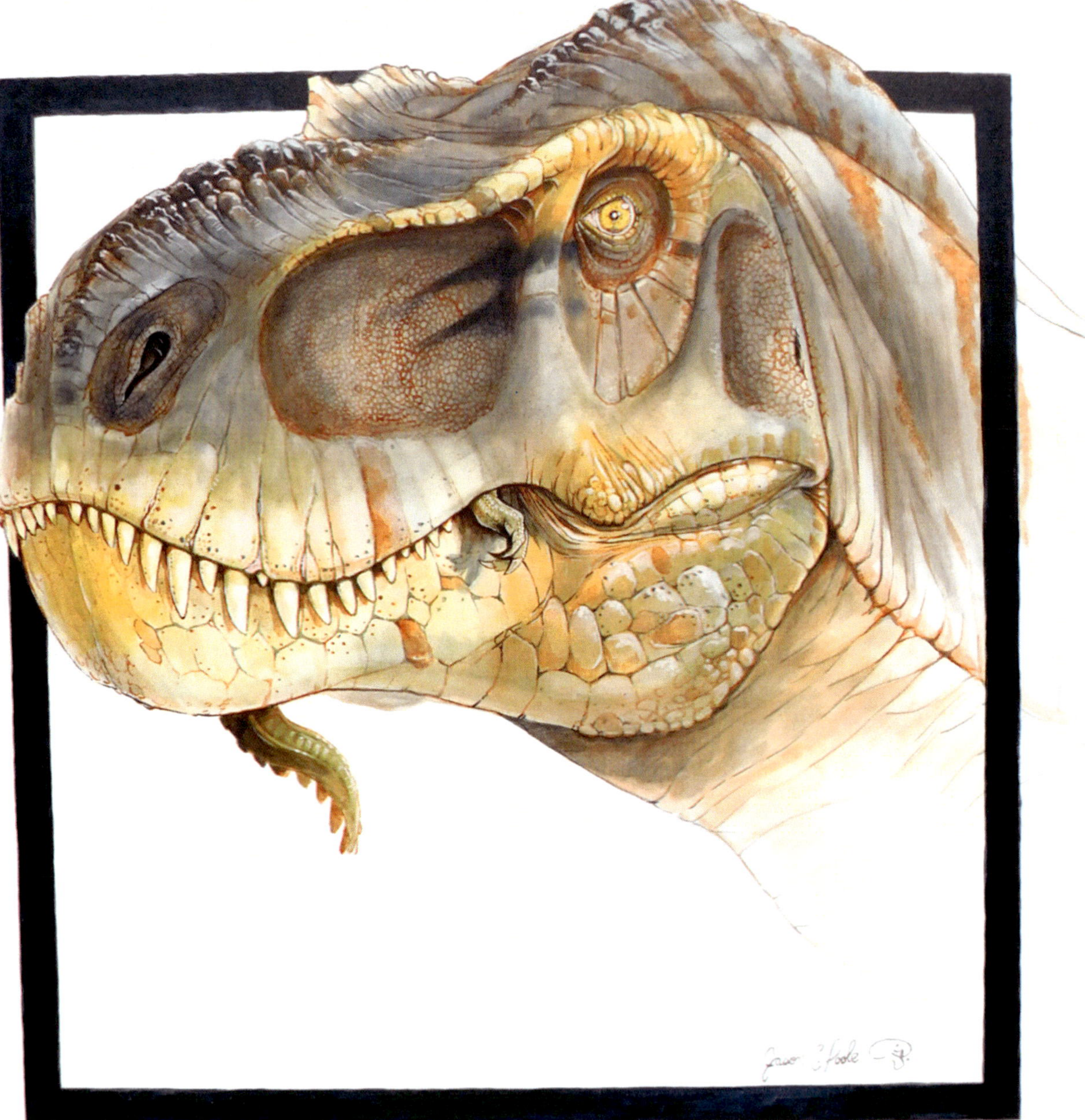

Dinosaur Fun

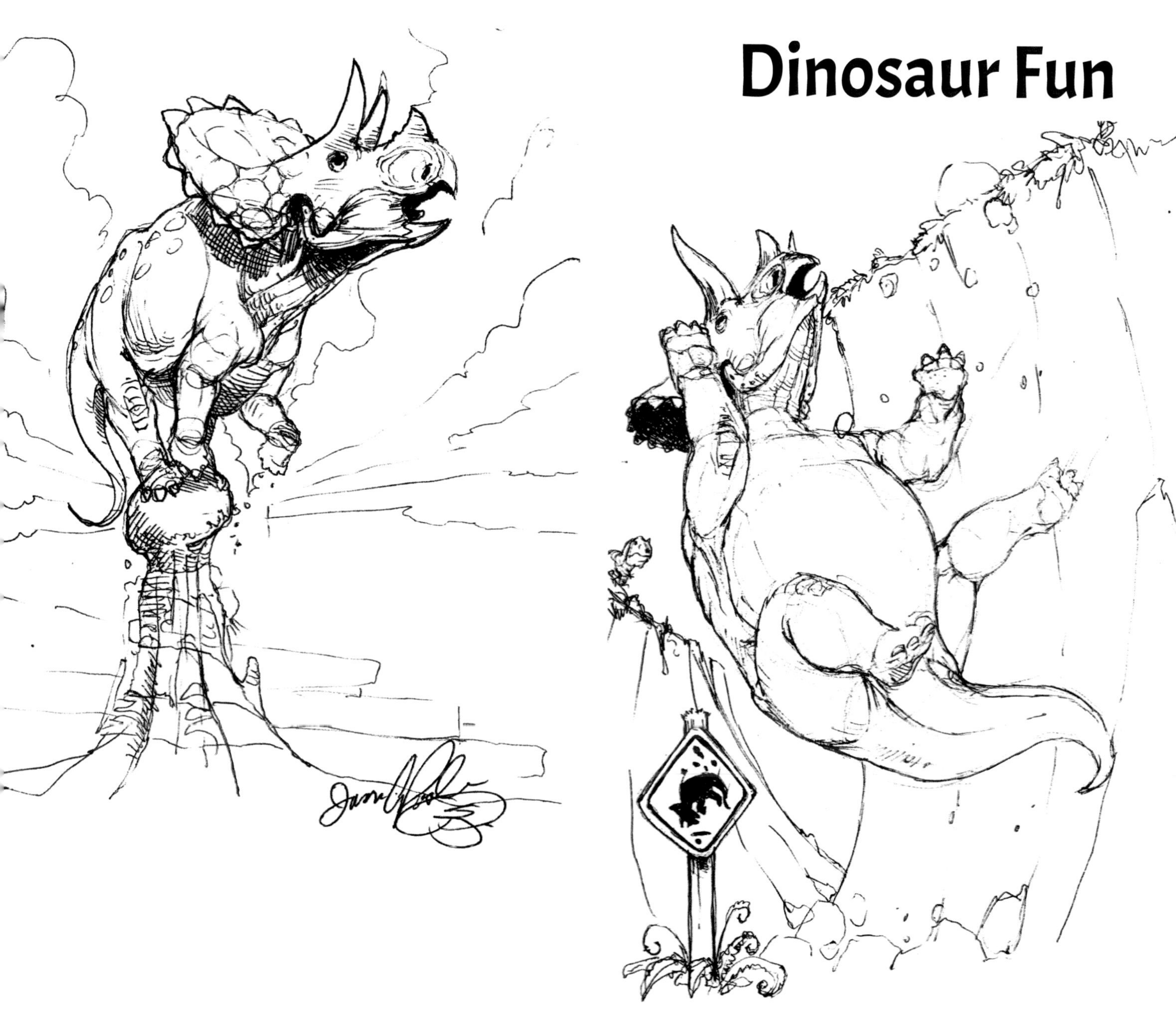

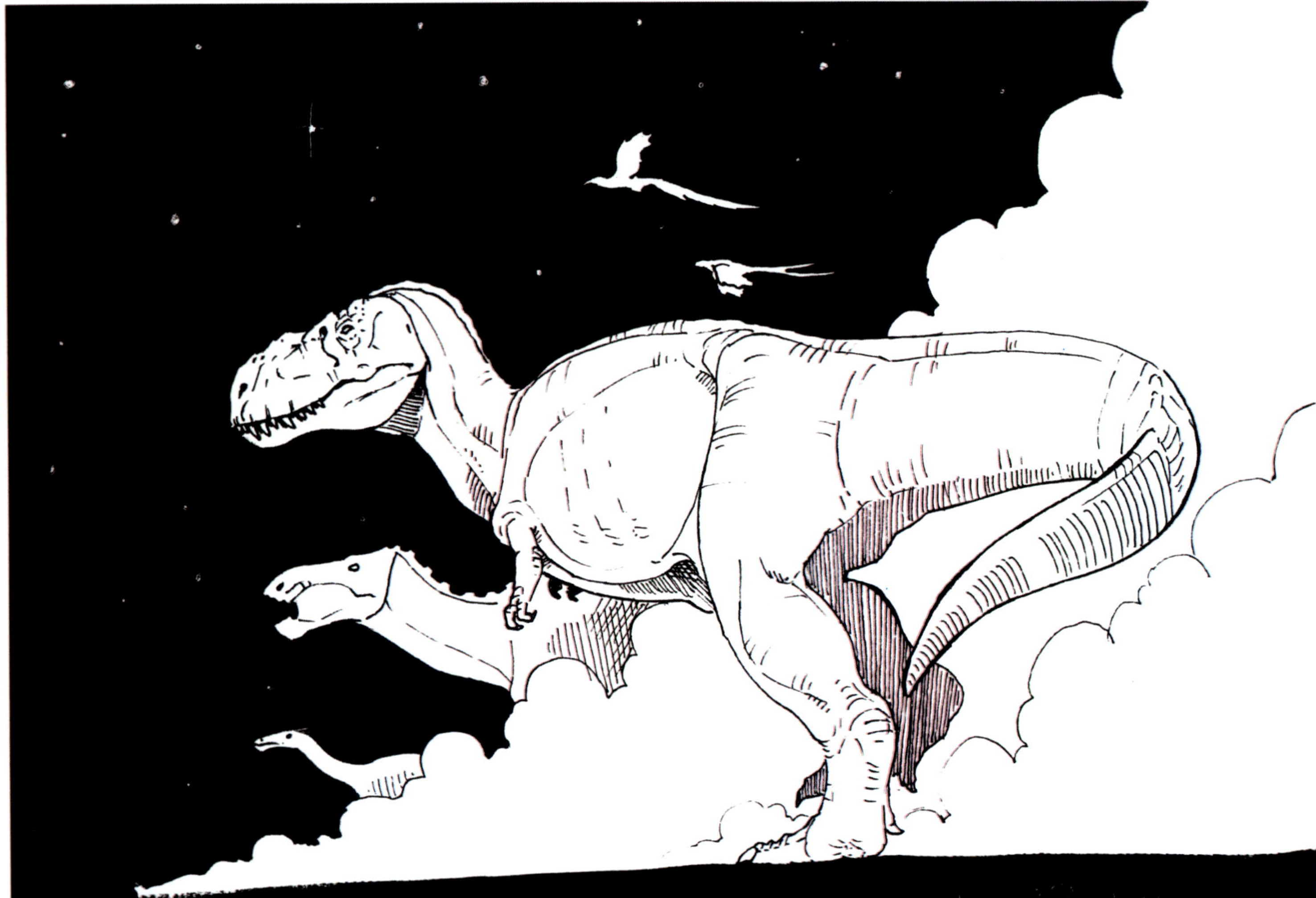

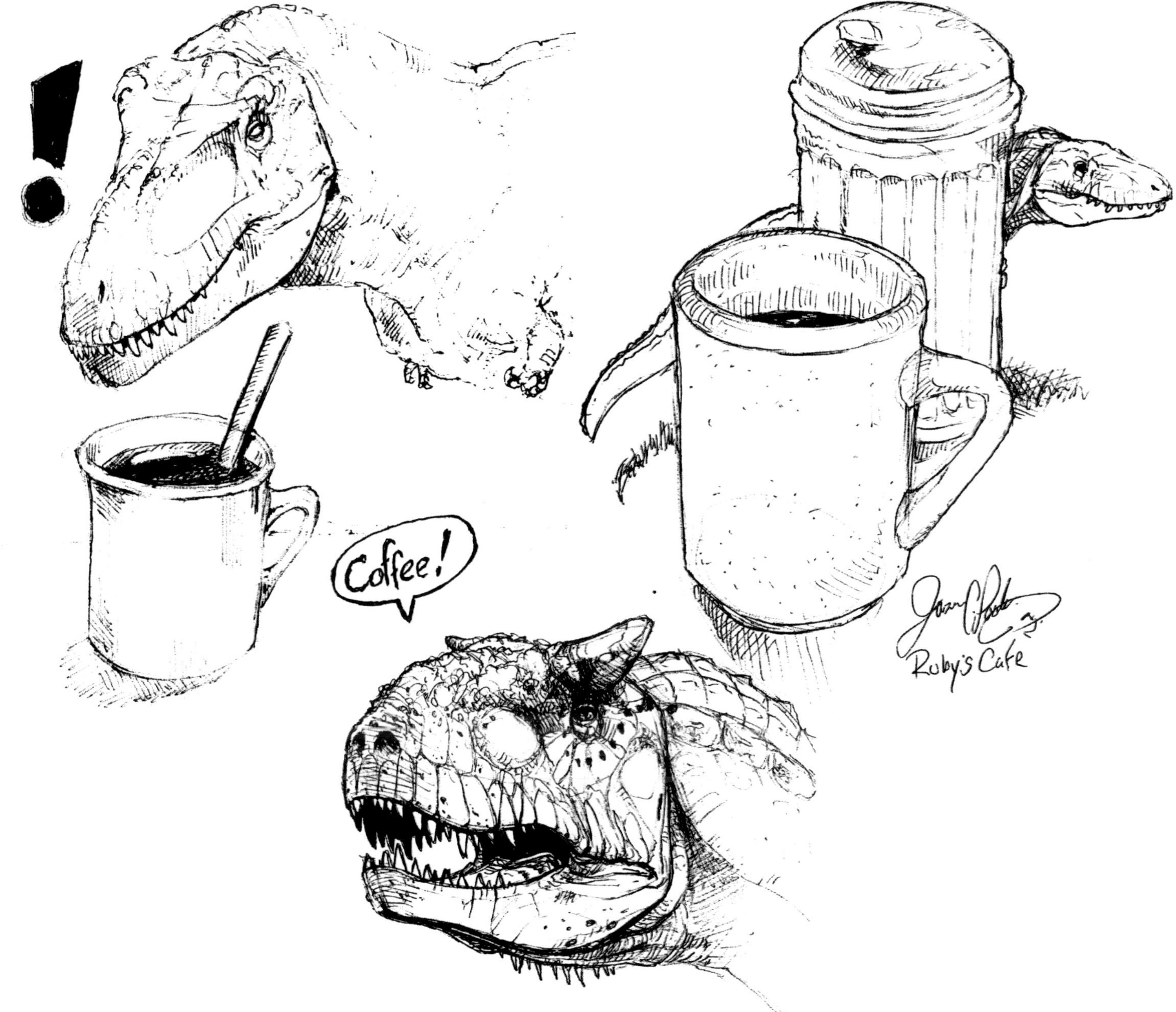
Coffee!
Ruby's Cafe

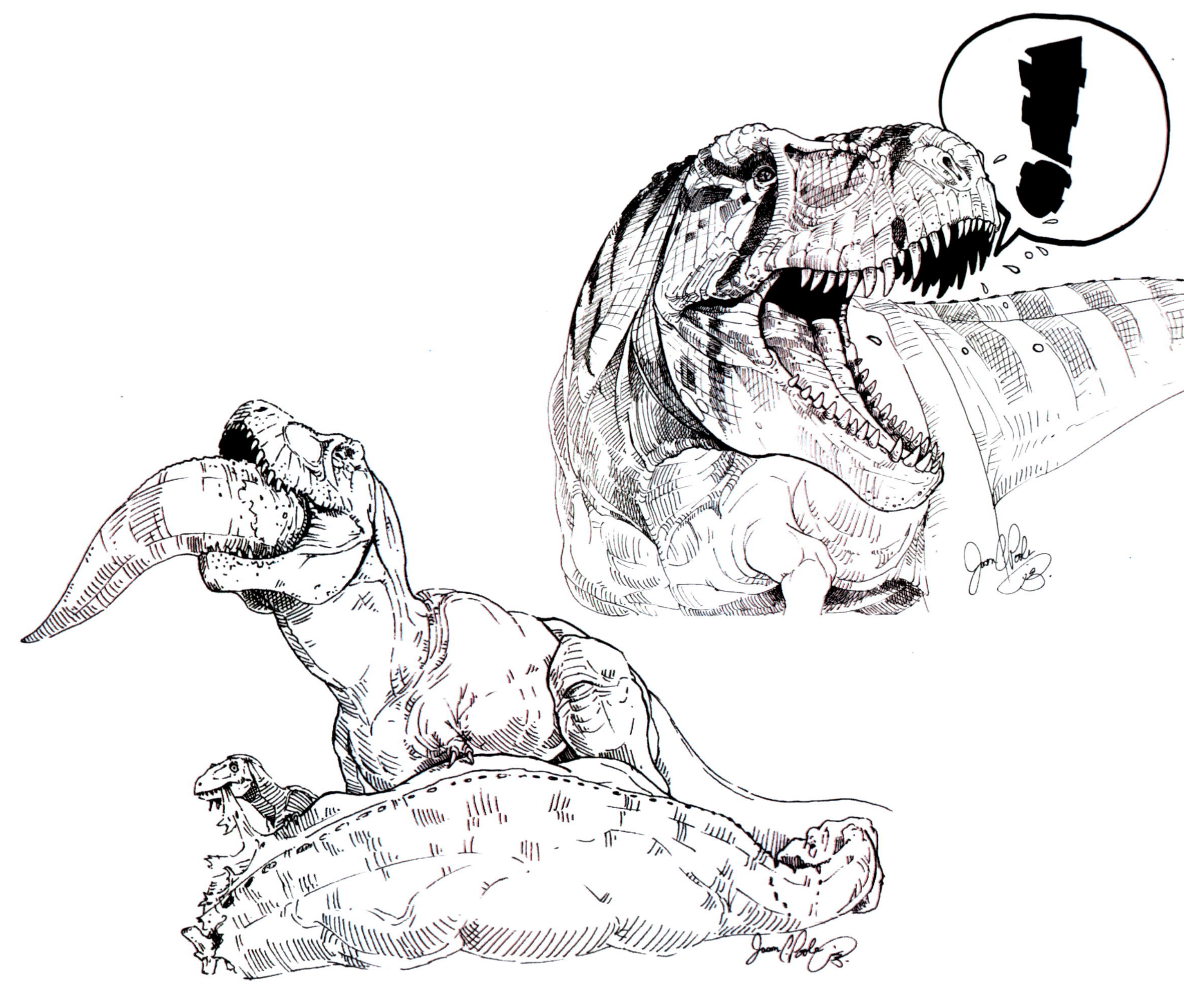

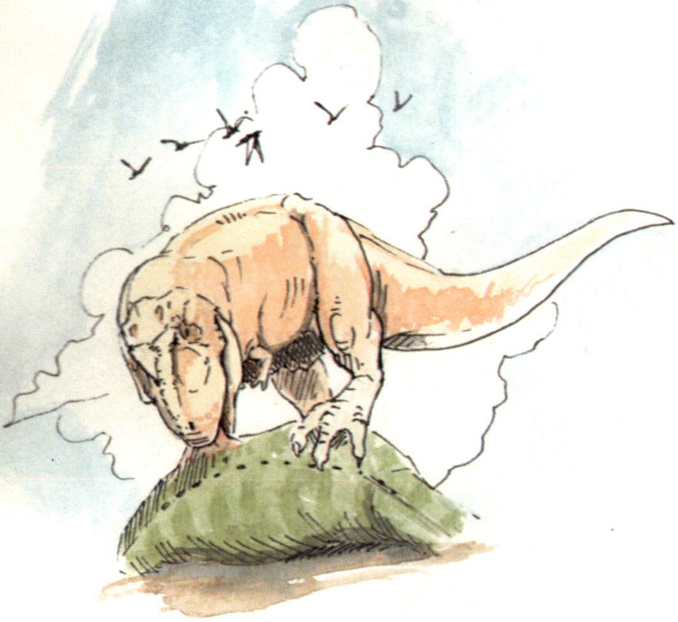

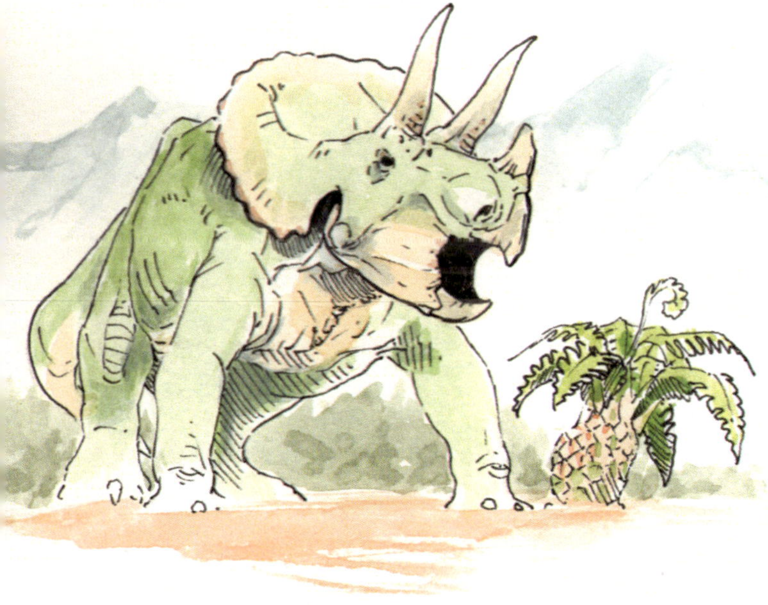

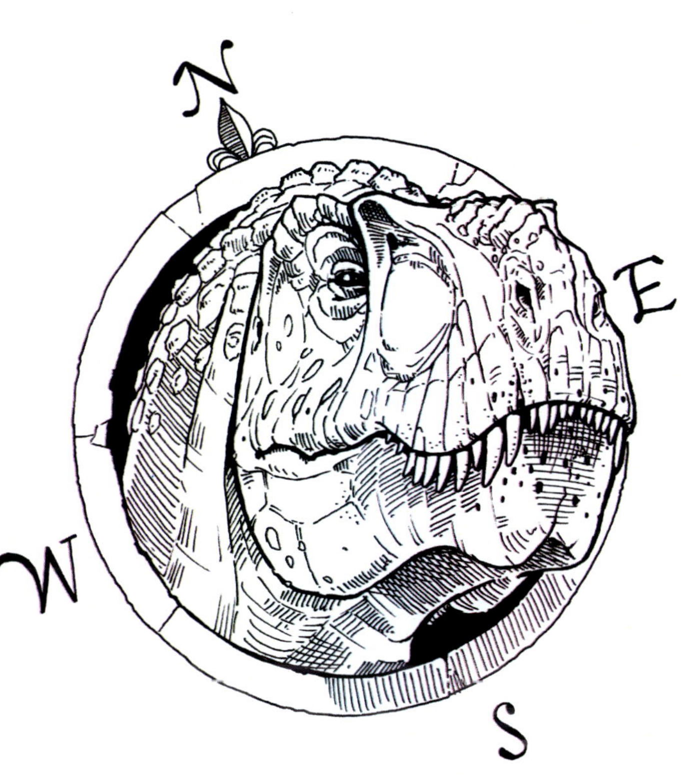

N
E
W
S

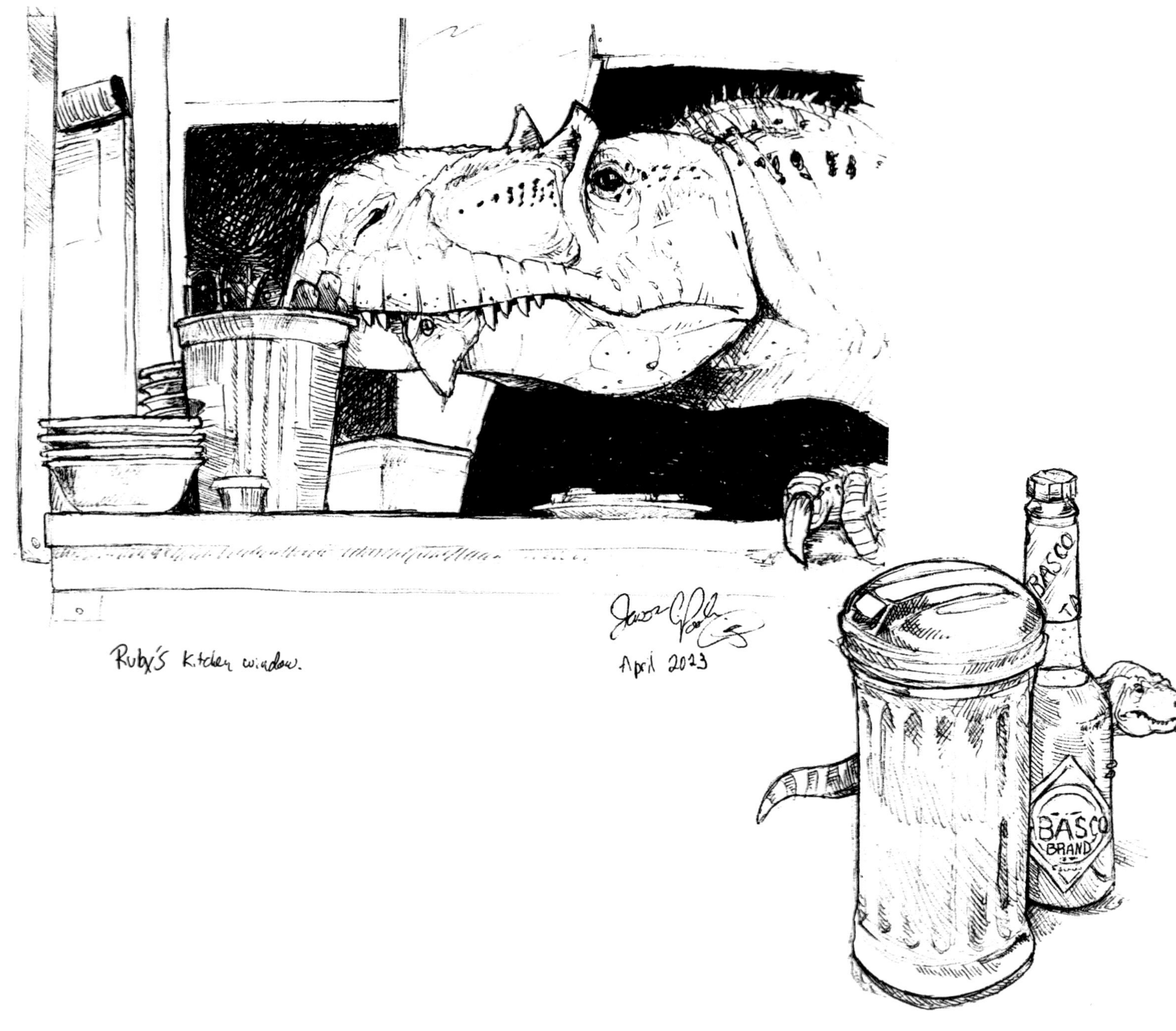

Ruby's kitchen window.

Our World

New Jersey 67 mya
Hadrosaurus foulkii
Gray Triggerfish
Atlantic Wolffish
Dryptosaurus

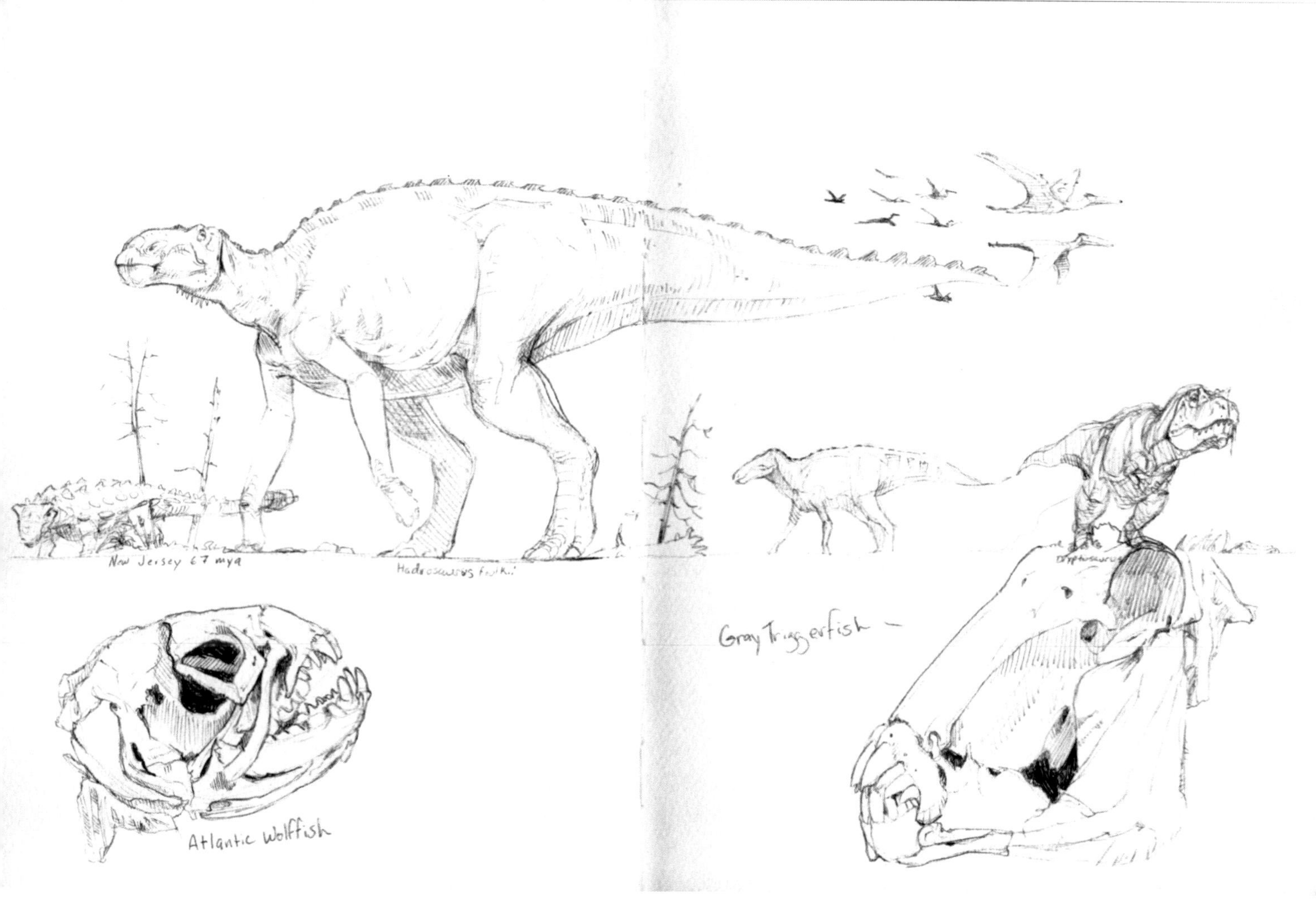

People

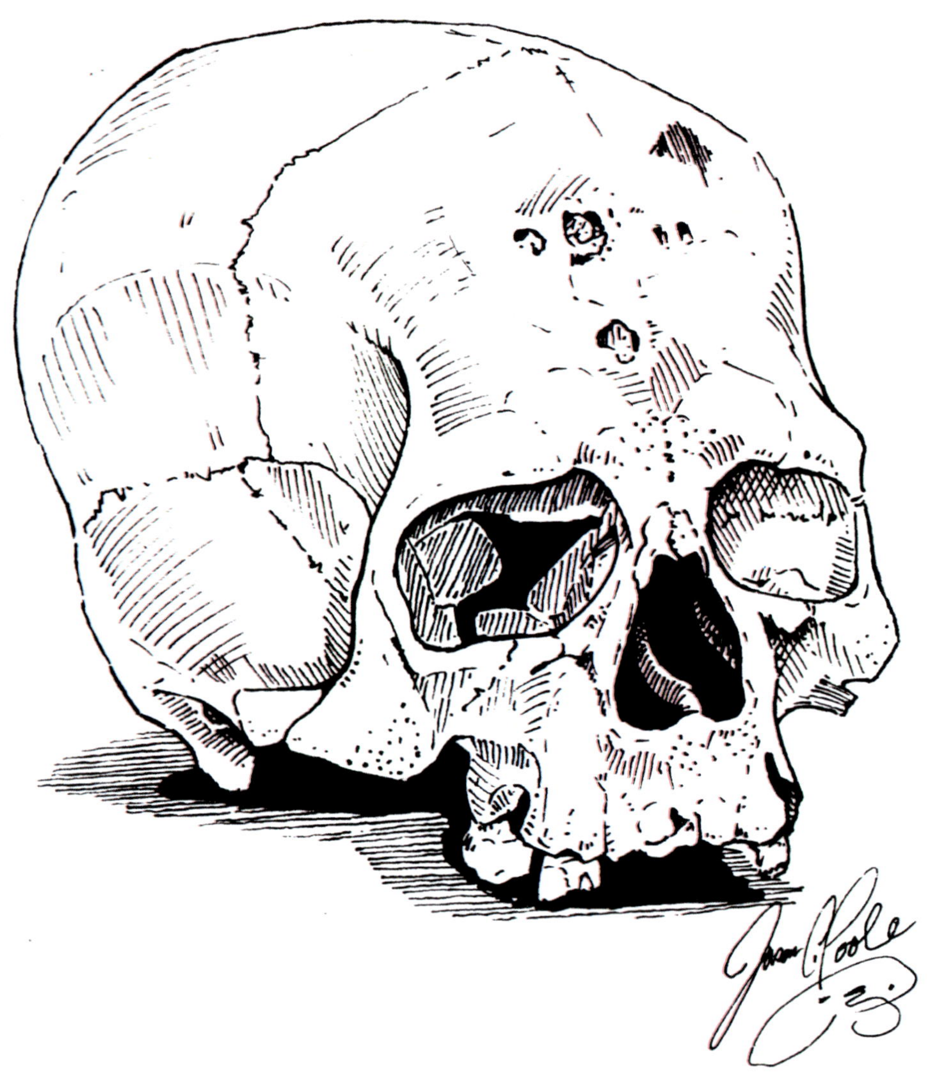

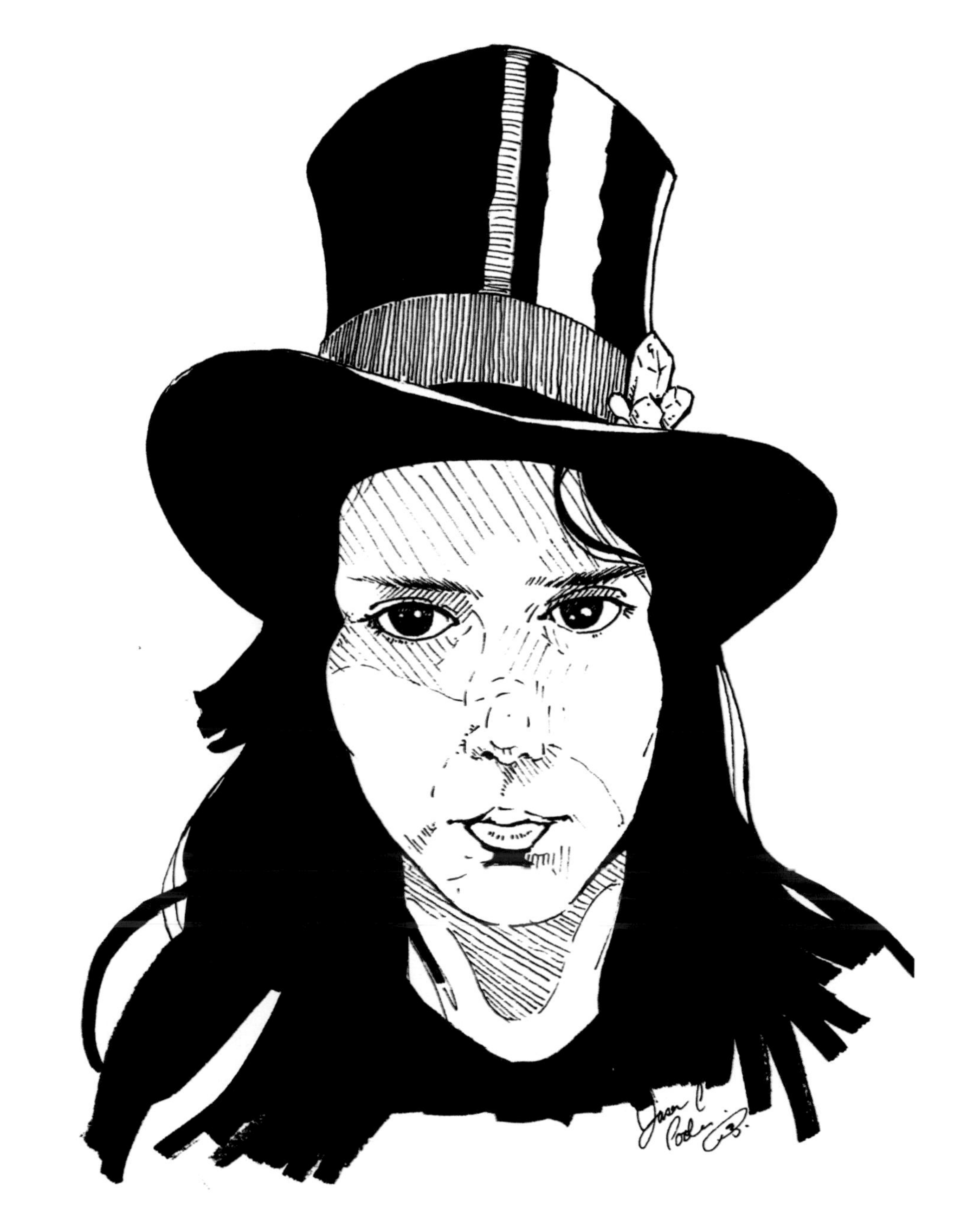

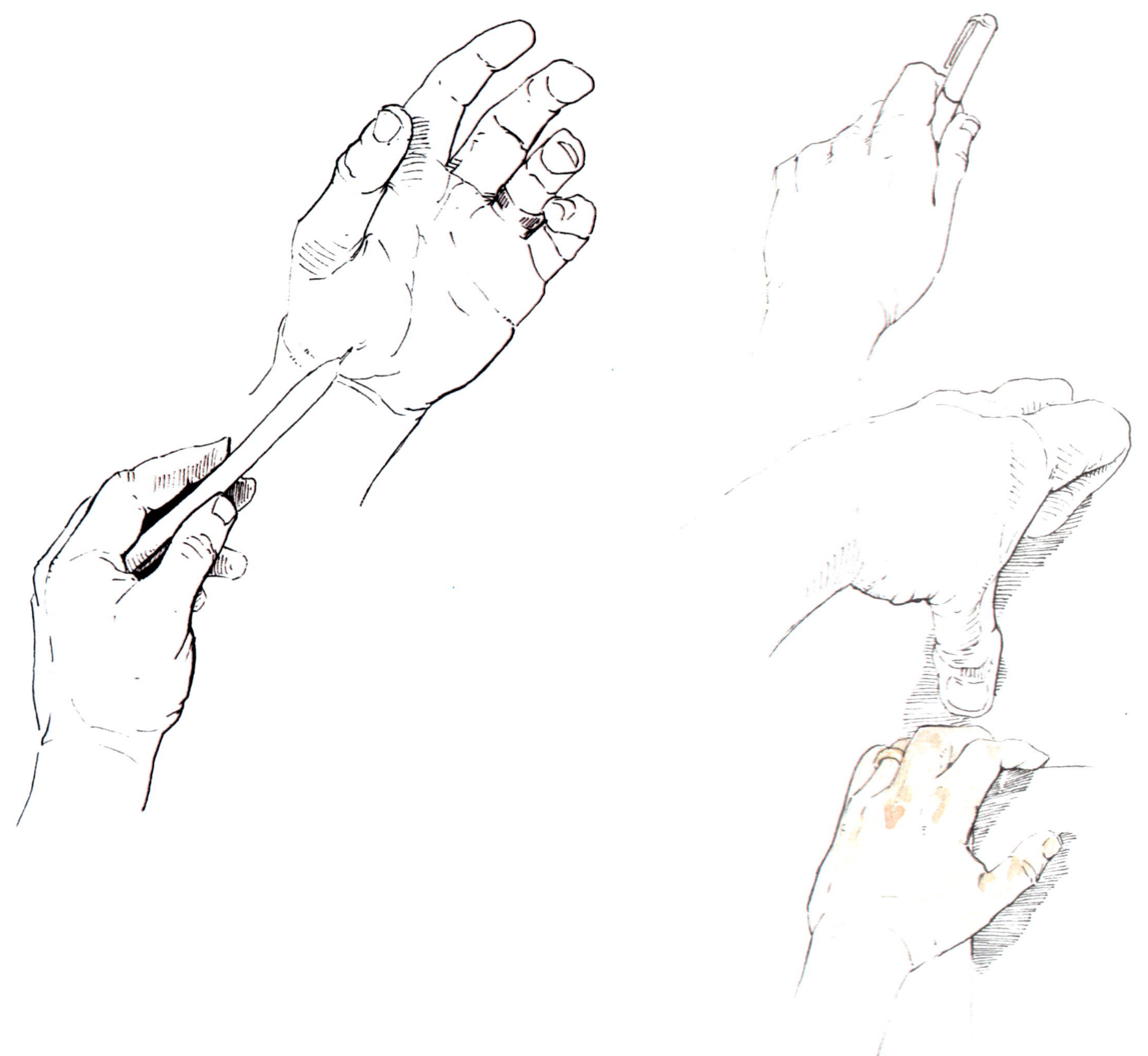

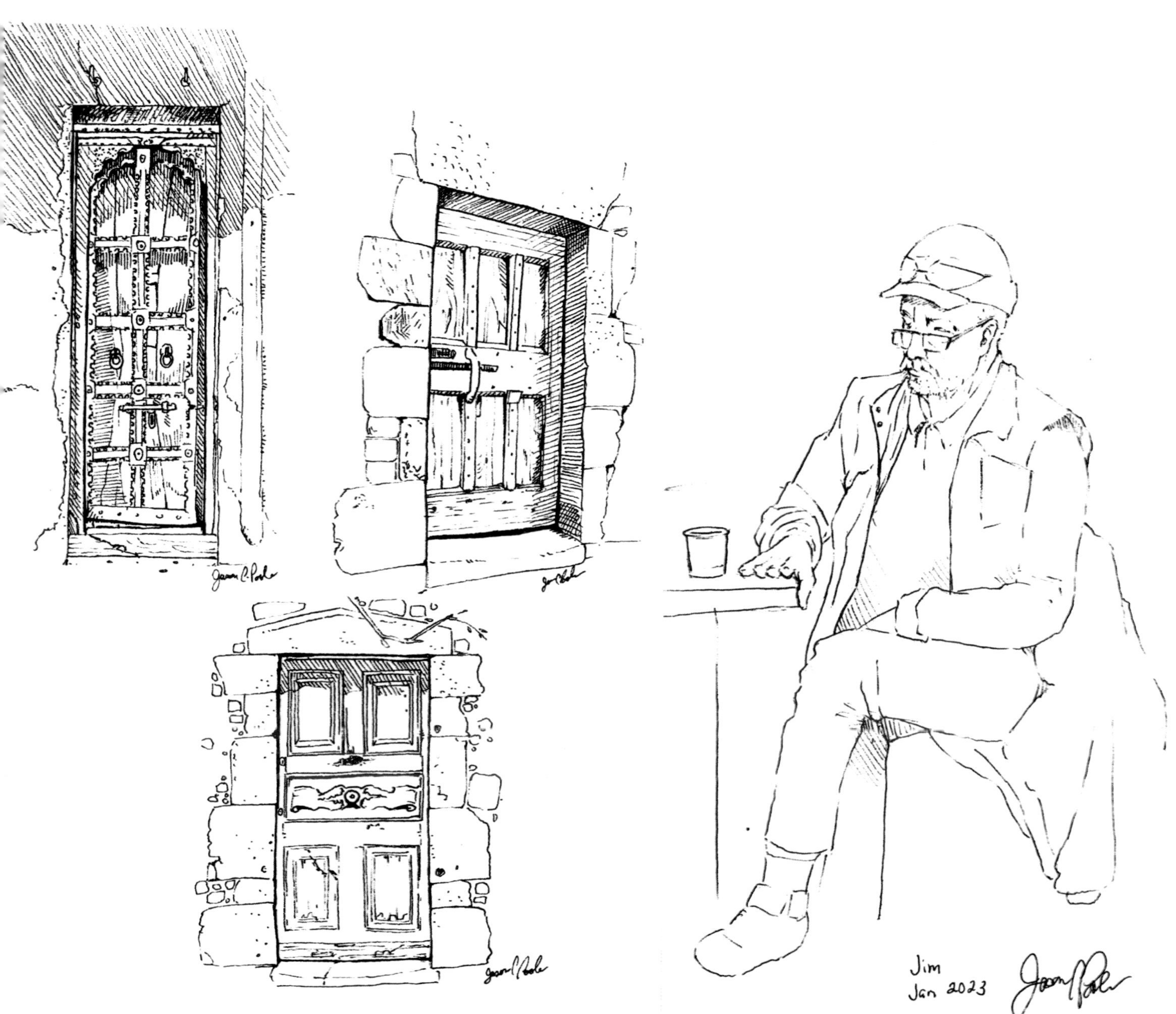
Jim
Jan 2023

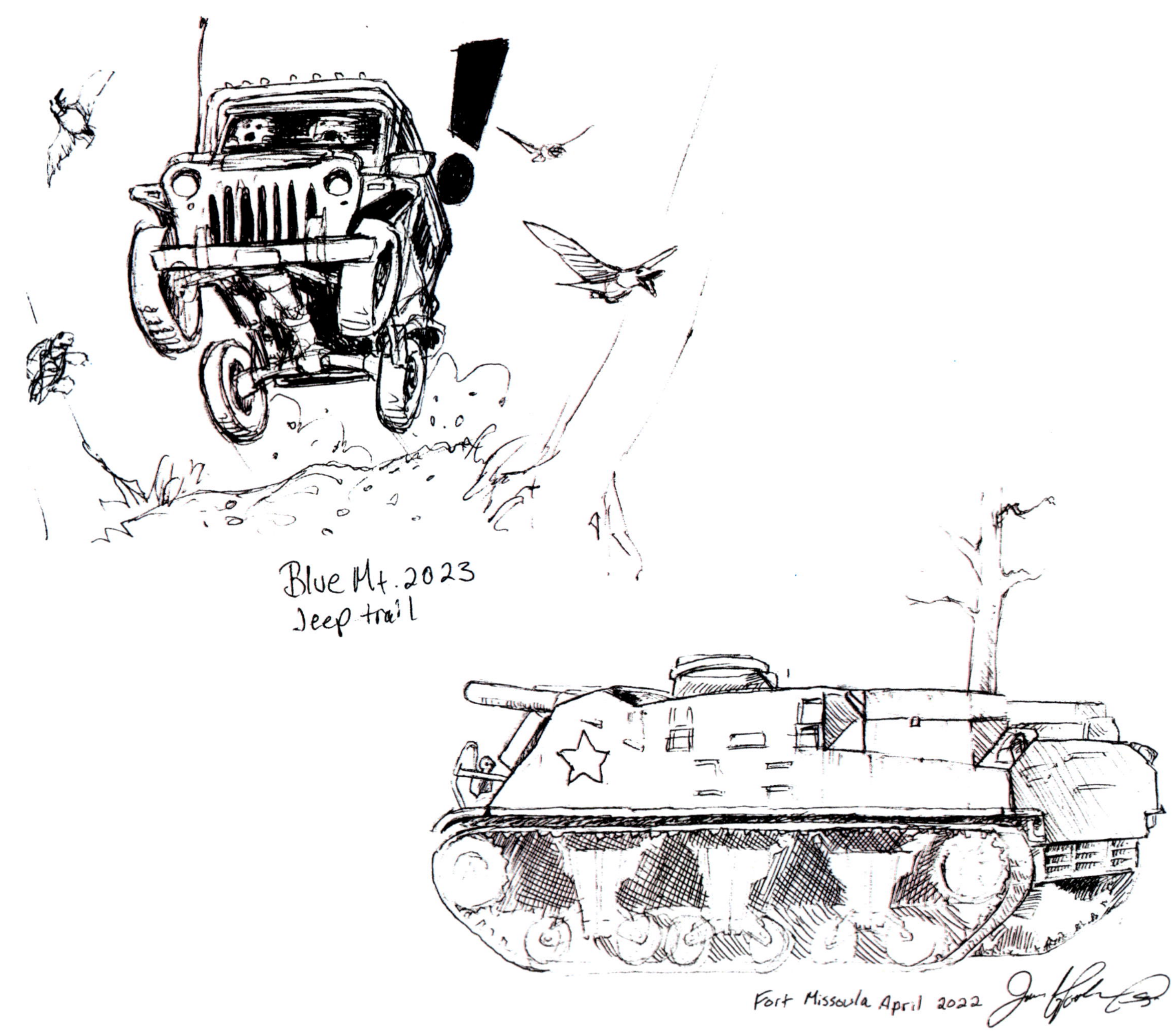

Blue Mt. 2023
Jeep trail
Fort Missoula April 2022

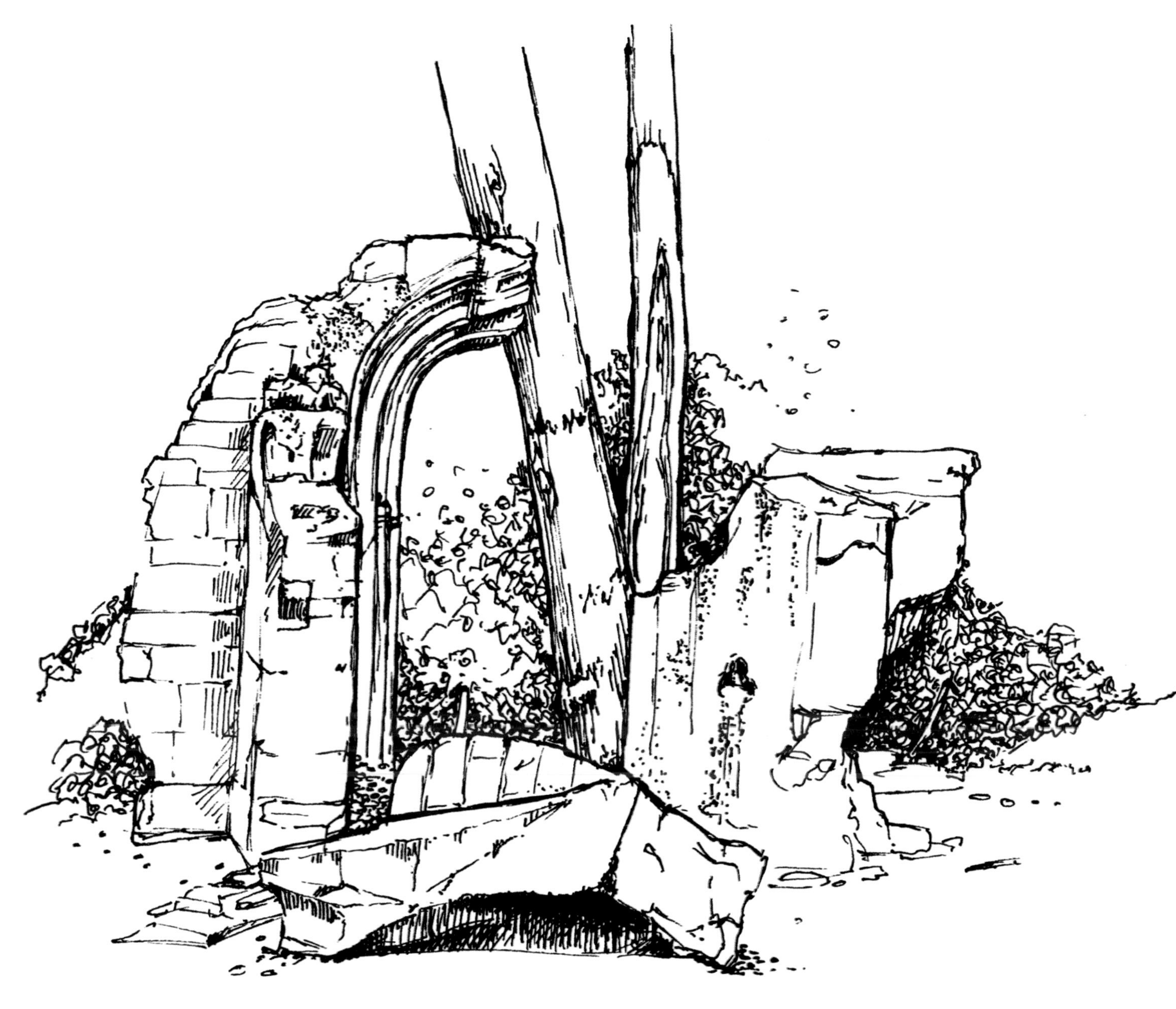

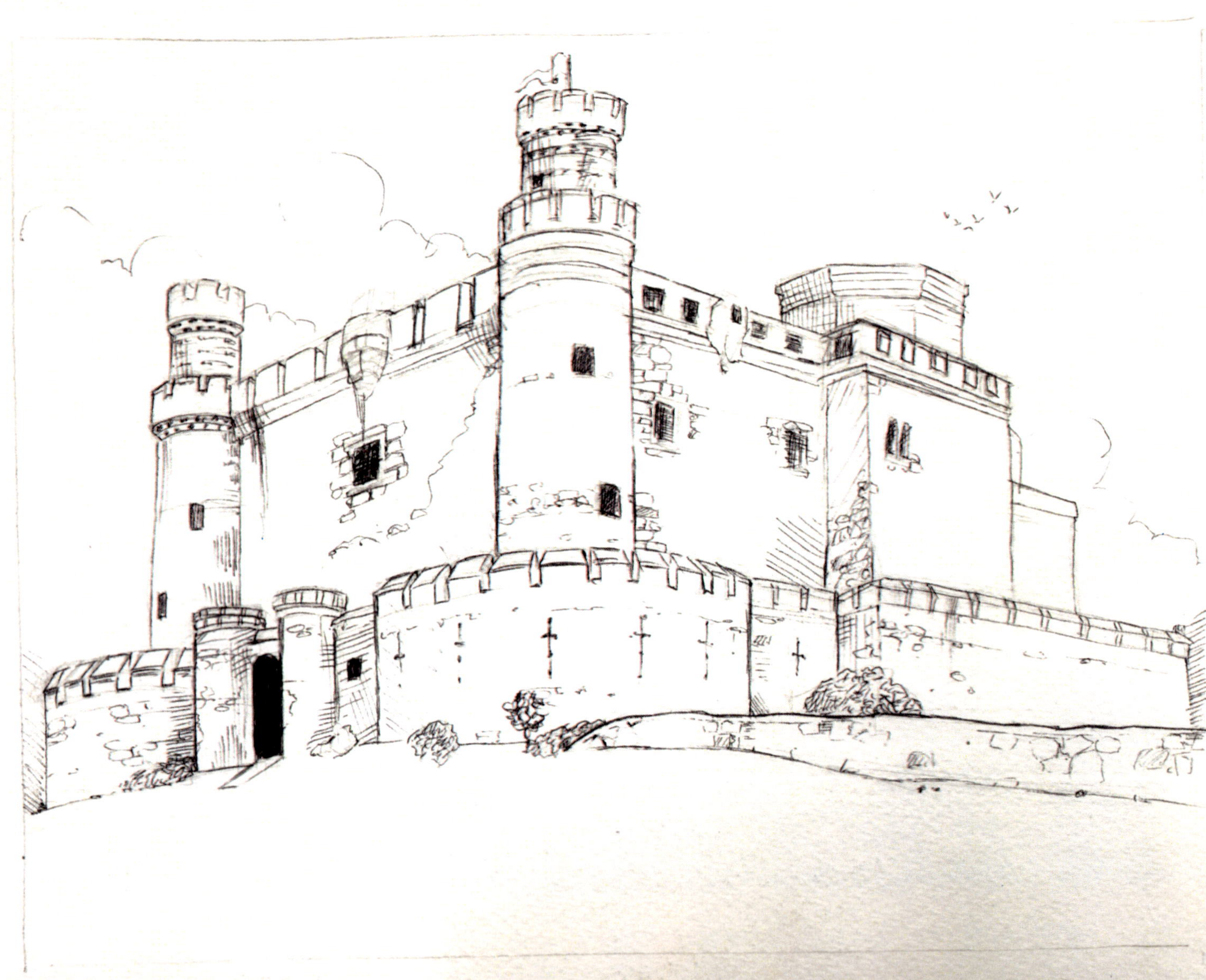

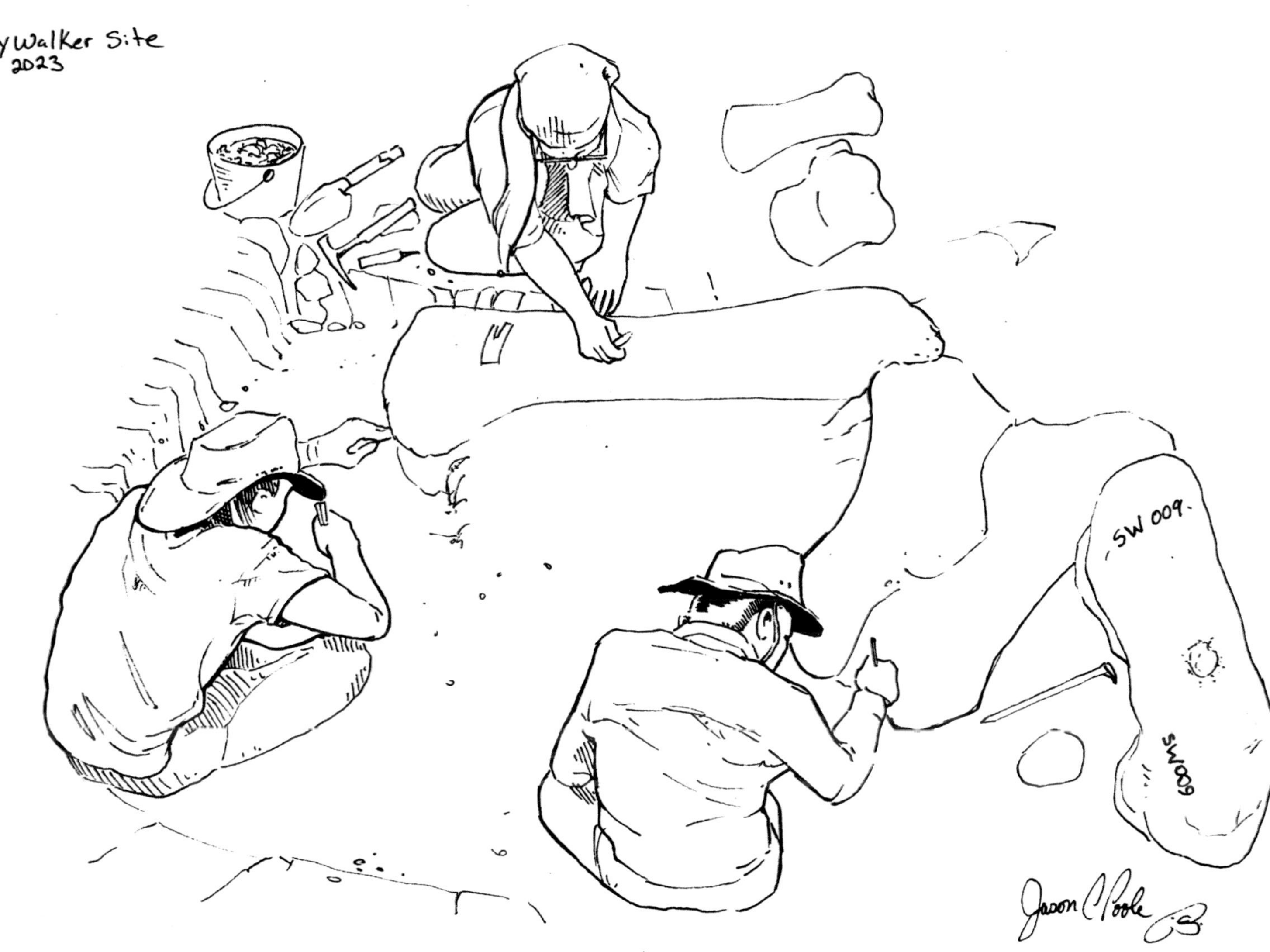

kyWalker Site
2023
SW 009
SW 009
Jason C Poole

Landscapes

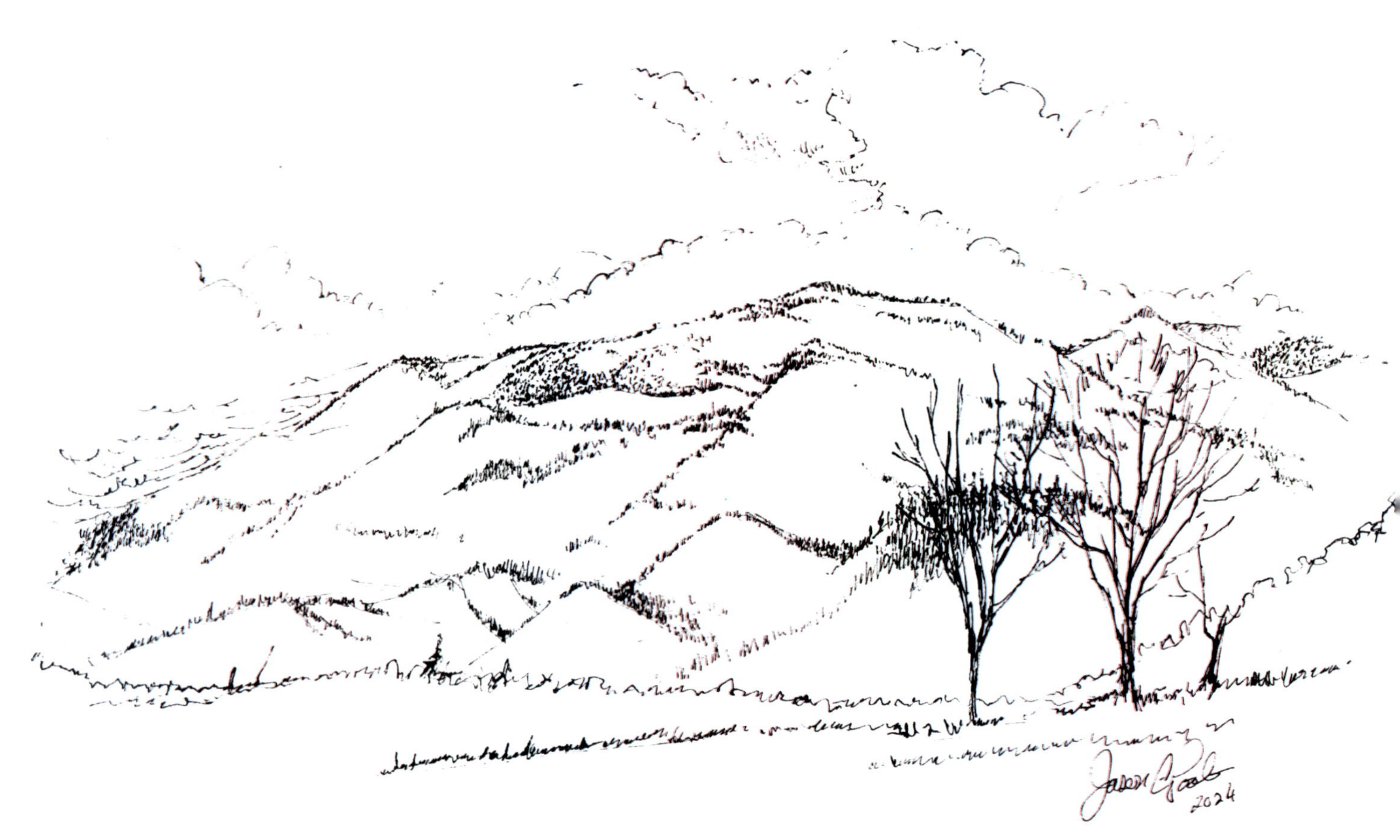

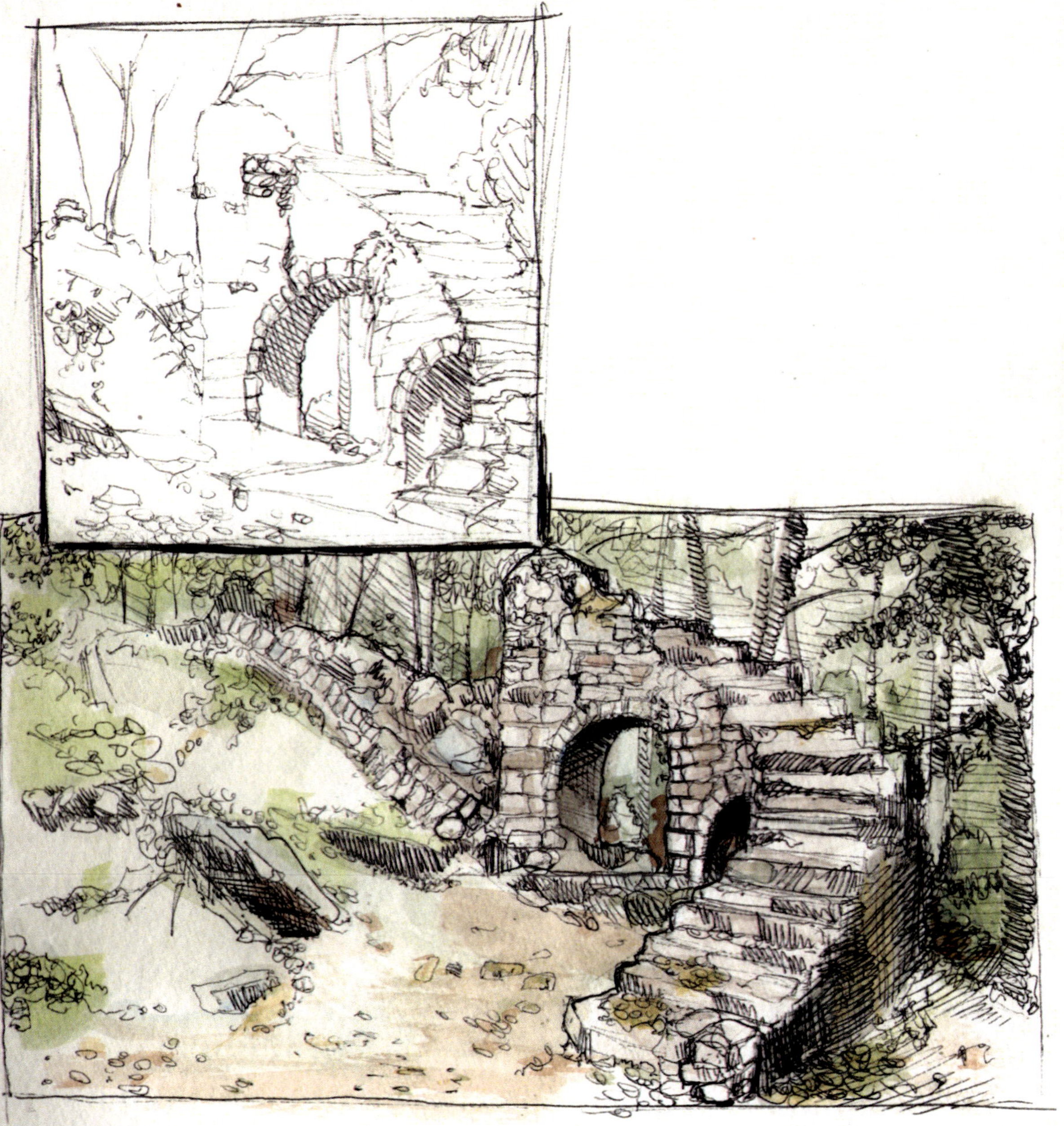

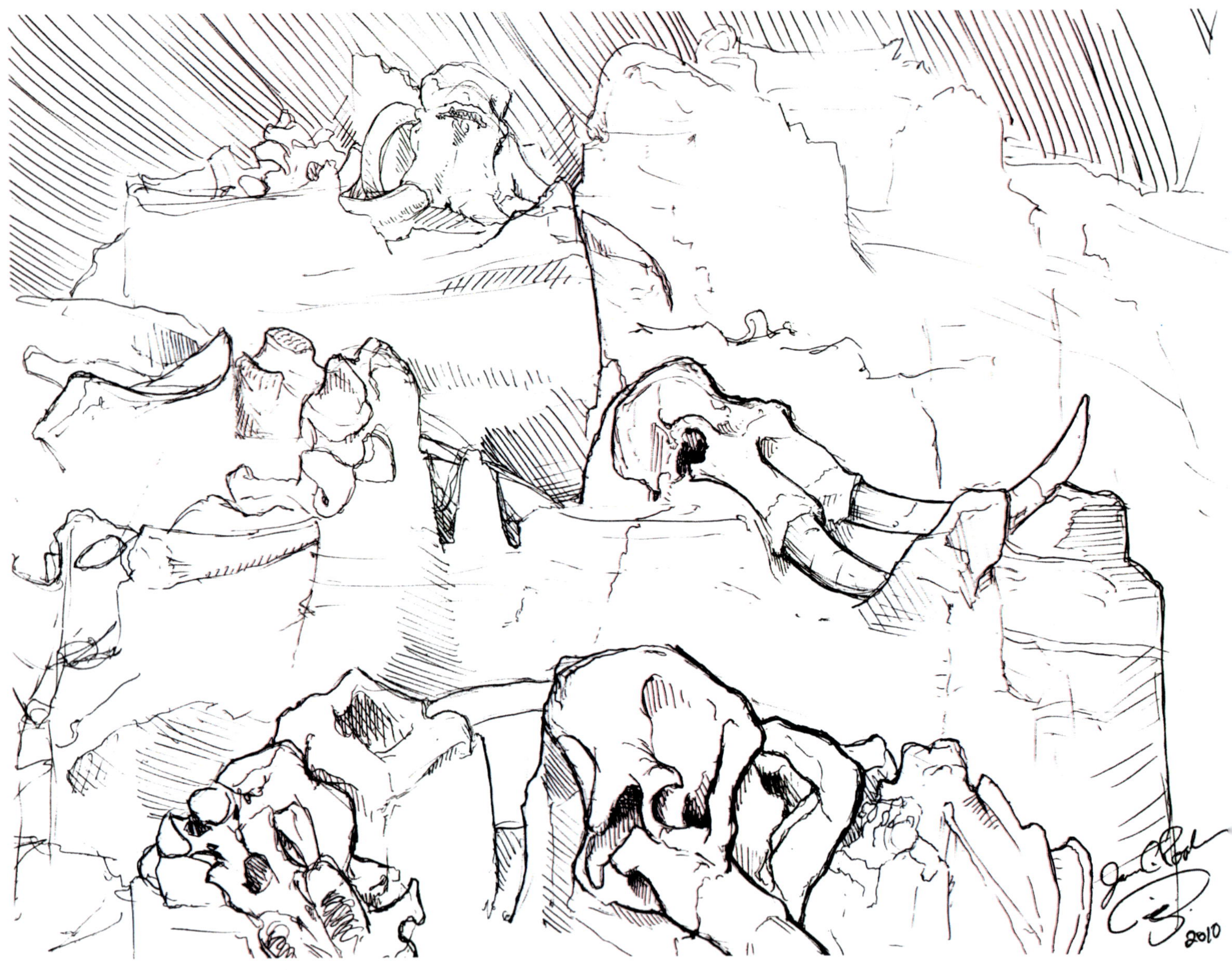

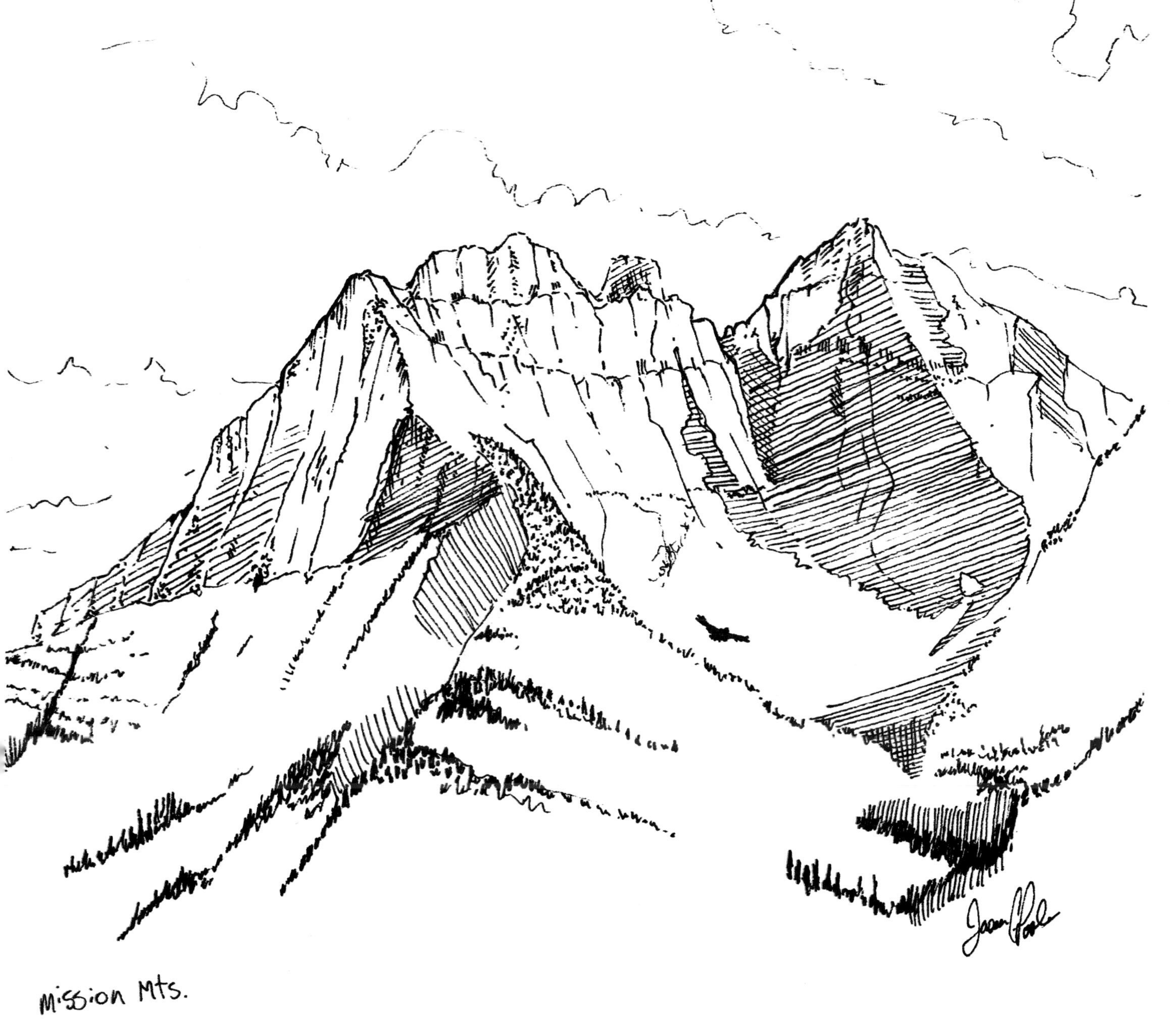

Mission Mts.

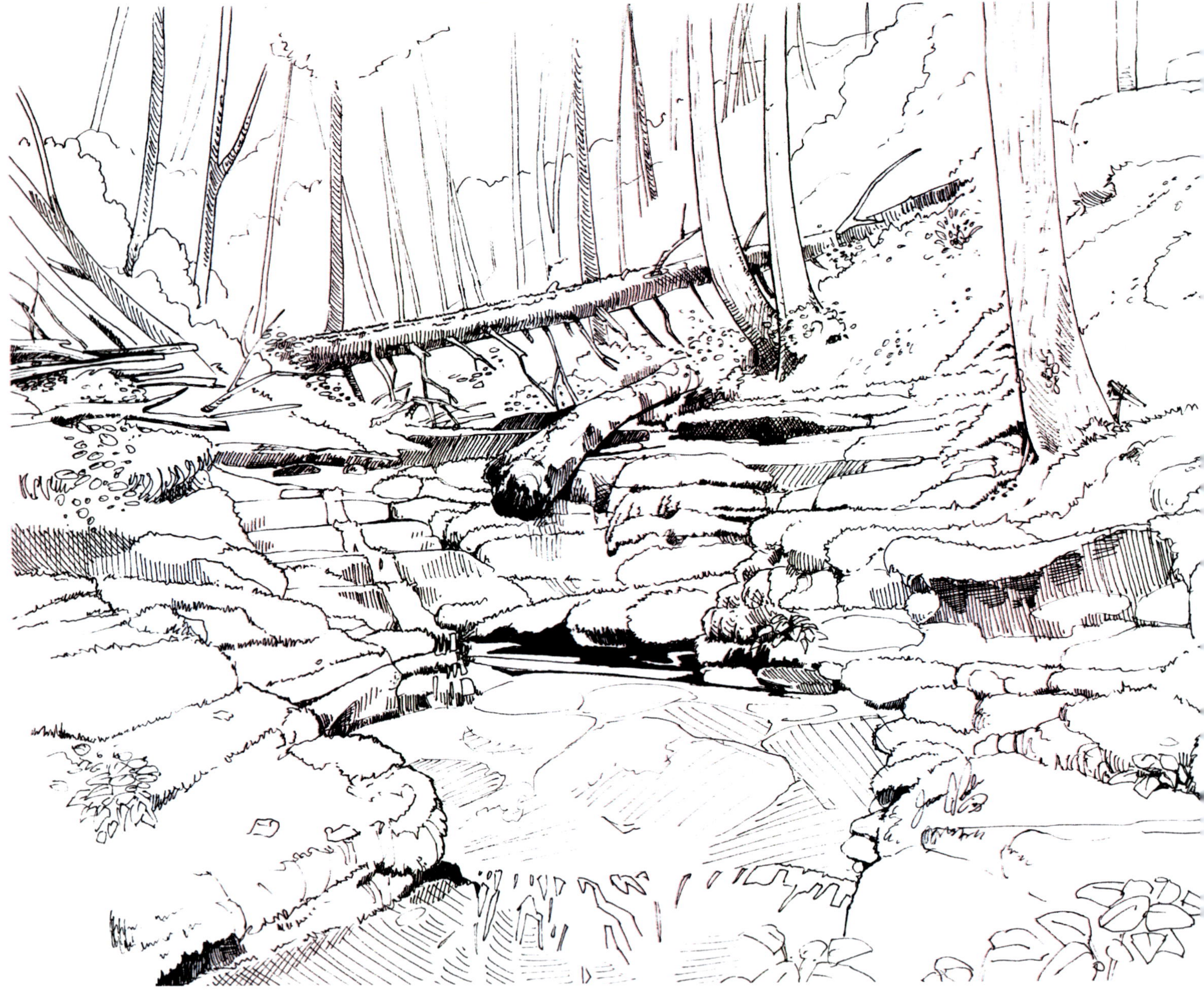

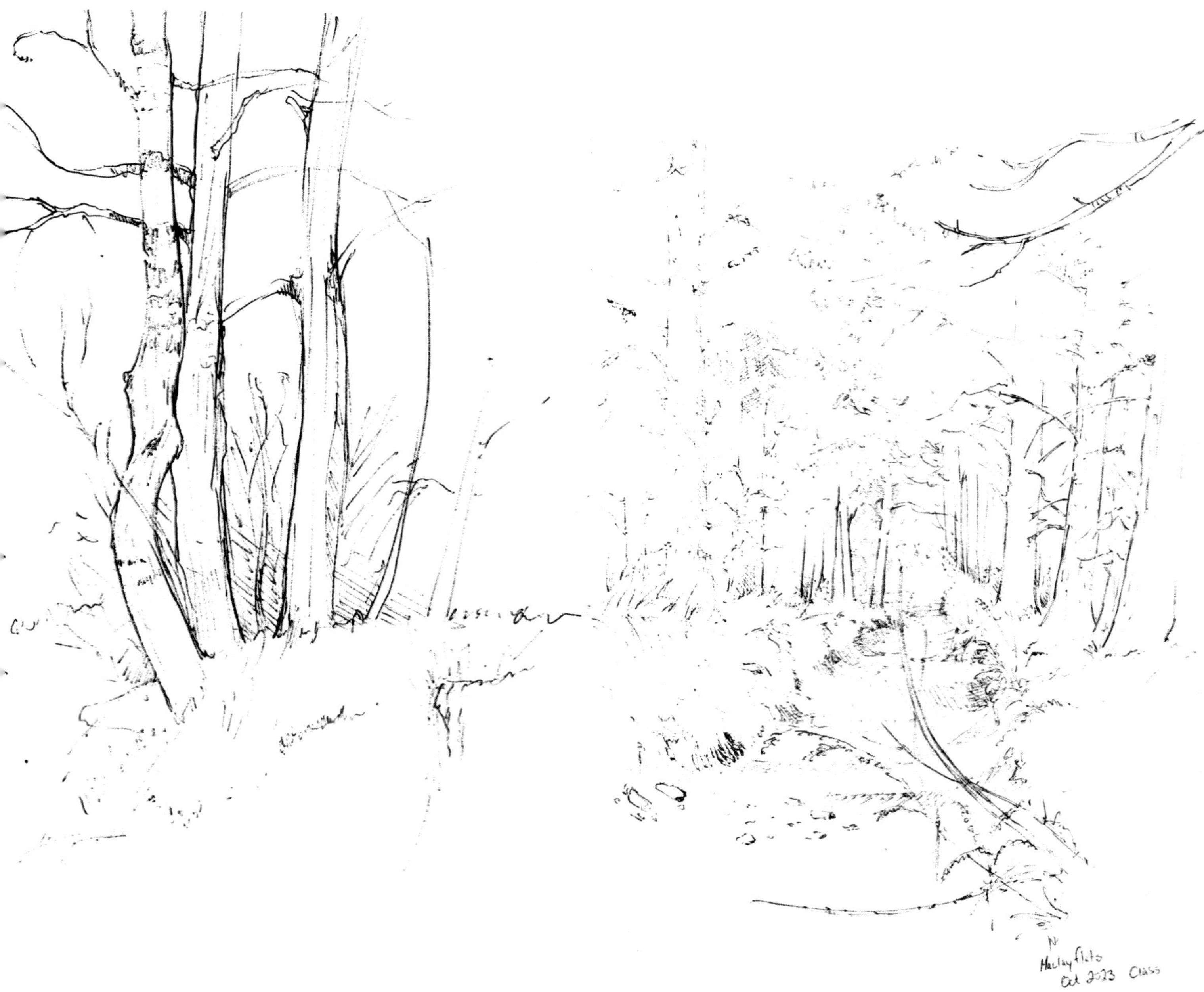

N
Maclay Flats
Oct 2023 Class

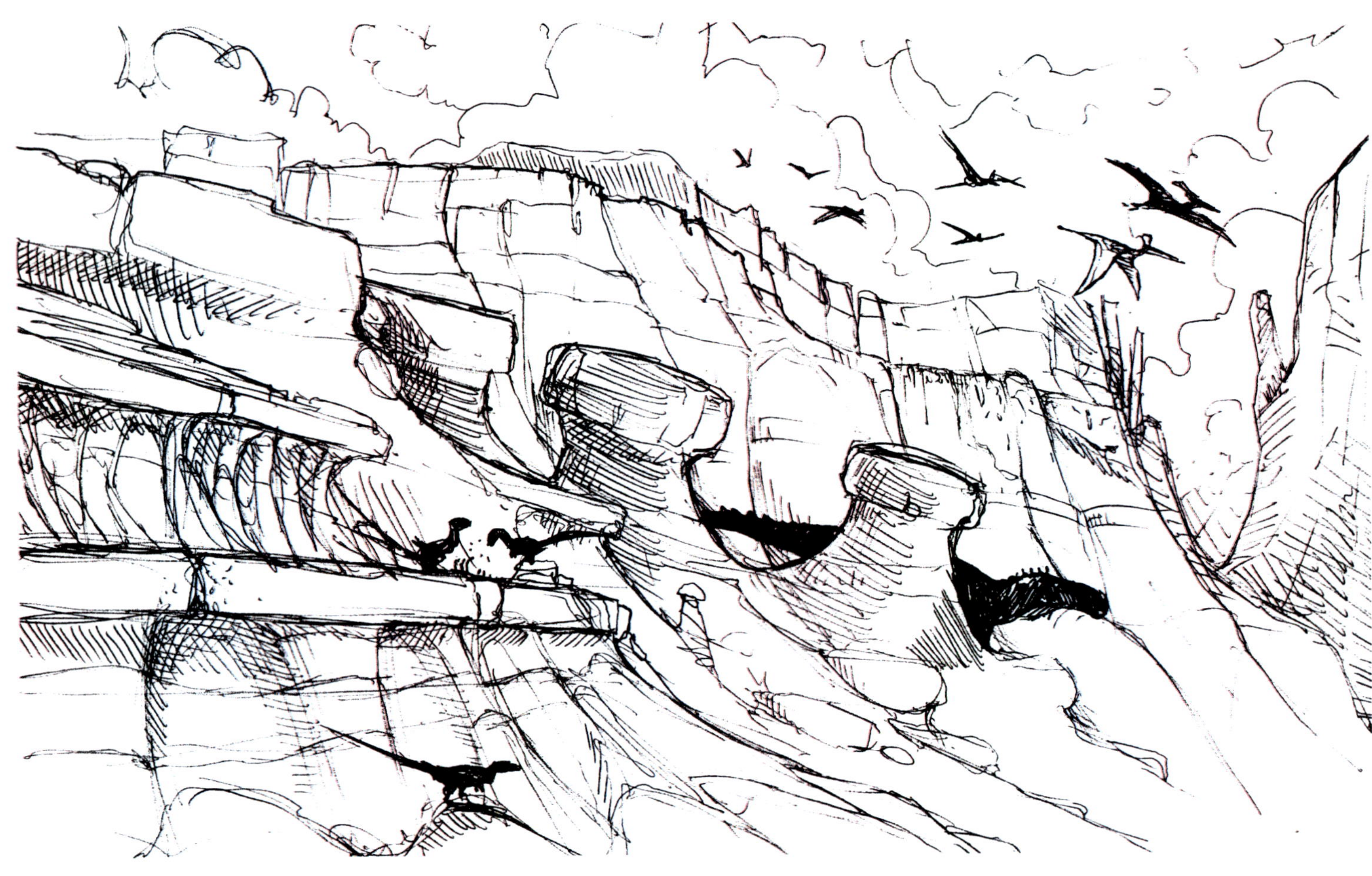

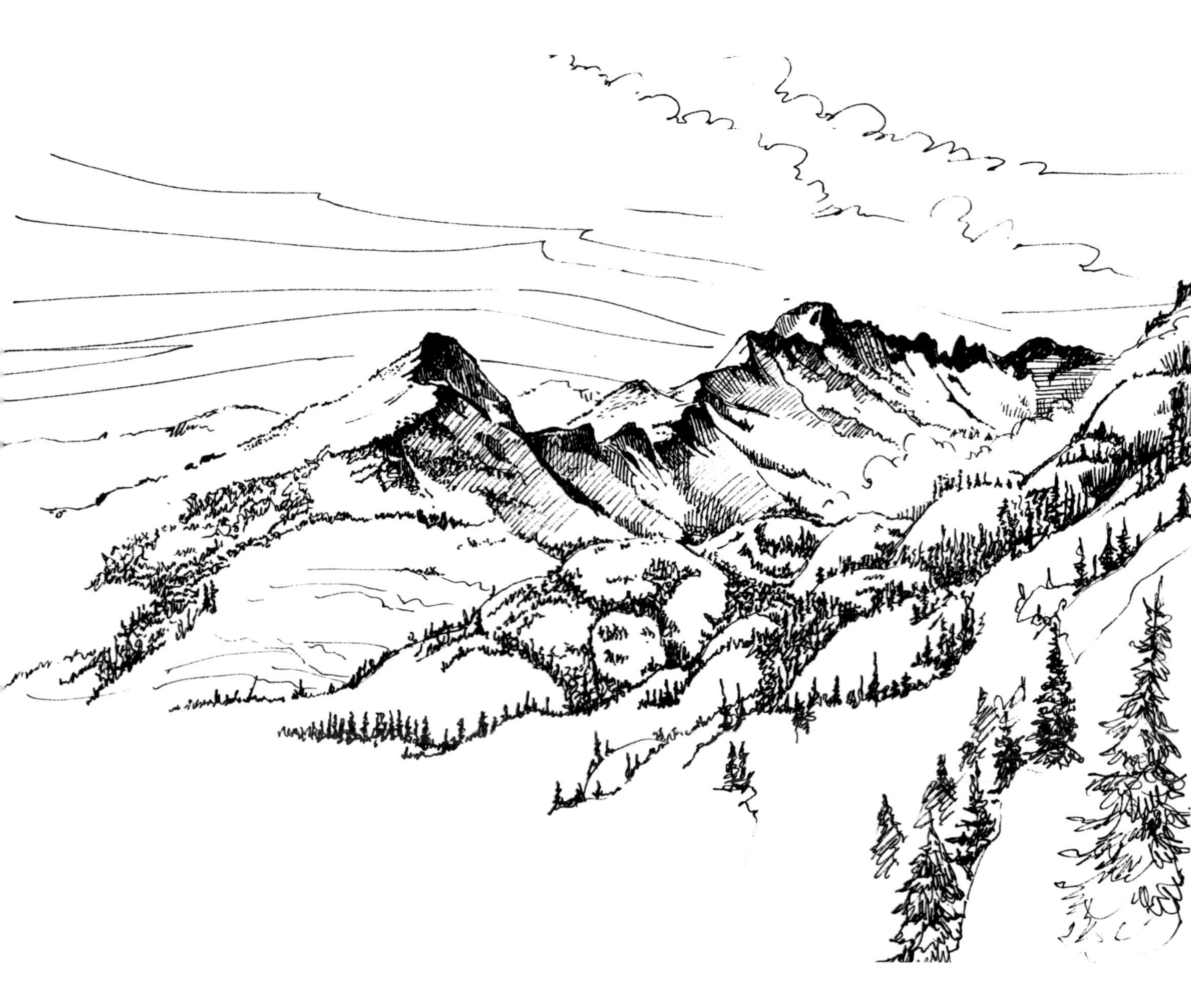

Feb 15, 2024 Thurs.
View from Ruby's Cafe front window
Snow is falling and Blowing a bit
23°f
The Horiz. lines in the side of the Mtr. are
water levels from the ~~Glacier~~ Glacier Missoula.
I omitted the walgreens across the street.
The Mt. dissapeared from view in the white-out
of falling snow.
    12 Noon

MH. Sentinel

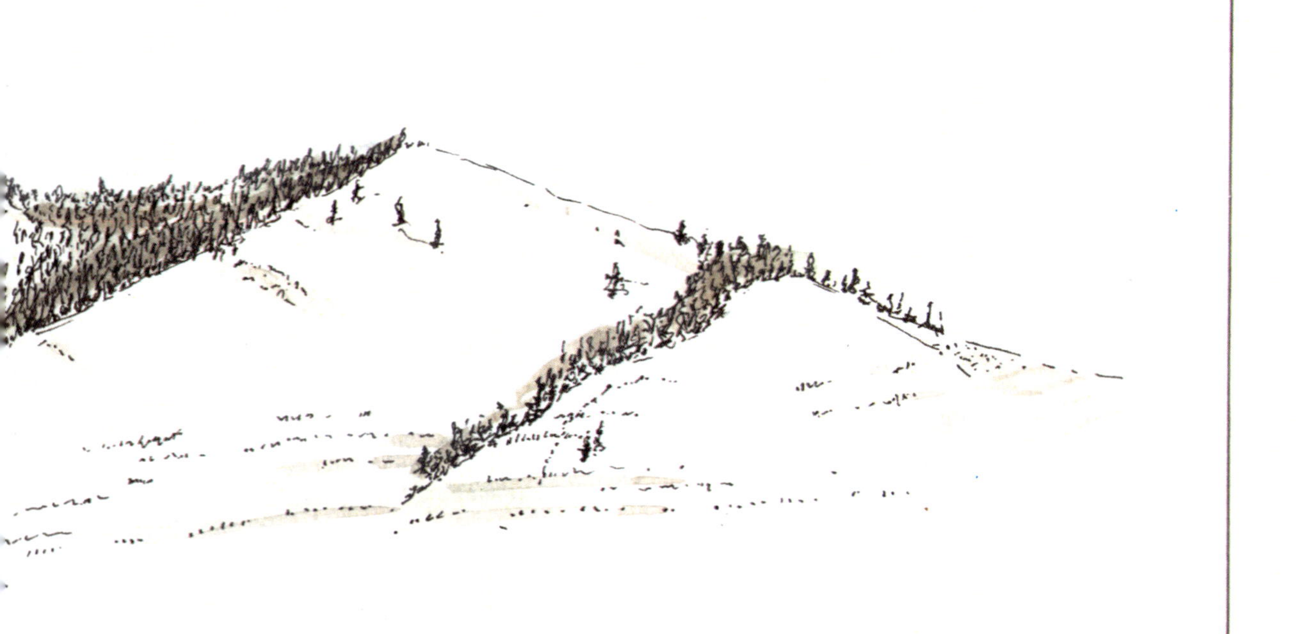

my friend Jim just commented
that the trees are not native to
where I have them as indiginous people
to this vally used to BURN the
Mt.s to favor grasses.
I need to check into this.

I imagine the ice age Mammoths
and other wooly creatures moving
across this landscape when the
lake Missoula was at it's highest.
Animals that where so well adopted to
life here and are now gone.
Jason C. Poole

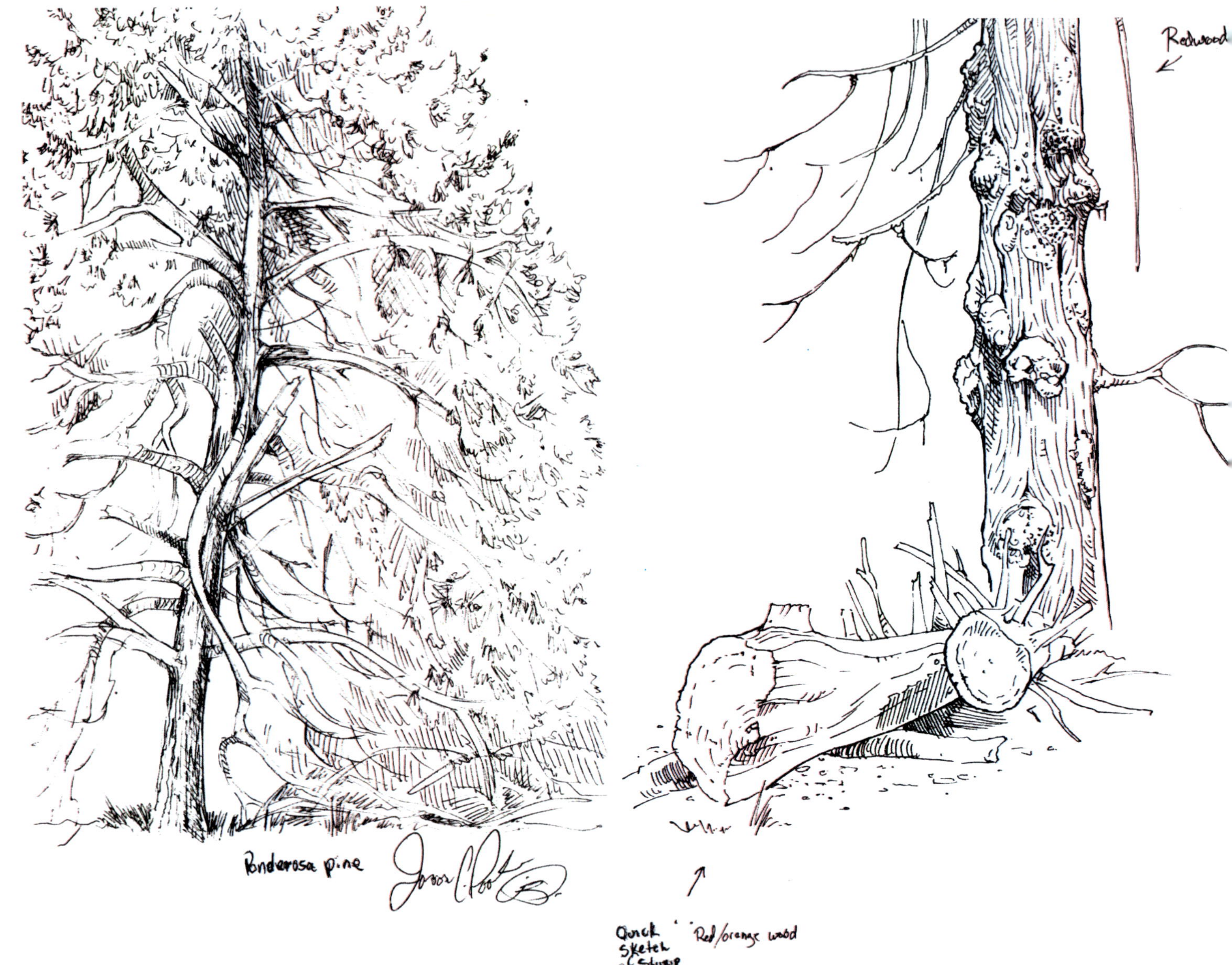

Redwood
Ponderosa pine
Red/orange wood
Quick
Sketch
at Stump
Morley Flats
11:45

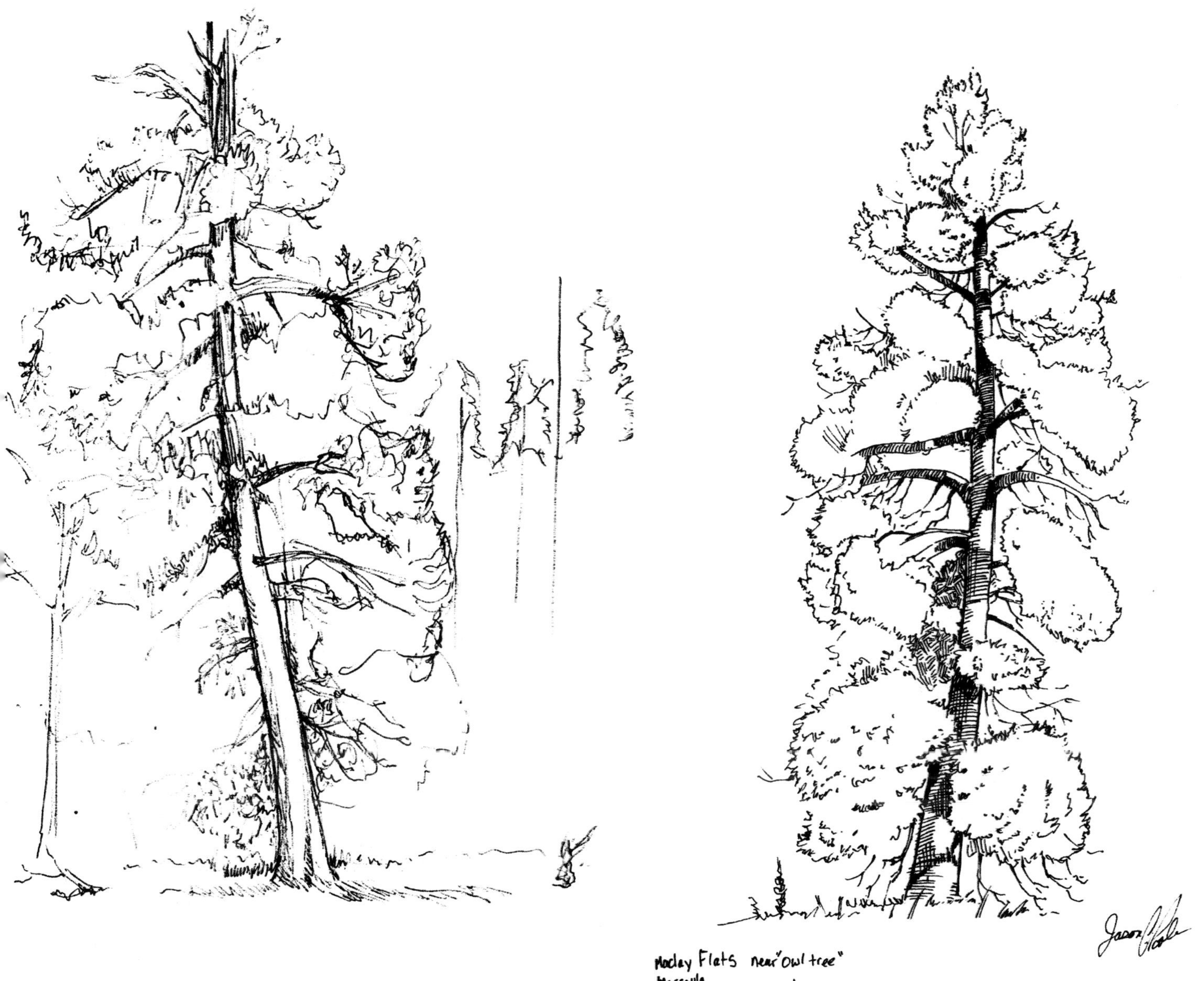

Maclay Flats near "Owl tree"
Missoula
10:15 Am clear day
Sketching outdoors class   Light from right side

<u>Fungi from a hike in Olympic National Park</u>

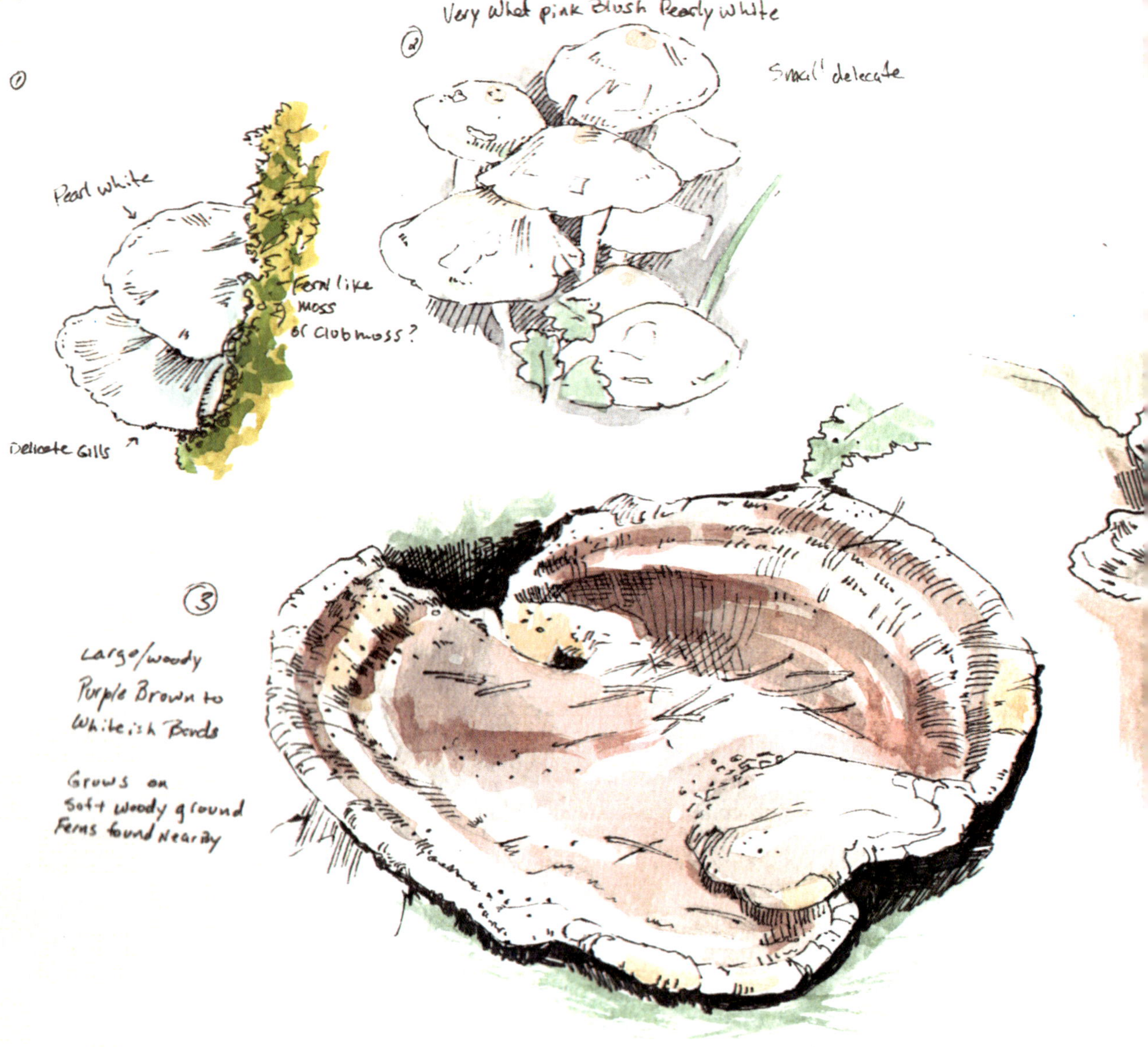

Very Whet pink Blush Pearly white

② Small delicate

① Pearl white

Fern like moss or clubmoss?

Delicate Gills

③ Large/woody Purple Brown to Whiteish Bands

Grows on Soft woody ground Ferns found Nearby

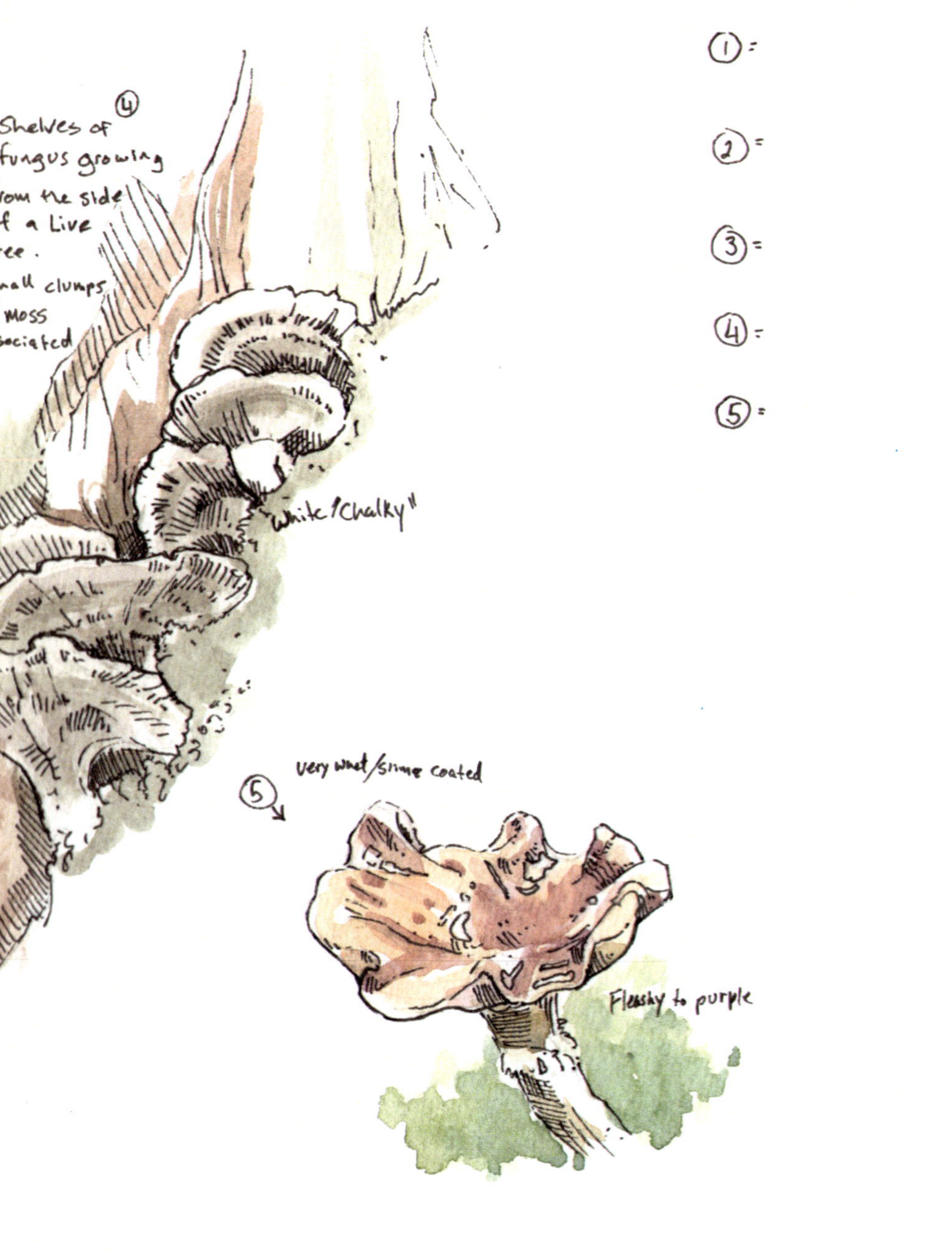

④
Shelves of
fungus growing
from the side
of a Live
Tree.
Small clumps
of moss
associated

White "Chalky"

① =
② =
③ =
④ =
⑤ =

⑤
very wet/slime coated

Fleshy to purple

Fungi of Lolo Wilderness area-

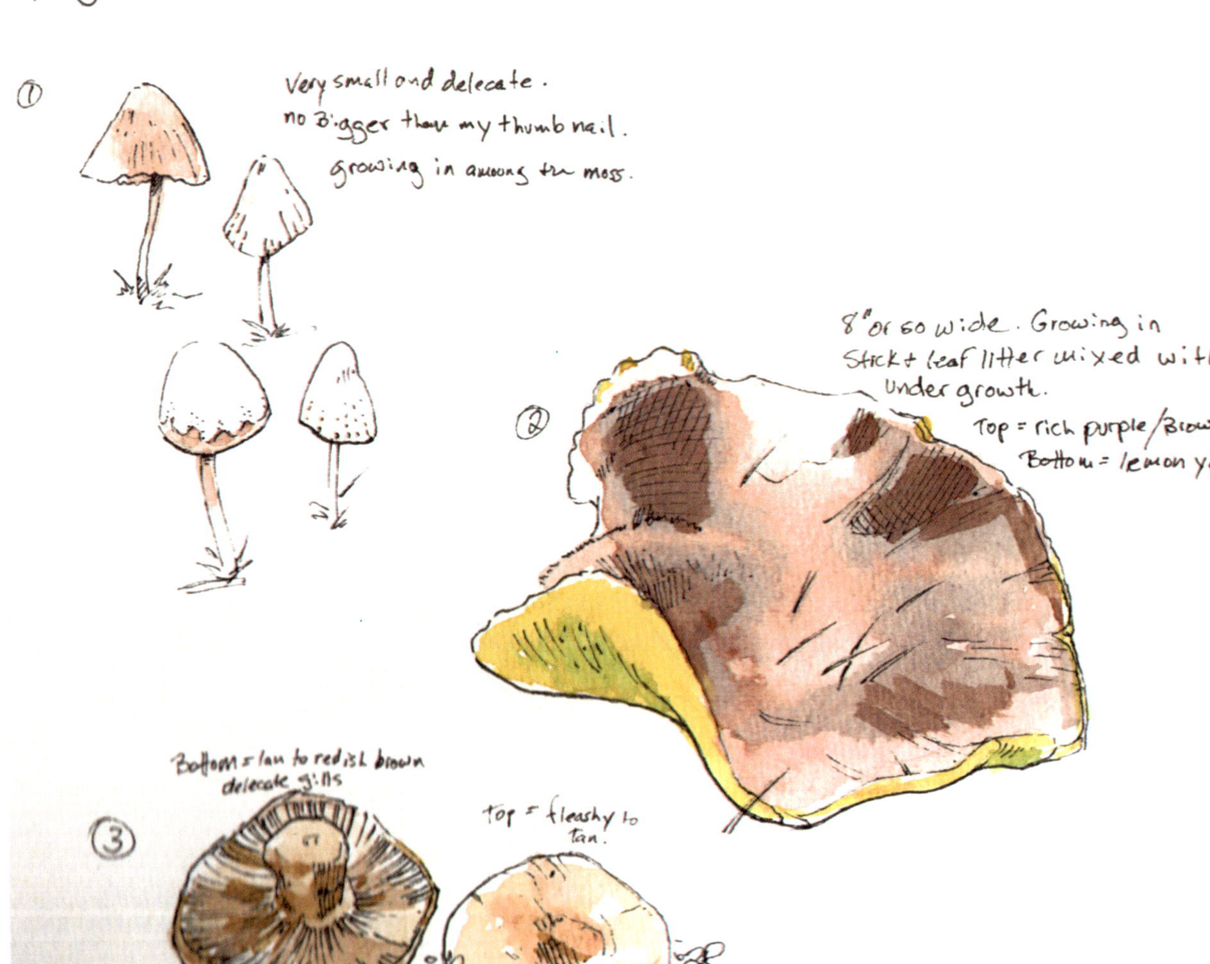

① Very small and delecate.
no Bigger than my thumb nail.
growing in among the moss.

② 8" or so wide. Growing in
Stick + leaf litter mixed with
Under growth.
Top = rich purple/Brown.
Bottom = lemon yellow.

③ Bottom = tan to redish brown
delecate gills
Top = fleashy to tan.
grows in undergrowth.

④ Fleashy outer edge / Pink/Purple inner surface
growing on a moss
bedt leaf litter.

①

②

③

④

⑤

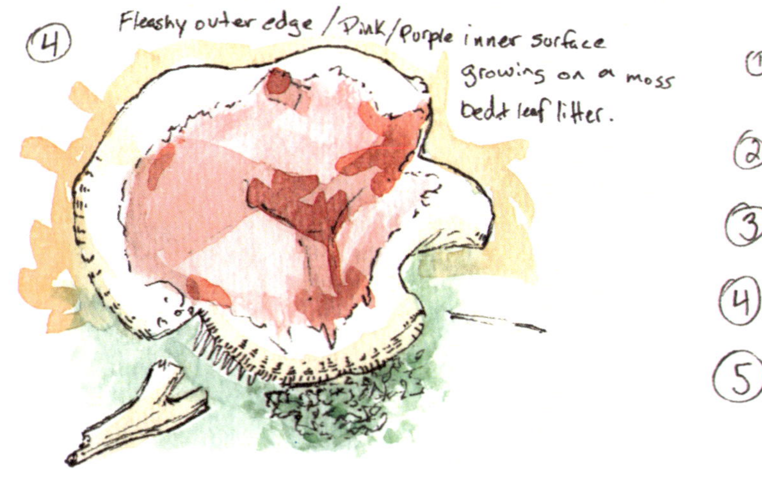
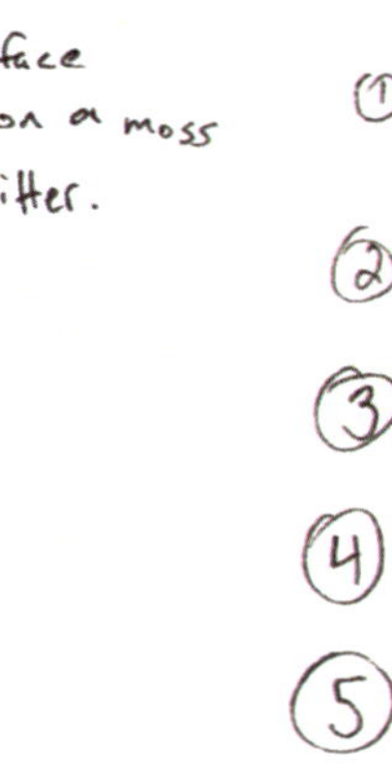

light-yellow to Brown

⑤

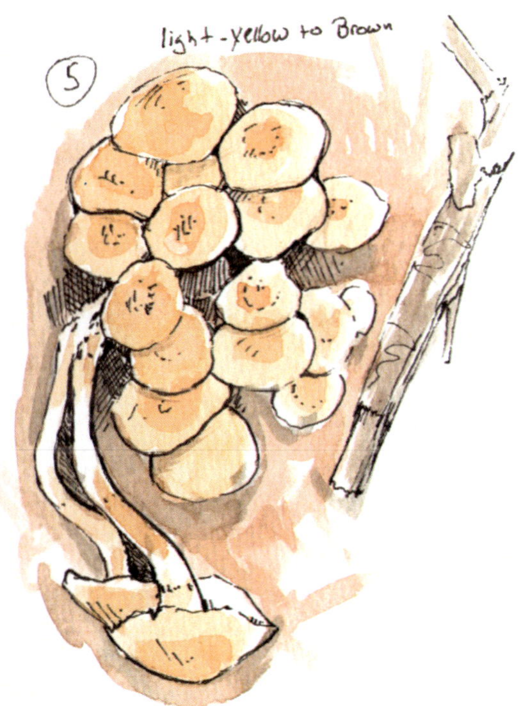

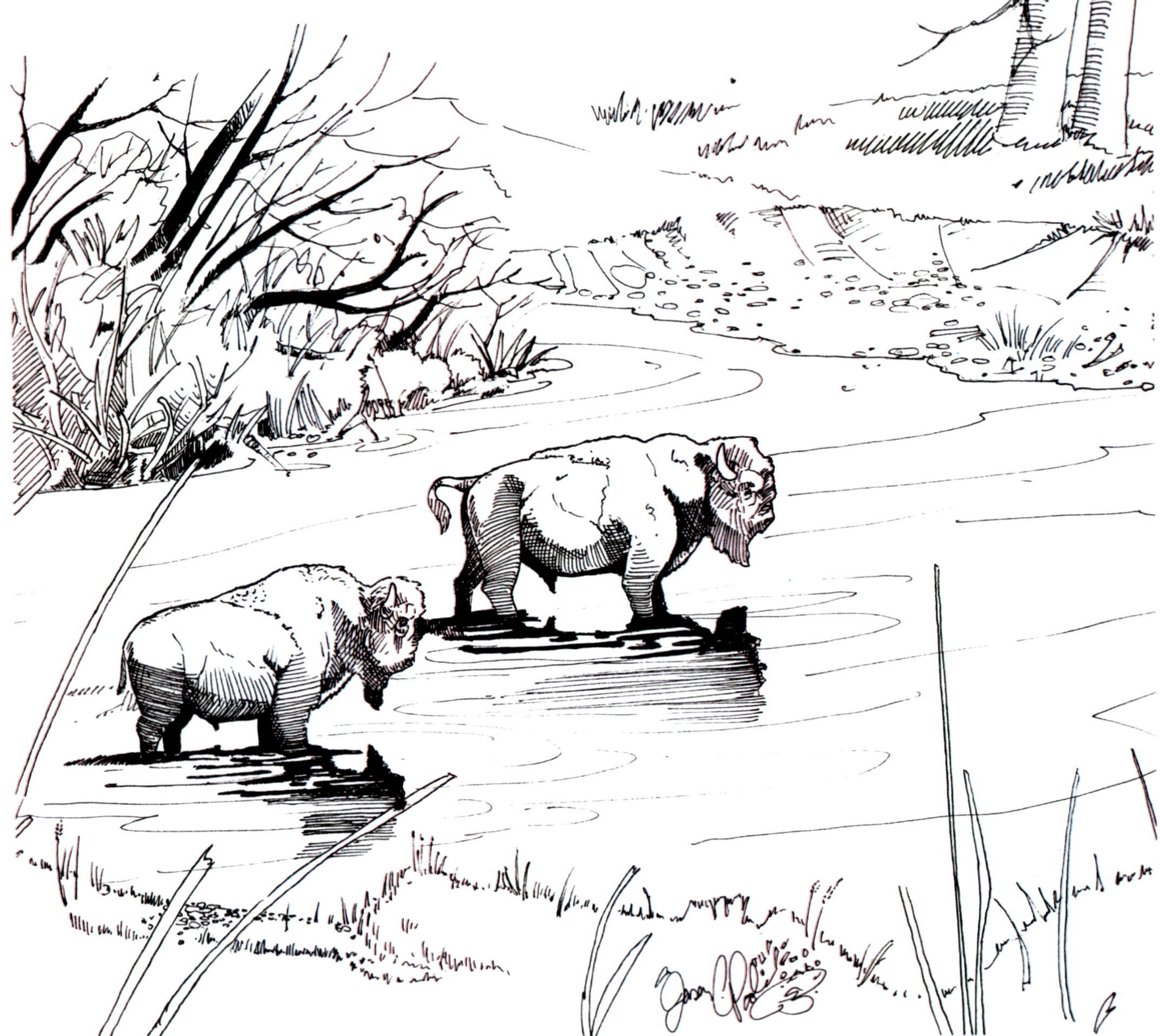

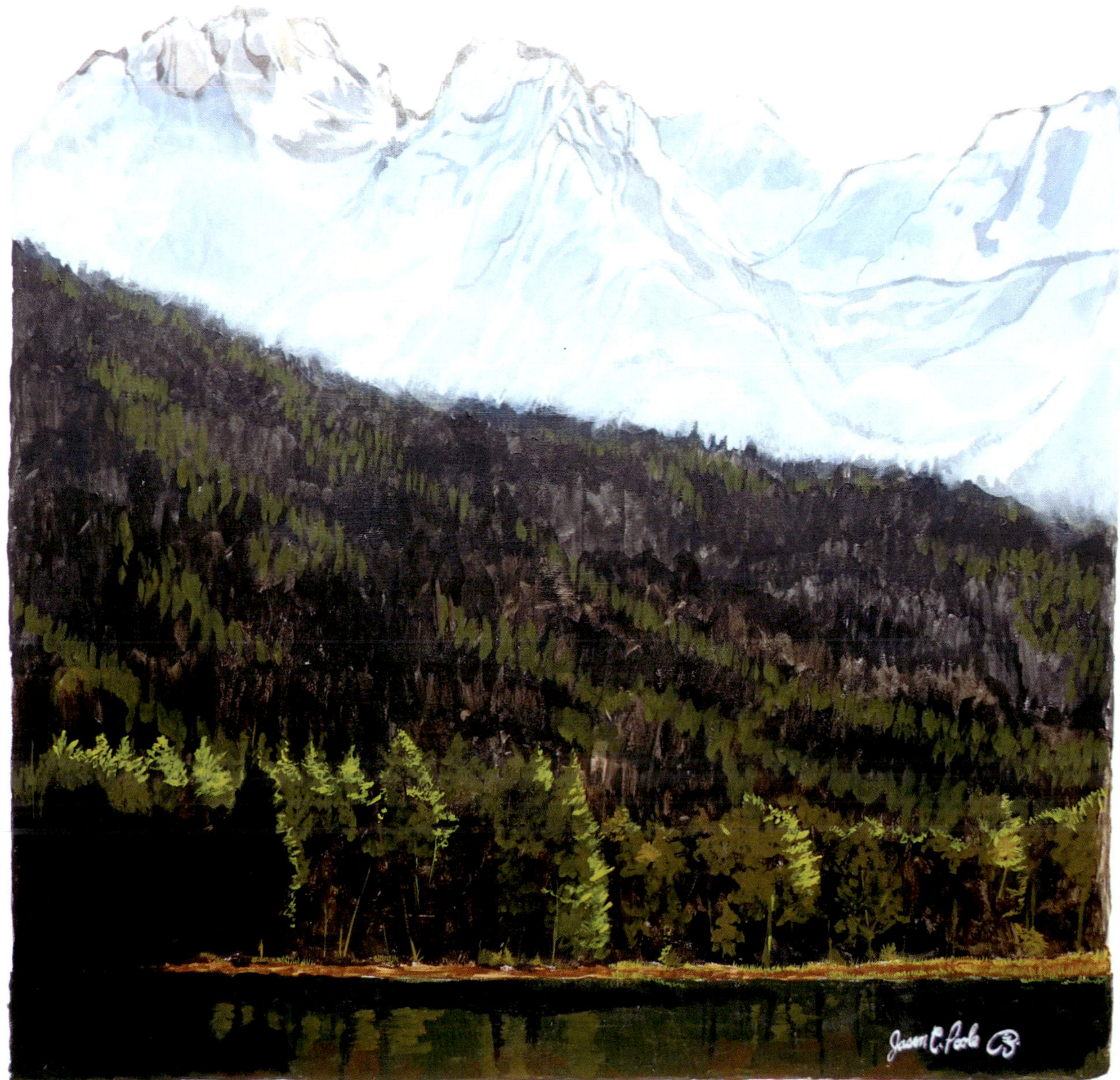
Jason C. Poole

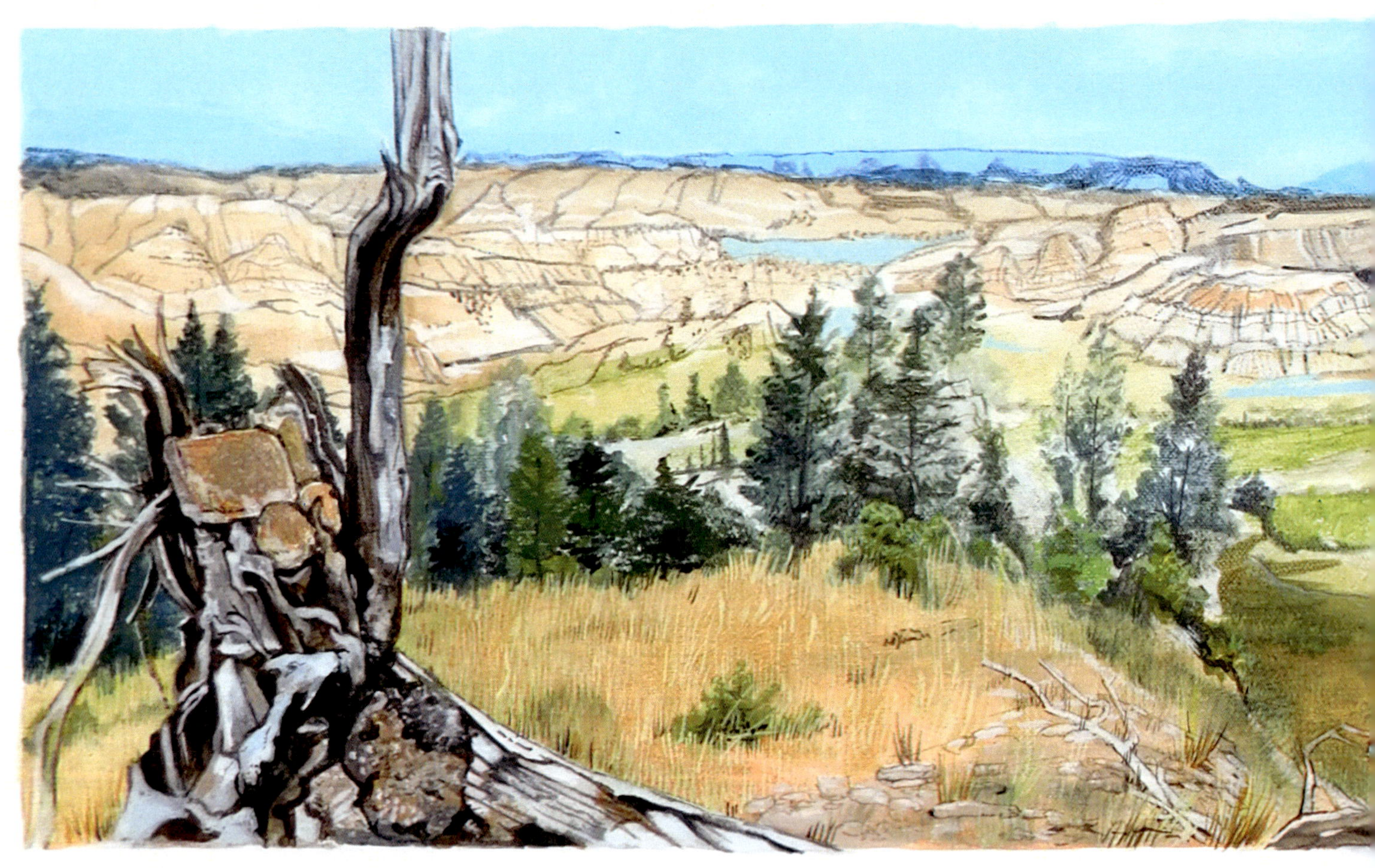

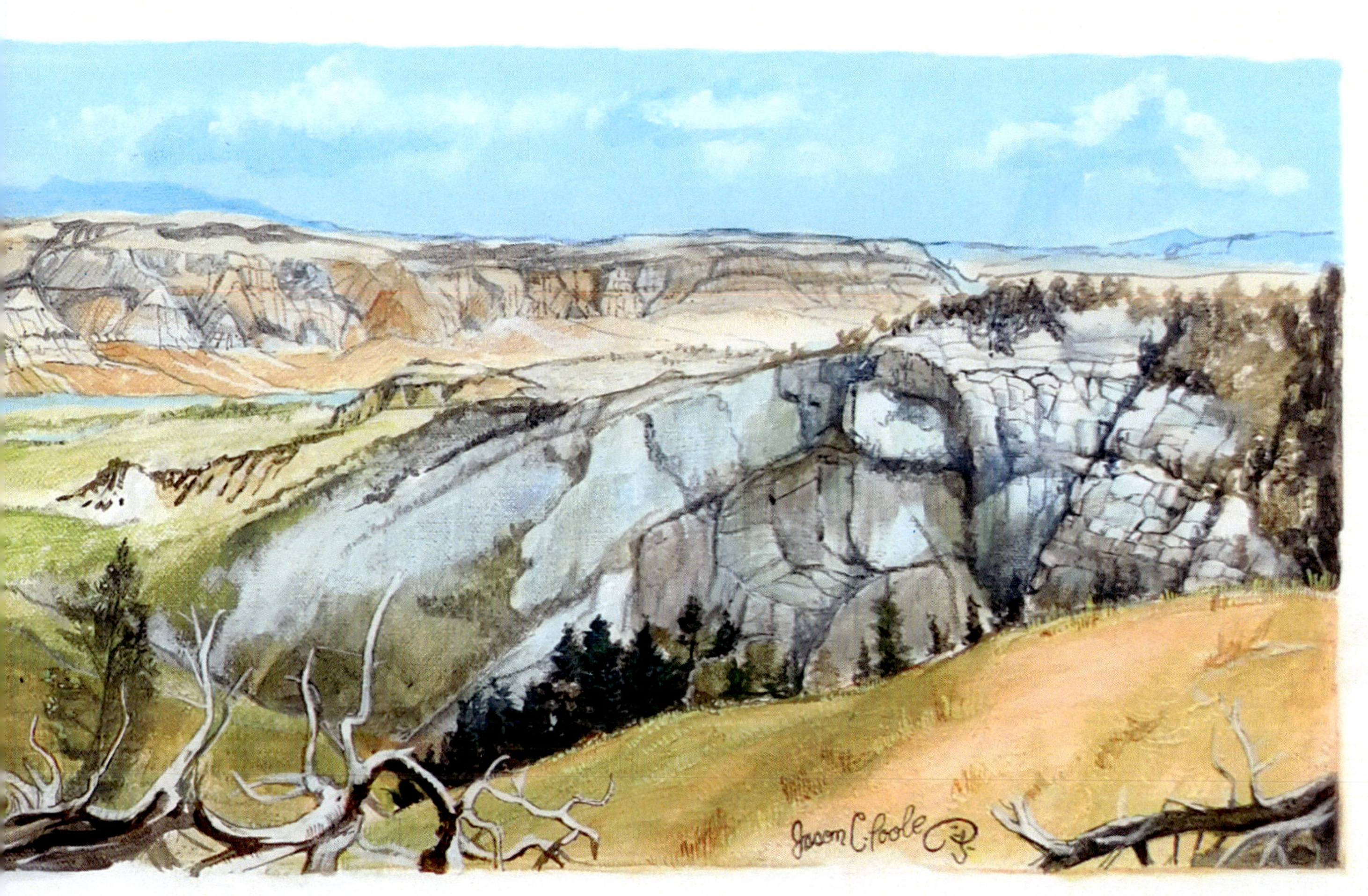

Jason C Poole

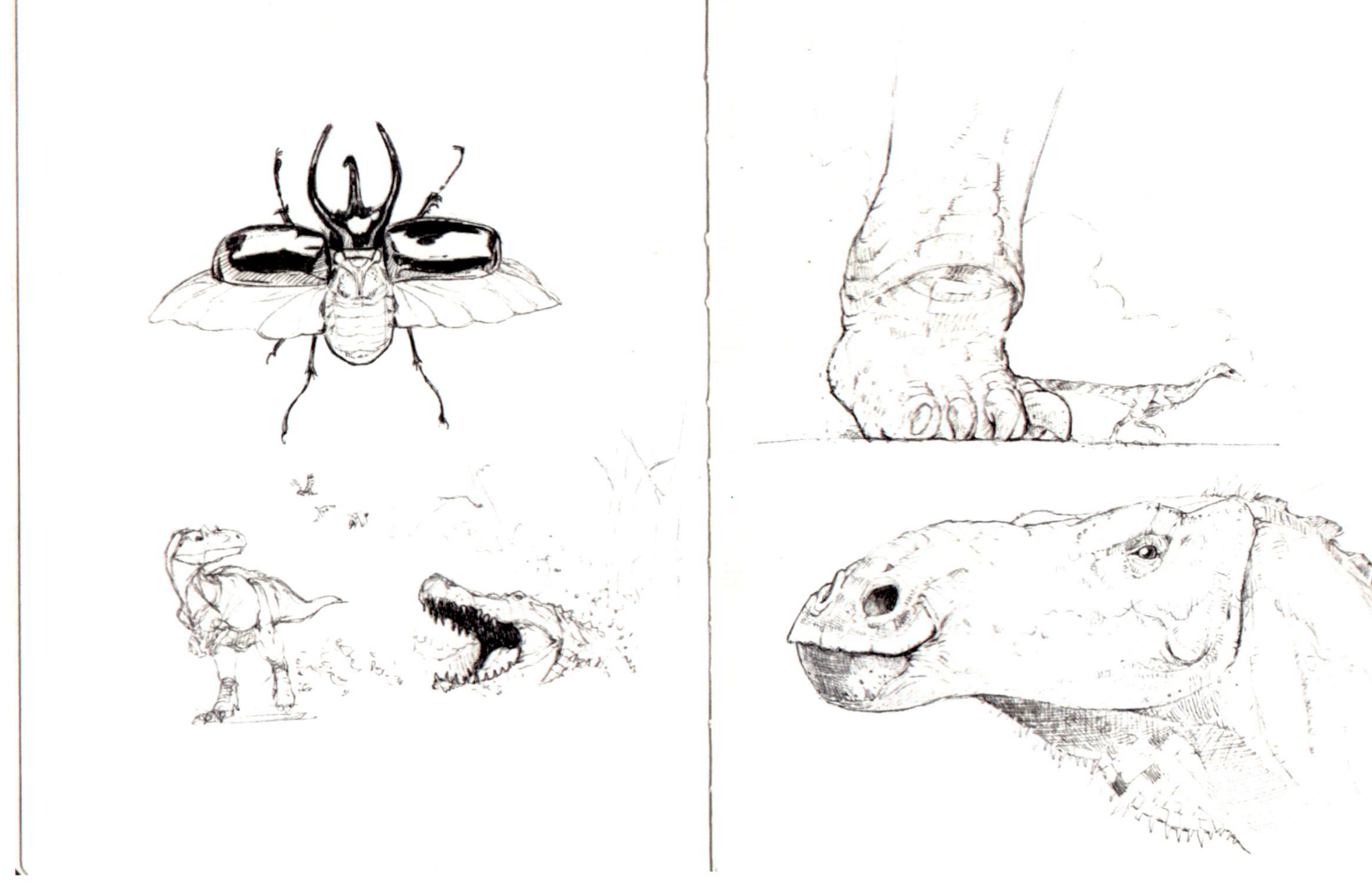

Animals

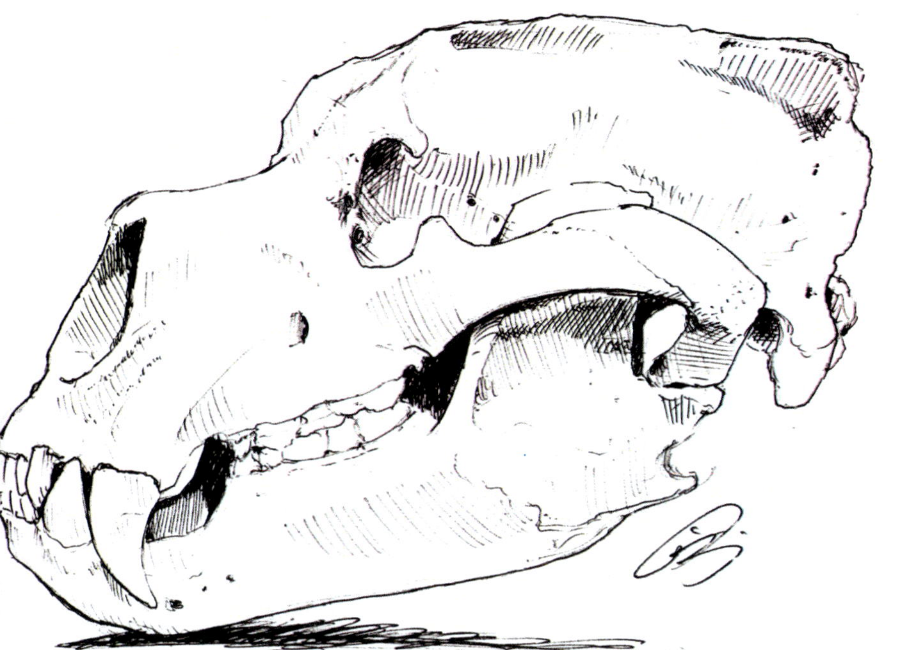

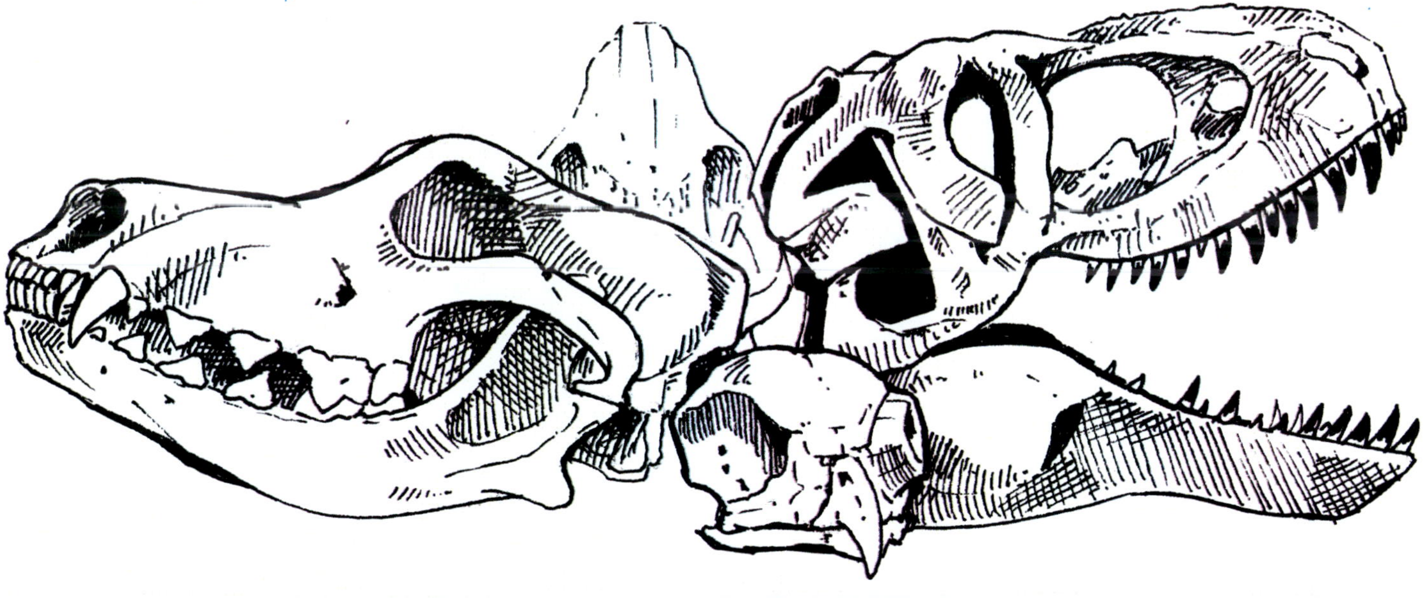

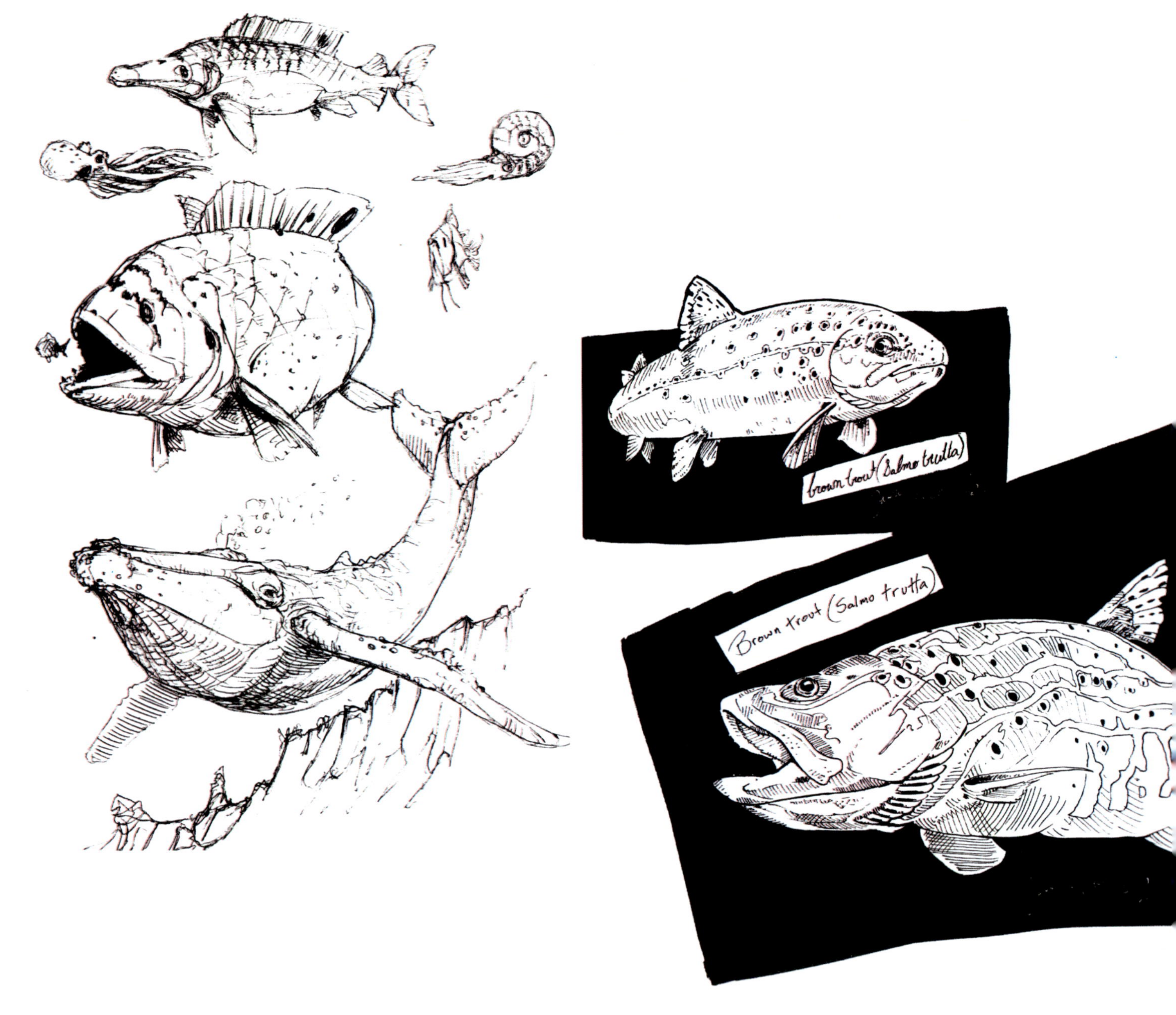

brown trout (Salmo trutta)
Brown trout (Salmo trutta)

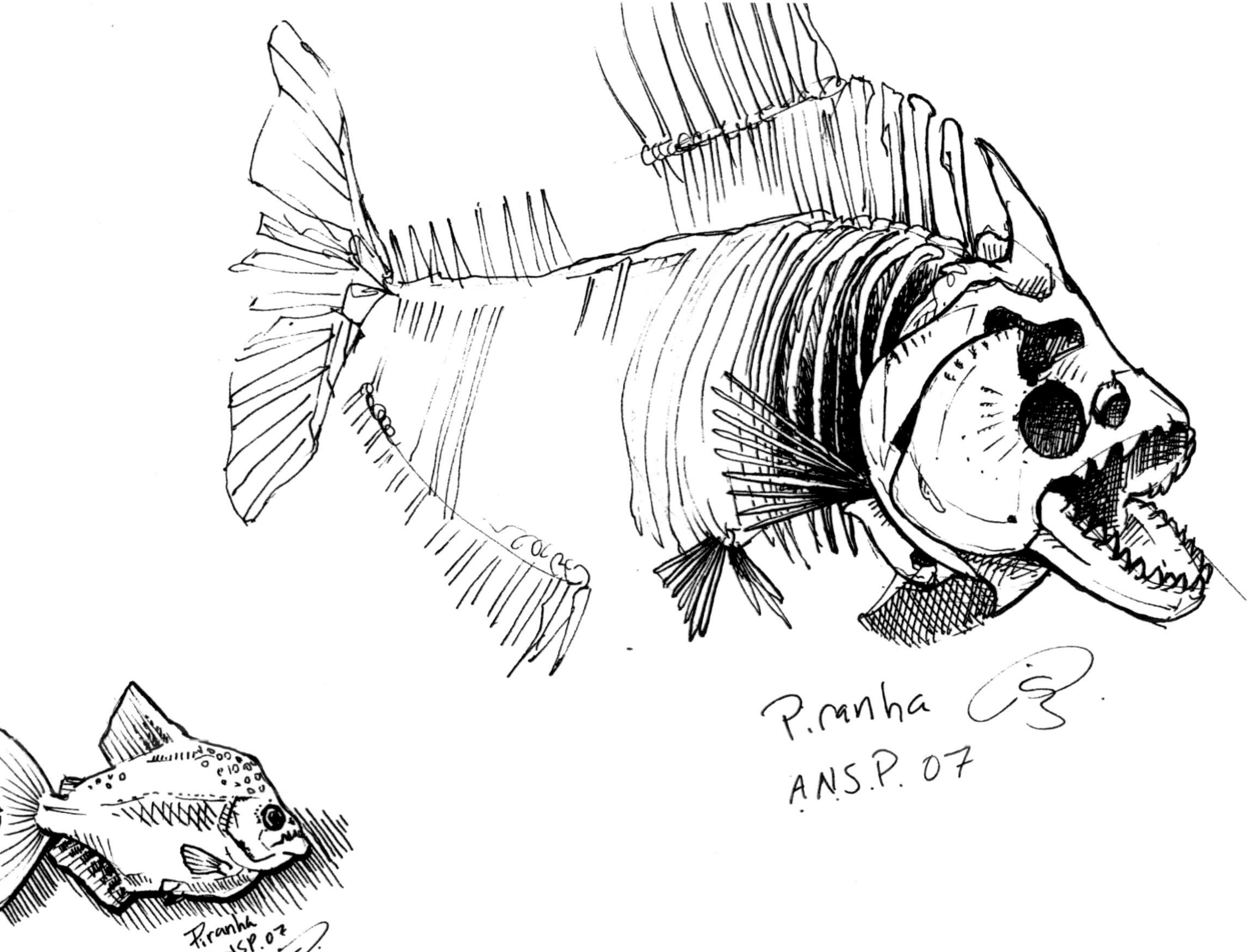

Piranha
A.N.S.P. 07
Piranha
A.N.S.P. 07

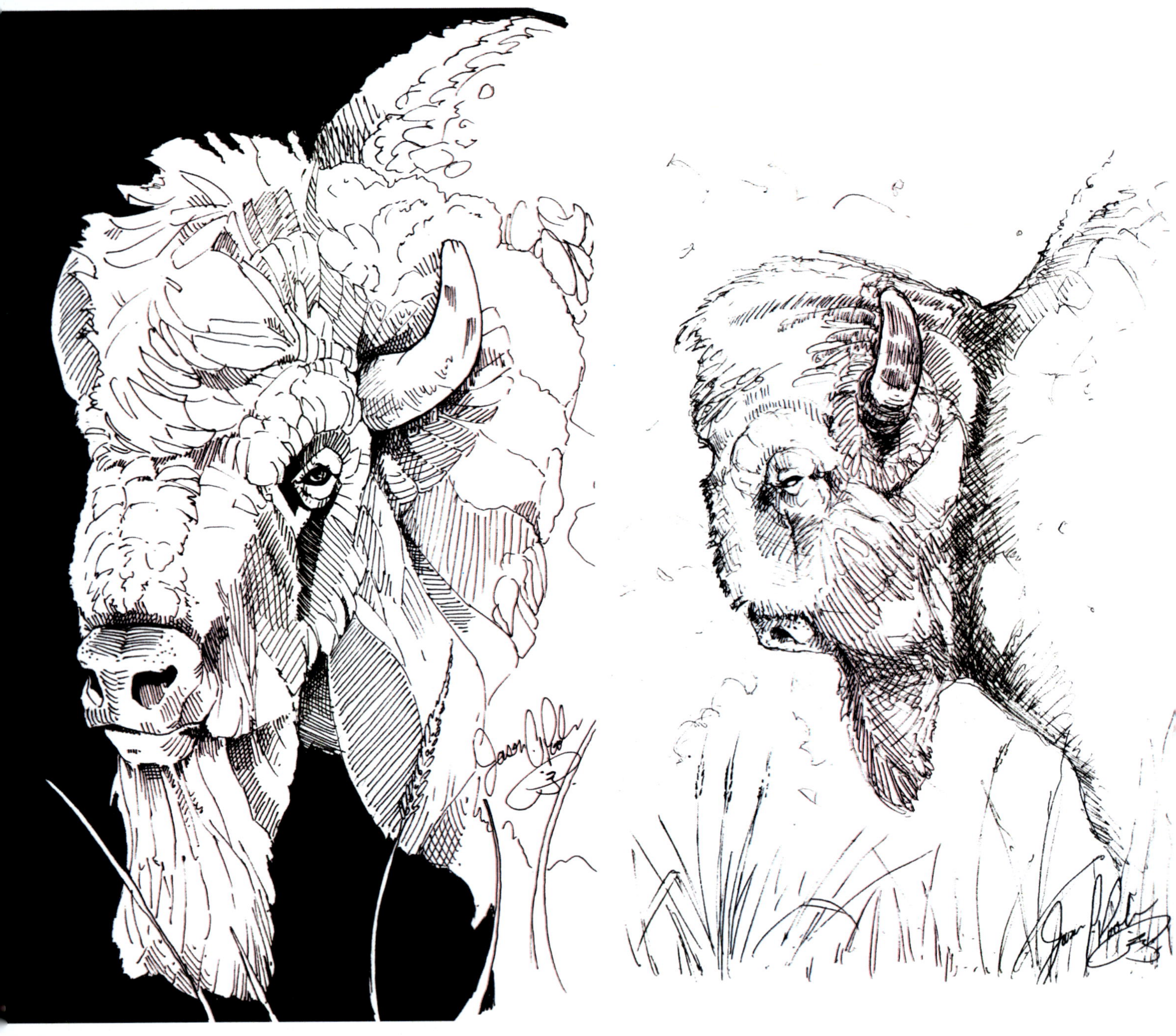

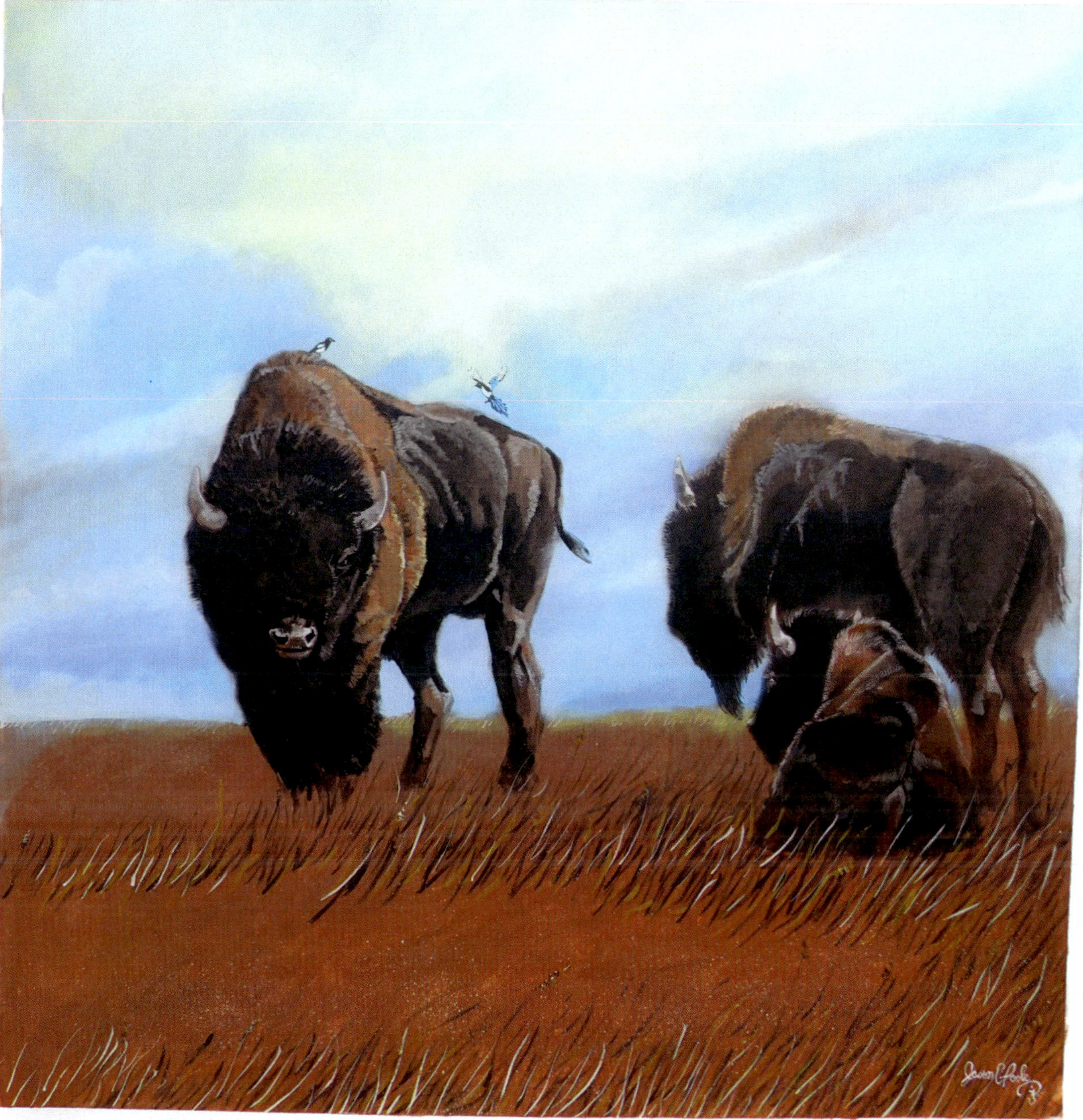

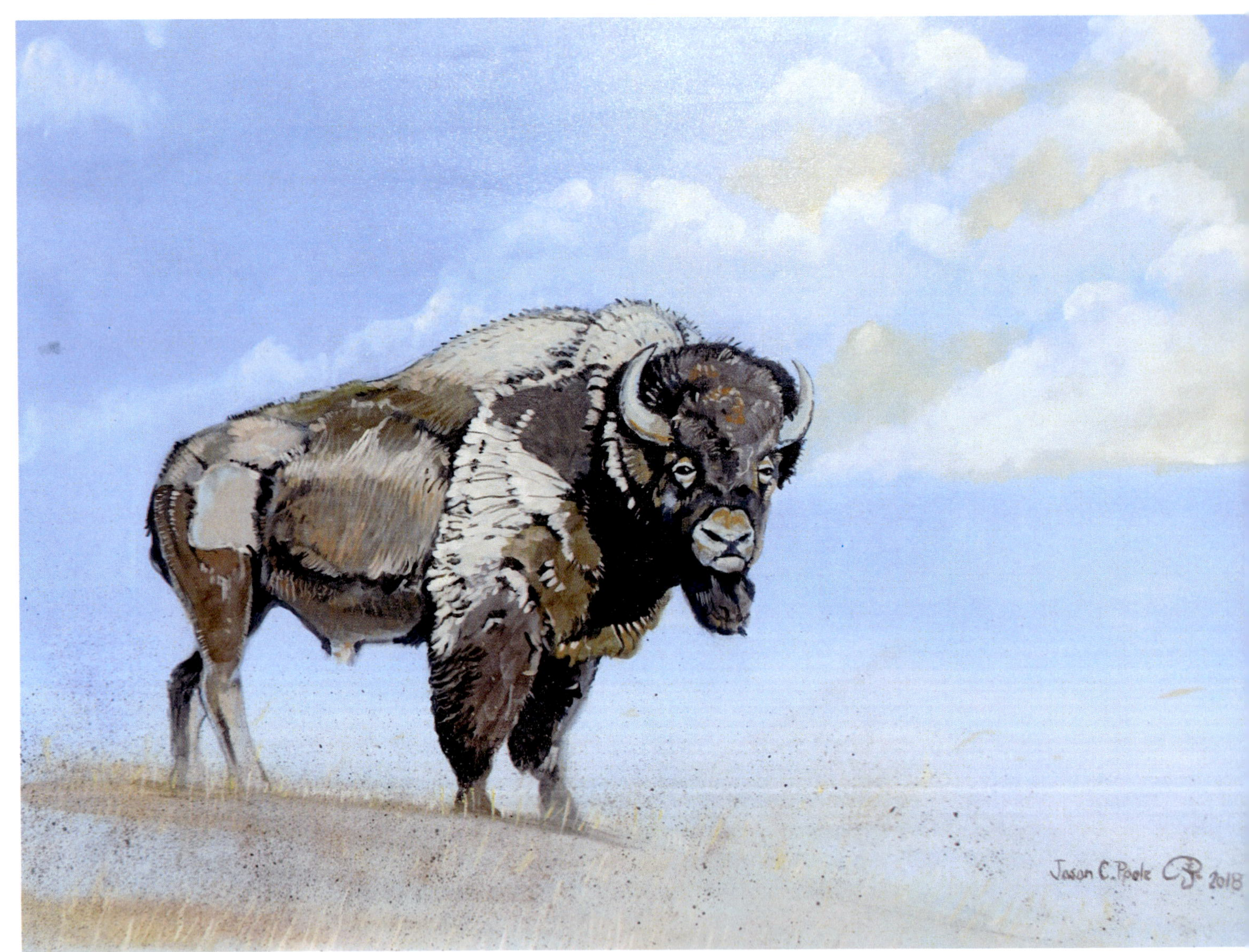
Jason C. Poole   2018

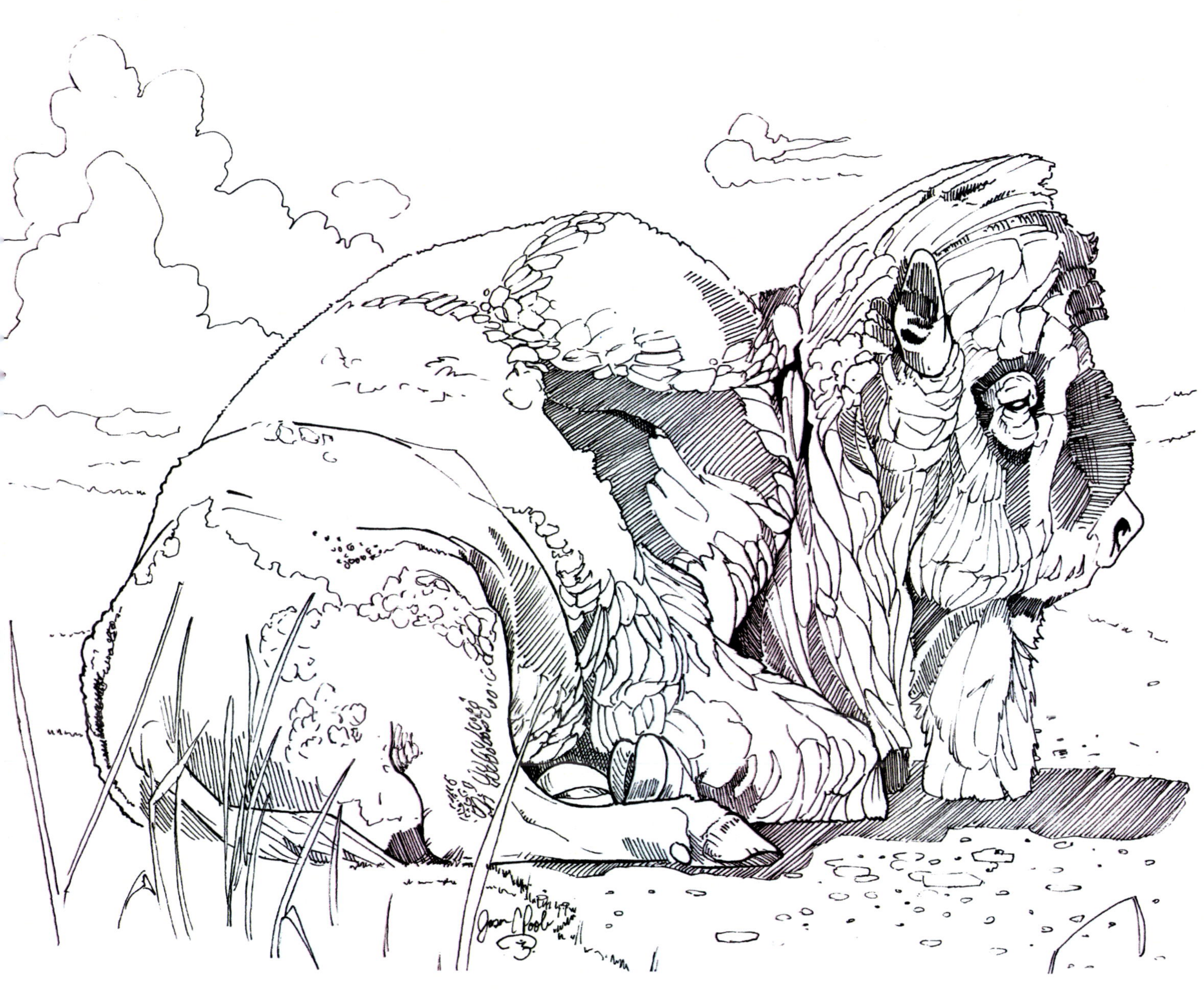

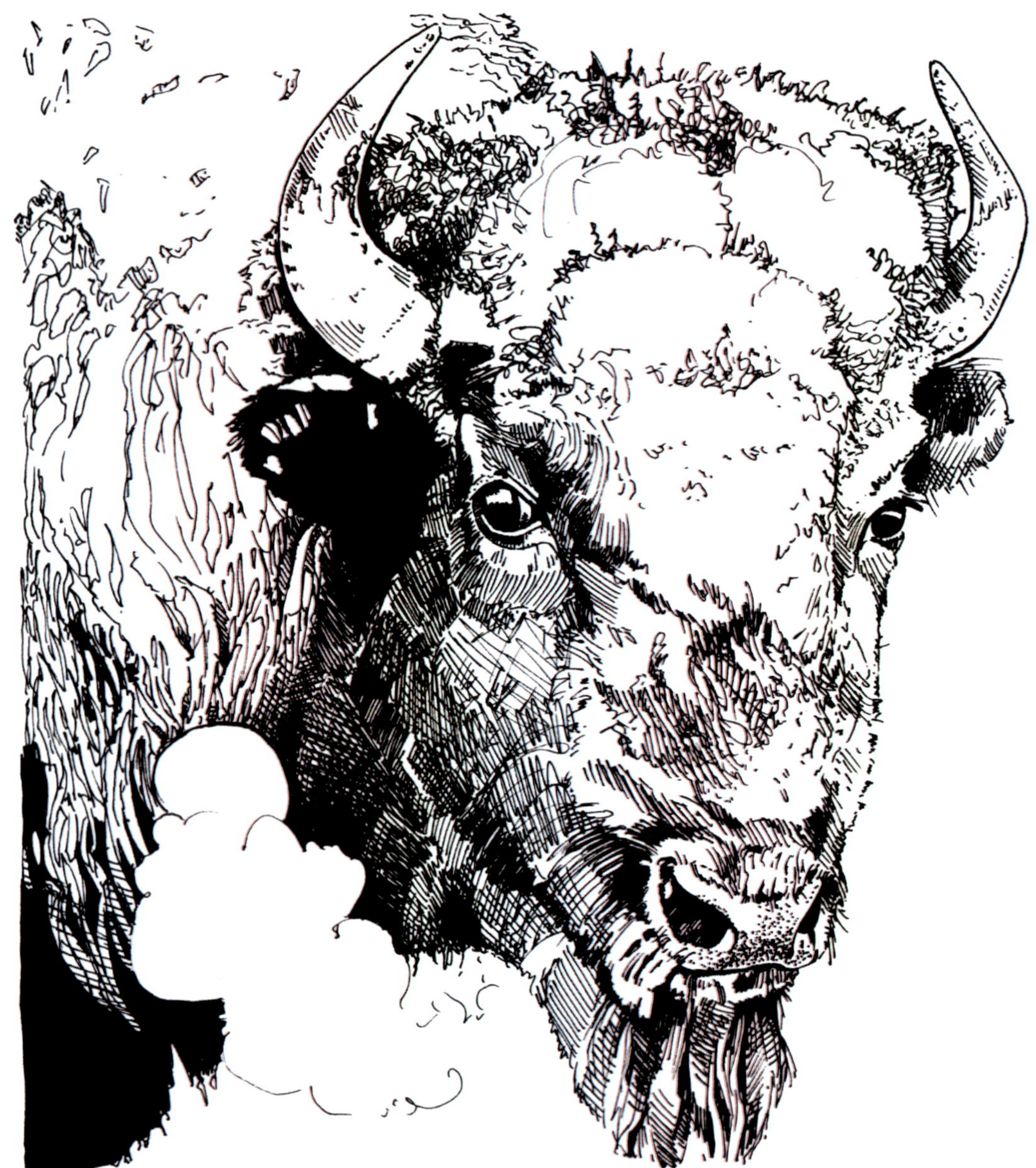

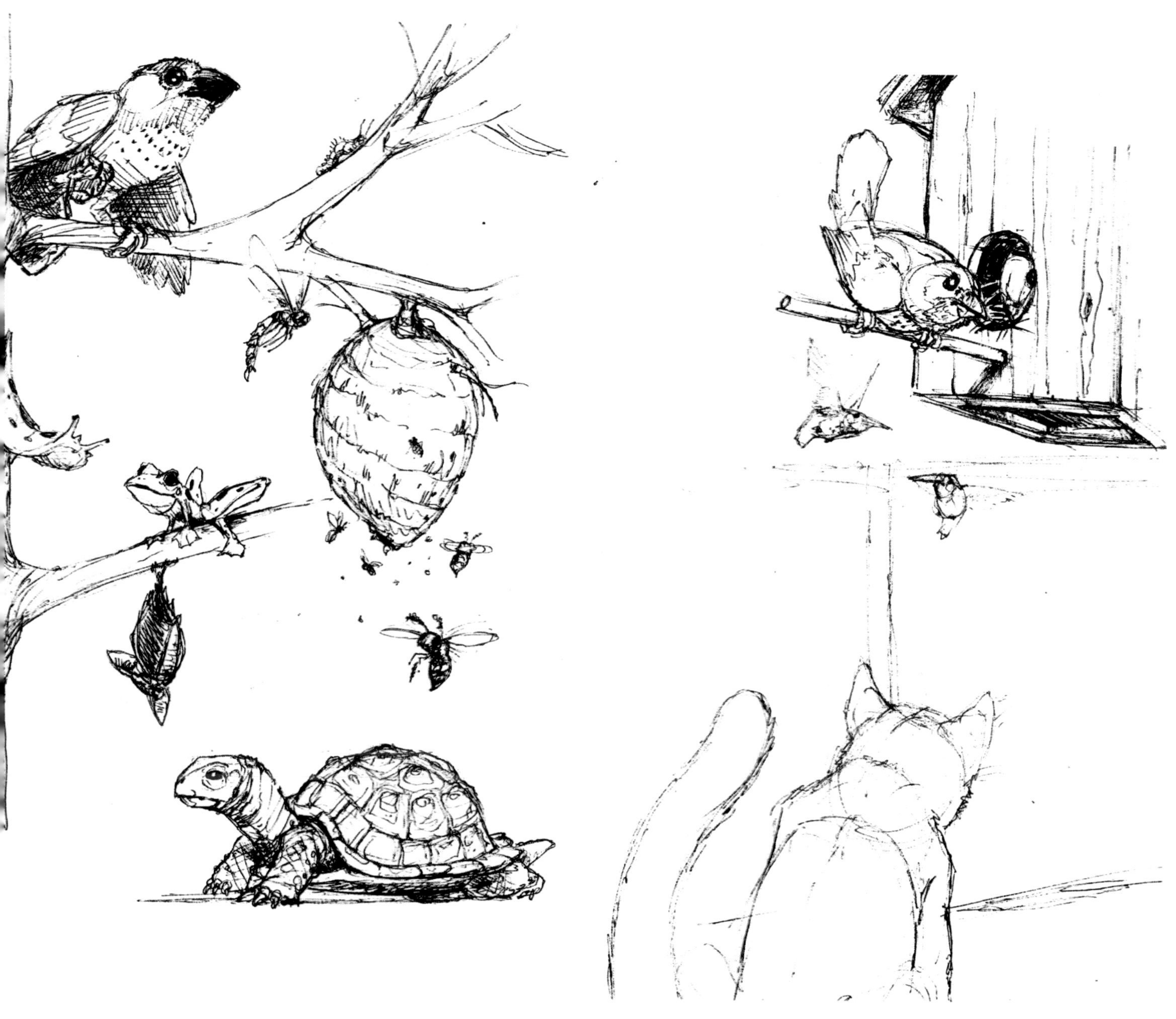

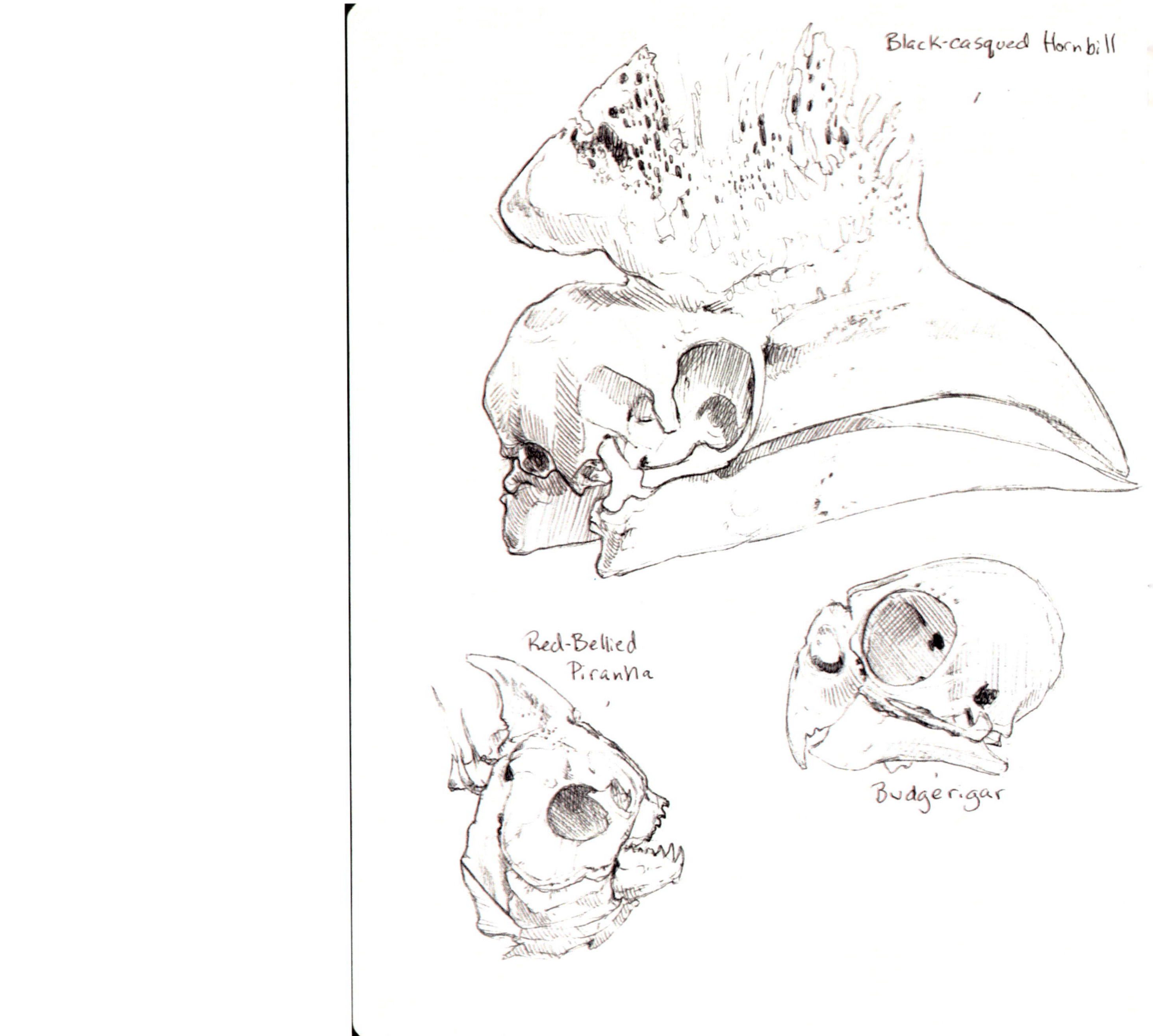
Black-casqued Hornbill
Red-Bellied Piranha
Budgerigar

Giant Moray

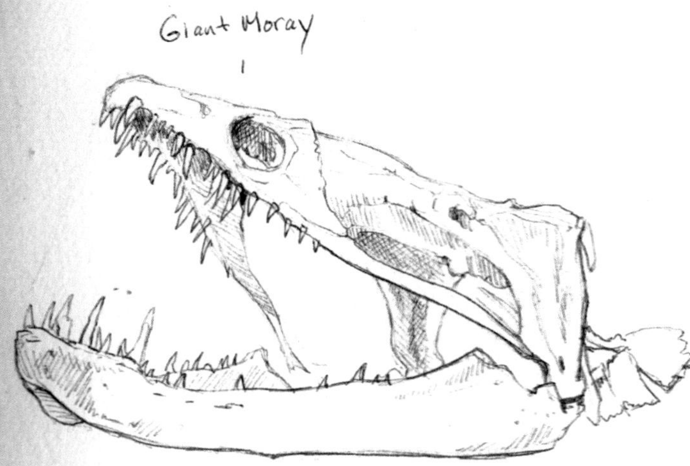

Potto

Chinese water Dragon

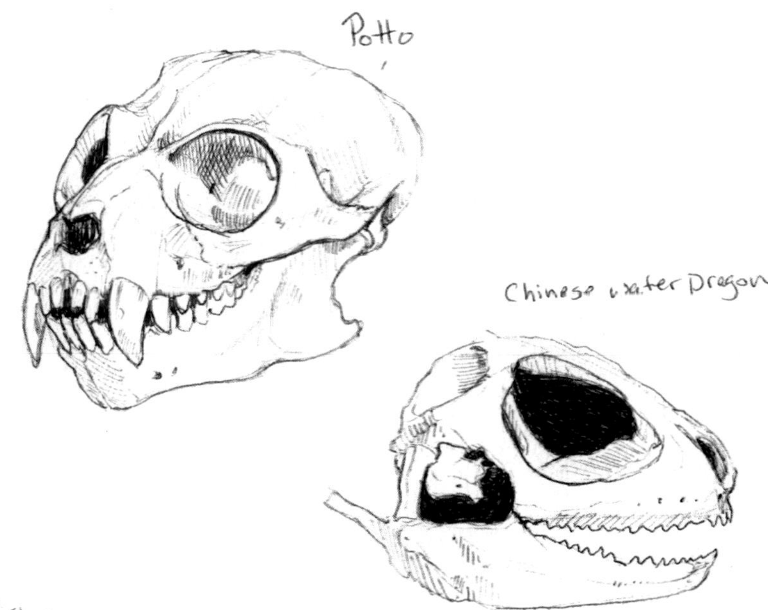

Karen Goerz Fisher

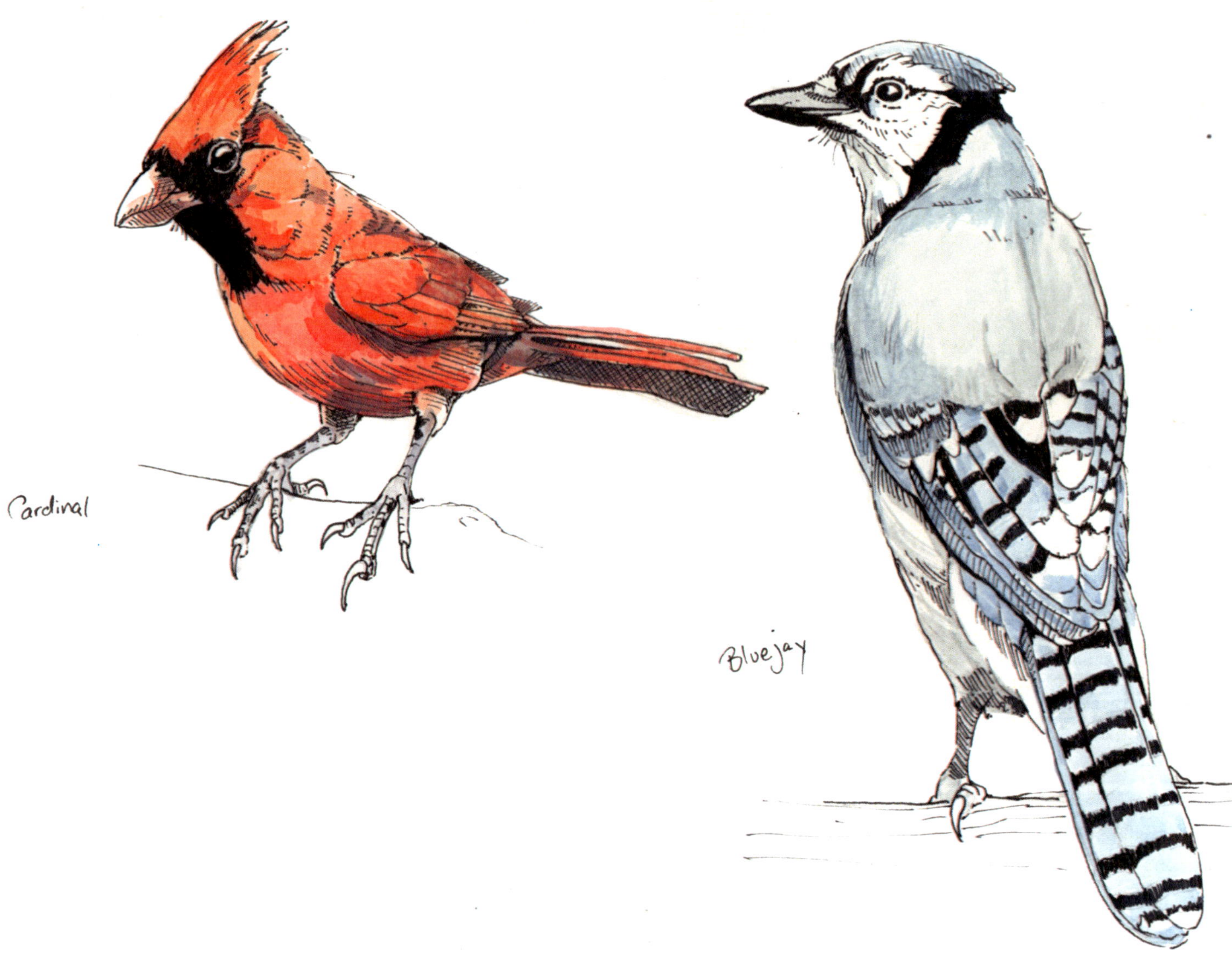
Cardinal
Bluejay

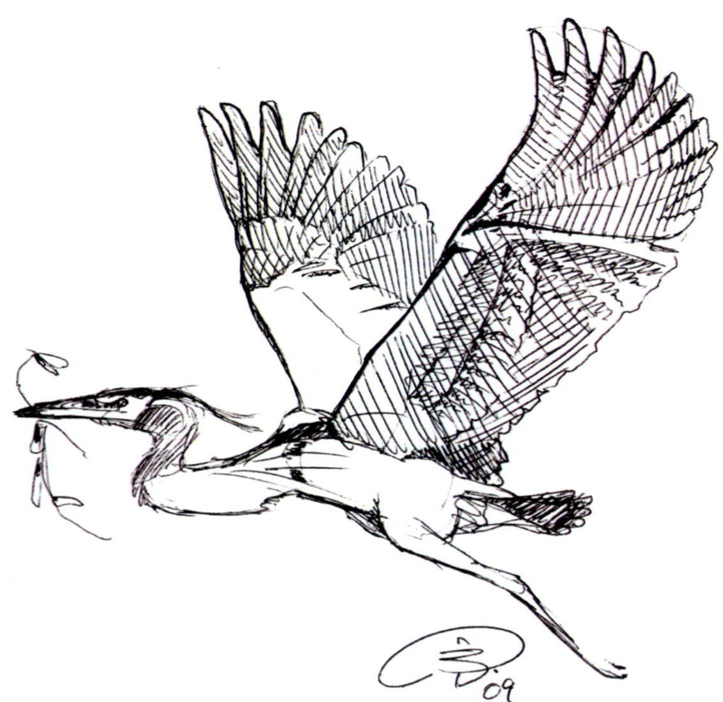

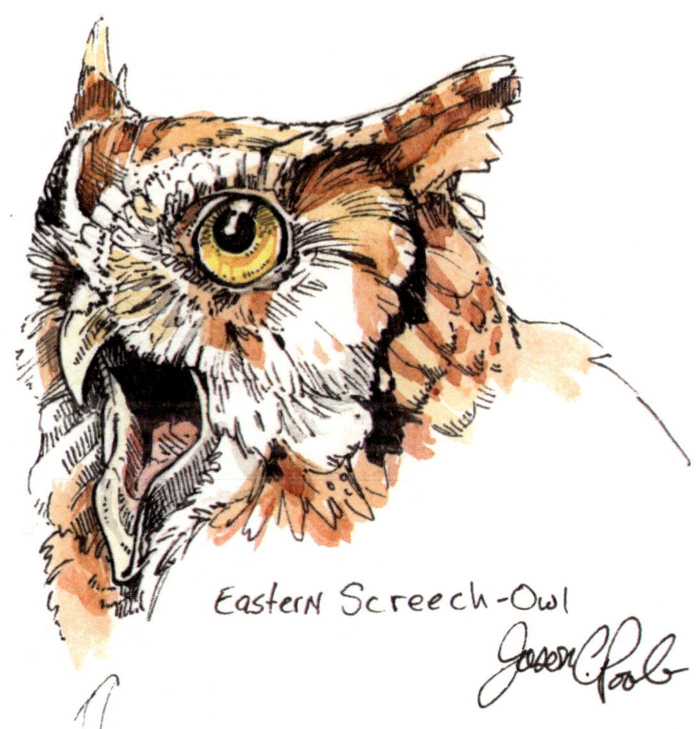

Eastern Screech-Owl

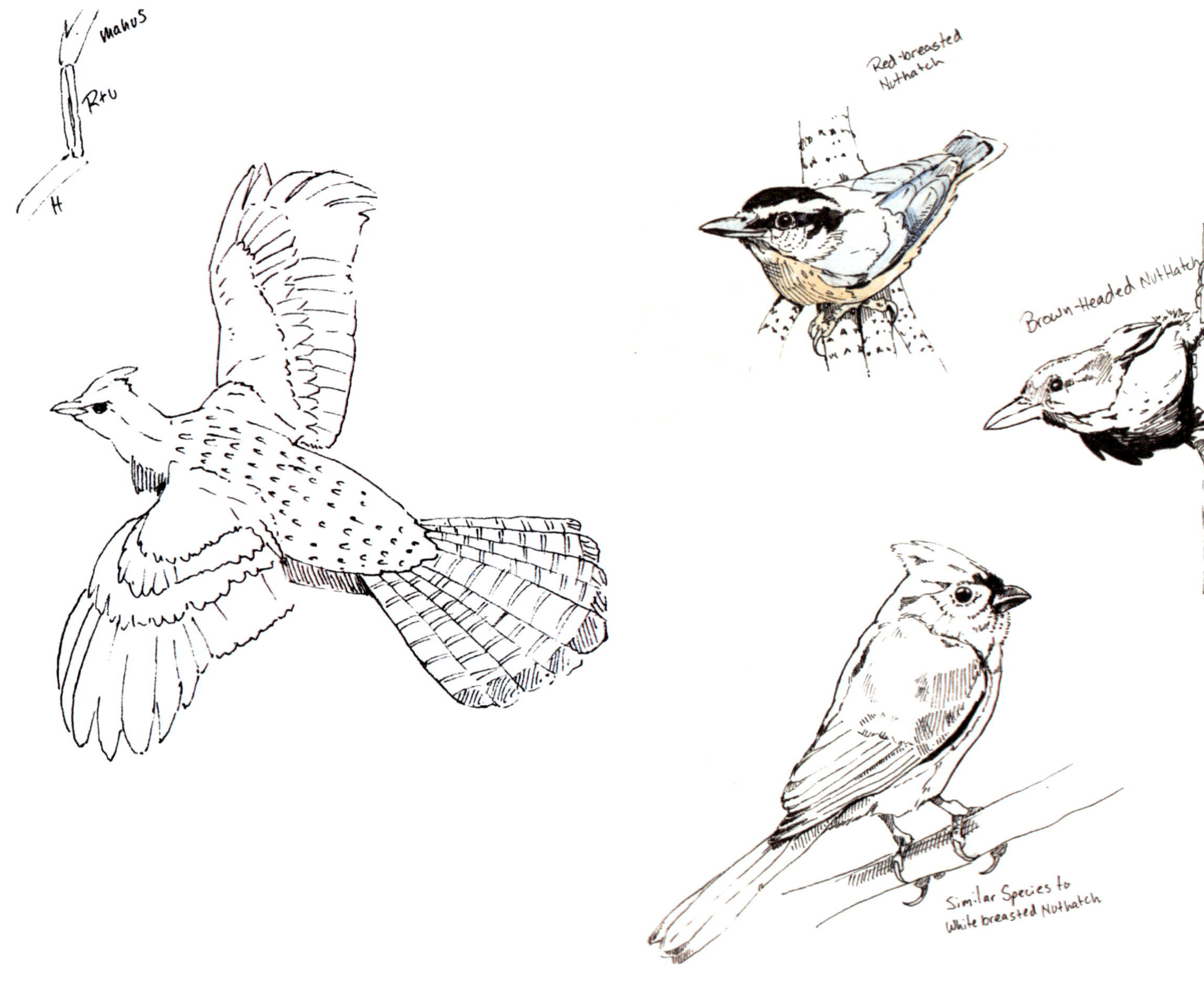

manus
R+u
H
Red-breasted Nuthatch
Brown-Headed Nuthatch
Similar Species to
White breasted Nuthatch

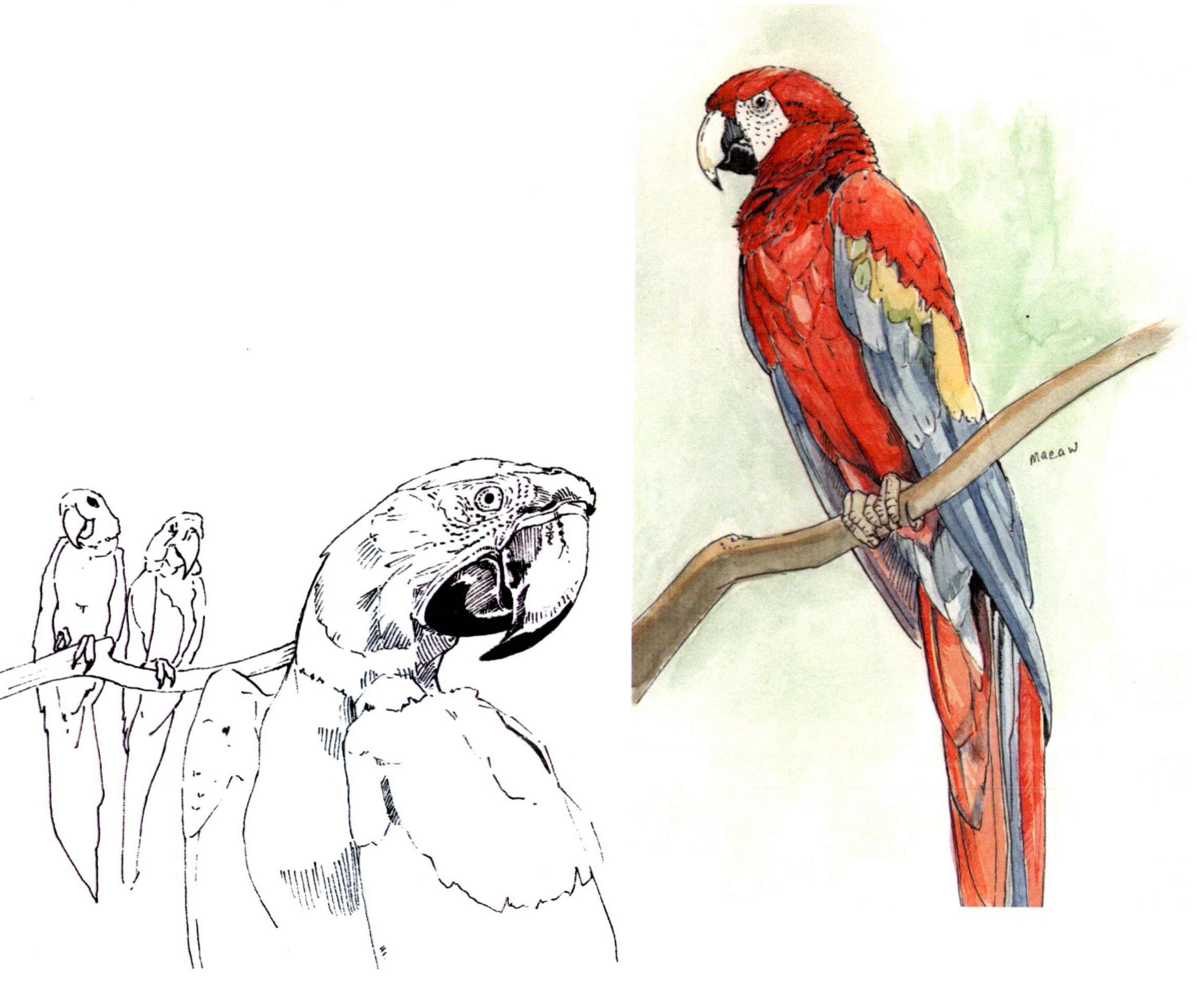
Macaw

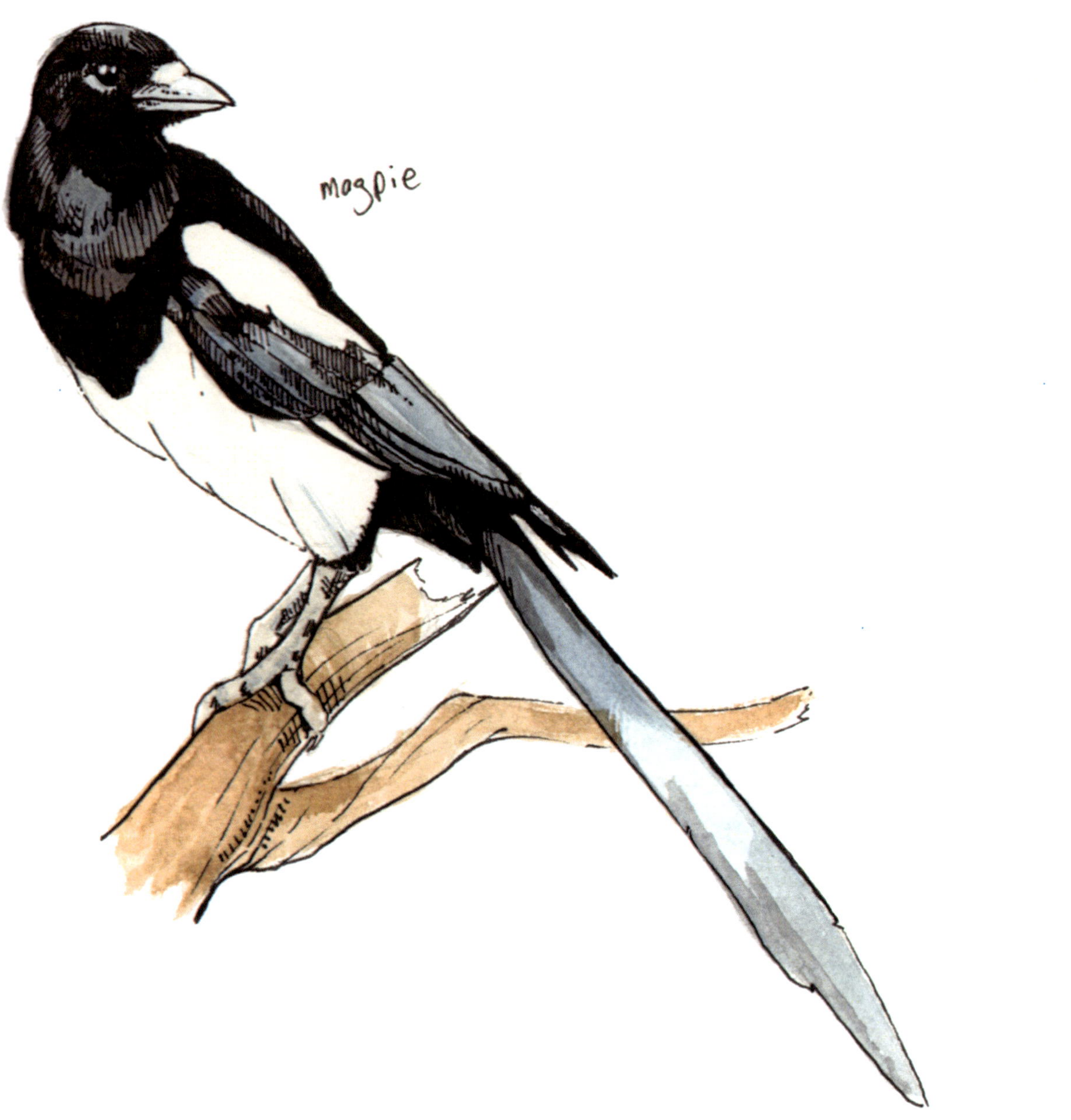

magpie

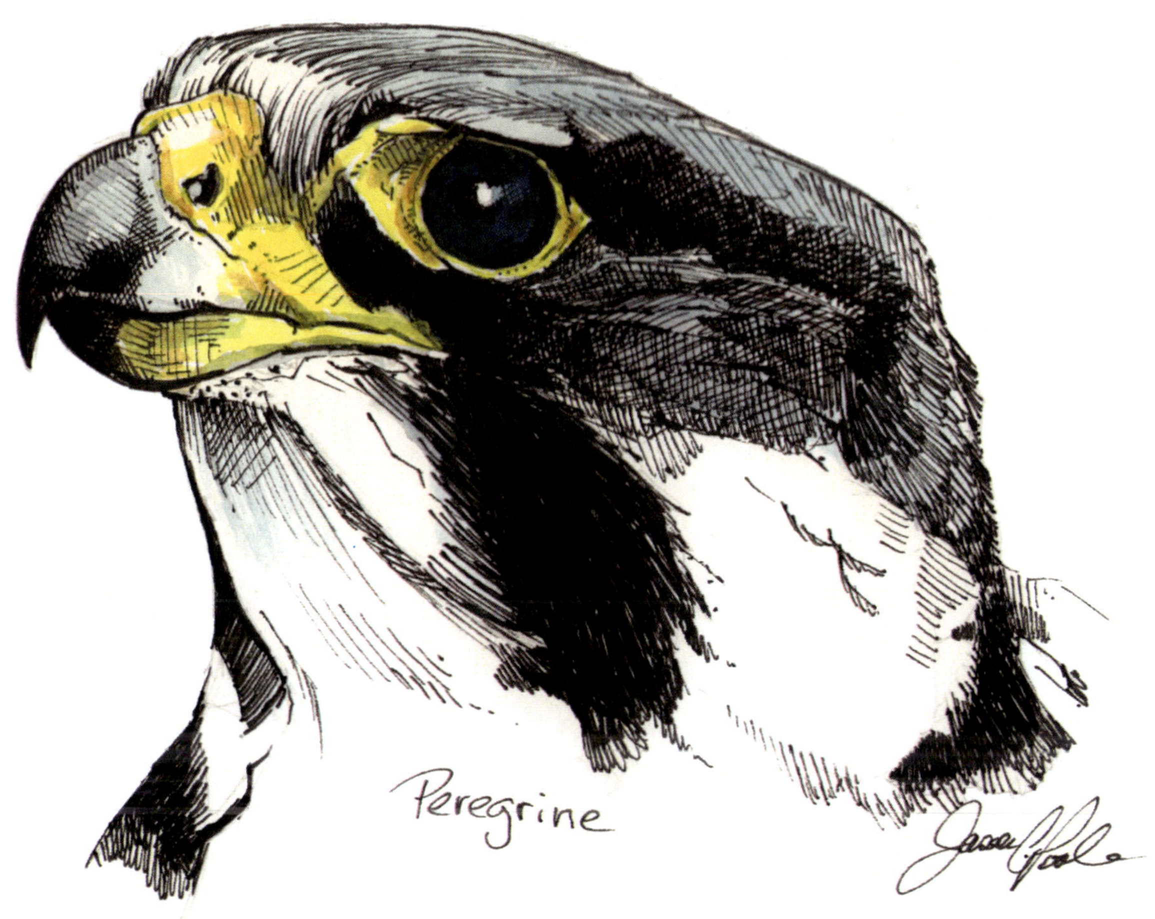

Peregrine

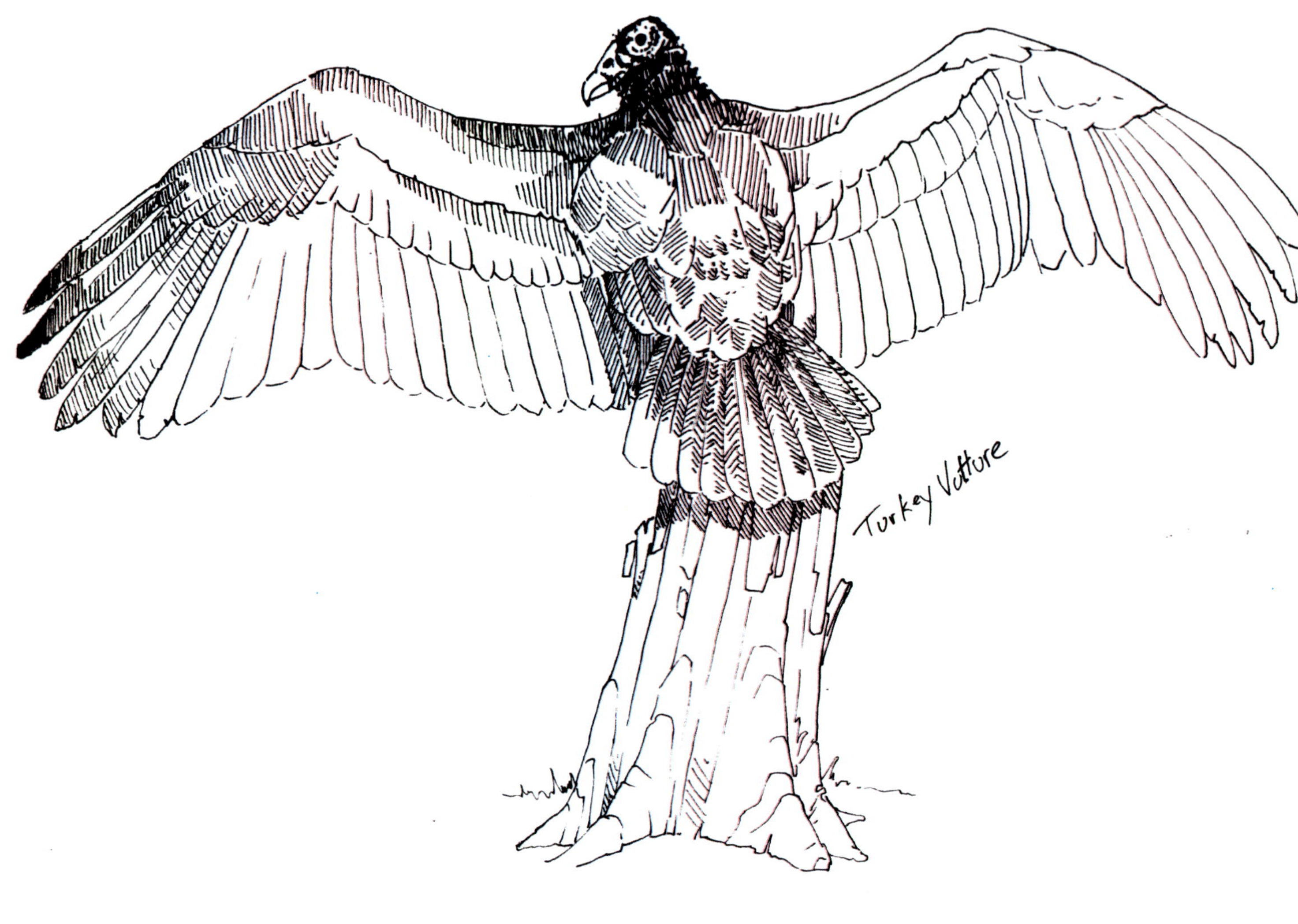
Turkey Vulture

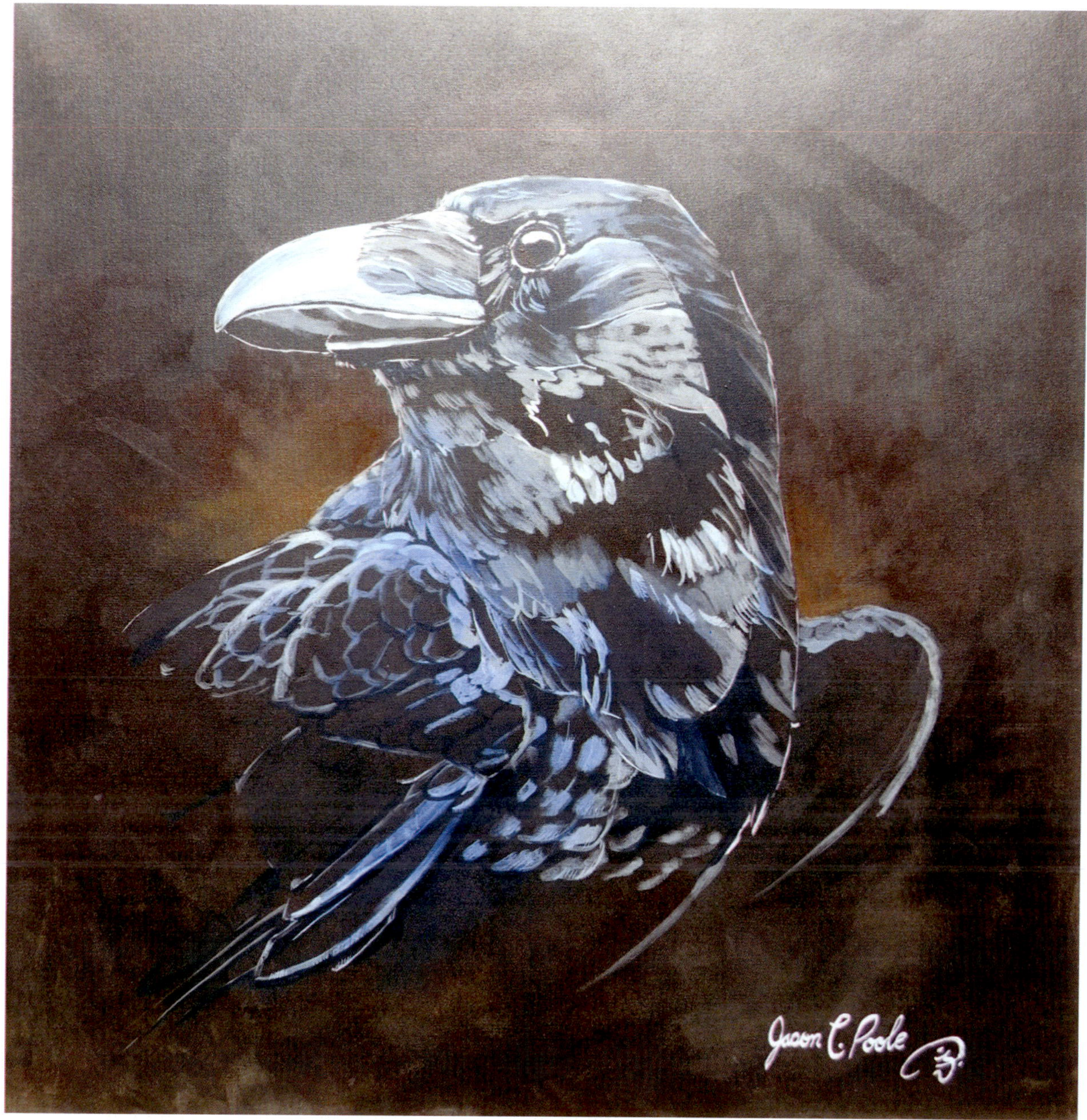

Jason C. Poole

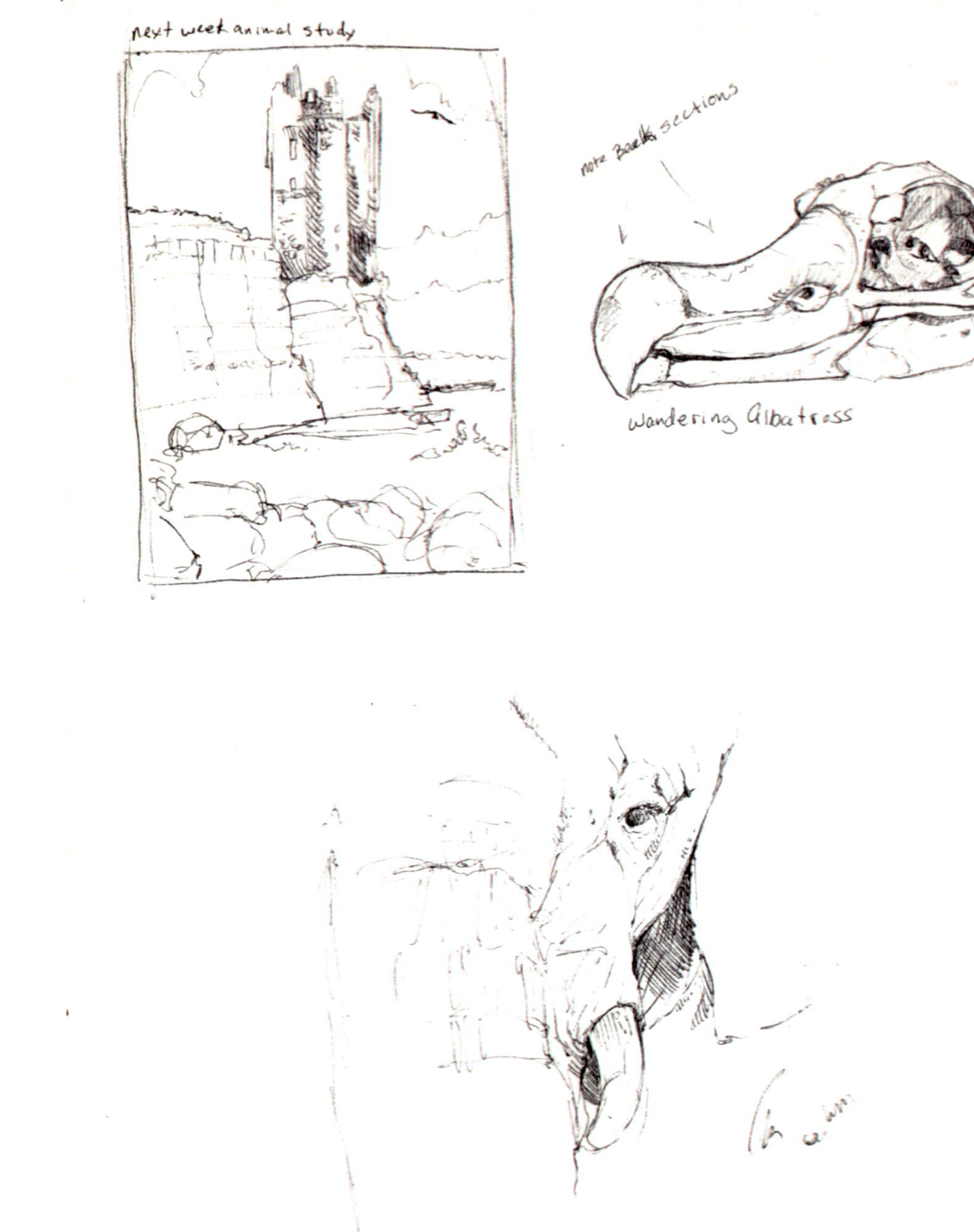
next week animal study
note Baella sections
wandering Albatross

9

Triassic
Period
248 —

Jurassic
Period
206 —

Cretaceous
Period
148 — 65

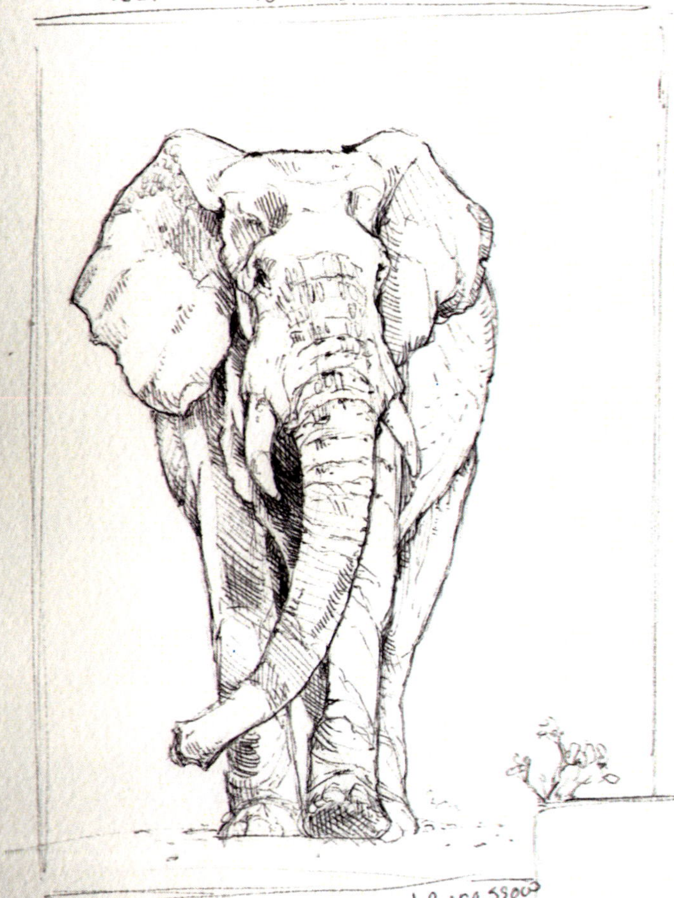

Helmeted Curassow

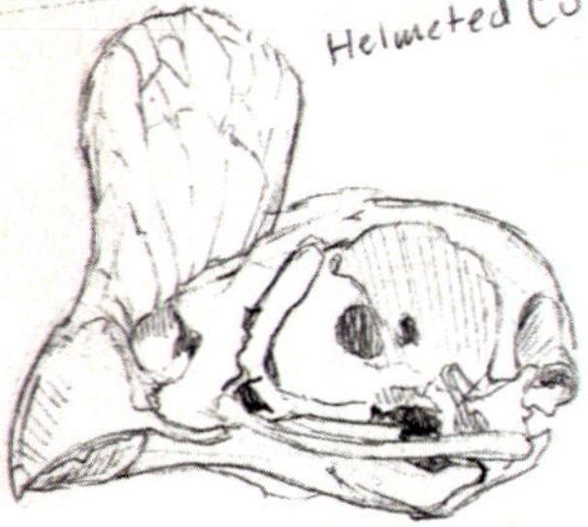

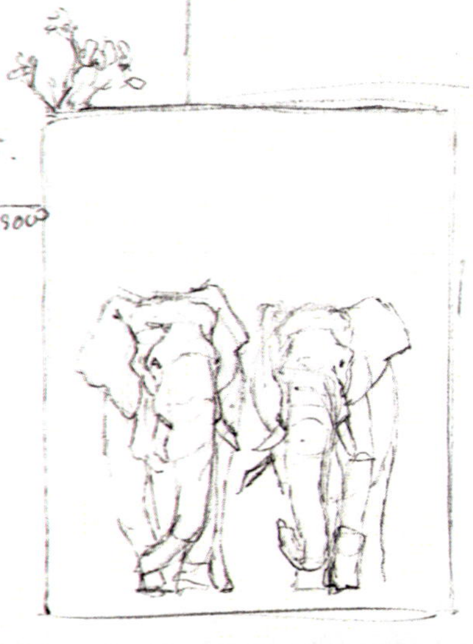

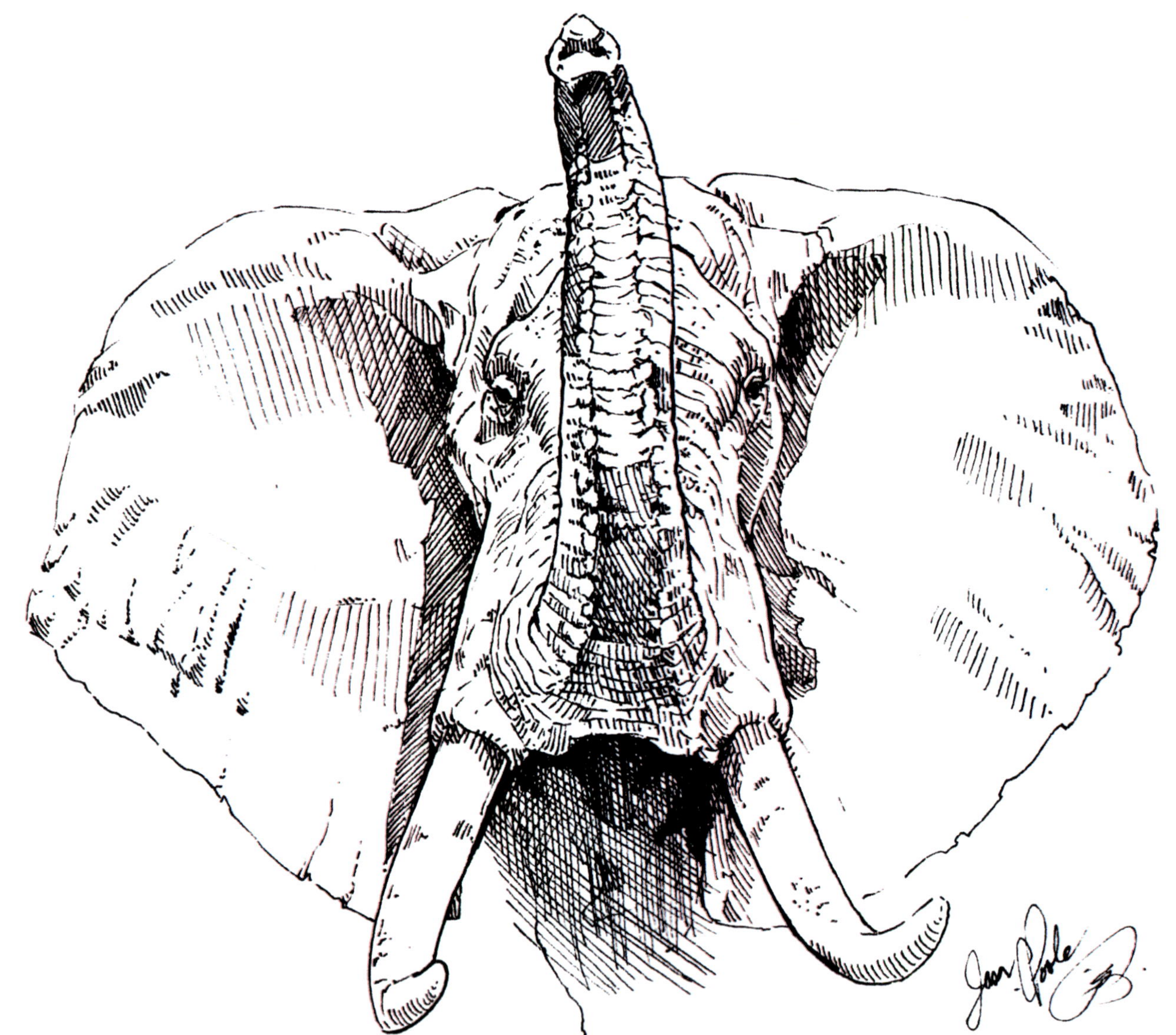

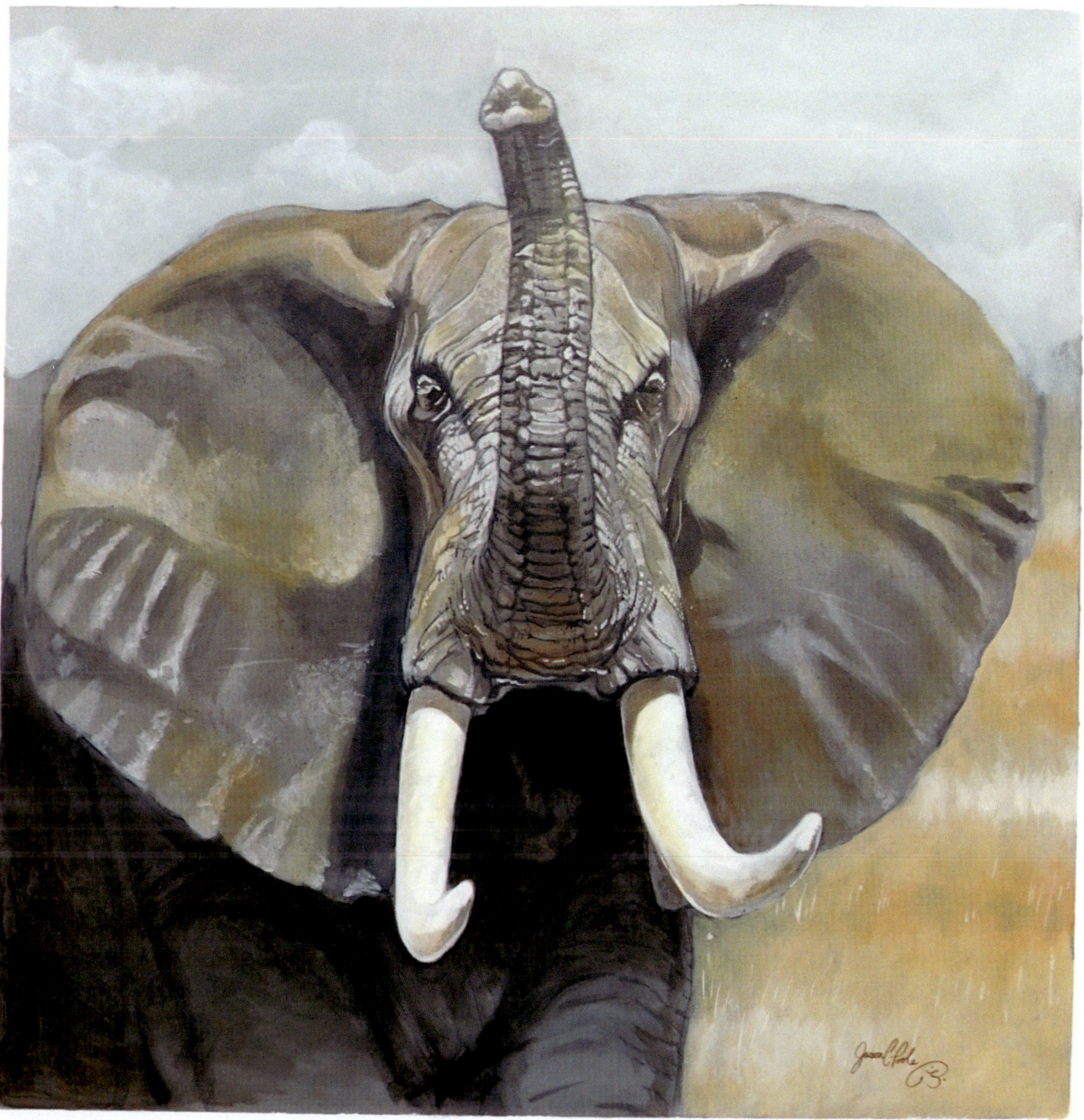

Joyce Poole
B.

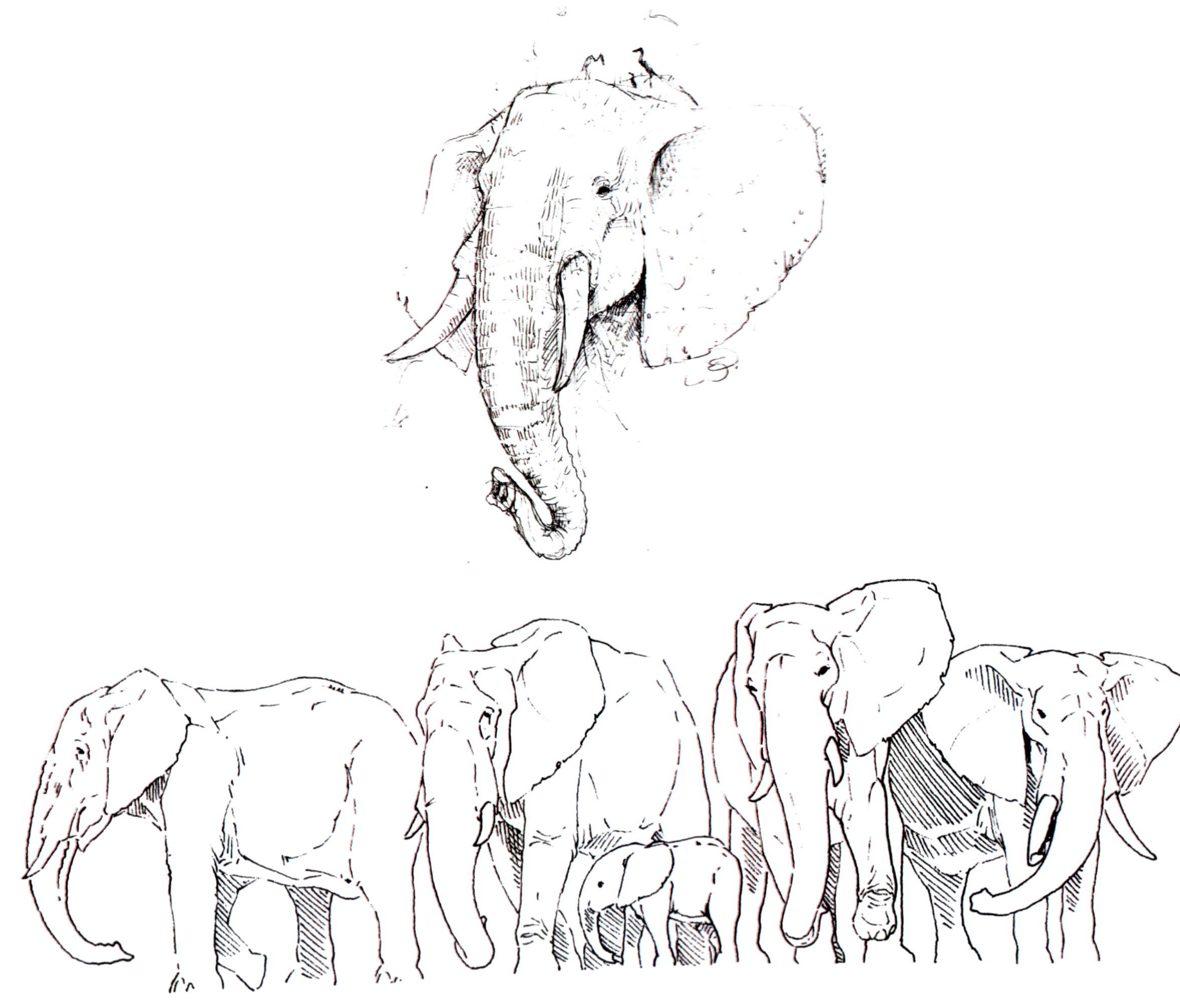

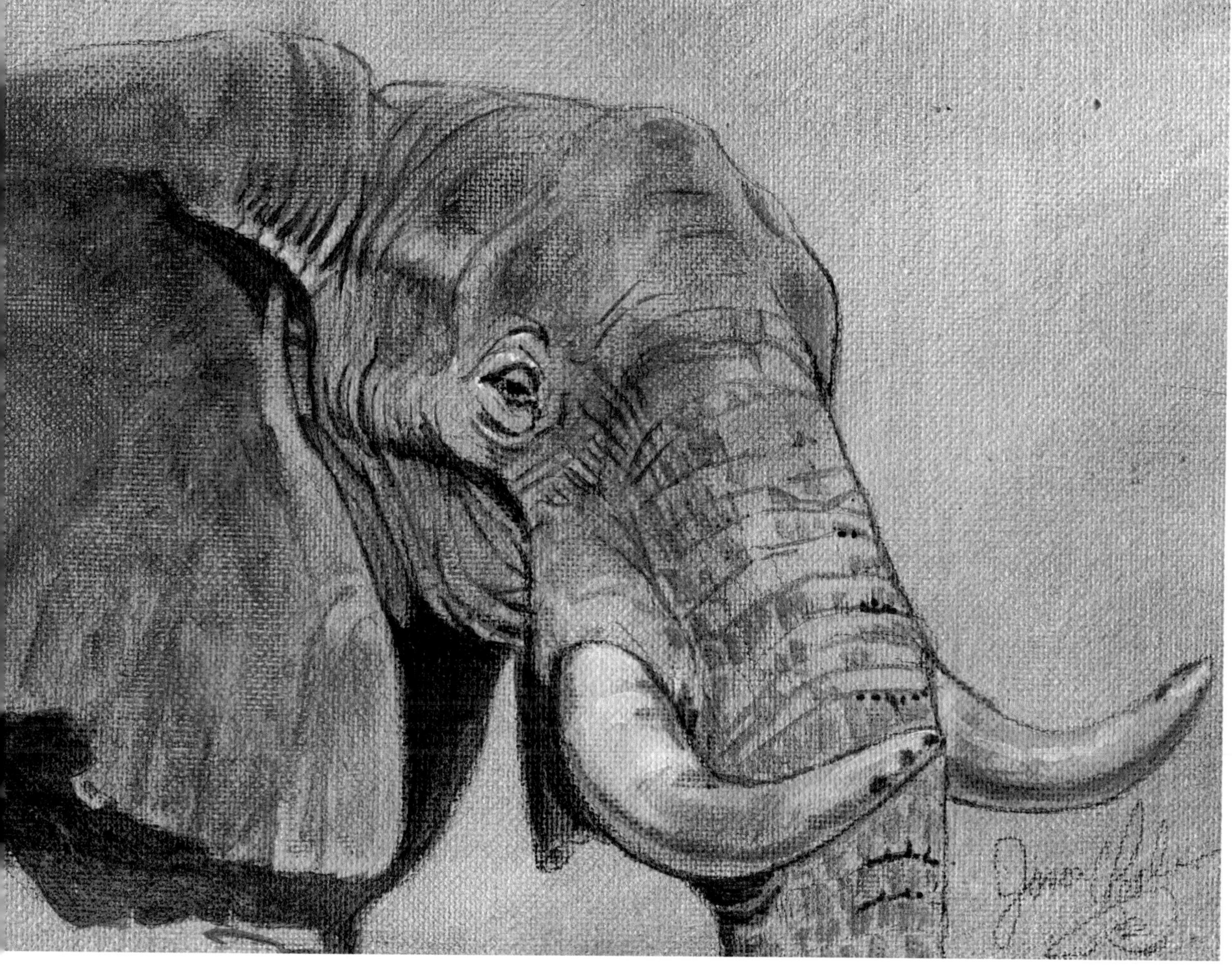

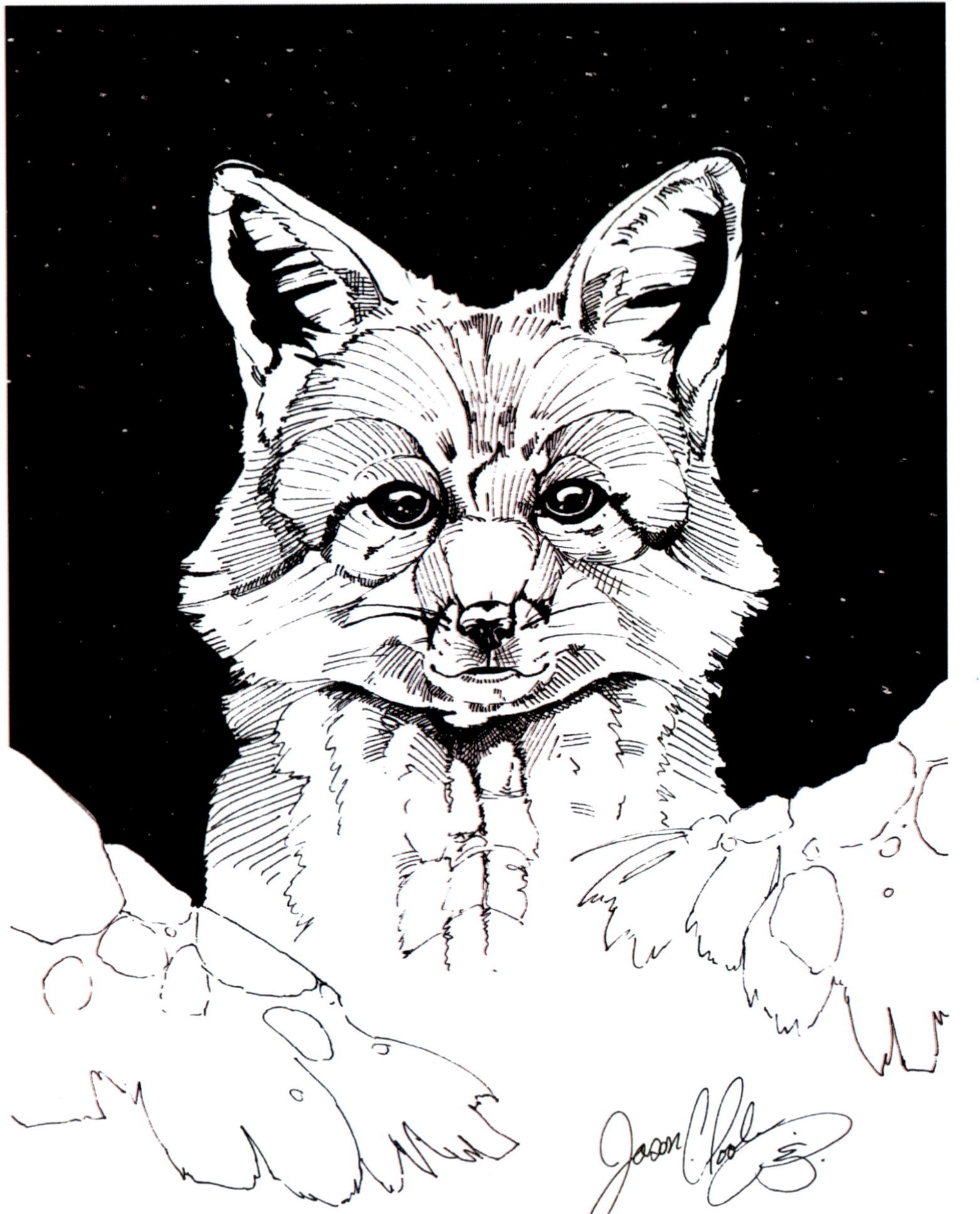

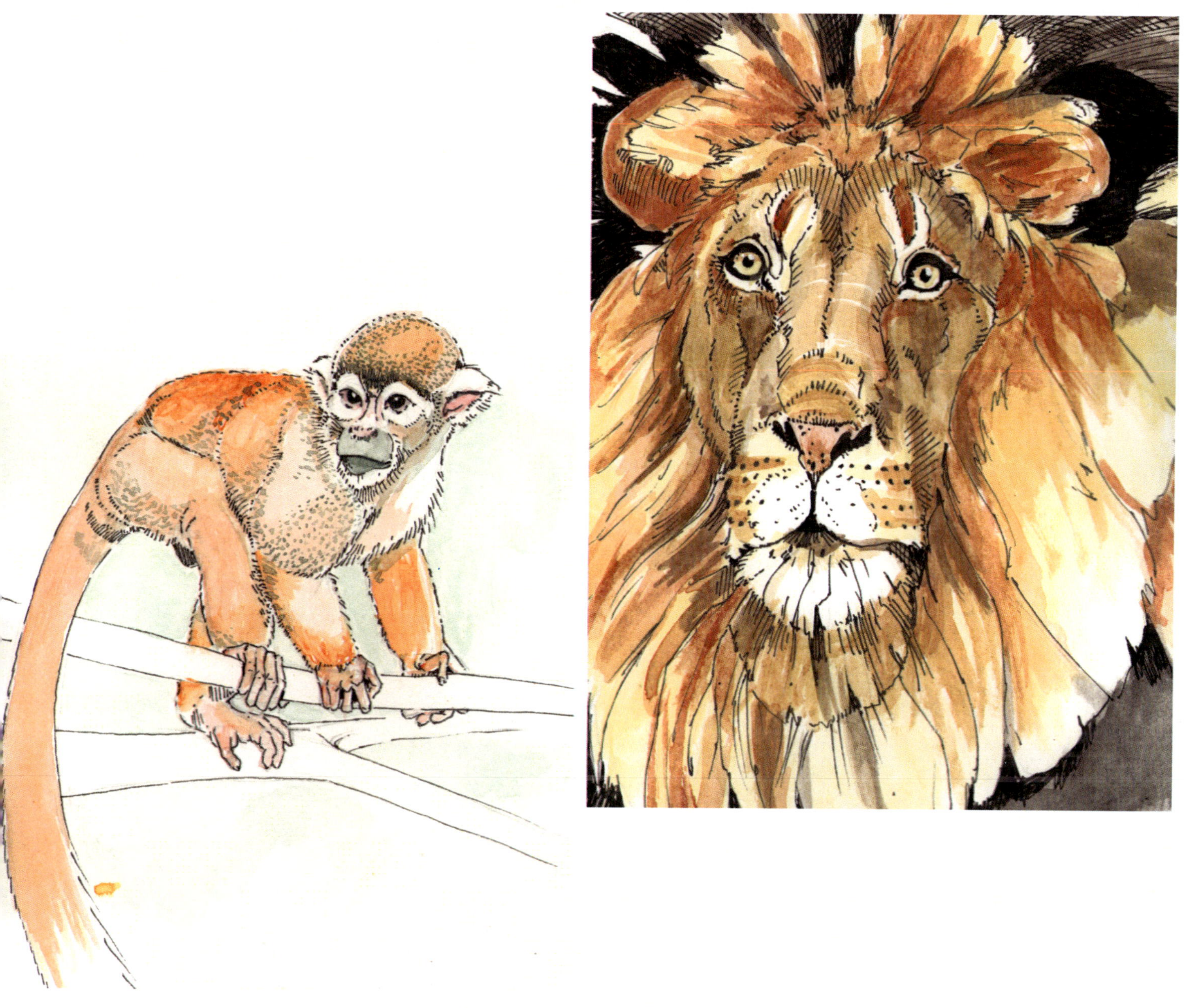

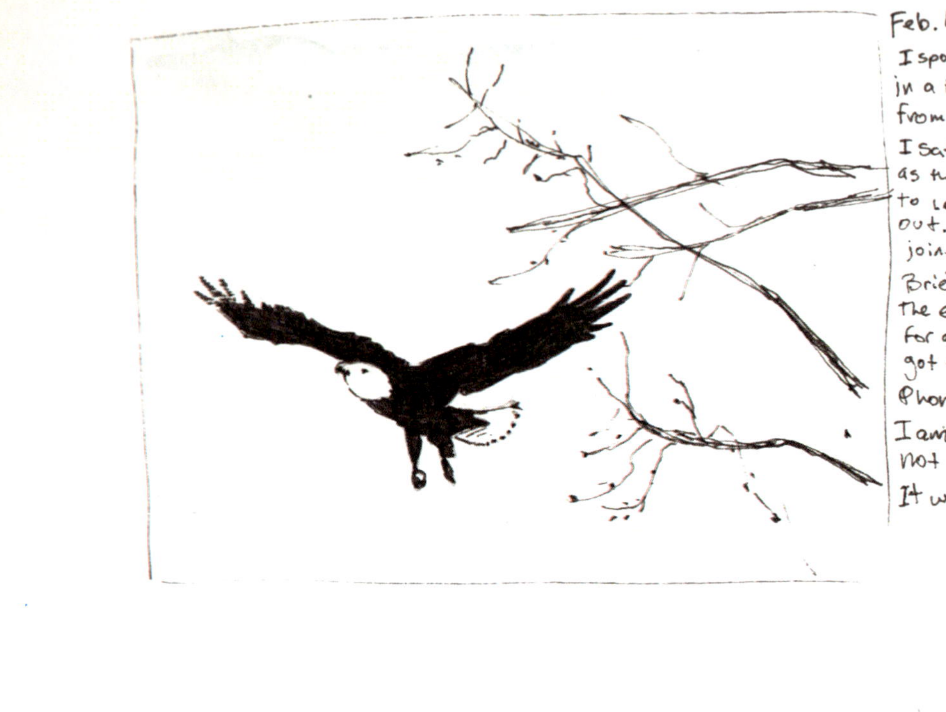

Feb. 10th 10:30-11:00 Am.
I spotted this Baldeagle
in a tree across the street
from my Home.
I sat from 10:30 Am.
as the clouds started
to let the sun come
out. The eagle was
joined By a magpie
Briefly.
The eagle suned it's self
for a bit then I finally
got this photo on my
Phone.
I am sore that I did
not Have my camera.
It was @ 35°F.

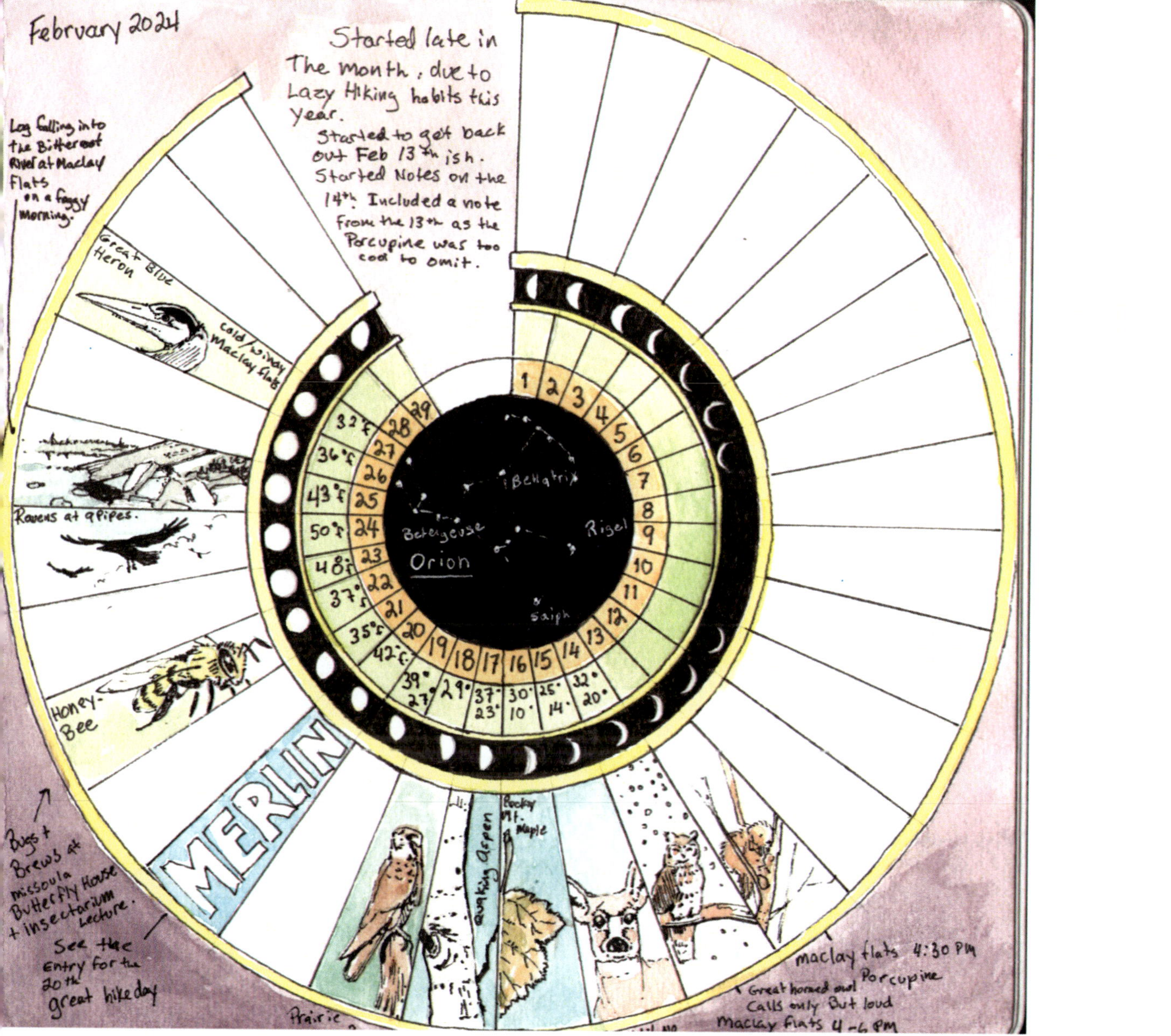

February 2024
Started late in the month, due to lazy hiking habits this year.
Started to get back out Feb 13th ish.
Started Notes on the 14th. Included a note from the 13th as the Porcupine was too cool to omit.
Log falling into the Bitterroot River at Maclay Flats on a foggy morning.
Great Blue Heron
cold/windy Maclay flats
Ravens at 9 Pipes.
Honey-Bee
Bugs + Brews at Missoula House Butterfly + Insectarium Lecture.
See the entry for the 20th great hike day
MERLIN
Prairie
Quaking Aspen
Rocky Mt. maple
Orion
Betelgeuse
Bellatrix
Rigel
Saiph
1 2 3 4 5 6 7 8 9 10 11 12 13 14 15 16 17 18 19 20 21 22 23 24 25 26 27 28 29
32°F 36°F 43°F 50°F 48°F 37°F 35°F 42°F
39° 27° 29° 37° 30° 25° 32° 20°
23° 10° 14°
Maclay flats 4:30 PM Porcupine
Great horned owl calls only But loud
Maclay flats 4-6 PM

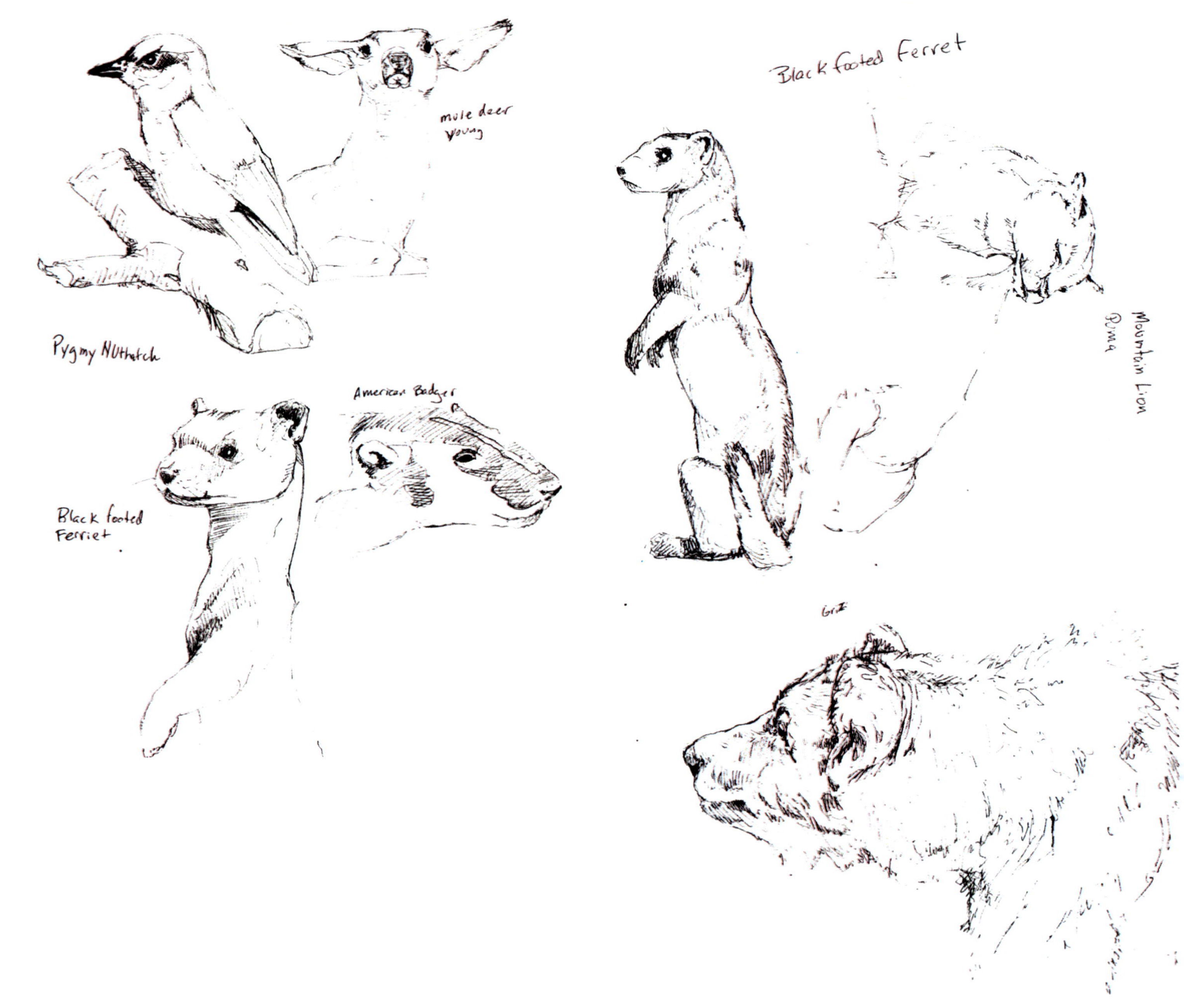

Black footed Ferret
mule deer young
Pygmy NUthatch
Mountain Lion
Puma
American Badger
Black footed Ferriet
Griz

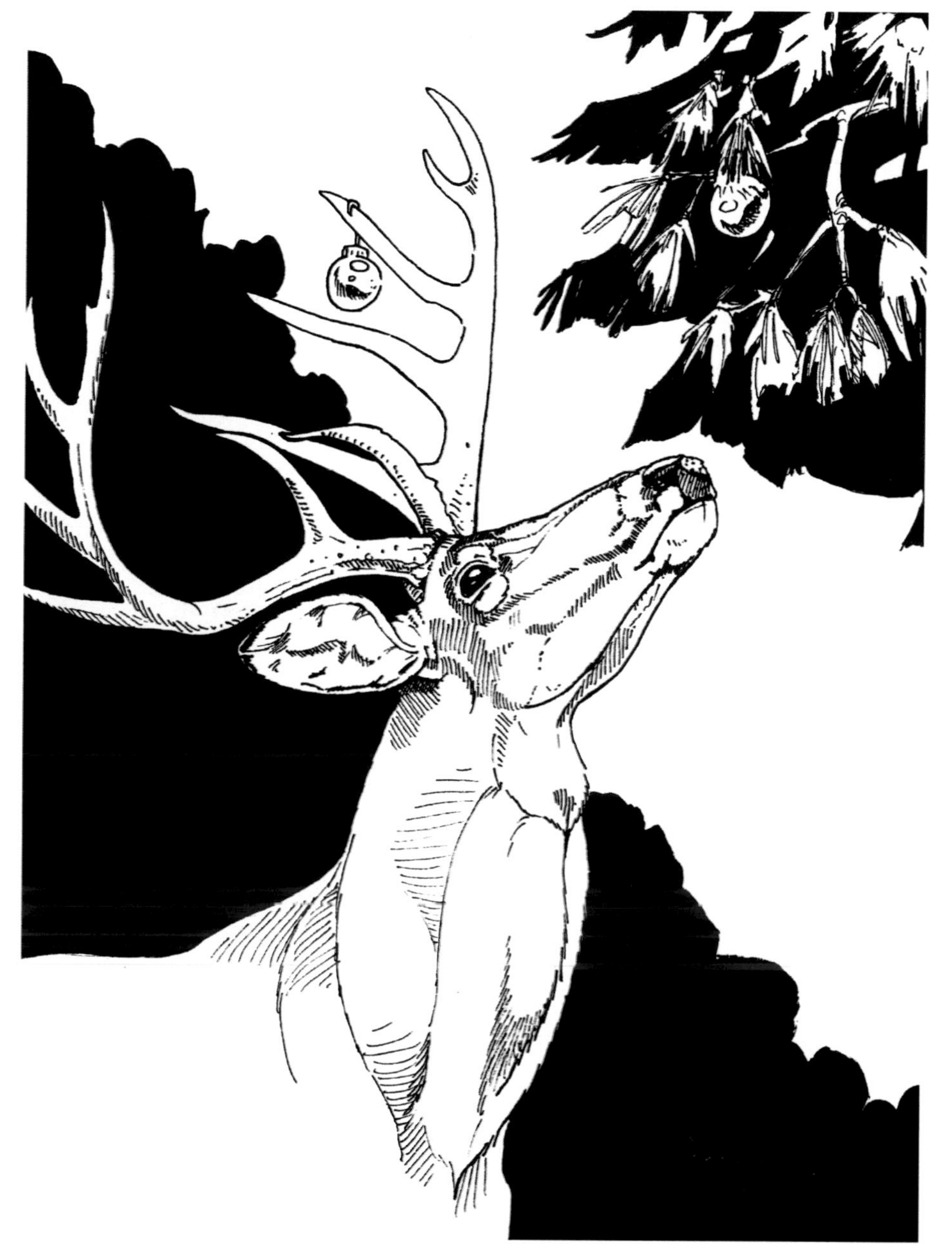

February 16. 2024   CB.

Locality: my residence
   104 Hearth ct. Missoula Mt.
Temp: 27°f Clear sky. Breezy
      Light snow on the ground.
Time : 10:30 Am

The males seem to have Shed thier
antlers.
The deer In the yard are pawing
at the snow to get at the grass and
fall leaves
They have become very tolerant of people
and will often watch me as I
walk to my car. Even the sound of
the motor seems only to be
cause for attention.

there are now young from this year
as well as last roaming around in
small pods.

Sometimes it feels like they are
just keeping an eye on us.

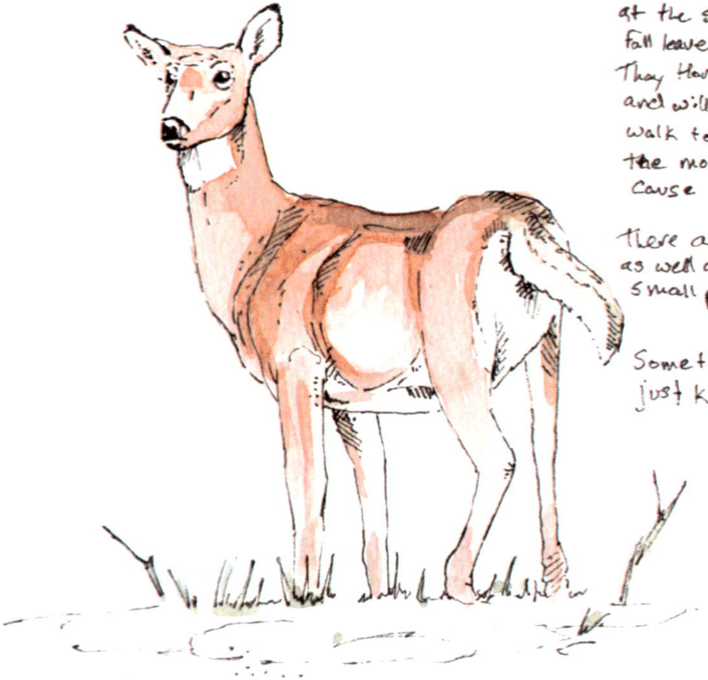

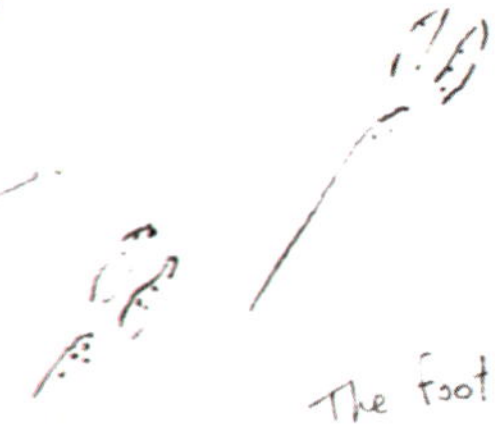

The foot Prints
Have a scuff or
drag even in very
light or shallow
snow

February 18. 2024

Surface anatomy of a Bird

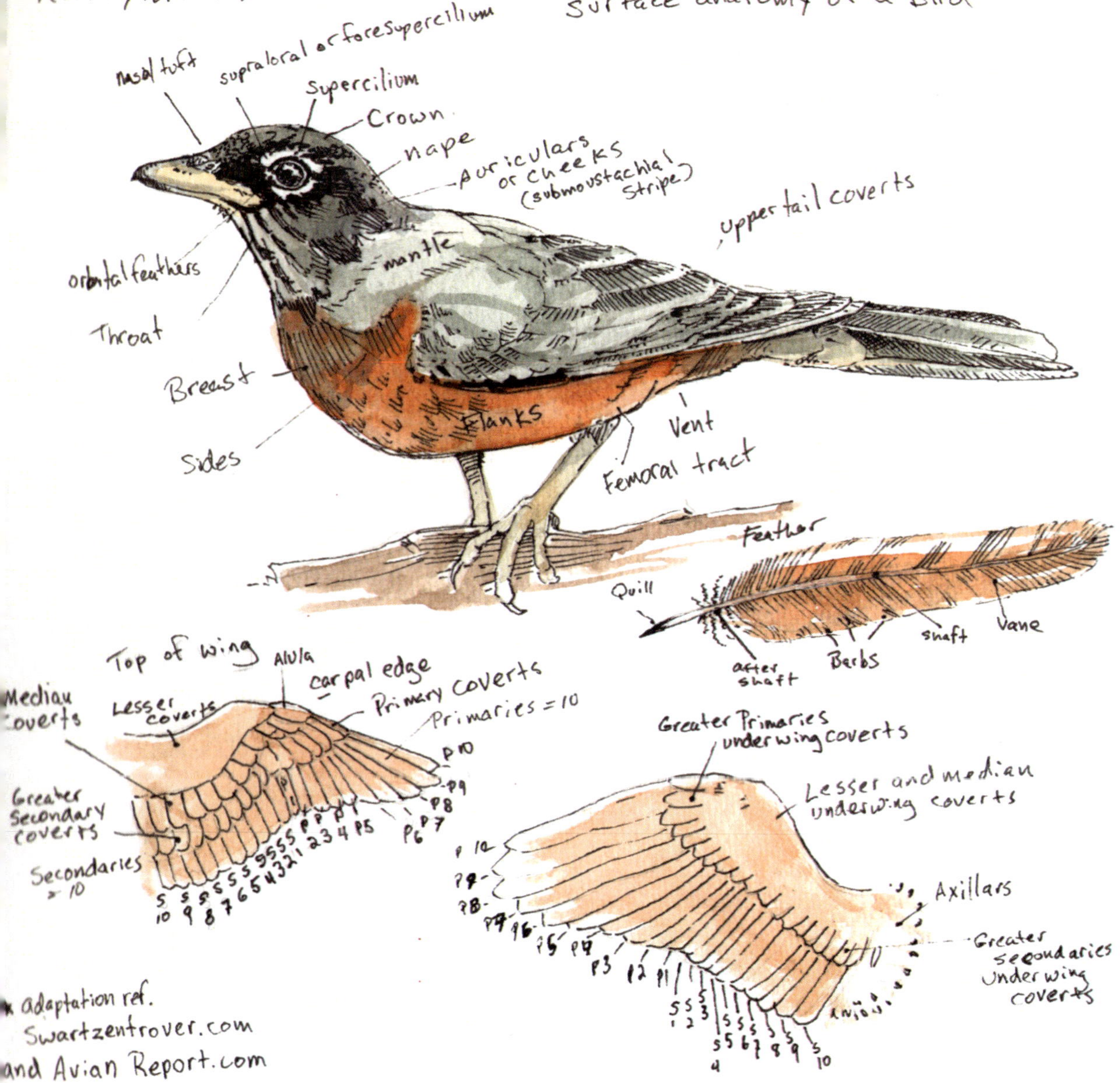

nasal tuft

supraloral or fore supercilium

supercilium

Crown

nape

Auriculars or cheeks (submoustachial stripe)

upper tail coverts

orbital feathers

mantle

Throat

Breast

Sides

Flanks

Vent

Femoral tract

Feather

Quill

after shaft

Barbs

shaft

Vane

Top of wing

Alula

carpal edge

Primary coverts

Primaries = 10

P10

P9

P8

P7

P6   P5

P P P
2 3 4

P1

Median coverts

Lesser coverts

Greater Secondary coverts

Secondaries = 10

S S S S S S
10 9 8 7 6 5

S S S S
4 3 2 1

Greater Primaries underwing coverts

Lesser and median underwing coverts

Axillars

Greater secondaries underwing coverts

P 12

P9

P8

P7

P6

P5   P4

P3   P2   P1

S S S
1 2 3

S S S
5 6 7

S
4

S S
8 9

S
10

adaptation ref.
Swartzentrover.com
and Avian Report.com

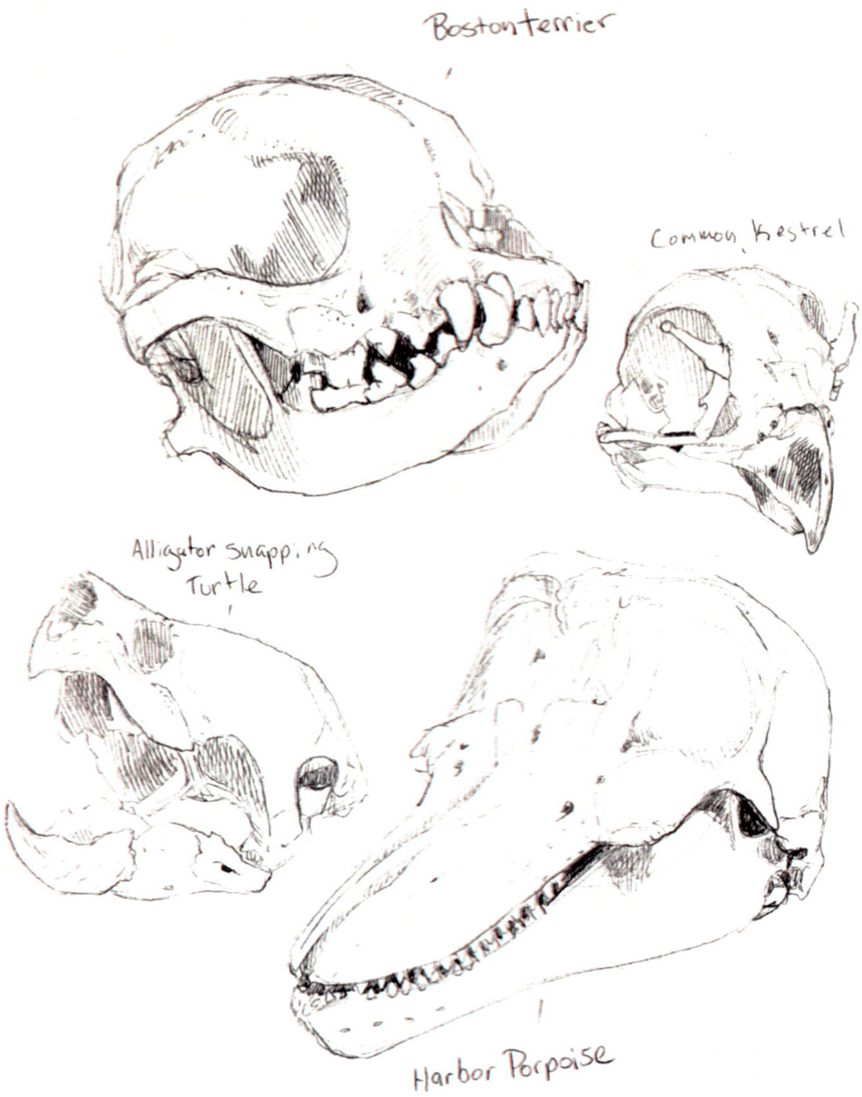

Boston terrier
Common Kestrel
Alligator snapping
Turtle
Harbor Porpoise

Razor-billed Curassow

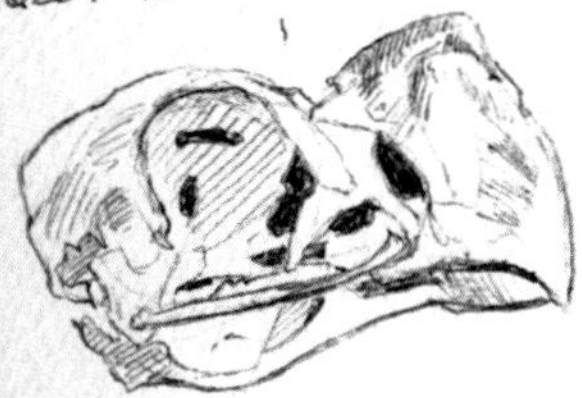

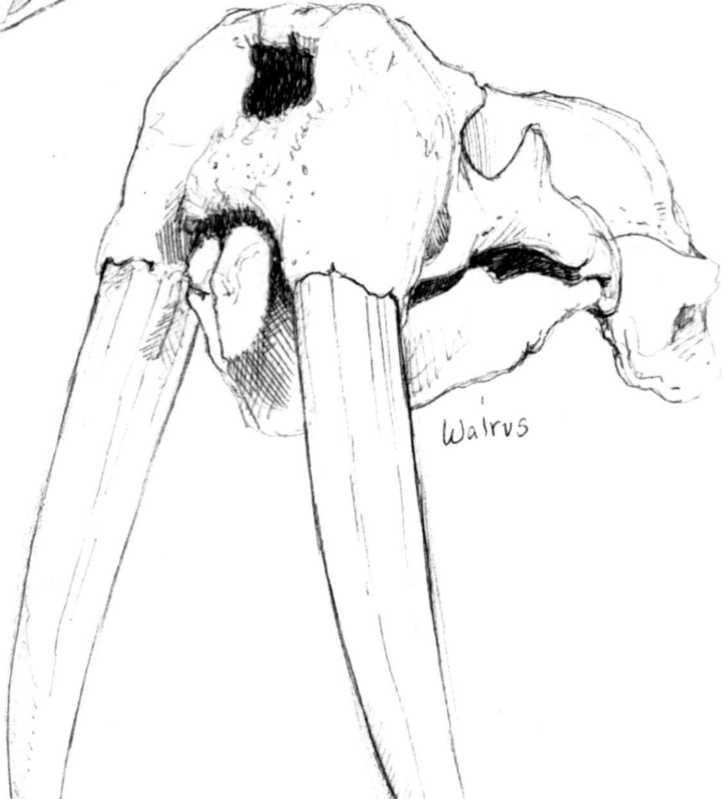

Walrus

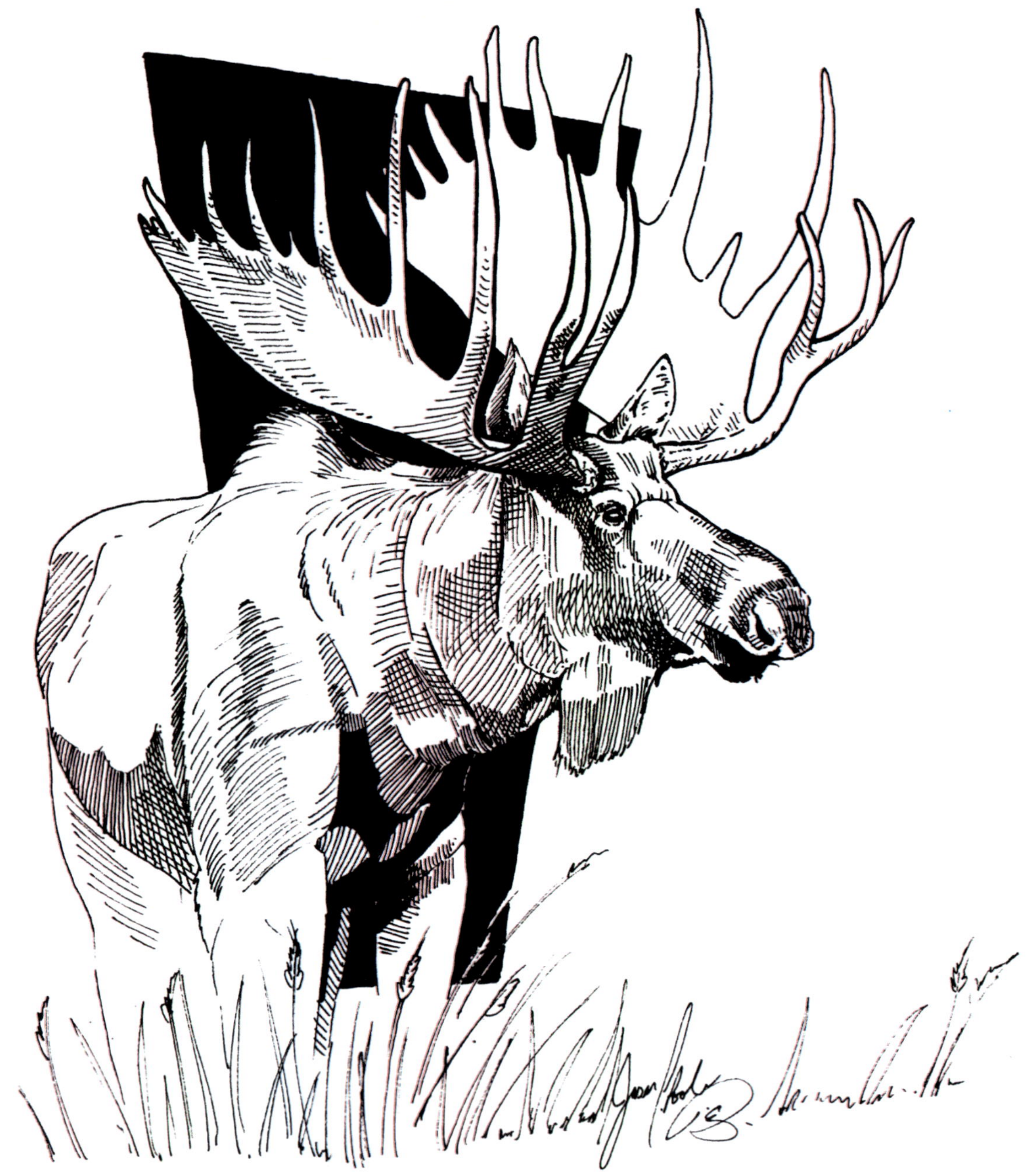

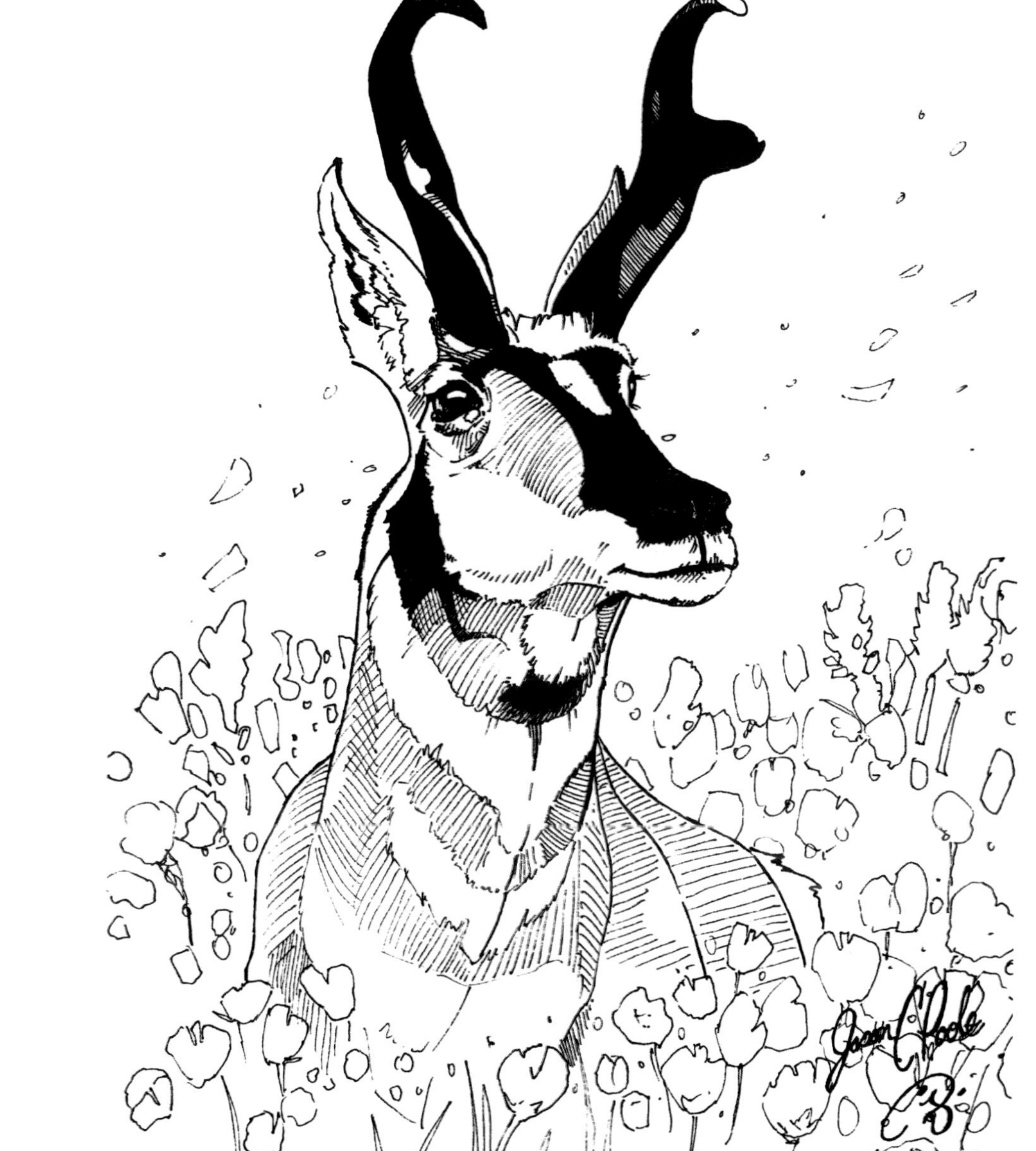

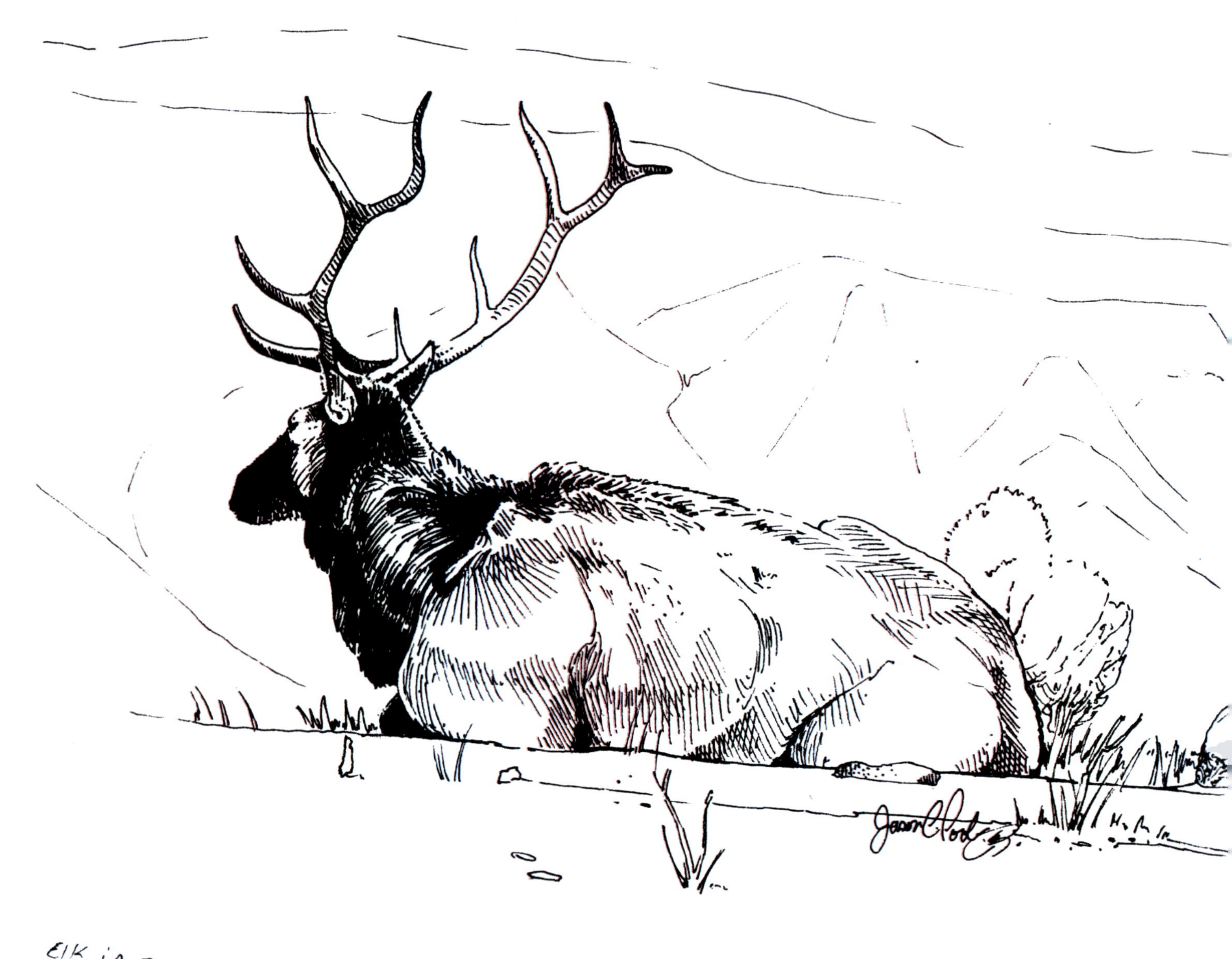

Elk in snowpatch at Yellostone 2023

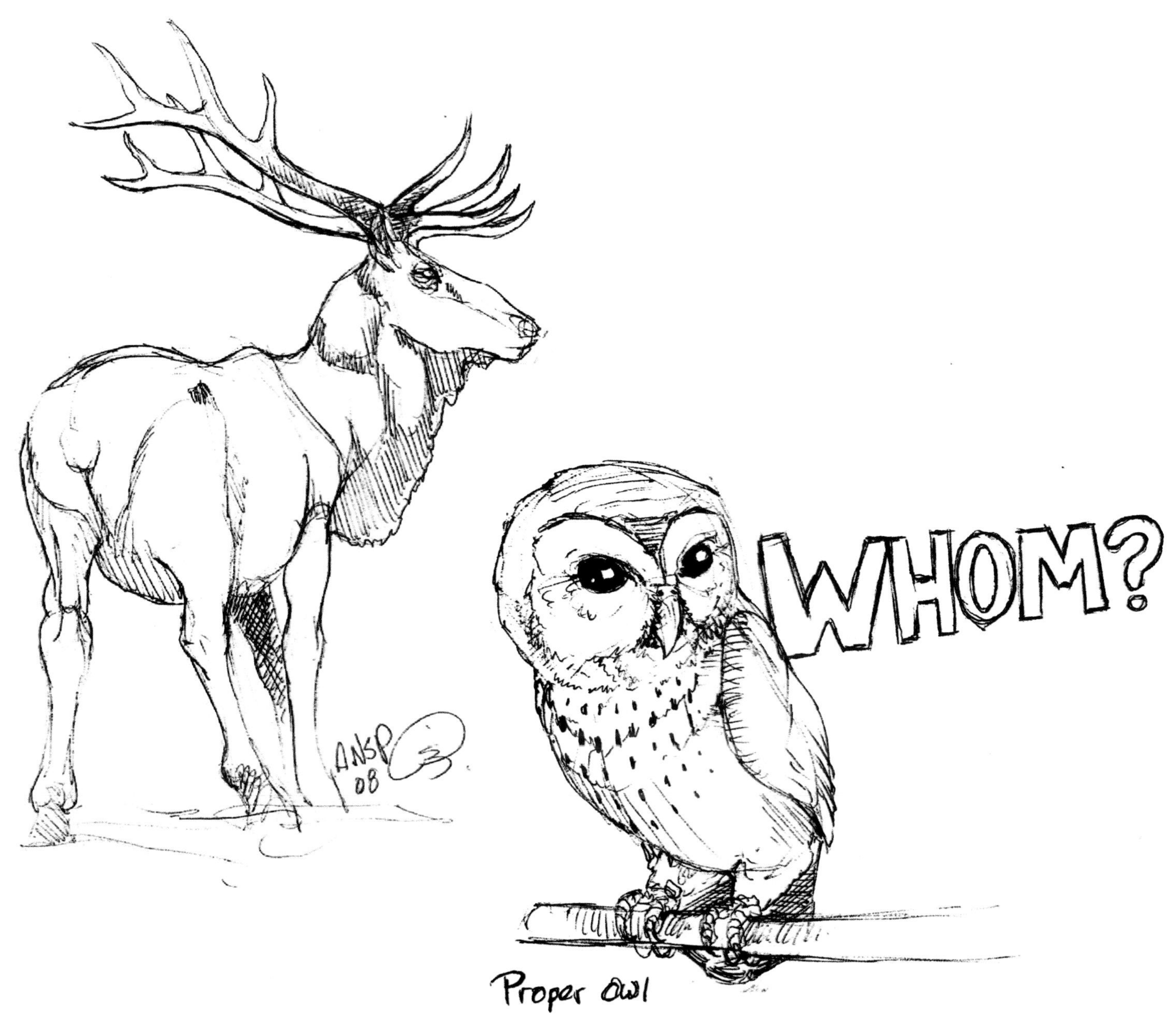

WHOM?
Proper Owl

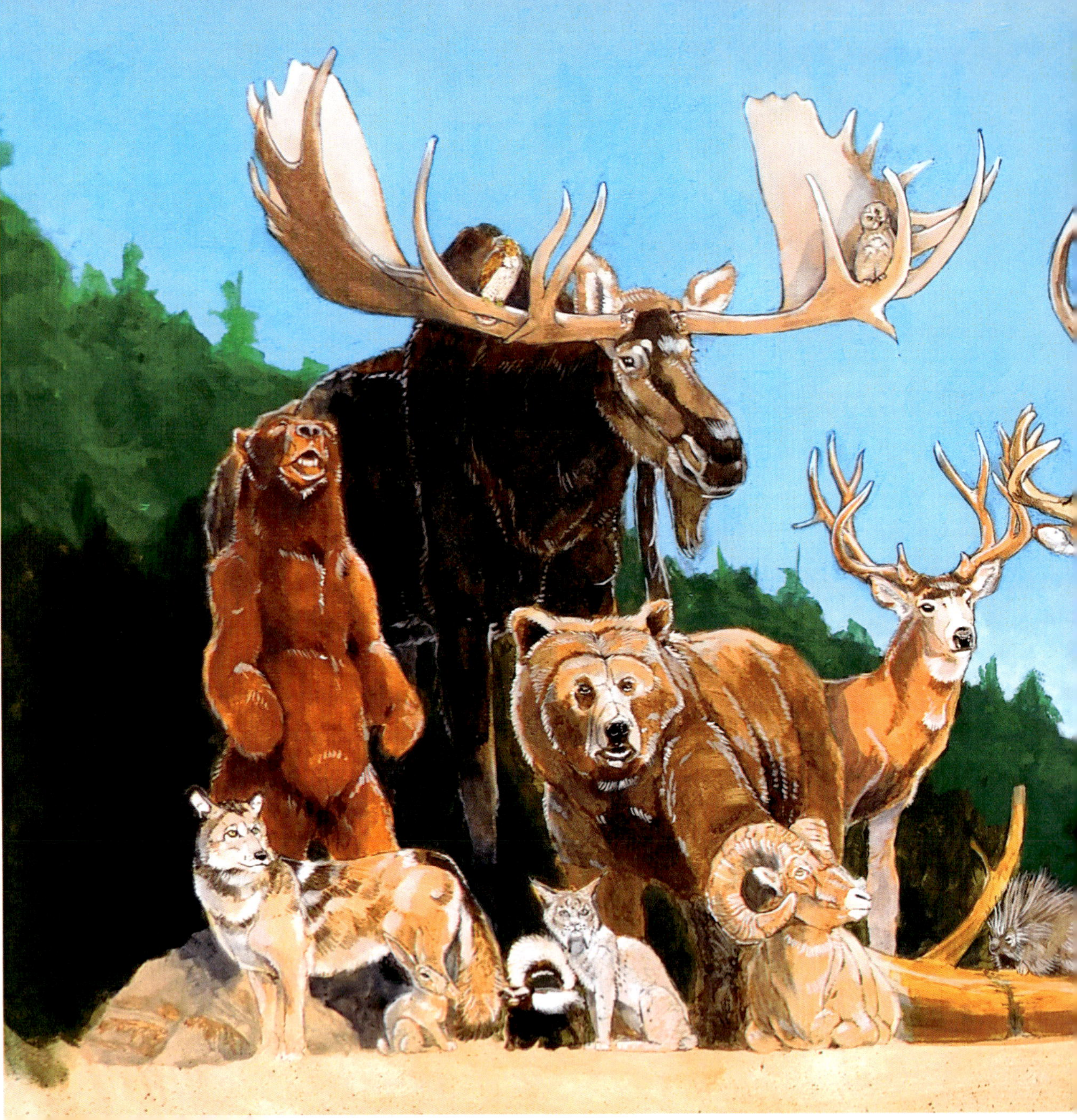

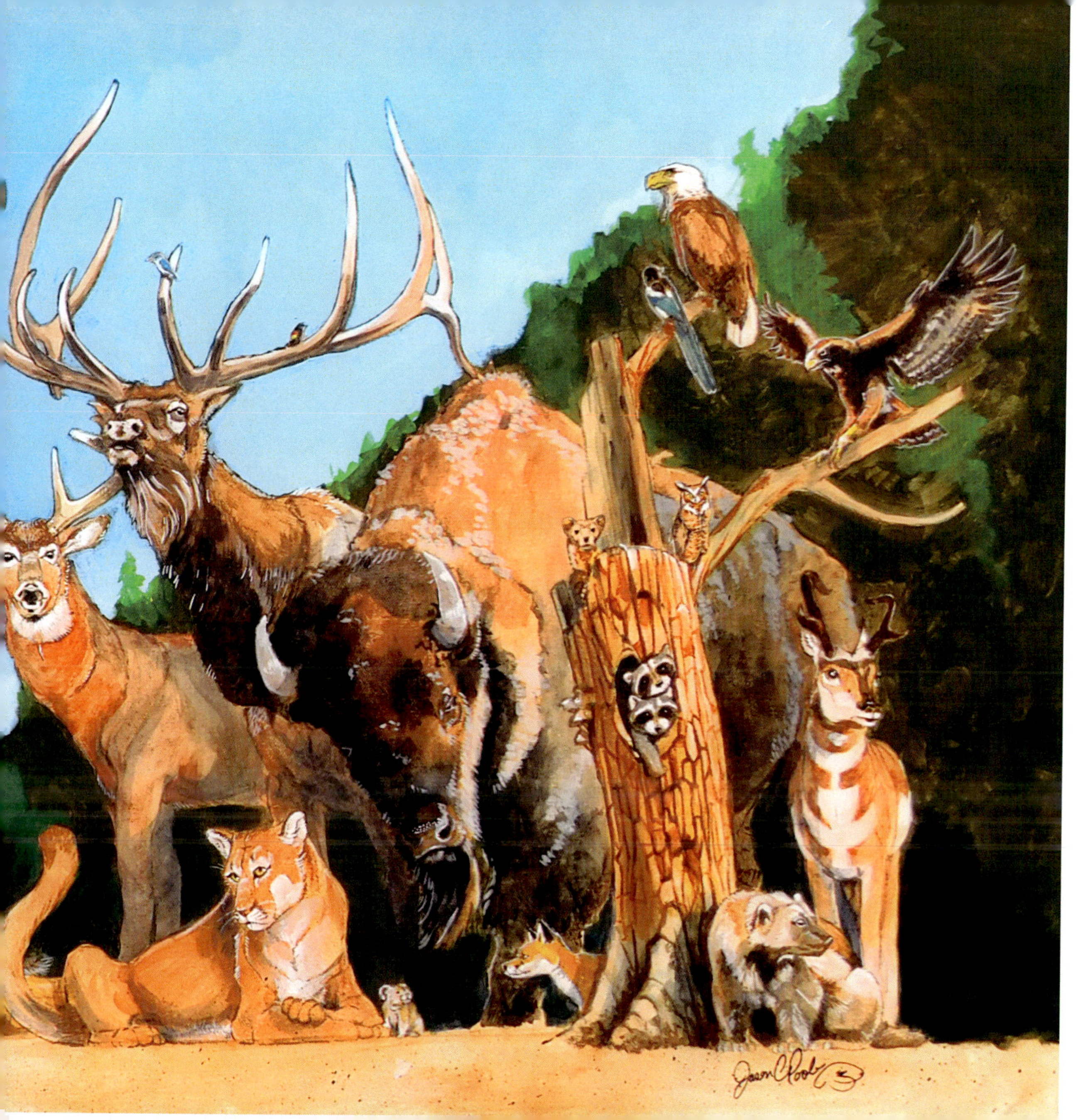

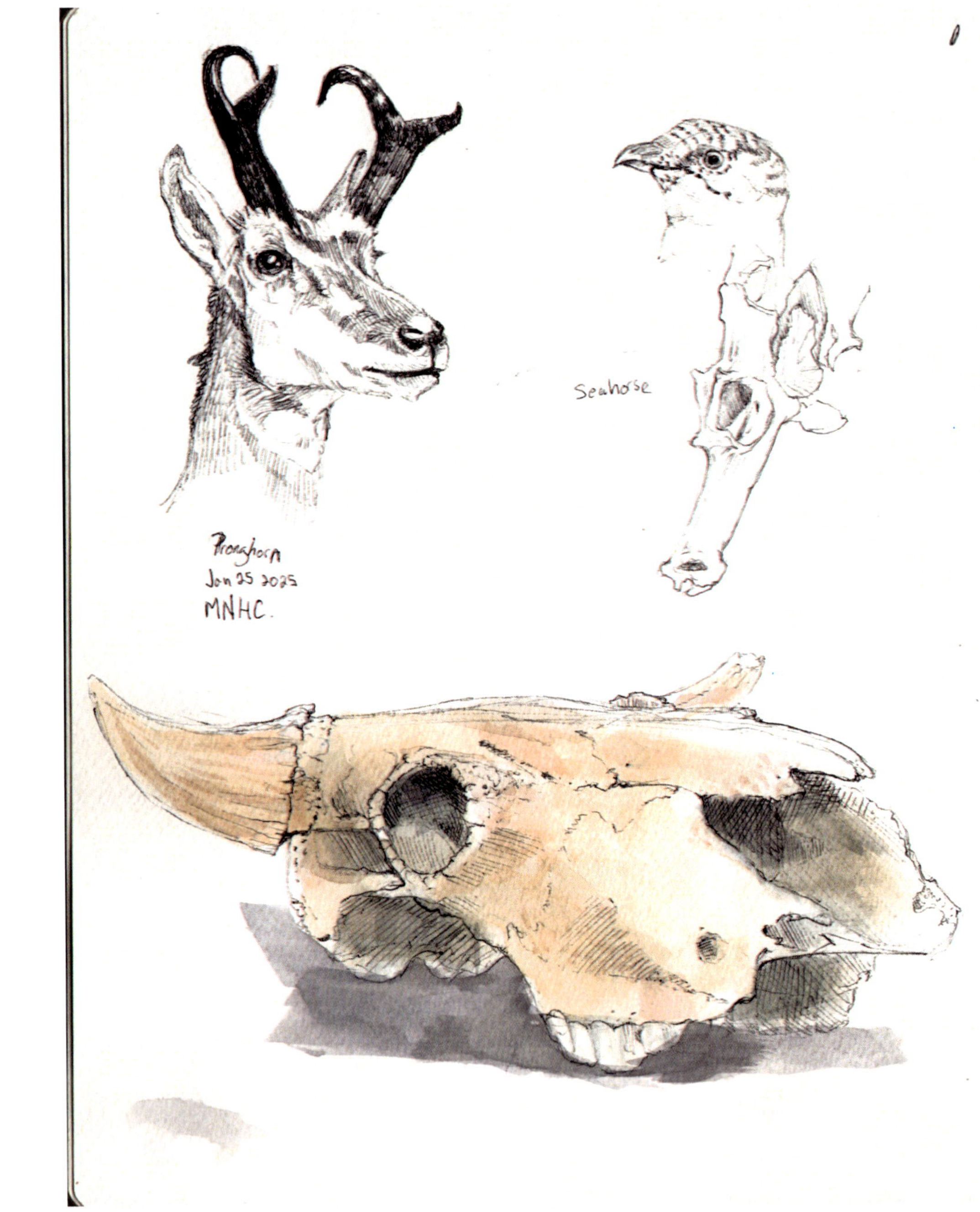

Seahorse
Pronghorn
Jan 25 2025
MNHC.

Water Color

Common Vampire Bat

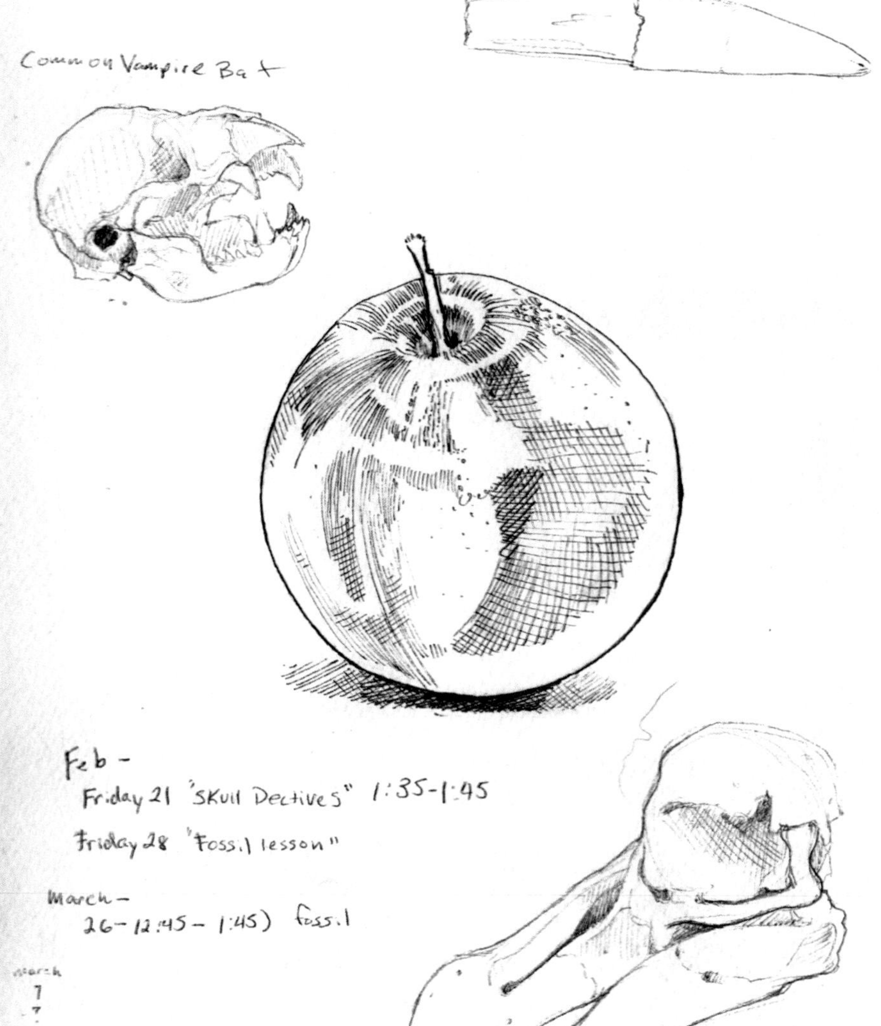

Feb -
   Friday 21 "Skull Dectives" 1:35-1:45

   Friday 28 "Fossil lesson"

 March—
   26- 12:45 - 1:45) fossil

March

Dodo
Raphus cucullatus

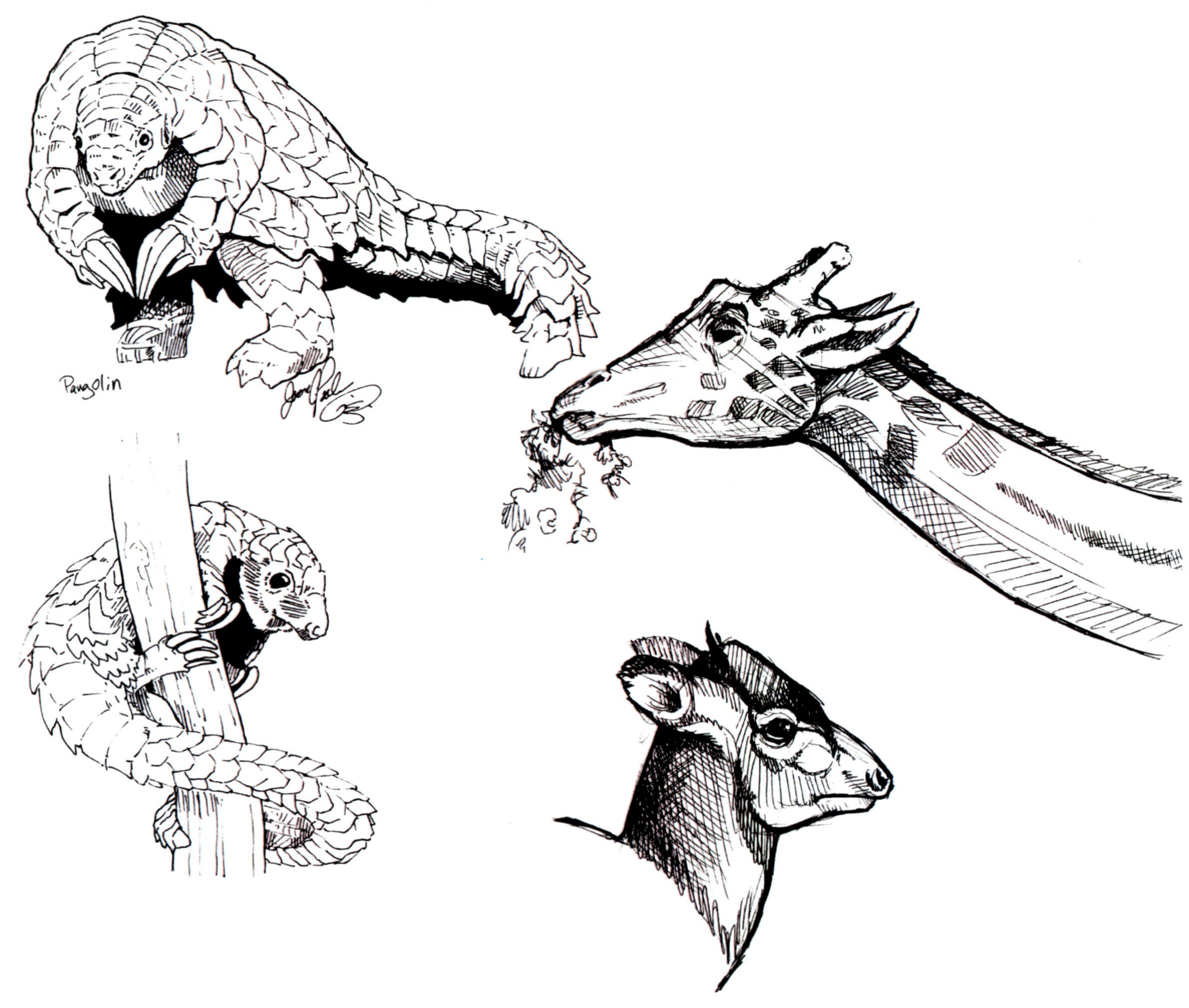
Pangolin

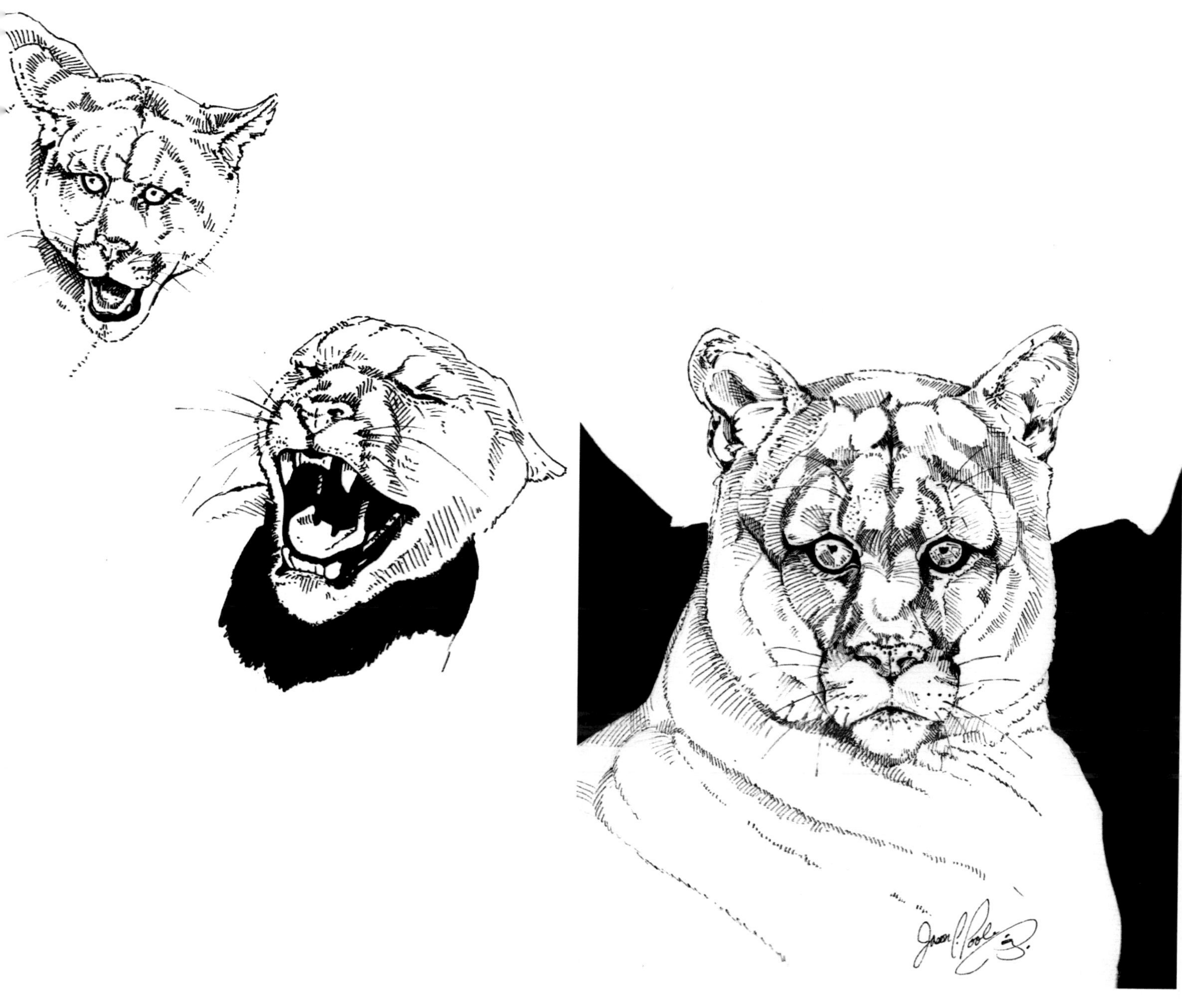

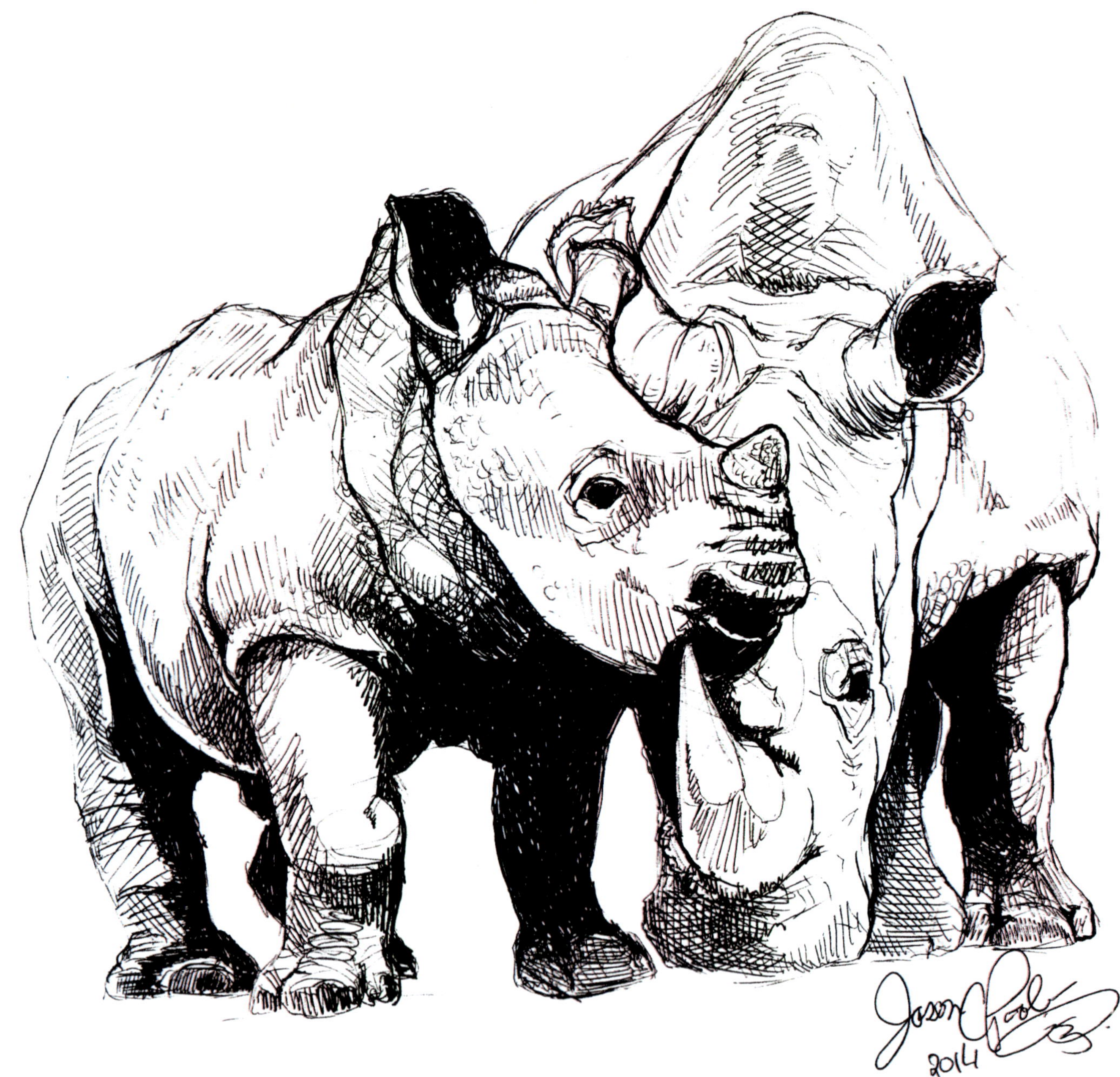

Jason Poole
2014

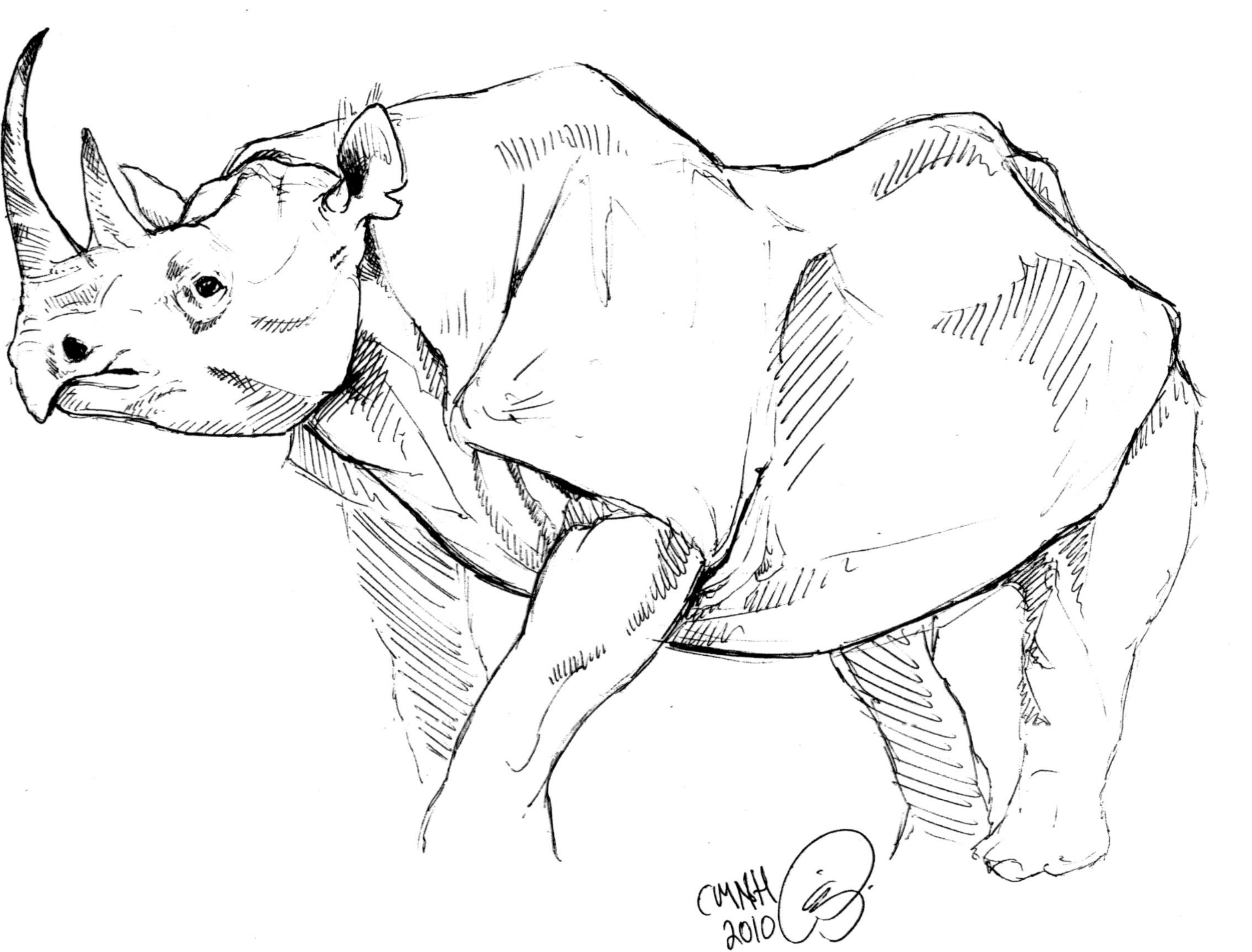
CMNH
2010

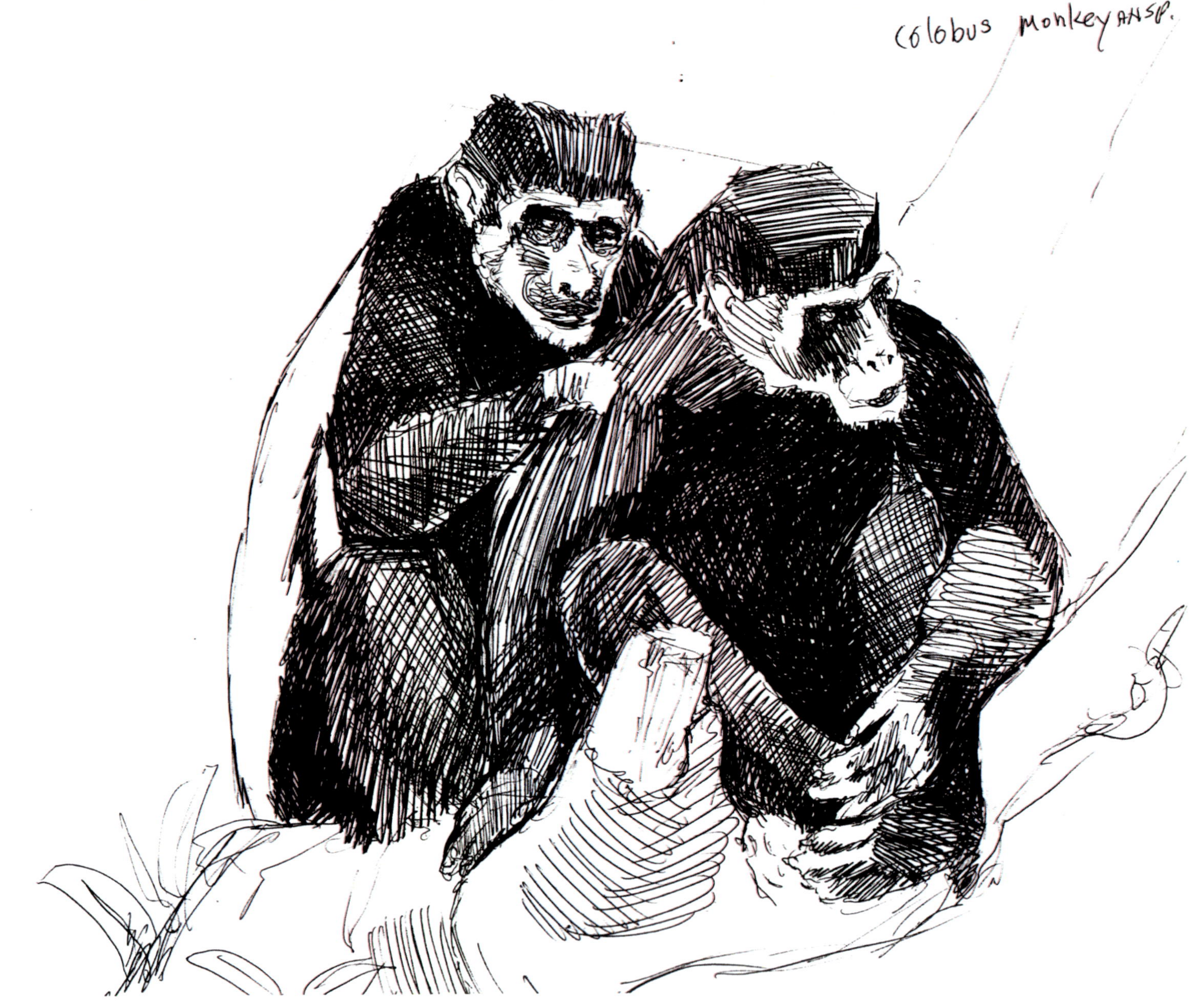

COLOBUS MONKEY AN SP.

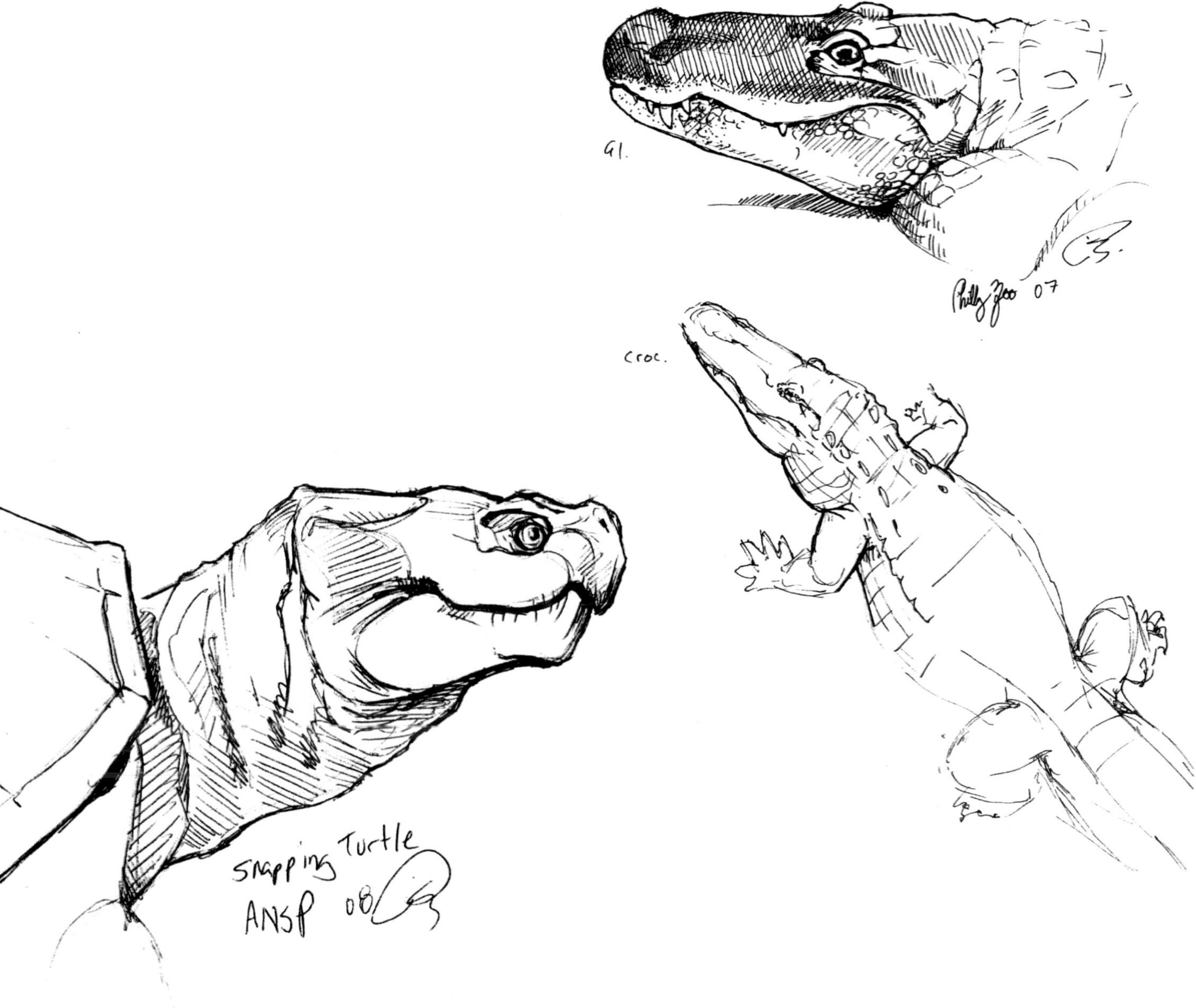

al.
Philly Zoo 07
croc.
snapping Turtle
ANSP 08

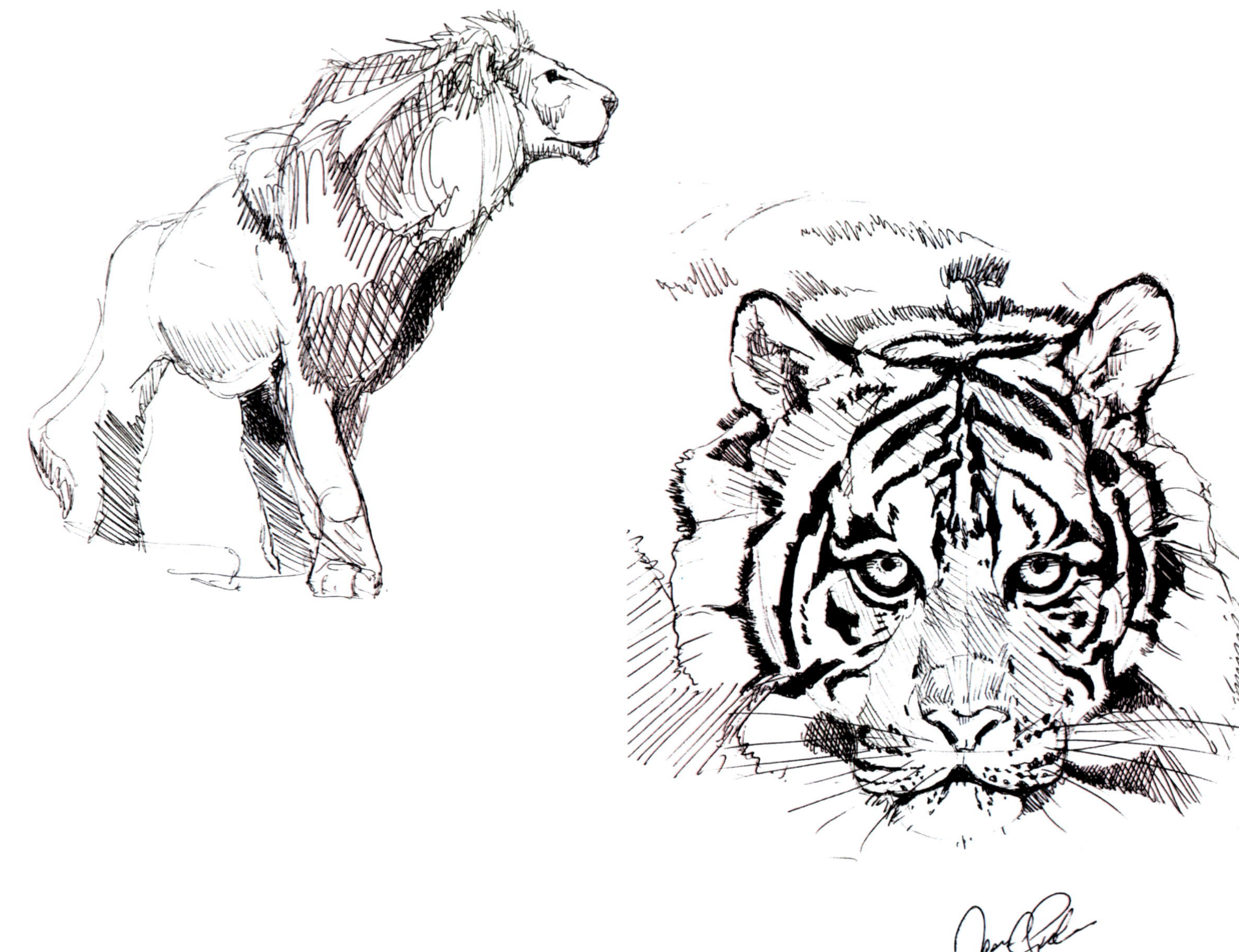
ANSP
2013

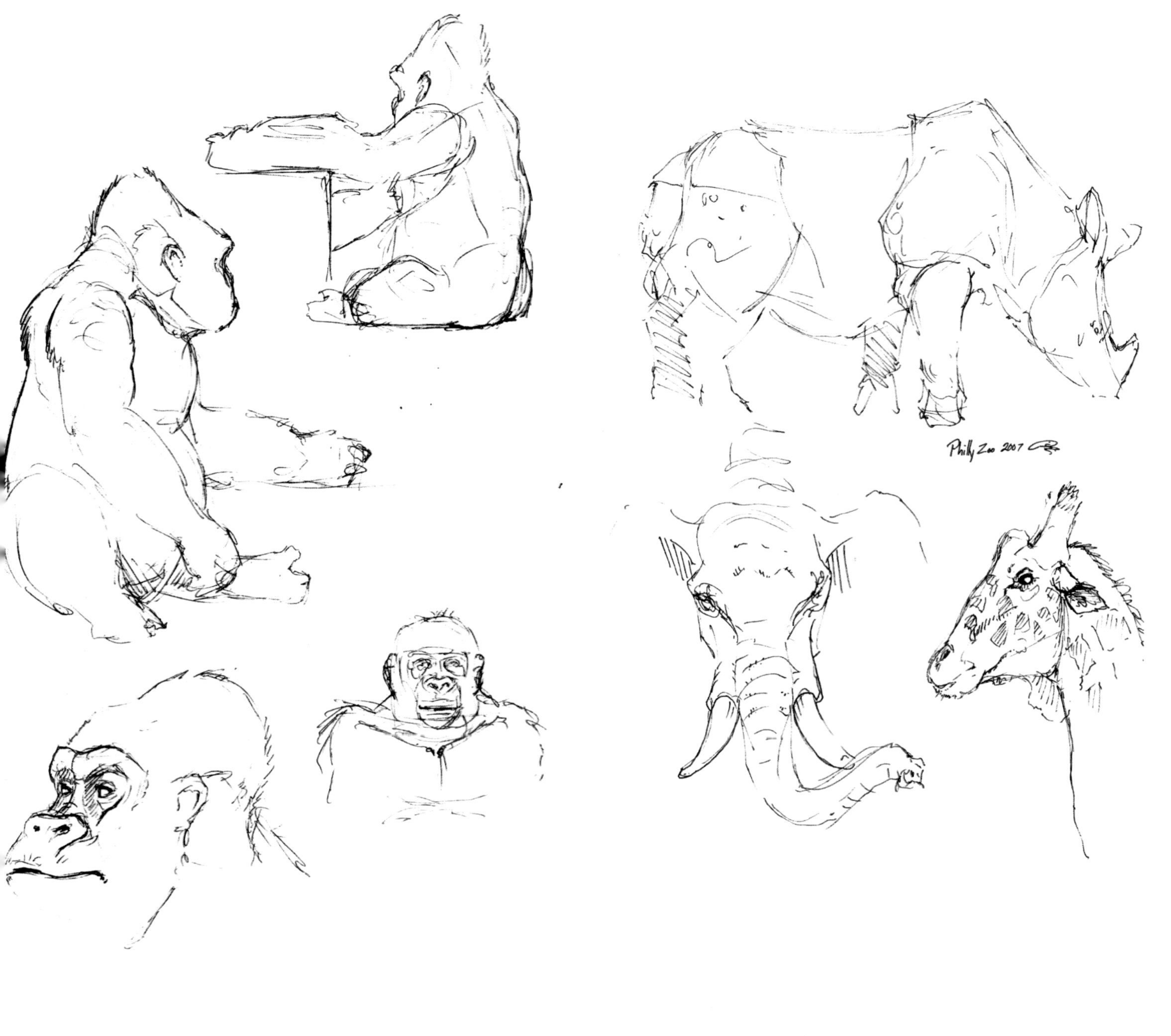

Philly Zoo 2007

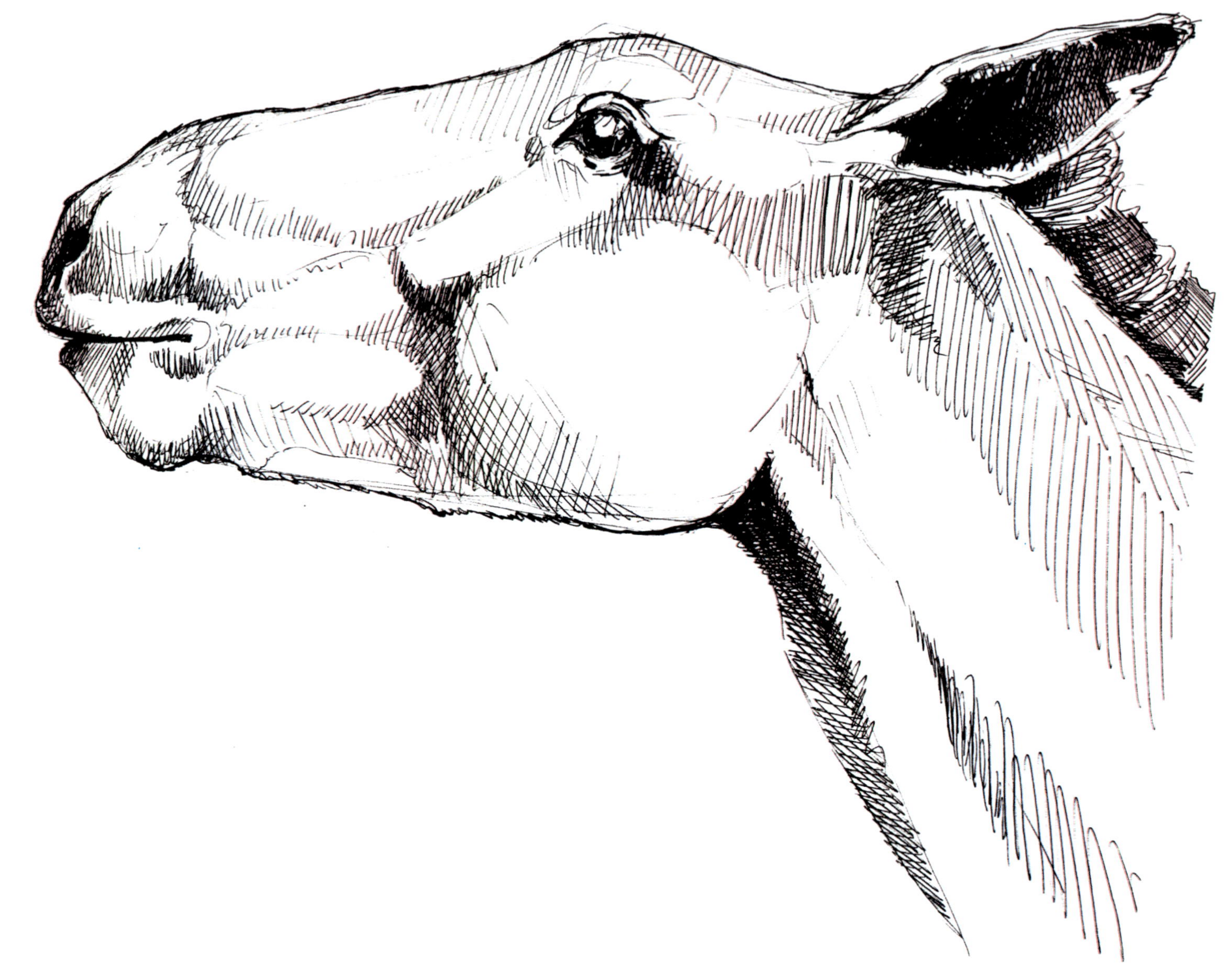

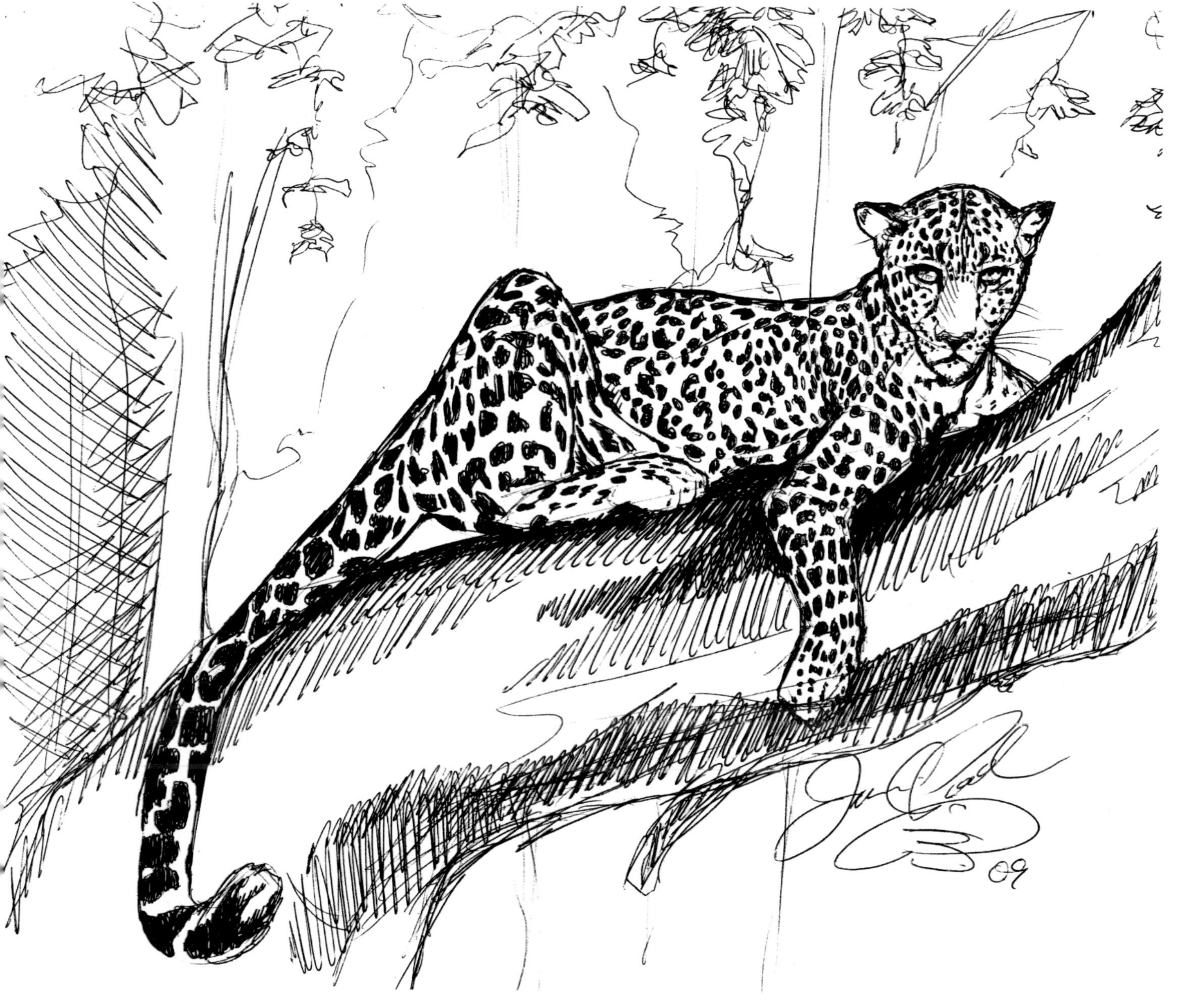

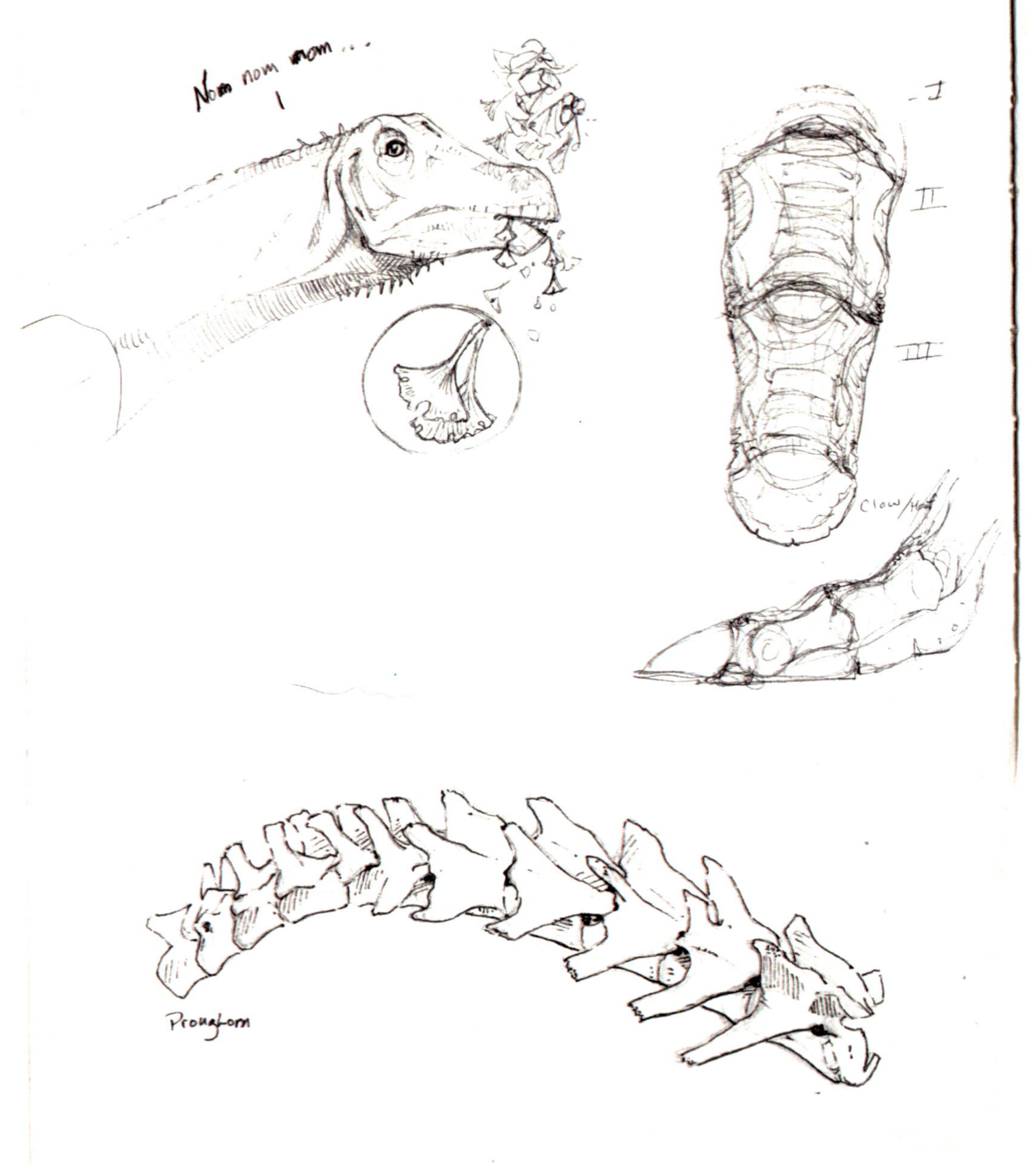

Nom nom nom . . .
I
II
III
Claw/Hoof
Pronaform

Other Worlds

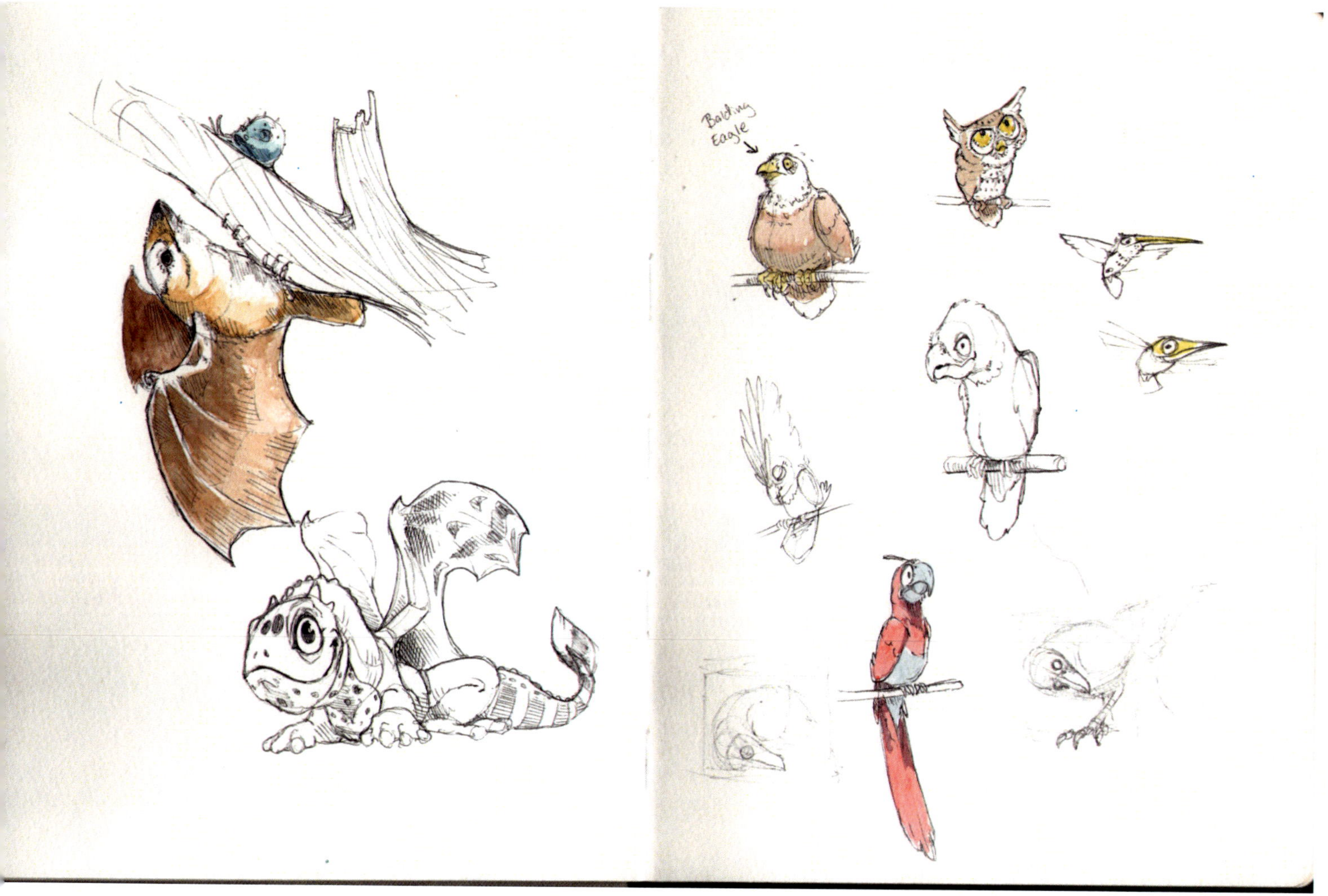

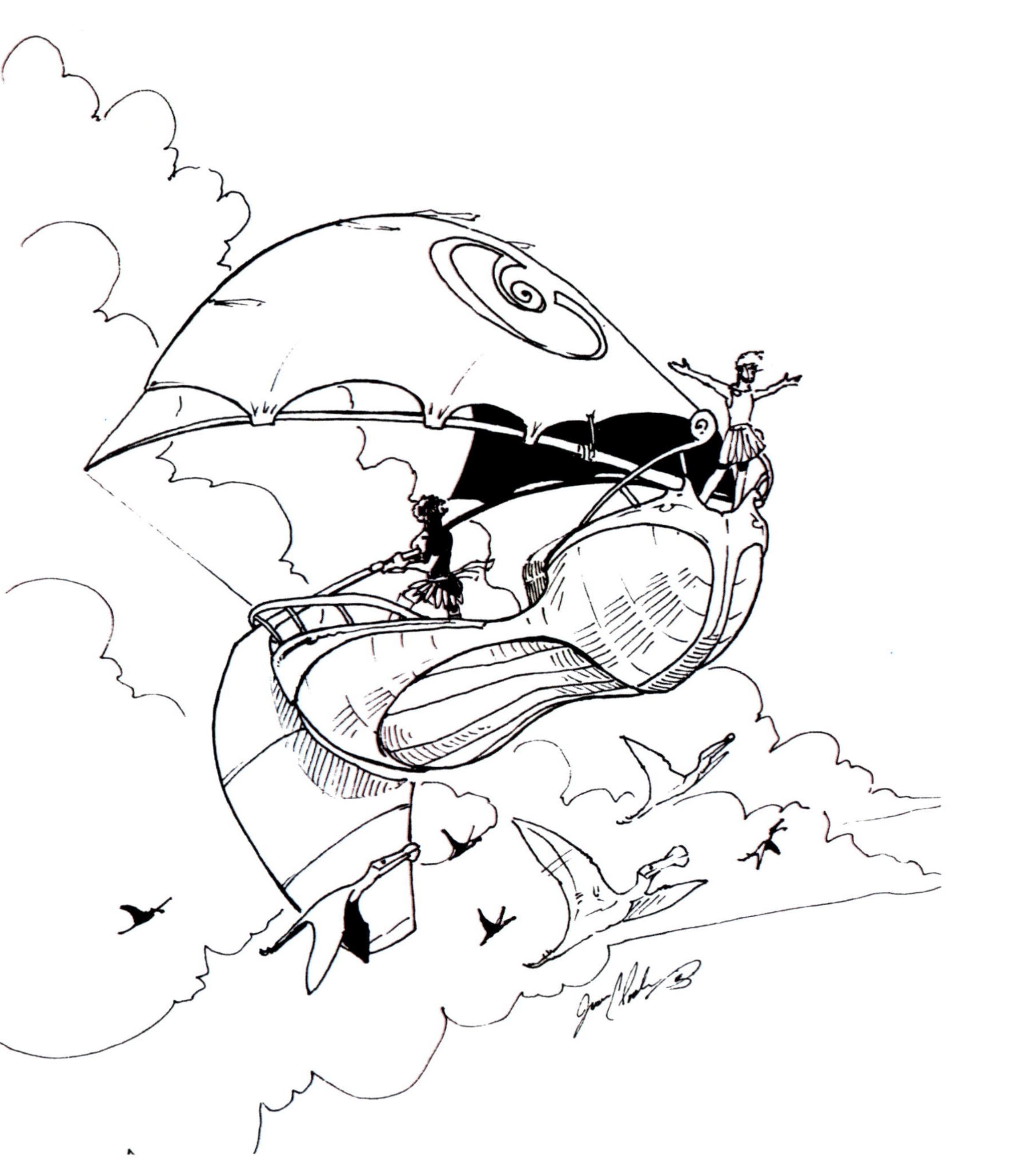

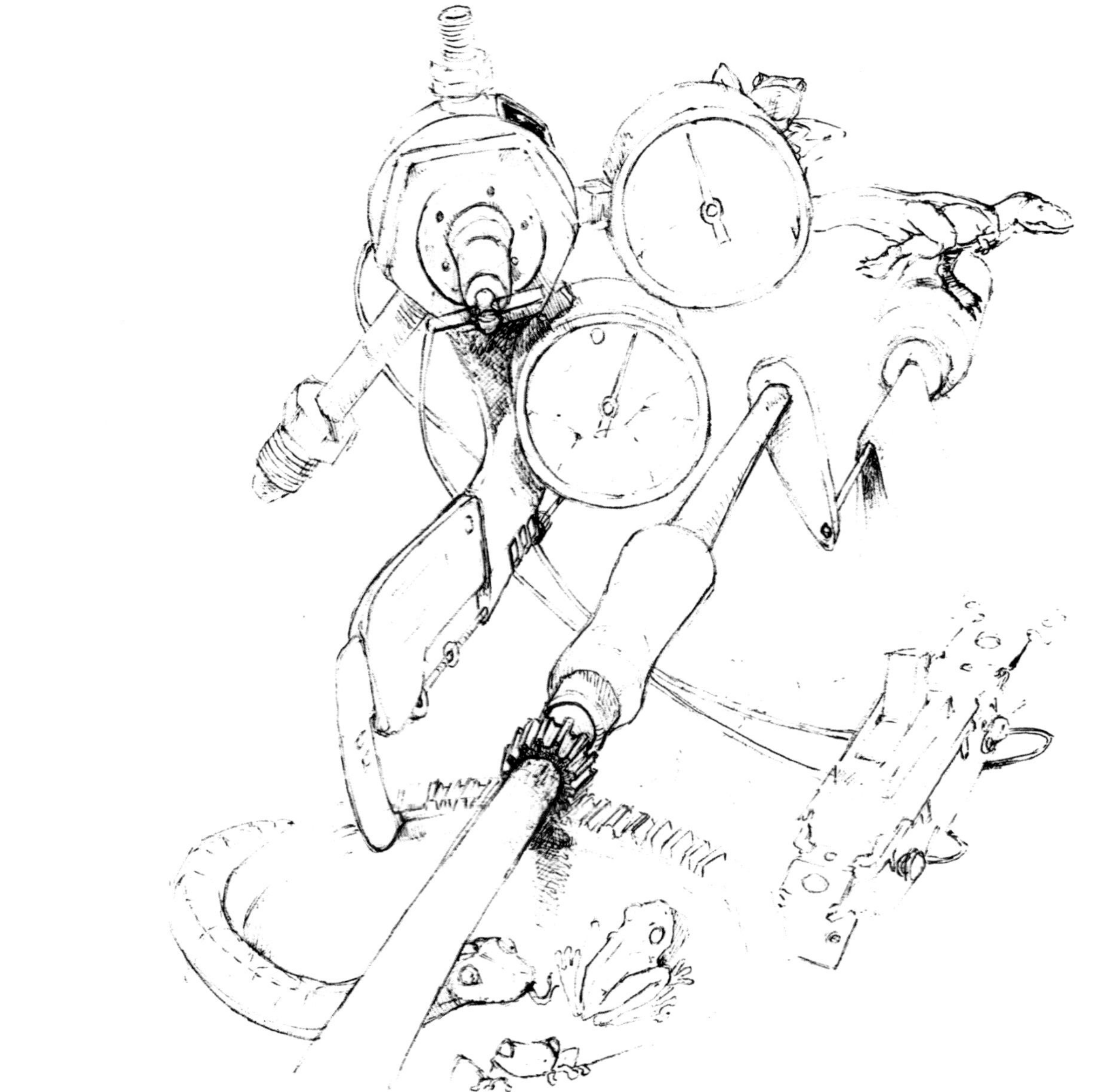

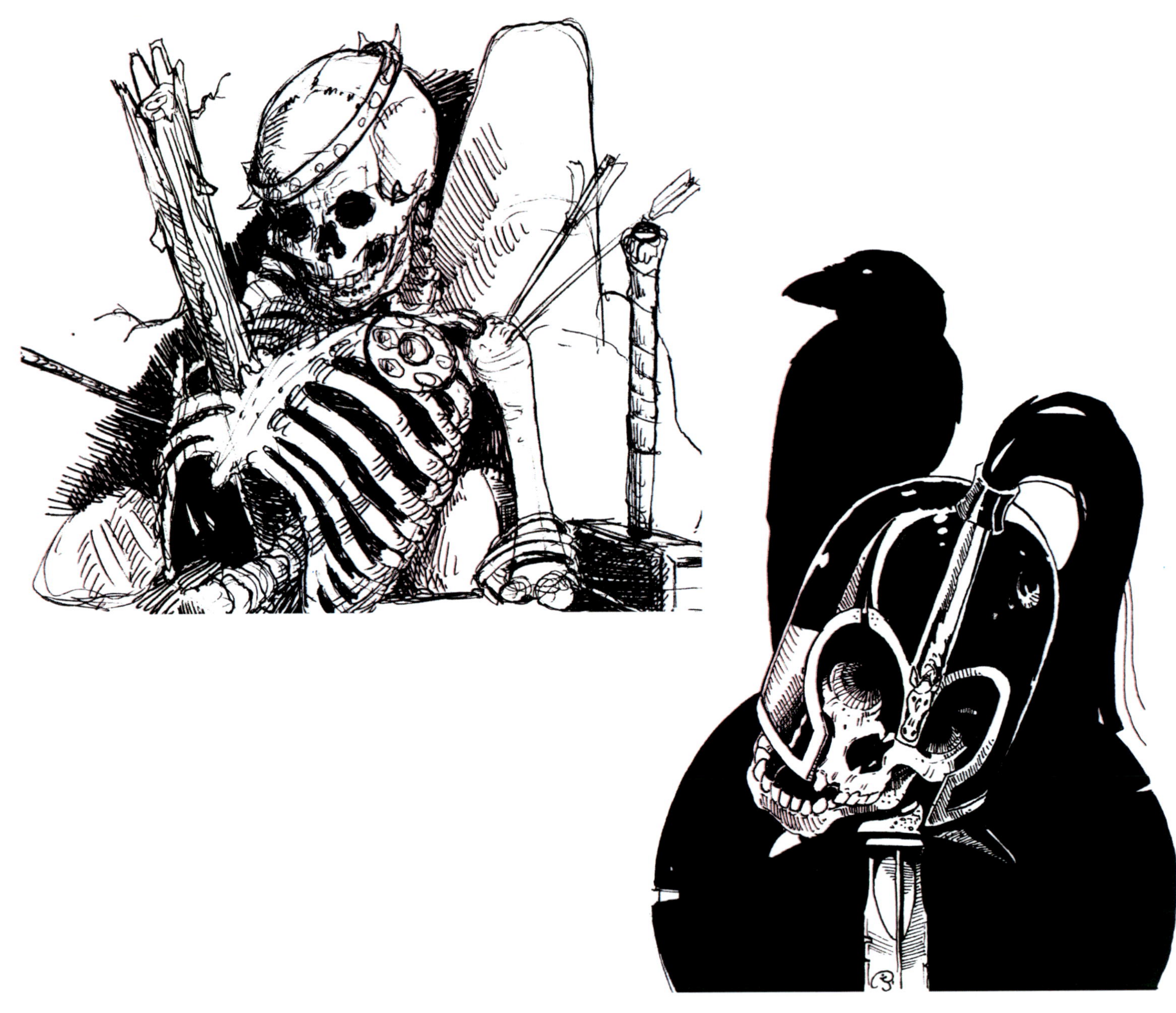

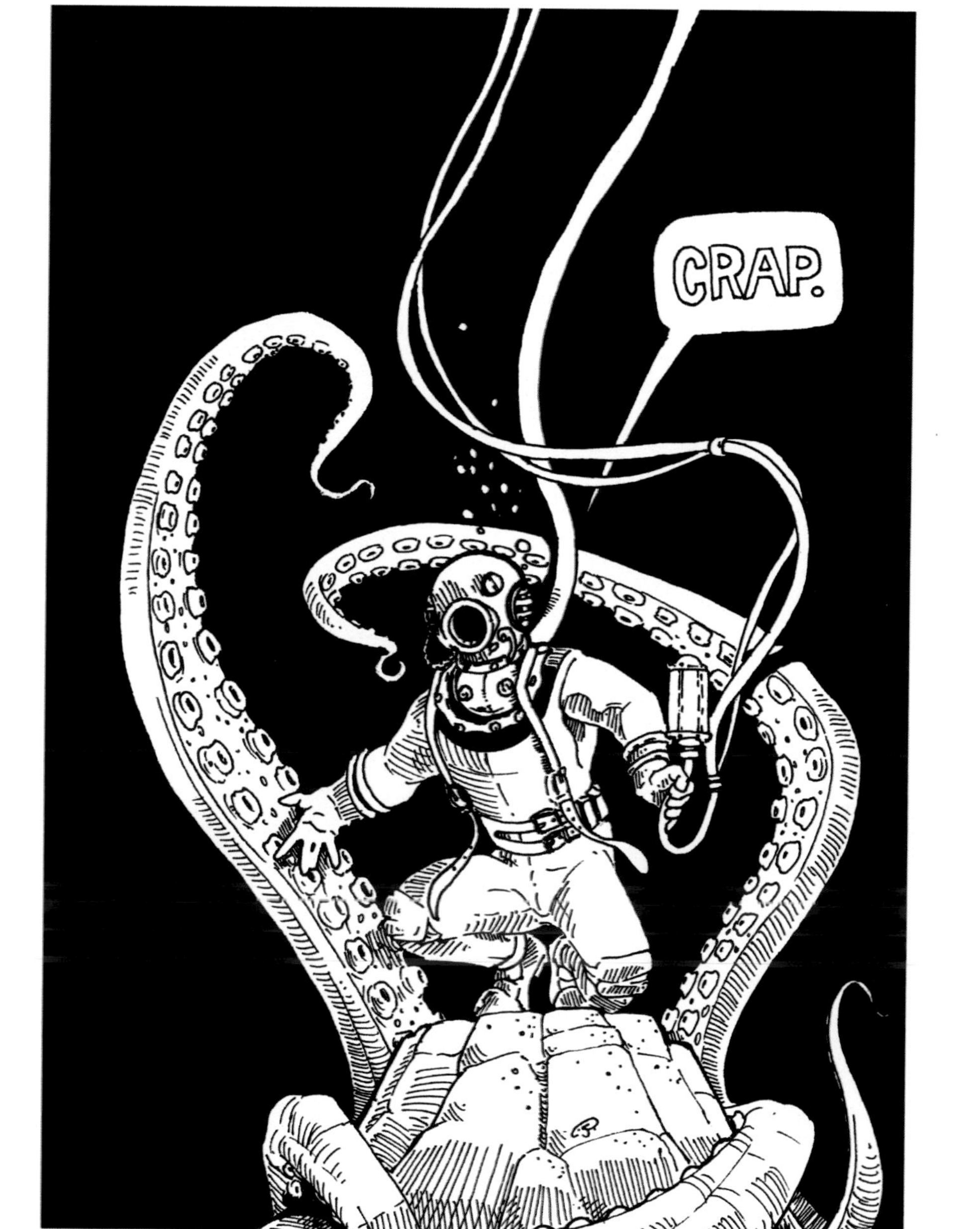

CRAP.

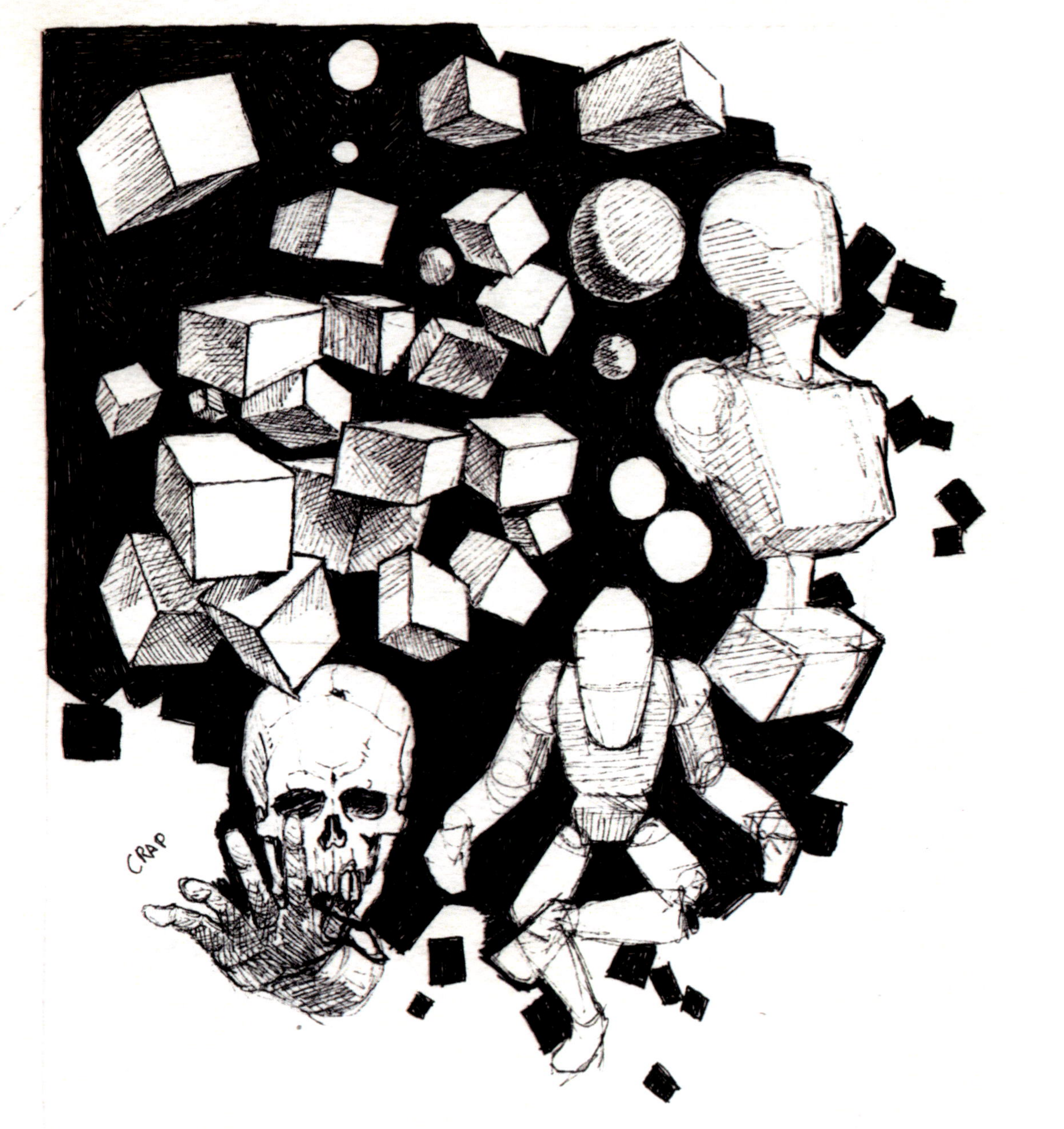

CRAP

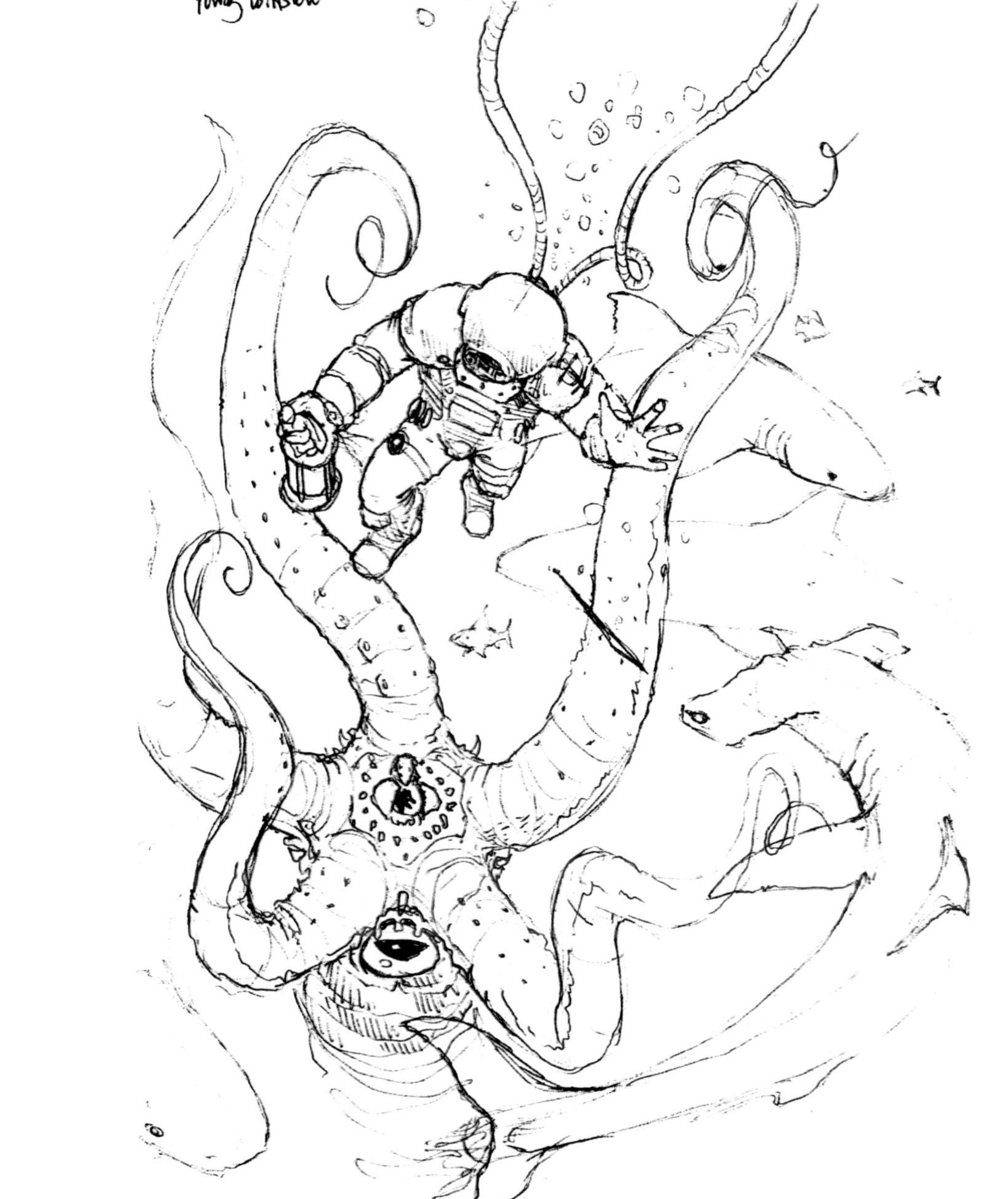
Young Winston

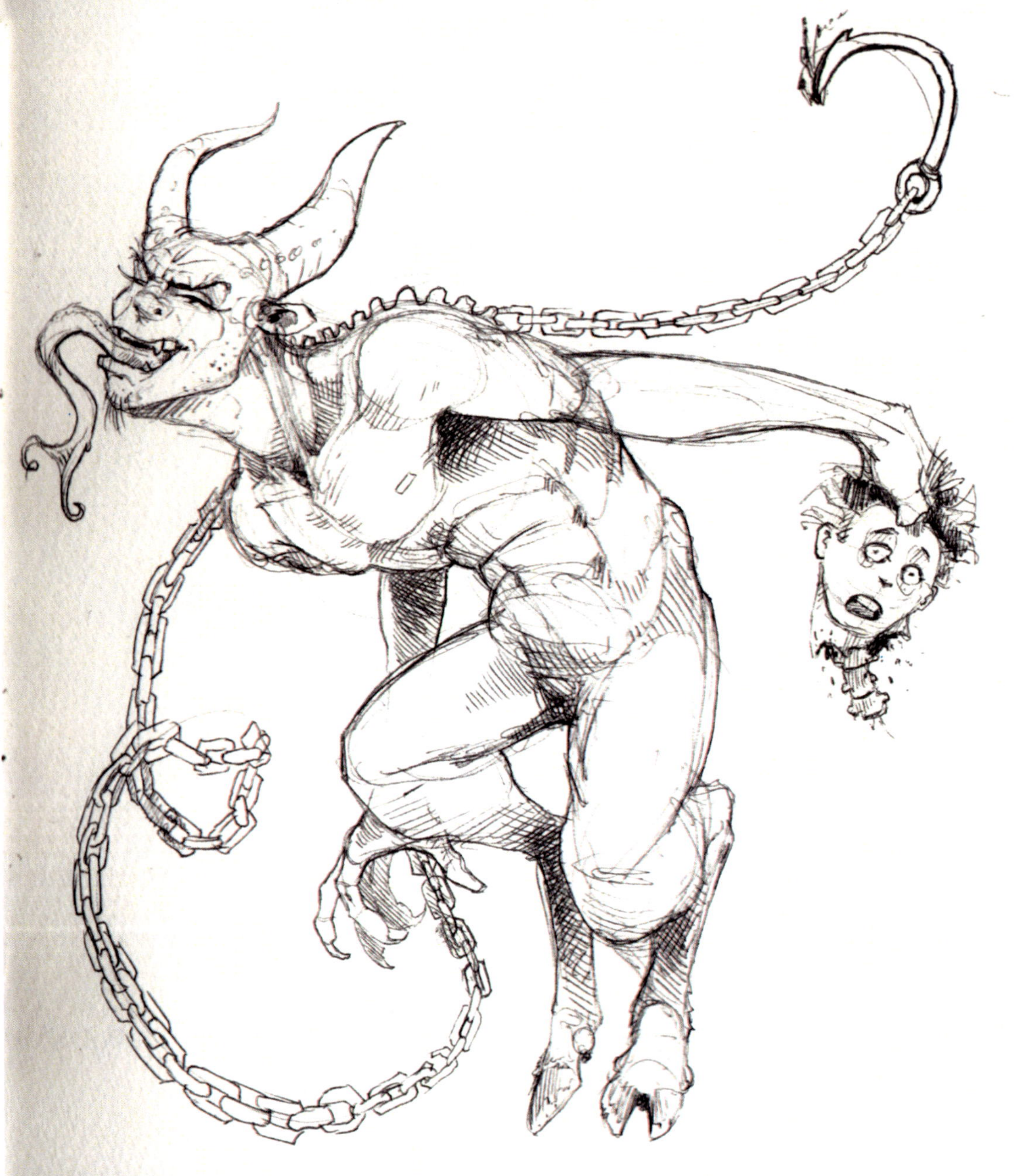

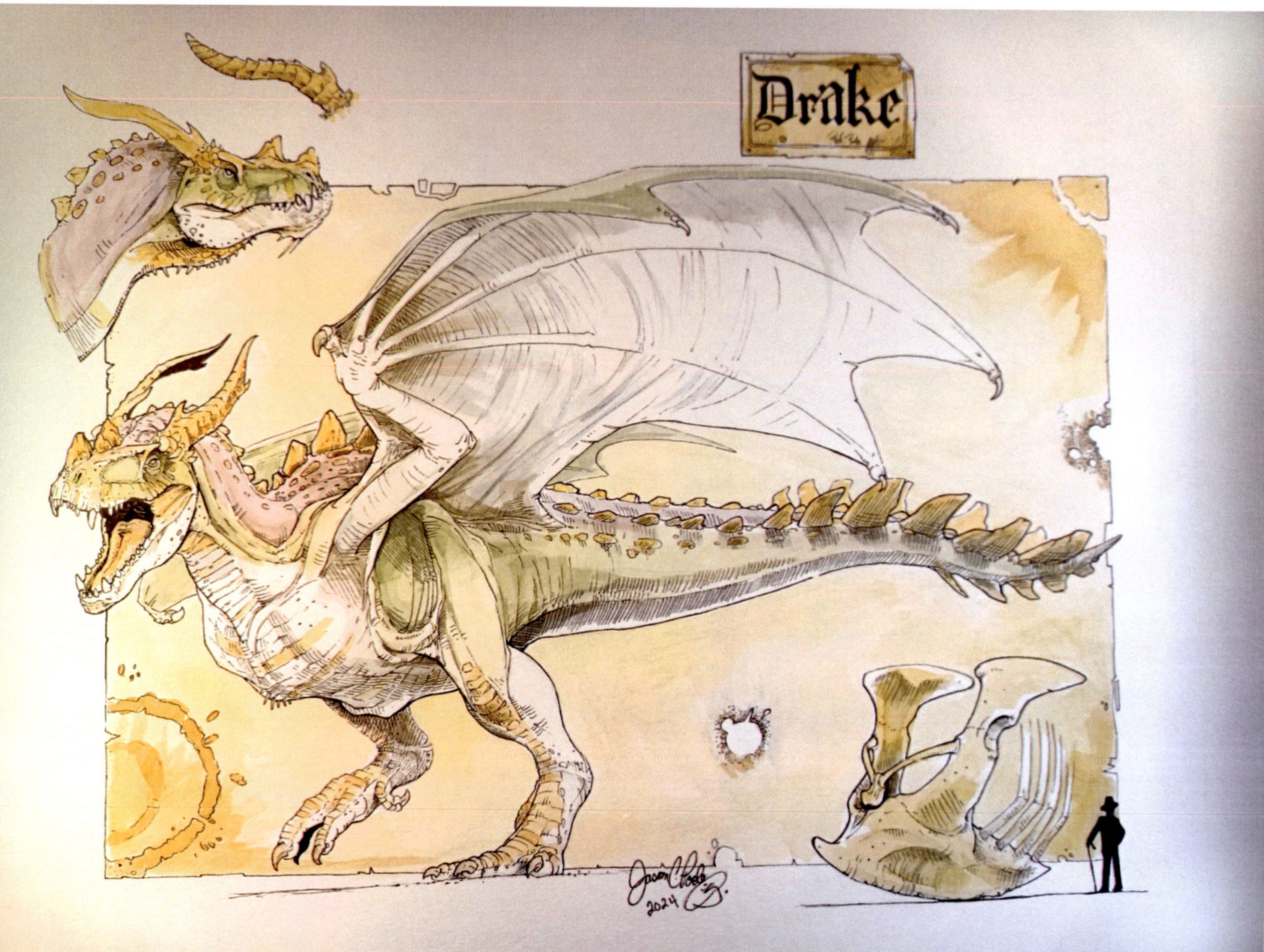

Drake
Jason Cloda
2024

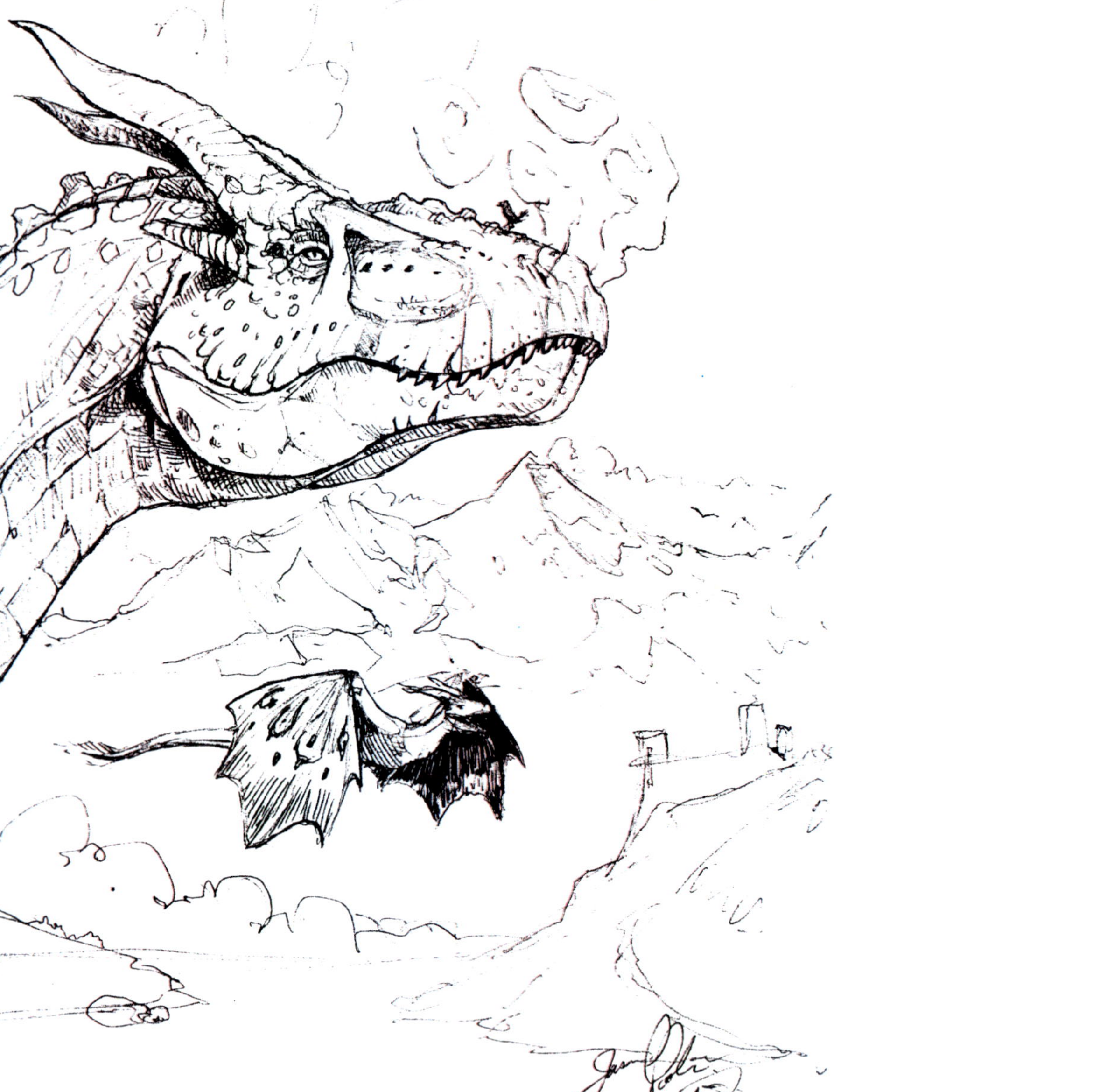

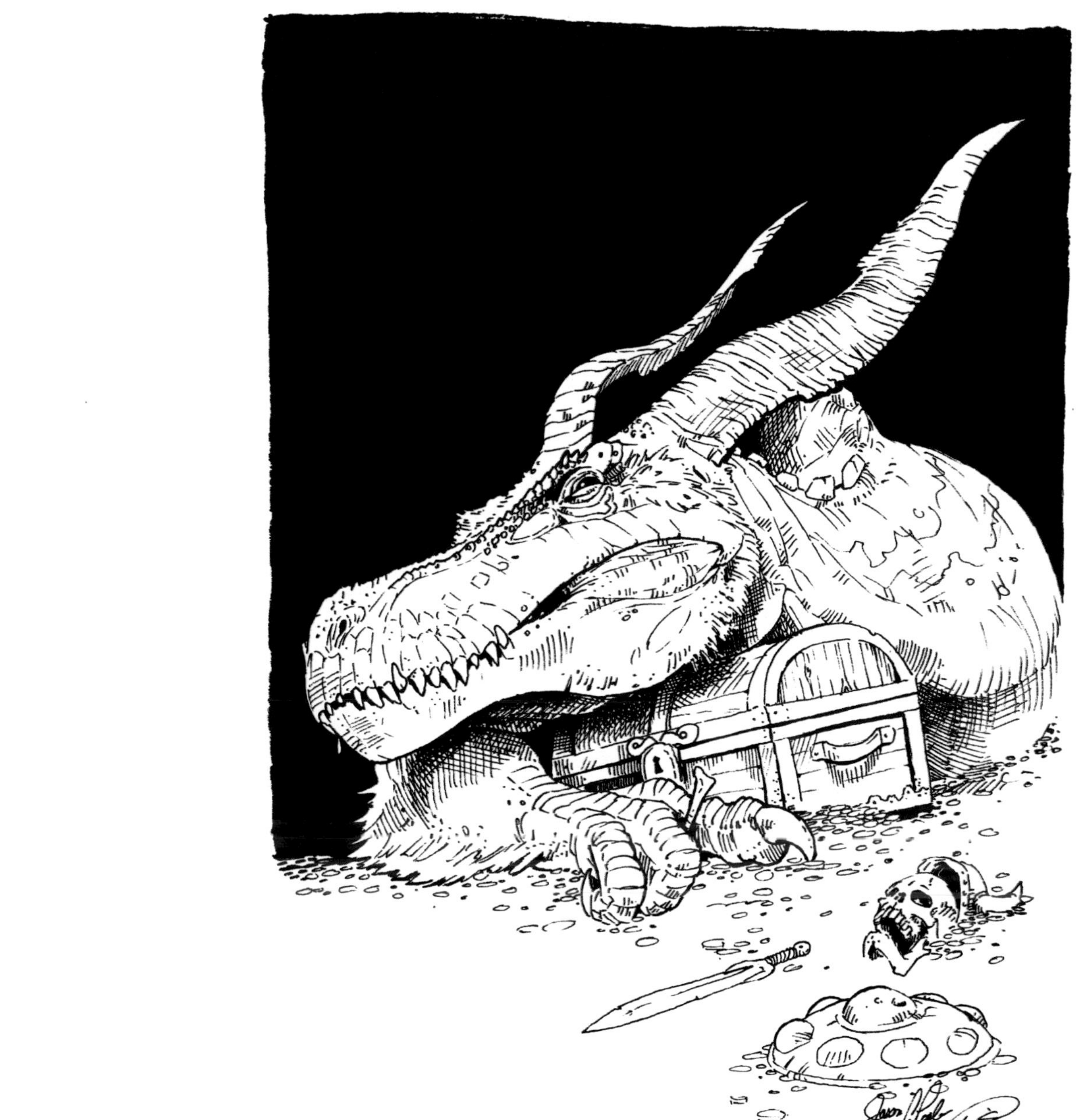

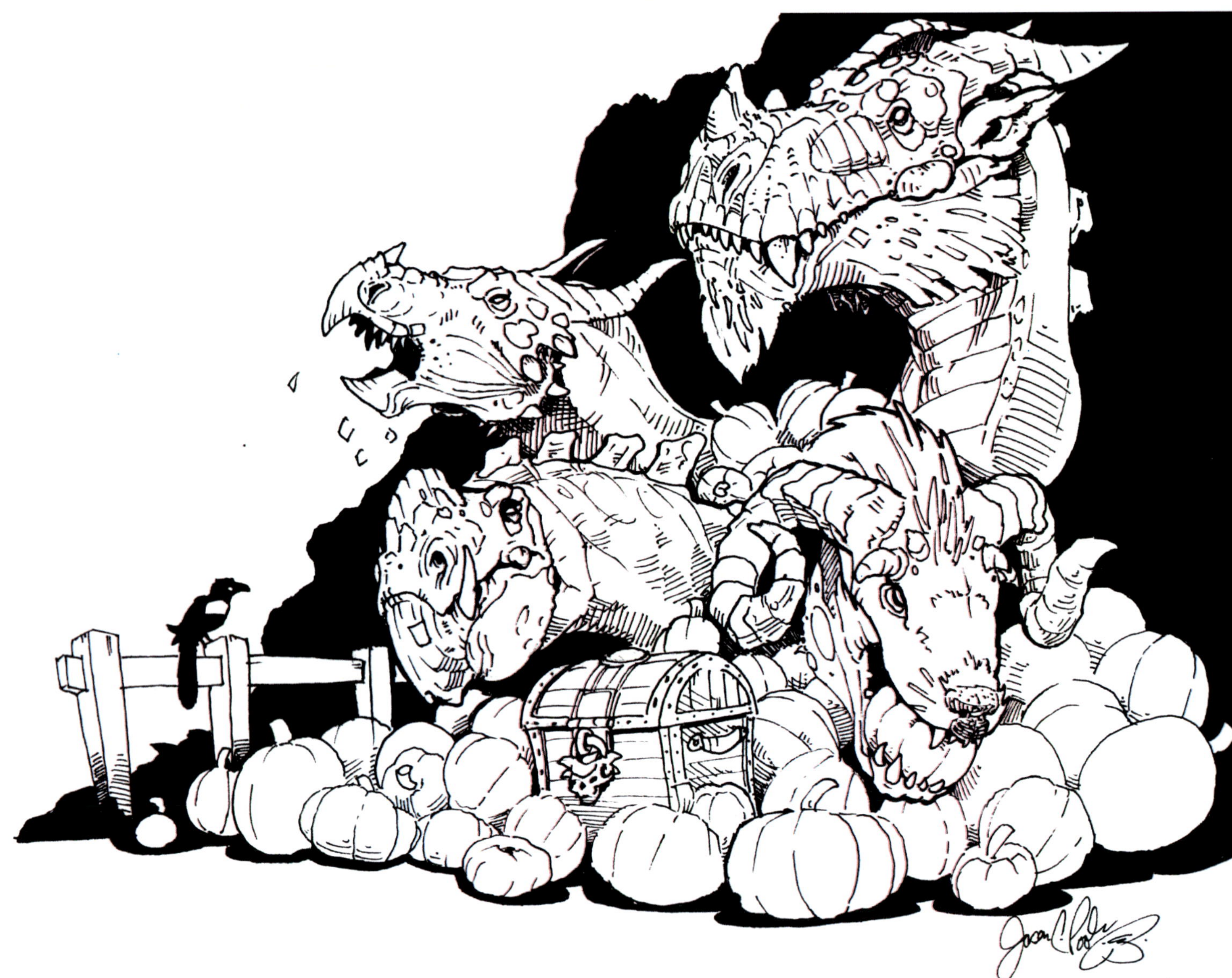

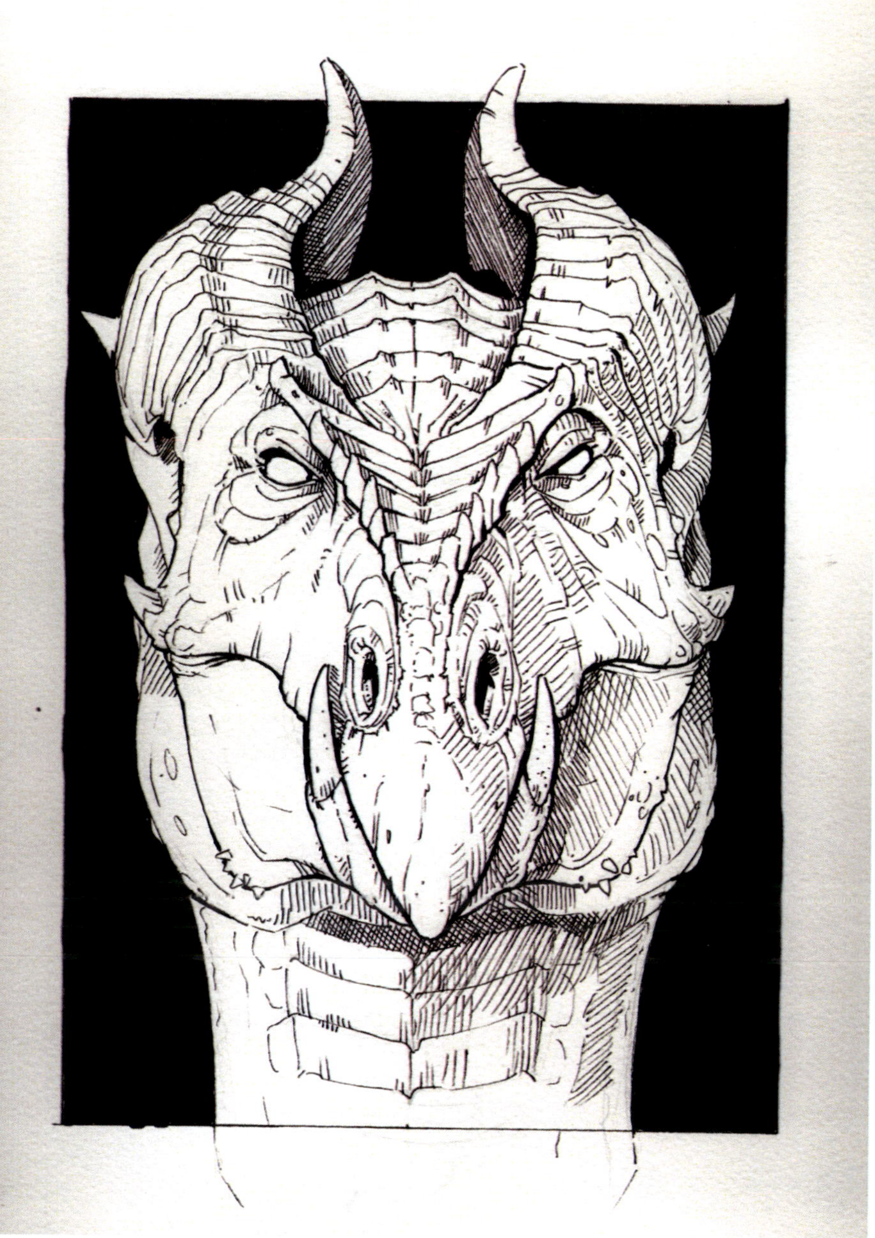

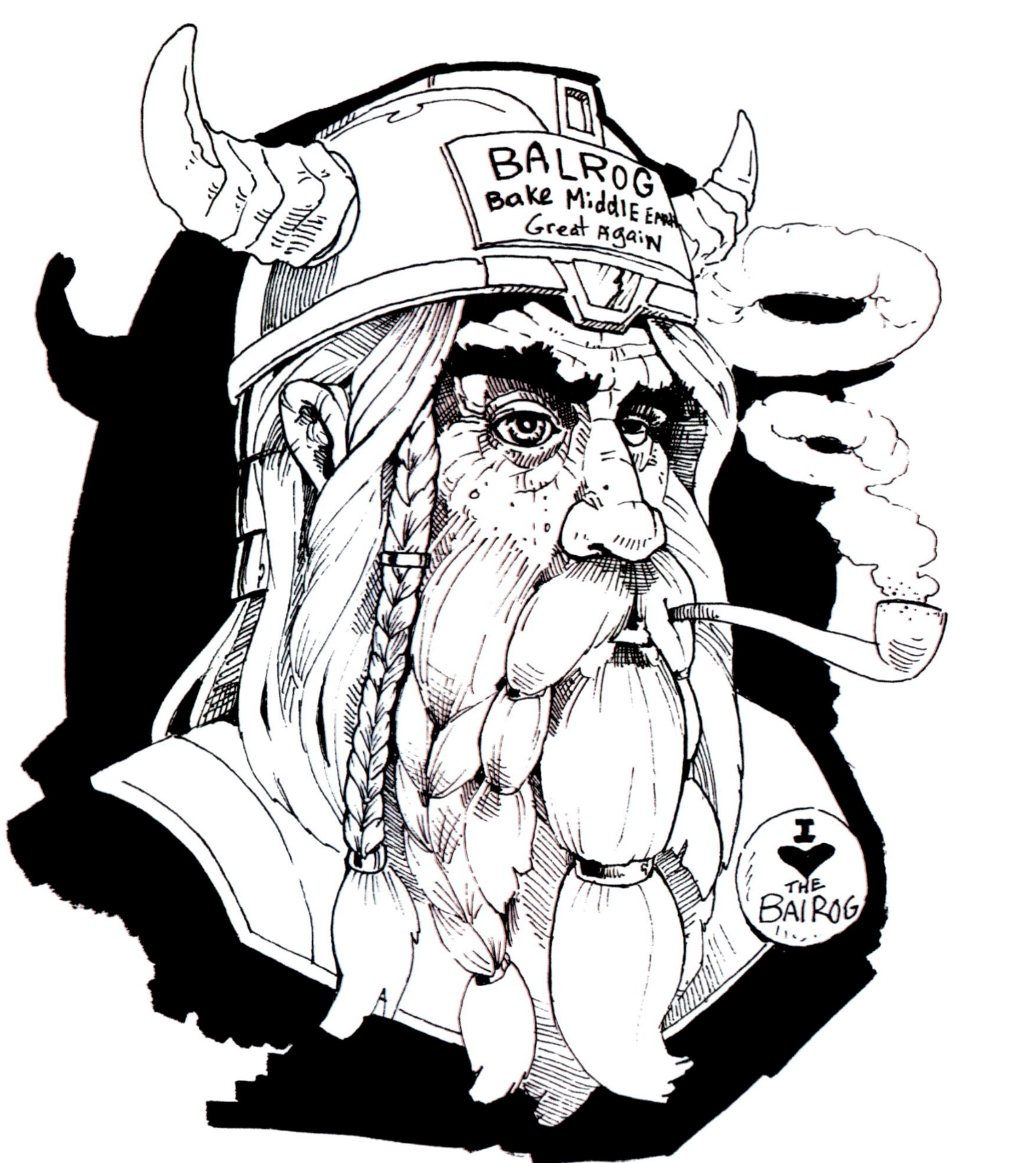

BALROG
Bake Middle Earth
Great Again
I ♥ THE BAIROG

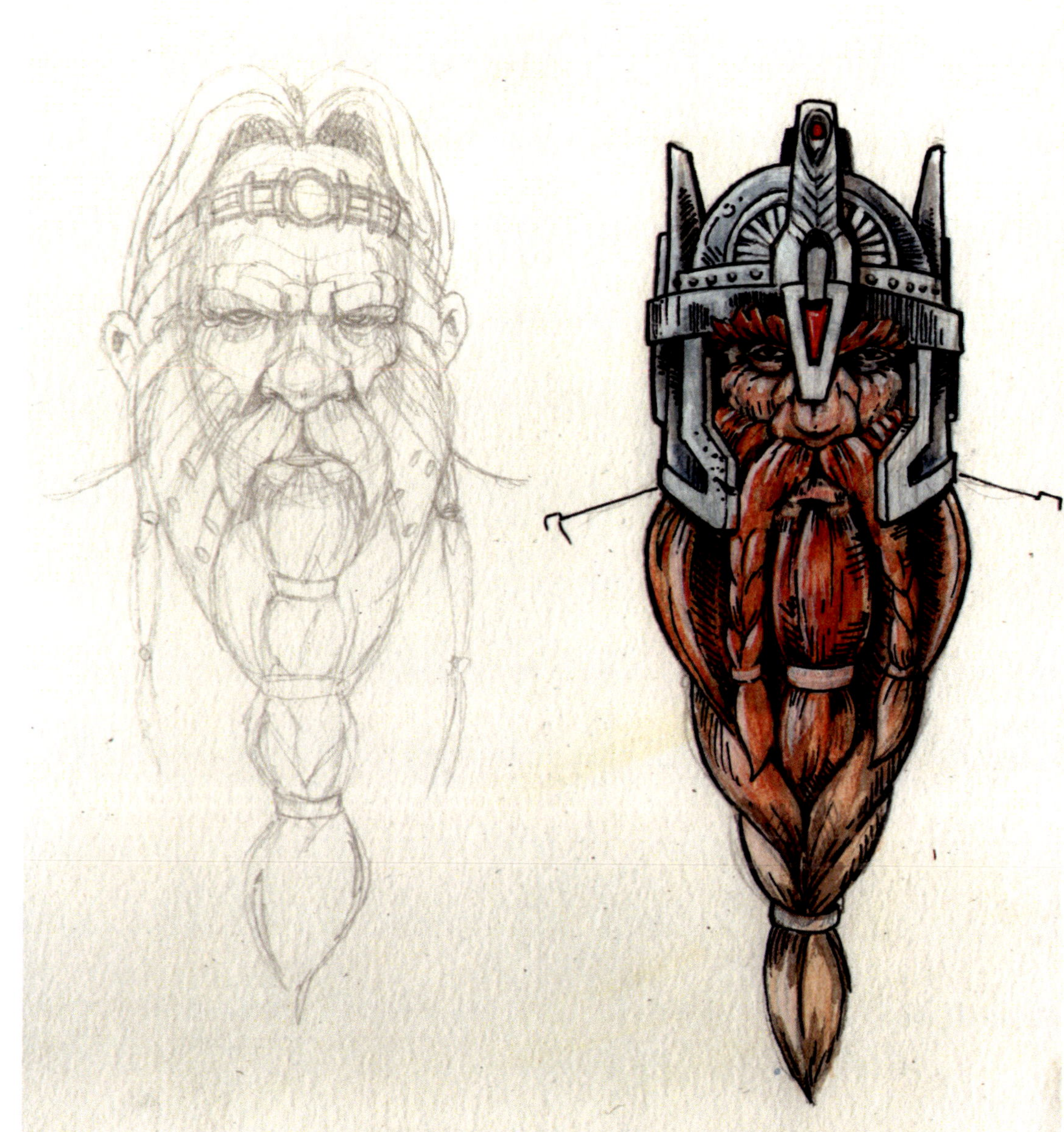

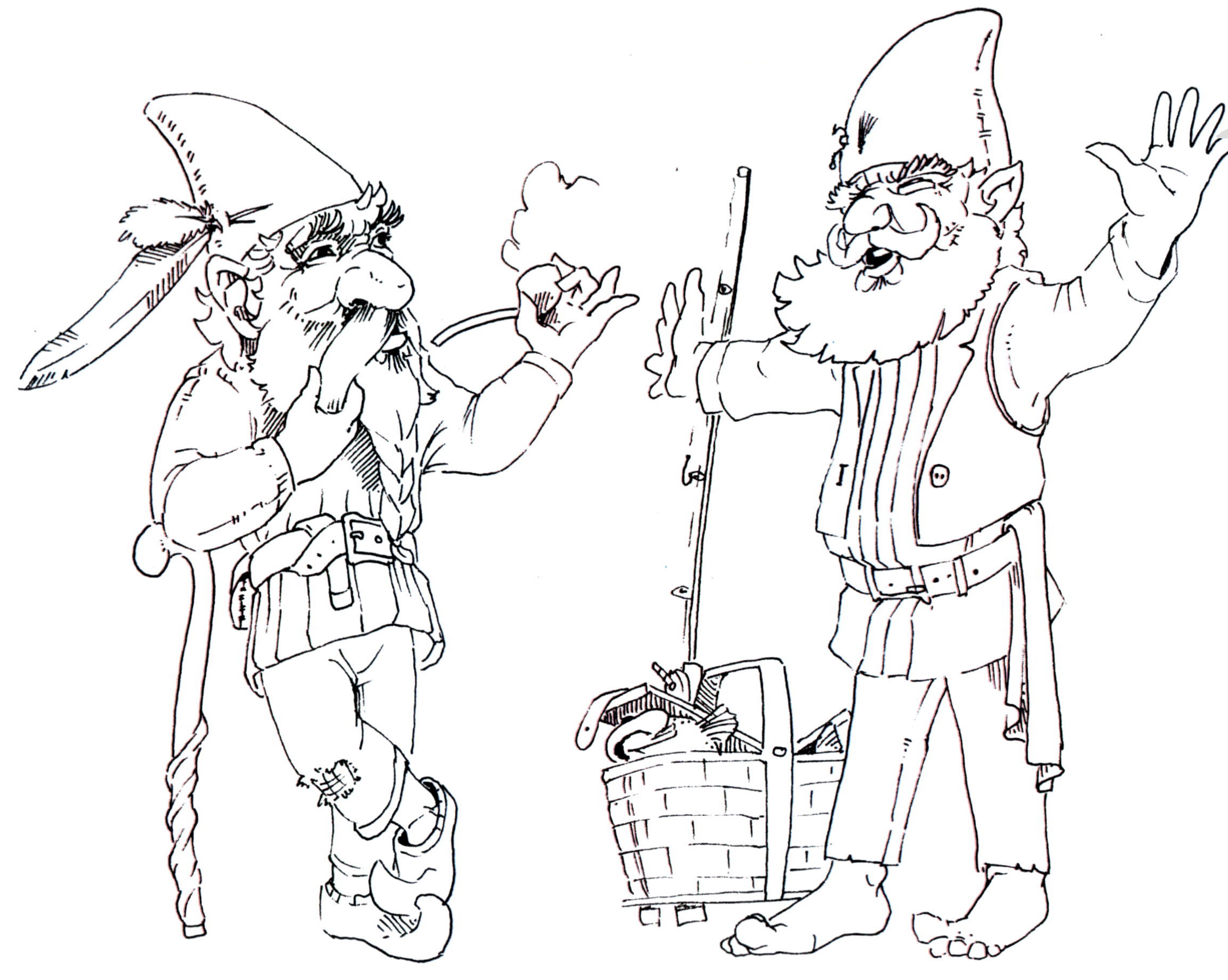

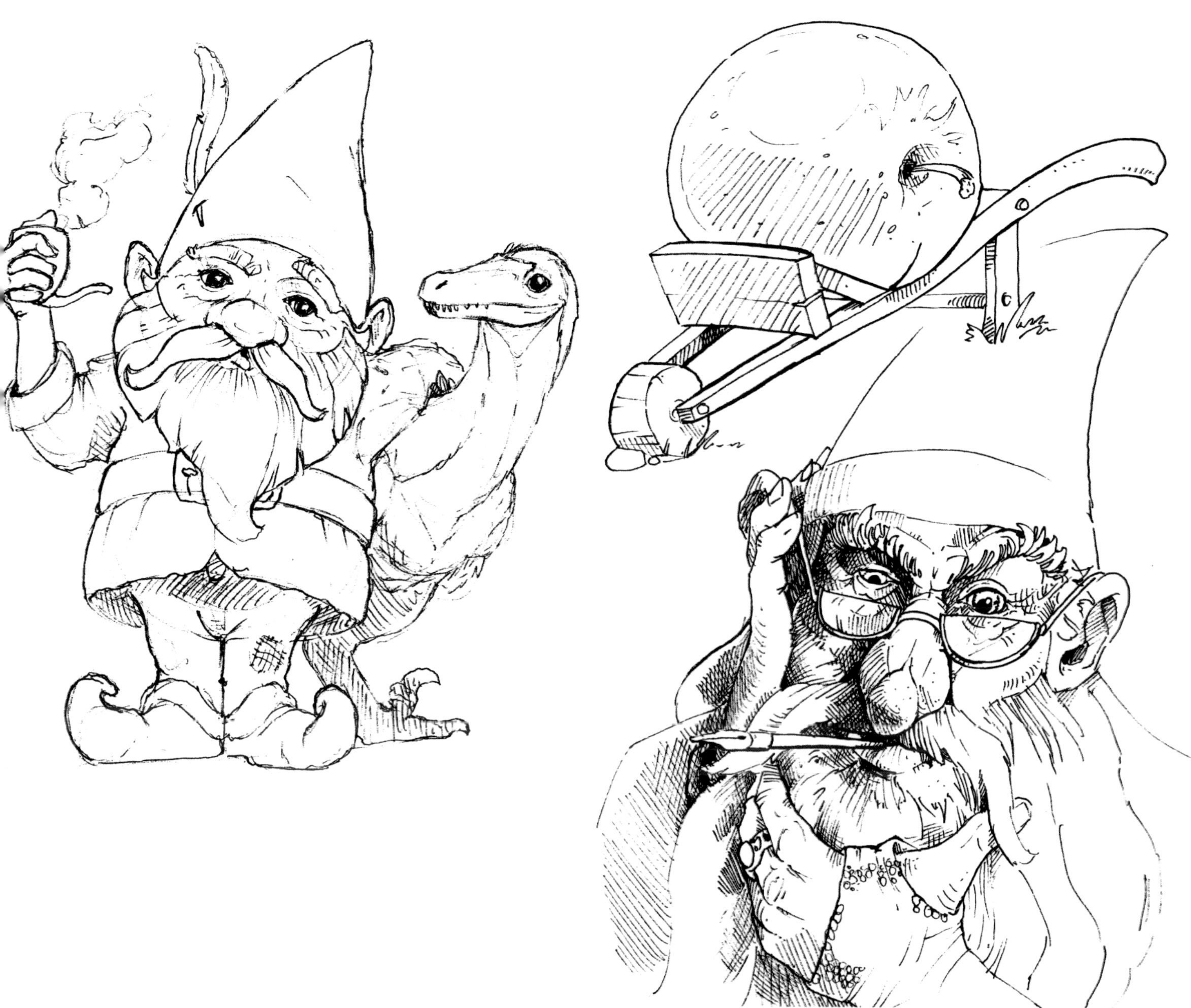

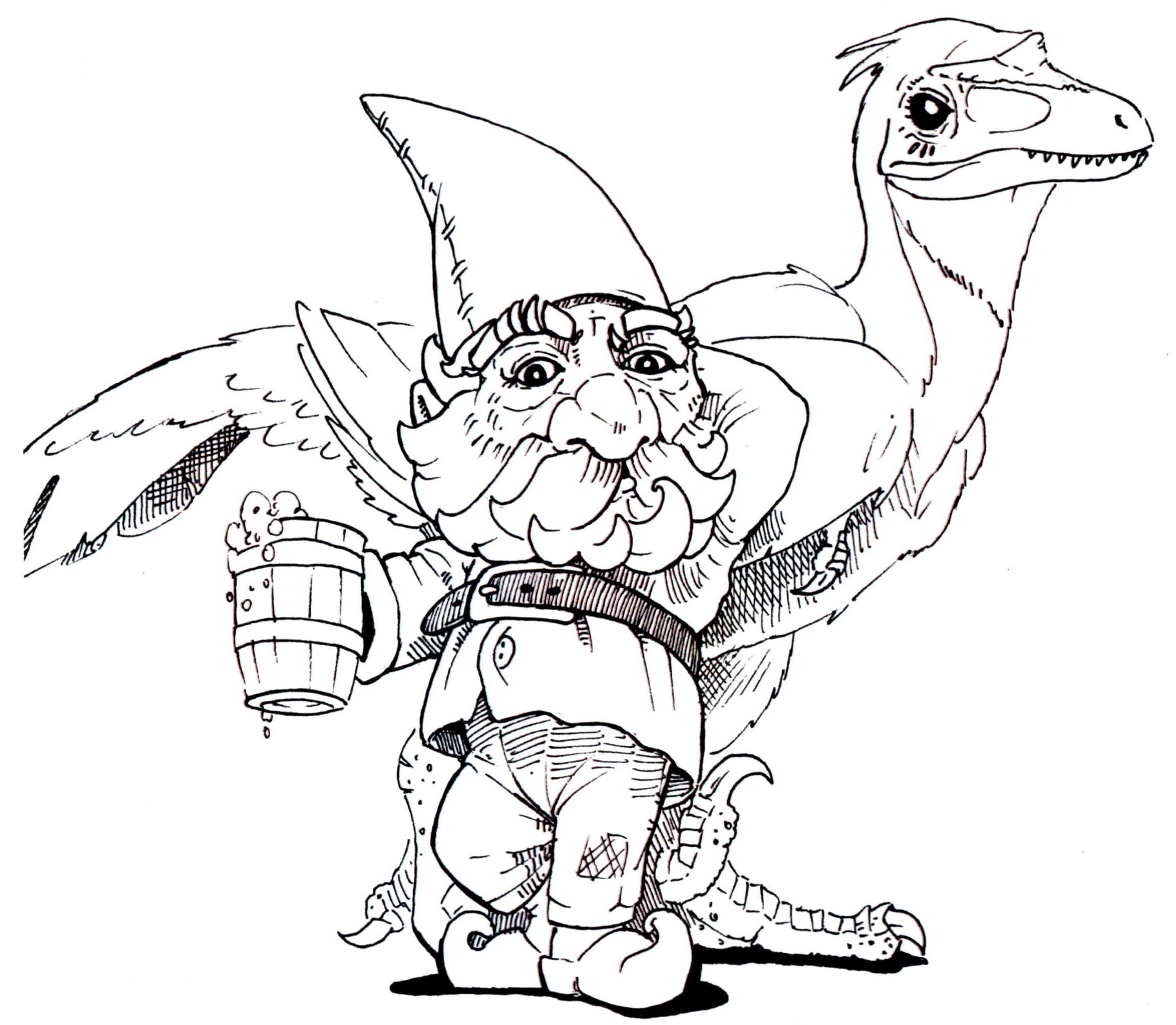

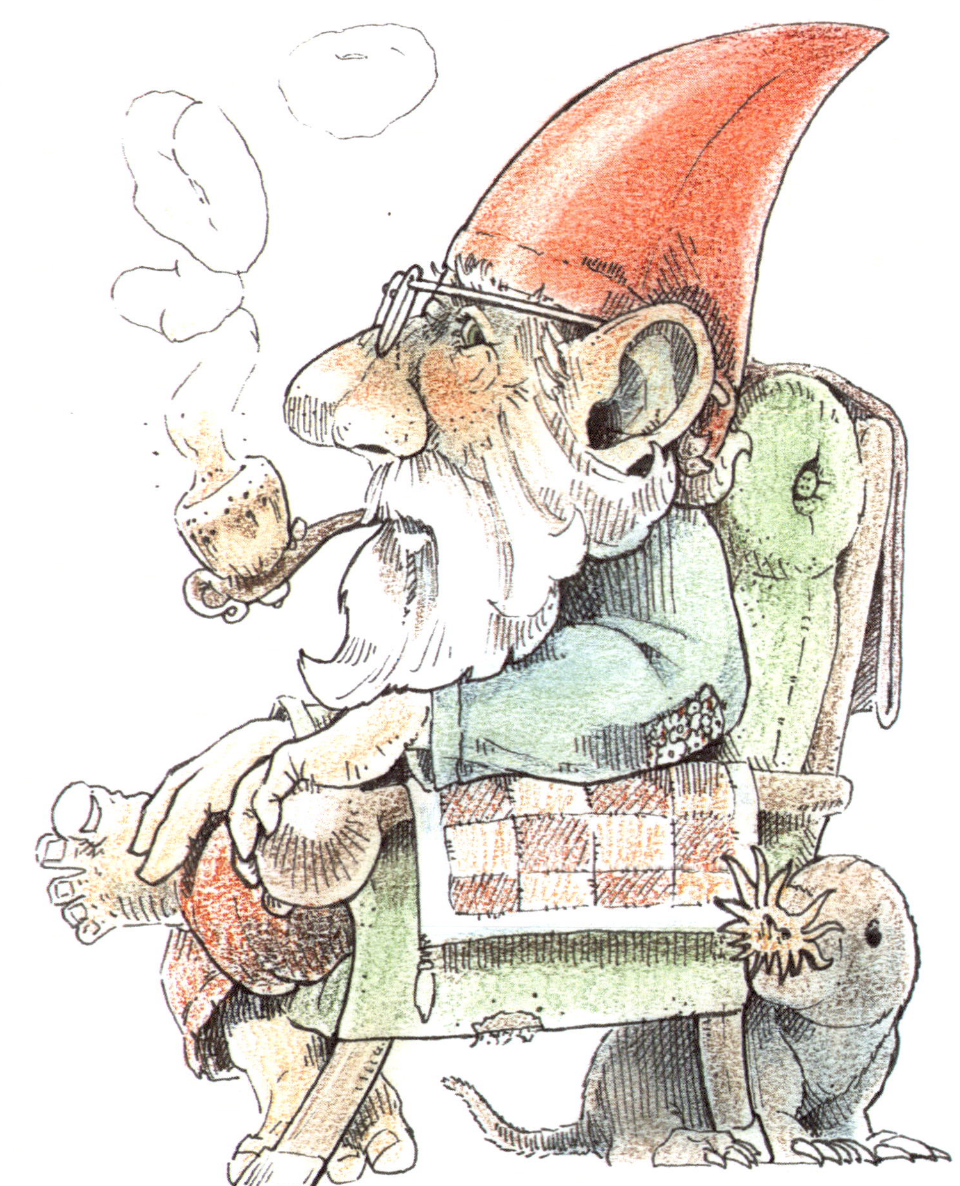

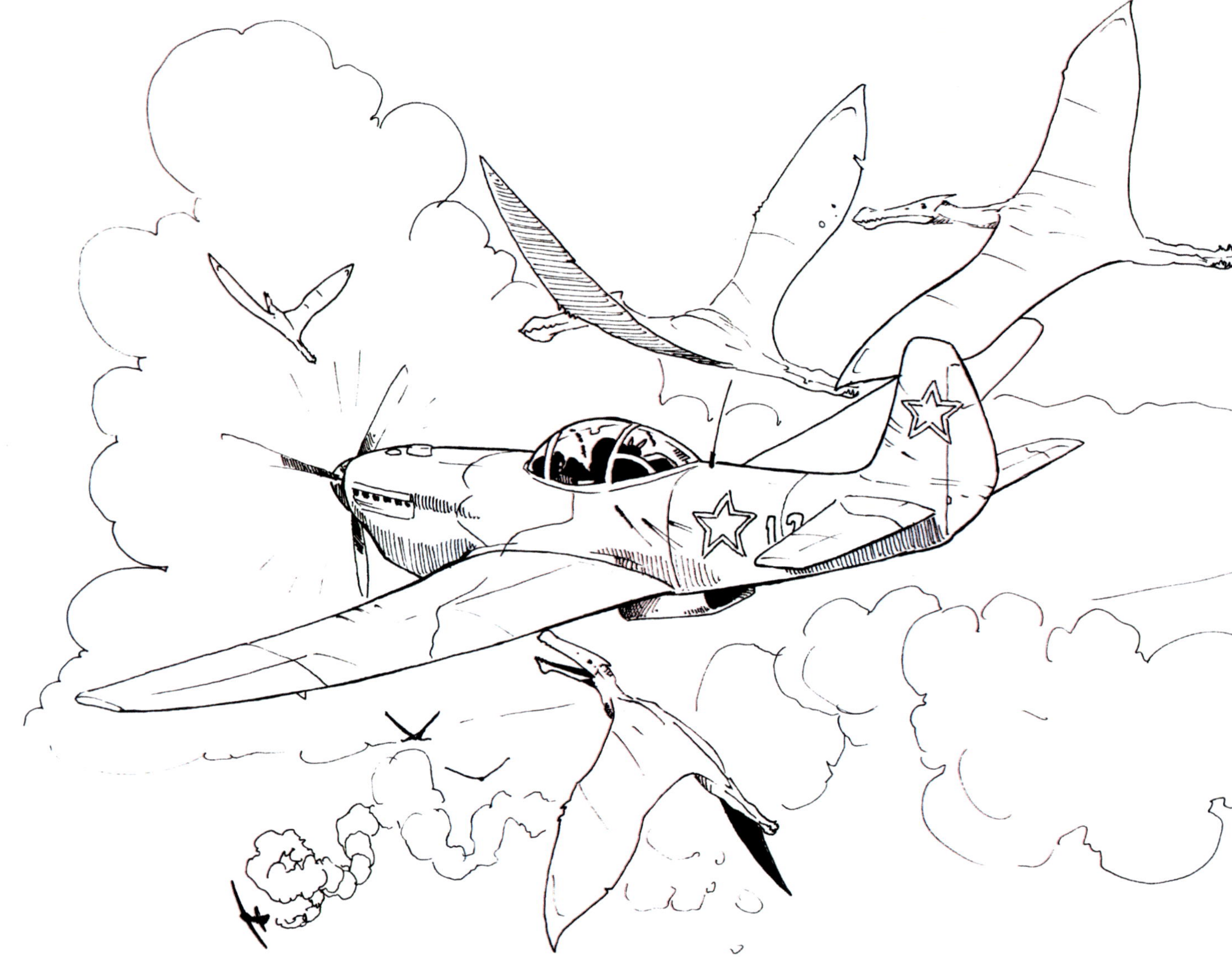

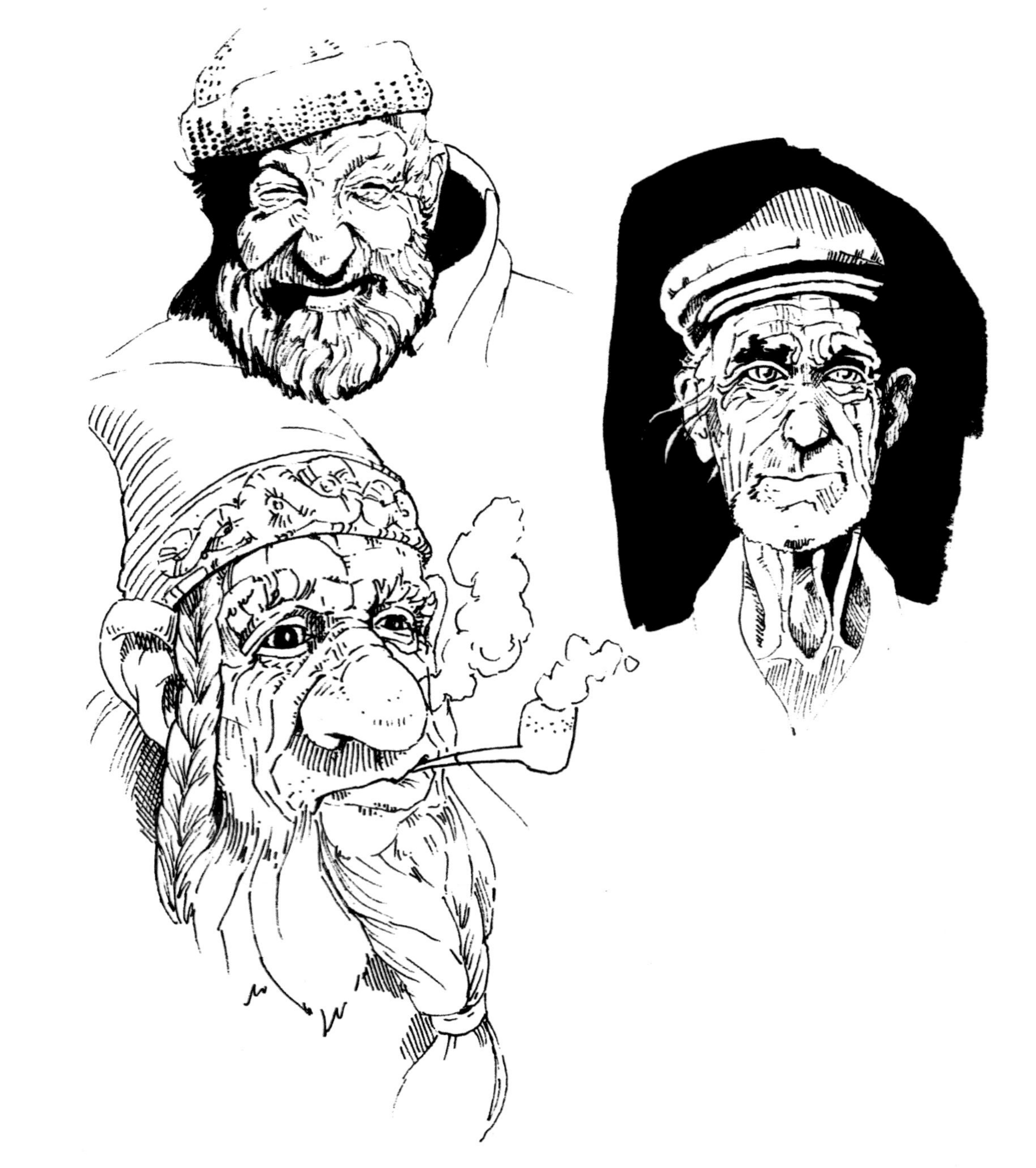

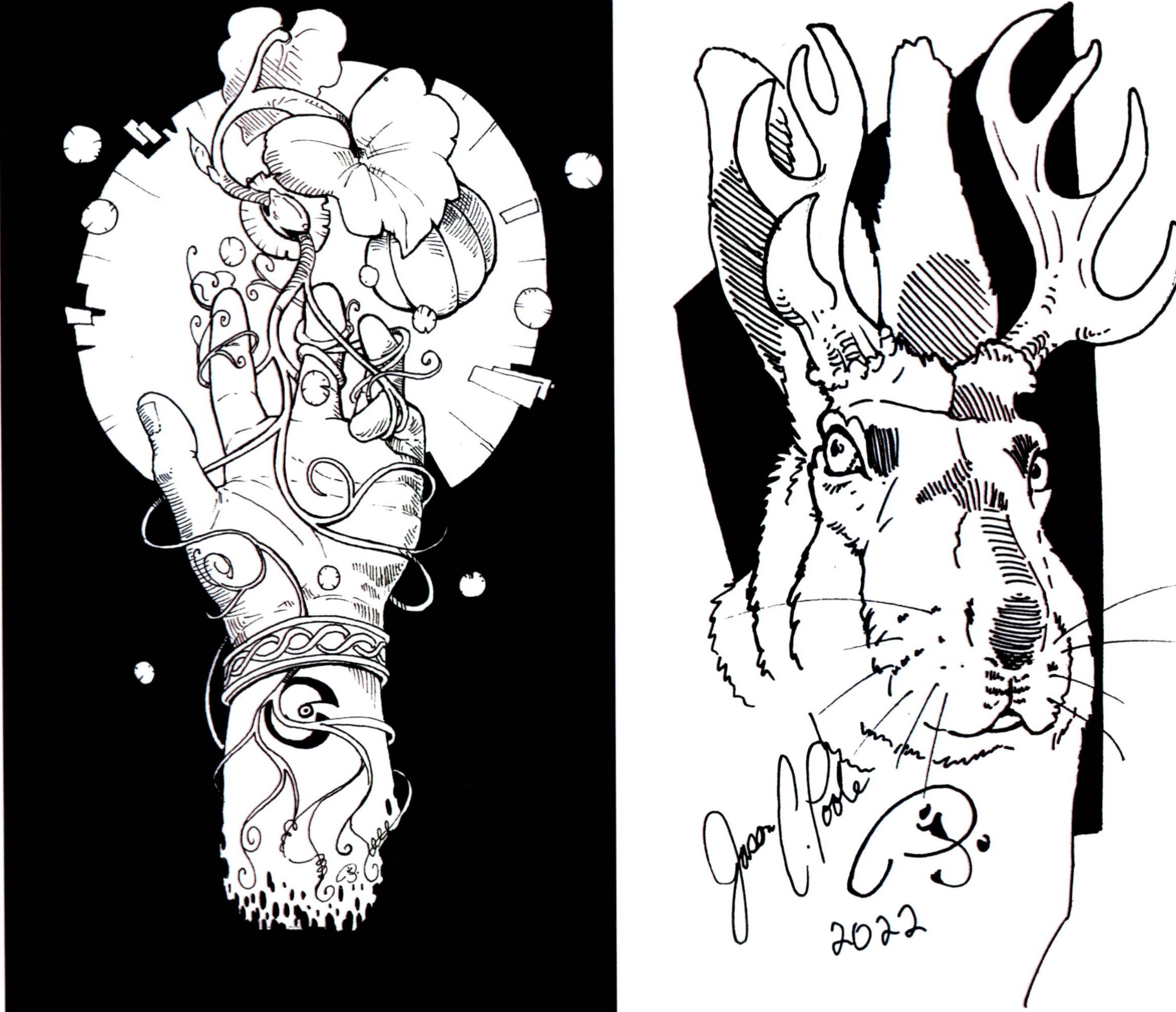
Jason C. Poole
2022

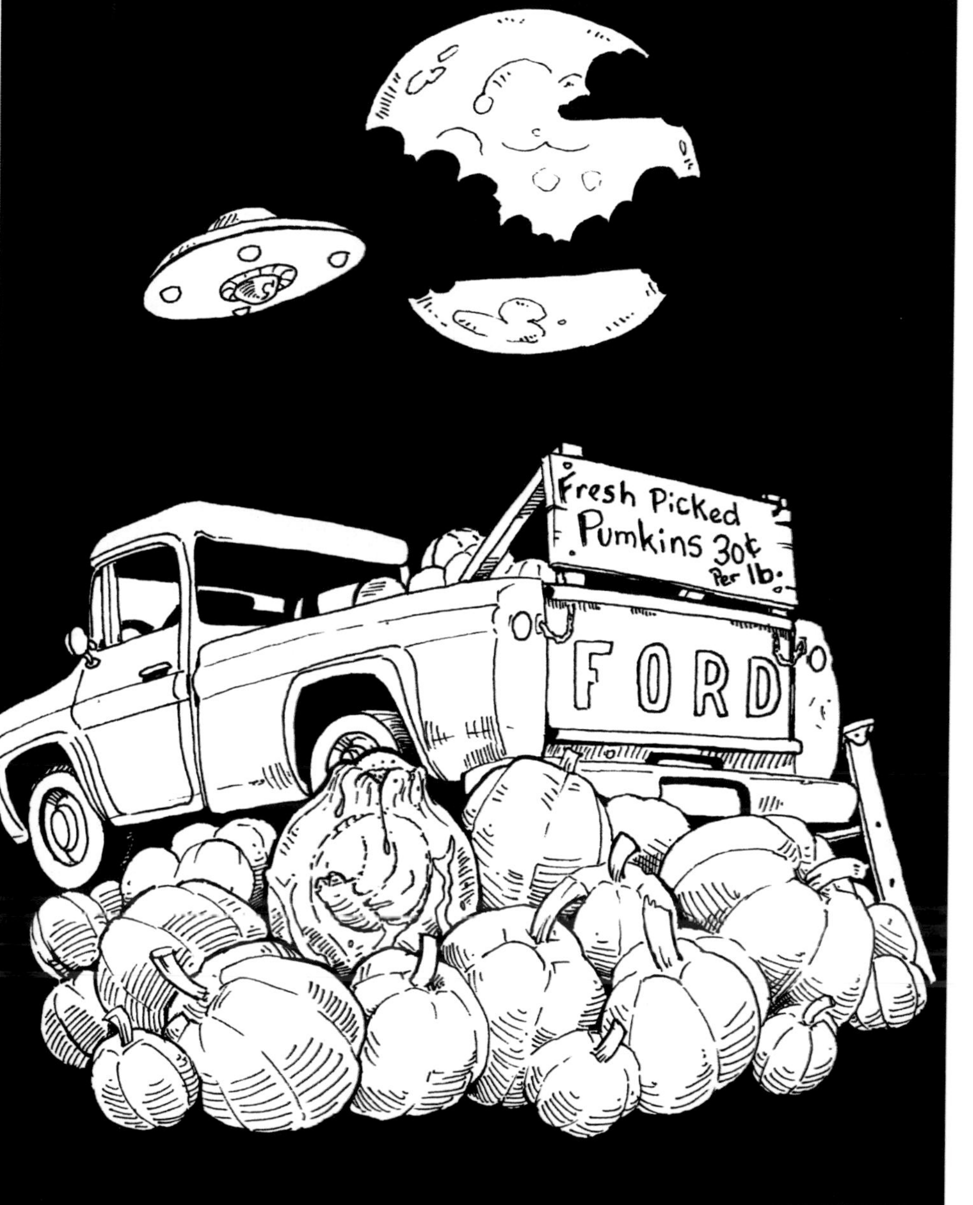

Fresh Picked
Pumkins 30¢
Per lb.
FORD

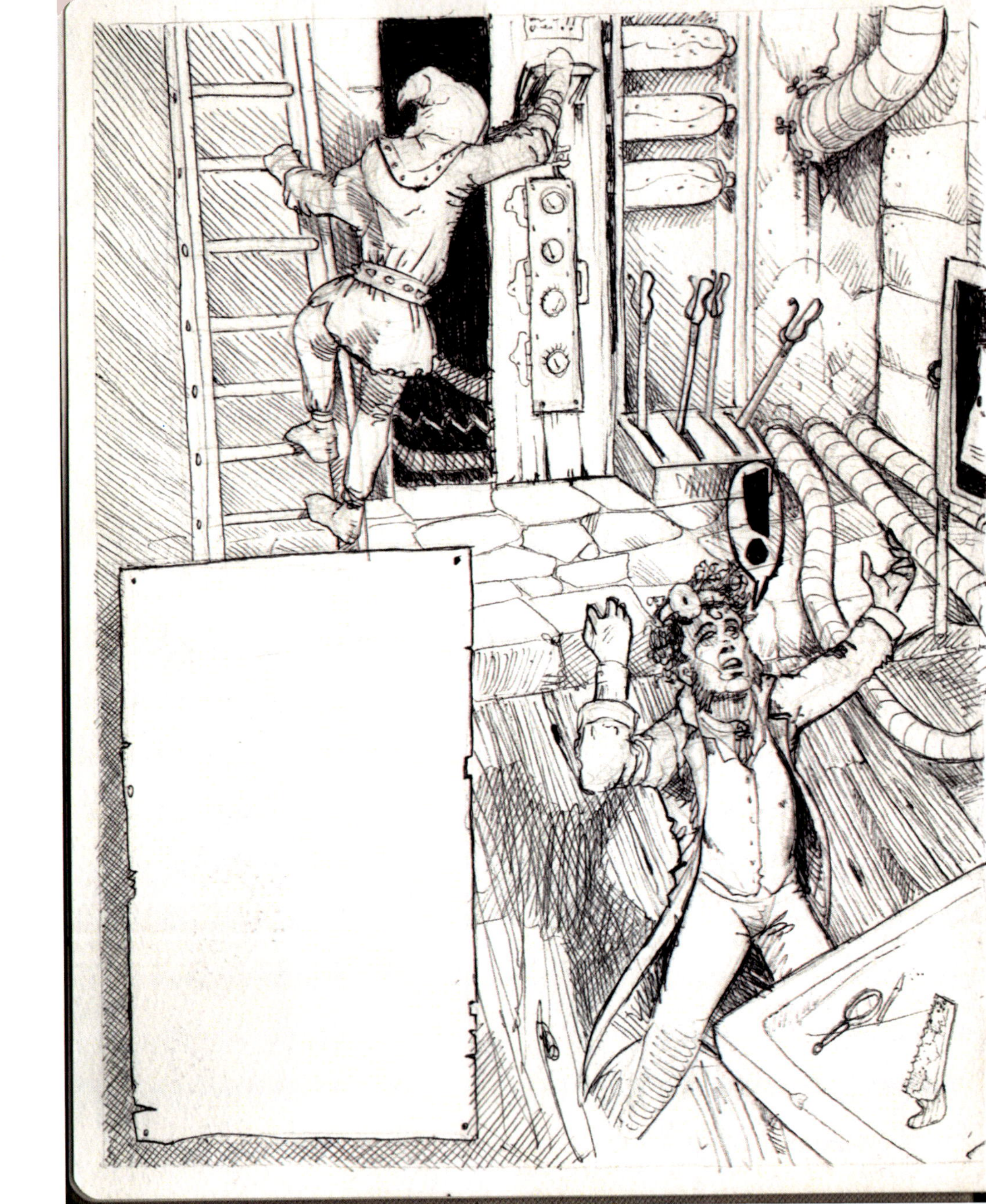

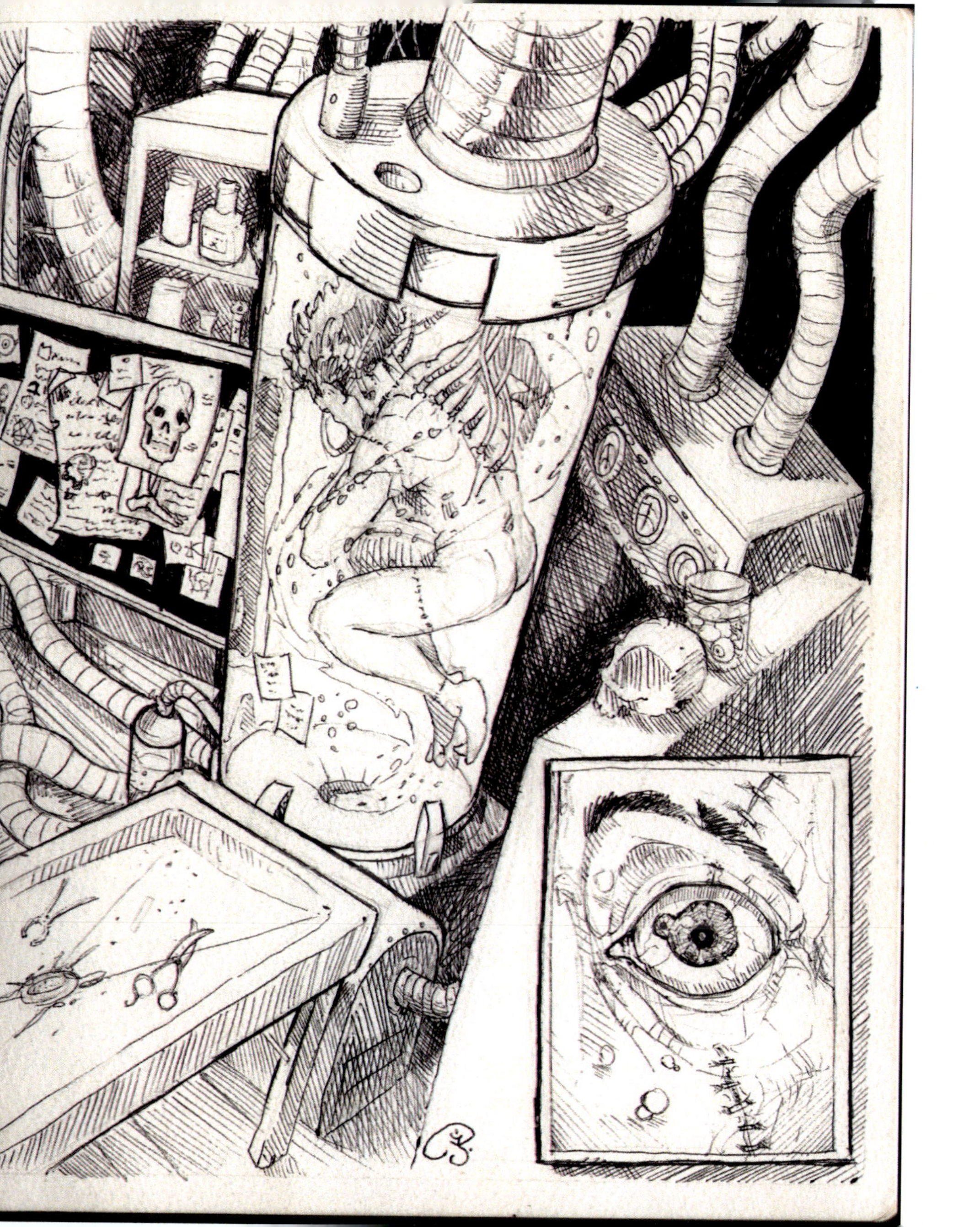

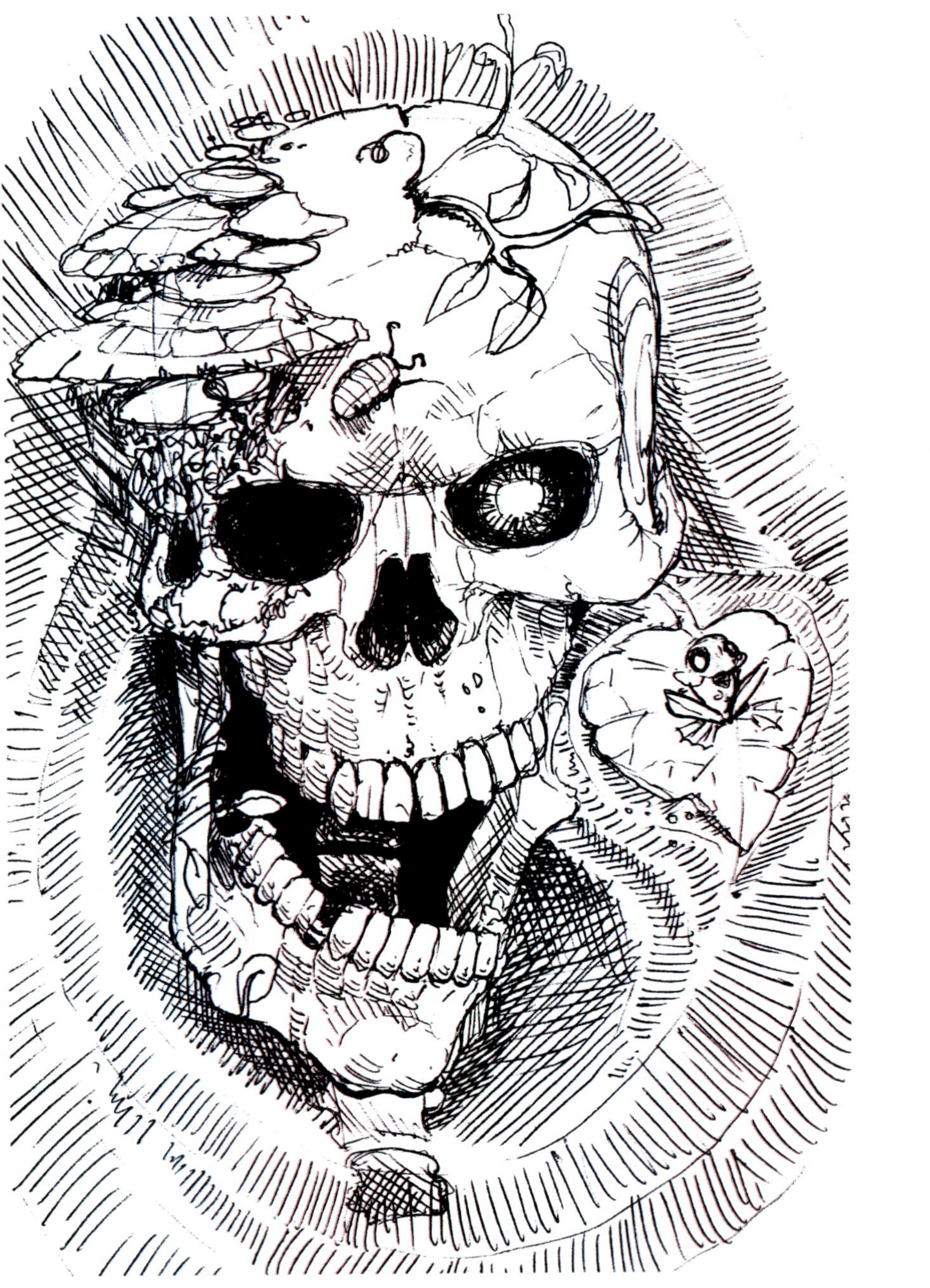

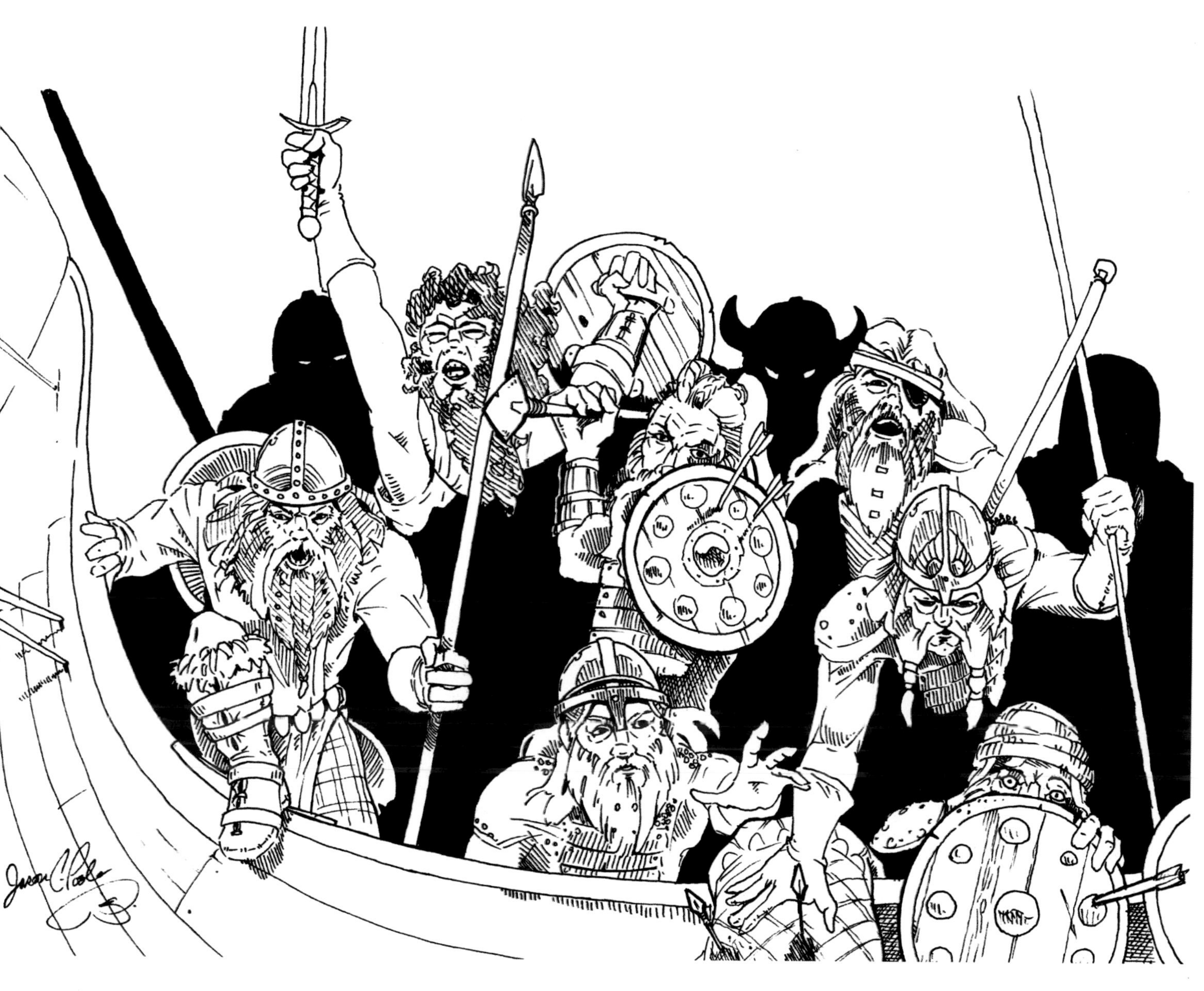

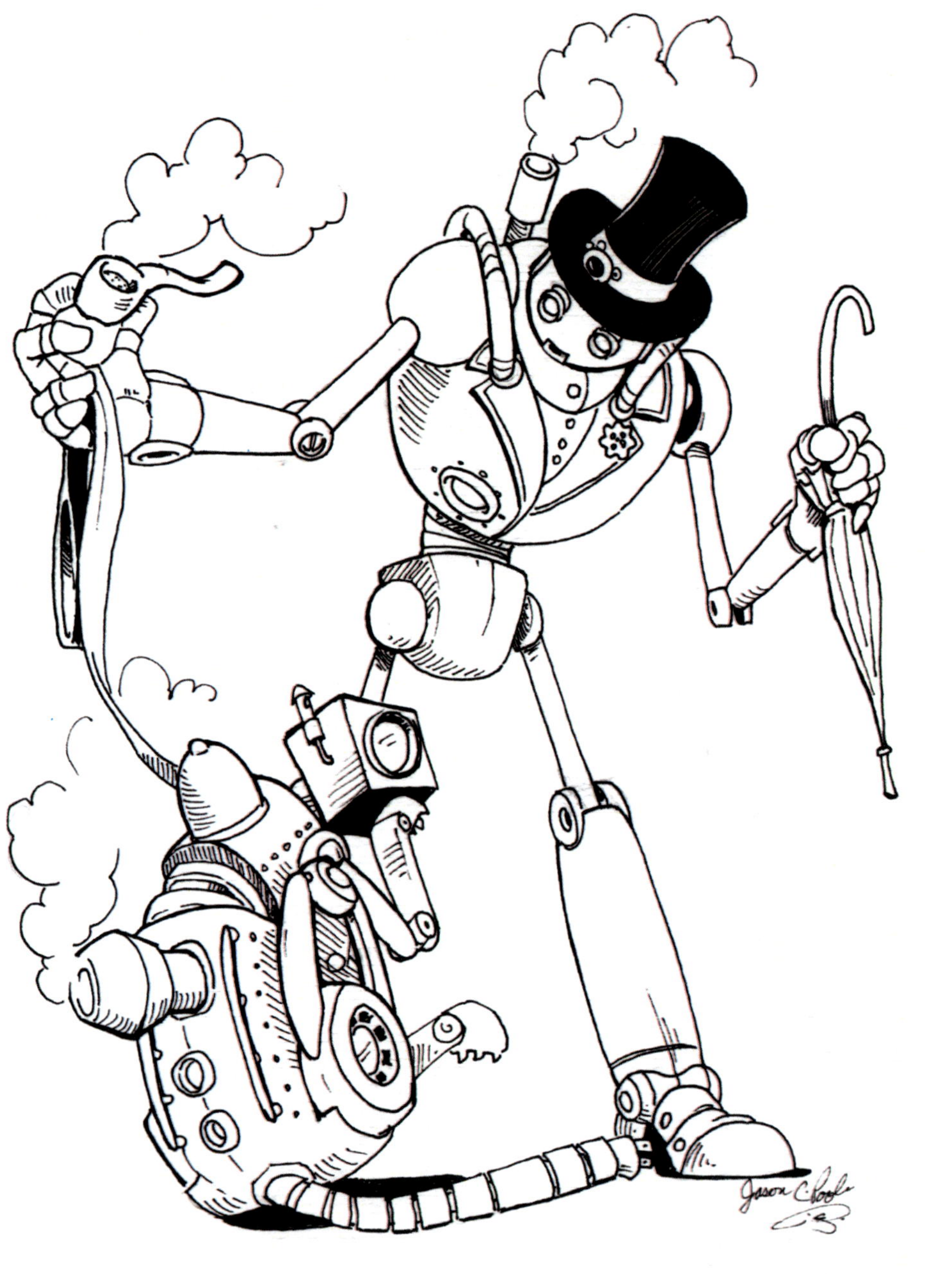

About the Artist

Jason C. Poole lives in Missoula Montana with his family, pets, and artwork. He encourages anyone to go outside, explore and to sketch often.